After Jonathan Edwards

The Courses of the New England Theology

———◦◖◗◦———

Edited by

OLIVER D. CRISP

and

DOUGLAS A. SWEENEY

OXFORD
UNIVERSITY PRESS

OXFORD
UNIVERSITY PRESS

Oxford University Press is a department of the University of Oxford.
It furthers the University's objective of excellence in research, scholarship,
and education by publishing worldwide.

Oxford   New York
Auckland   Cape Town   Dar es Salaam   Hong Kong   Karachi
Kuala Lumpur   Madrid   Melbourne   Mexico City   Nairobi
New Delhi   Shanghai   Taipei   Toronto

With offices in
Argentina   Austria   Brazil   Chile   Czech Republic   France   Greece
Guatemala   Hungary   Italy   Japan   Poland   Portugal   Singapore
South Korea   Switzerland   Thailand   Turkey   Ukraine   Vietnam

Oxford is a registered trademark of Oxford University Press
in the UK and certain other countries.

Published in the United States of America by
Oxford University Press
198 Madison Avenue, New York, NY 10016

Library of Congress Cataloging-in-Publication Data
After Jonathan Edwards : the courses of the New England theology /
edited by Oliver D. Crisp and Douglas A. Sweeney.
p. cm.
Includes index.
ISBN 978-0-19-975629-2 — ISBN 978-0-19-975630-8
1. Edwards, Jonathan, 1703–1758.   2. Edwards, Jonathan, 1703–1758—Influence.
3. New England theology—History.   4. Calvinism.
5. Congregational churches—Doctrines.
6. Theology—United States—History.
I. Crisp, Oliver.   II. Sweeney, Douglas A.
BX7260.E3A58 2012
230'.5874—dc23
2012003849

ISBN 978-0-19-975629-2
ISBN 978-0-19-975630-8

1 3 5 7 9 8 6 4 2
Printed in the United States of America
on acid-free paper

To Wilson Kimnach and Ken Minkema,
facilitators of scholarship on Edwards and his legacies
than which none greater have been conceived

Contents

PART THREE: *Edwardsian Light Refracted*

Acknowledgments

THE EDITORS WOULD like to thank Cynthia Read of Oxford University Press for her patience and assistance. They would also like to thank their respective families for their encouragement and support. In addition, the following individuals have been of considerable help at various stages of this project: David Barshinger, Heber Campos, Mark Hamilton, Dongsoo Han, Paul Helm, Bernard Ho, David Kirkpatrick, Liz Kiszonas, Ernie Klassen, David Kling, Xiao-Xiao (Sharon) Lei, Cesar Lopes, Michael McClymond, Kenneth Minkema, Adriaan Neele, Tom Oey, and William Purinton.

Contributors

James P. Byrd is the associate dean for graduate education and research at Vanderbilt University Divinity School in Nashville, Tennessee. His current book project, under contract with Oxford University Press, focuses on the Bible and patriotism in Revolutionary America. In addition to various articles and reviews, he has previously published two books, *Jonathan Edwards for Armchair Theologians* (WJK, 2008) and *The Challenges of Roger Williams* (Mercer University Press, 2002).

Oliver D. Crisp is professor of systematic theology at Fuller Theological Seminary in Pasadena, California. He has written *Jonathan Edwards and the Metaphysics of Sin* (Ashgate, 2005) and *Jonathan Edwards on God and Creation* (Oxford University Press, 2013) and with Paul Helm has co-edited *Jonathan Edwards: Philosophical Theologian* (Ashgate, 2003). He is currently completing *Jonathan Edwards: An Introduction to His Thought* (T&T Clark, 2013). He has also published a number of essays and articles on the theology of Jonathan Edwards and the New Divinity.

Allen Guelzo is Henry Luce III Professor of the Civil War Era at Gettysburg College in Gettysburg, Pennsylvania. Among his many publications are *Edwards and the Will: A Century of Theological Debate* (Wesleyan University Press, 1989). With Douglas Sweeney he co-edited *The New England Theology: From Jonathan Edwards to Edwards Amasa Park* (Baker Academic, 2006).

Charles Hambrick-Stowe is pastor of the First Congregational Church of Ridgefield, Connecticut. His publications include a number of articles and book chapters on Jonathan Edwards, the Great Awakening, and the New Divinity. He is the author of *The Practice of Piety: Puritan Devotional Disciplines in Seventeenth-Century New England* (University of North Carolina Press, 1982), *Early New England Meditative Poetry: Anne Bradstreet and Edward Taylor* (Paulist Press, 1988), and *Charles G. Finney and the Spirit of American Evangelicalism* (Eerdmans, 1996); he co-edited, with Douglas A. Sweeney, *Holding on to the Faith: Confessional Traditions in American Christianity* (University Press of America, 2008).

D. G. Hart is visiting professor of history at Hillsdale College, Michigan, and is the author of a number of books on Christianity in the United States, including *From Billy Graham to Sarah Palin: Evangelicals and the Betrayal of American Conservatism* (Eerdmans, 2011), *Deconstructing Evangelicalism: Conservative Protestantism in the Age of Billy Graham* (Baker Academic, 2005), and *The Lost Soul of American Protestantism* (Rowman & Littlefield, 2004). With Sean Michael Lucas and Stephen Nichols, he co-edited *The Legacy of Jonathan Edwards: American Religion and Evangelical Tradition* (Baker Academic, 2003). He is currently writing a global history of Calvinism for Yale University Press.

Michael A. G. Haykin is professor of church history and biblical spirituality and director of the Andrew Fuller Center for Baptist Studies in the Southern Baptist Theological Seminary in Louisville, Kentucky. His publications include *One Heart and One Soul: John Sutcliff of Olney, His Friends, and His Times* (Evangelical Press, 1994); *Kiffin, Knollys and Keach: Rediscovering Our English Baptist Heritage* (Reformation Today Trust, 1996); *'At the Pure Fountain of Thy Word': Andrew Fuller as an Apologist* (Paternoster Press, 2004); *Jonathan Edwards: The Holy Spirit in Revival* (Evangelical Press, 2005); *The God Who Draws Near: An Introduction to Biblical Spirituality* (Evangelical Press, 2007).

Paul Helm is a Teaching Fellow at Regent College, Vancouver, B.C., Canada, and emeritus professor of the history and philosophy of religion, University of London. He edited *Jonathan Edwards, Treatise on Grace and Other Posthumous Writings Including Observations on the Trinity* (London, James Clarke, 1971); and he co-edited with Oliver Crisp *Jonathan Edwards: Philosophical Theologian* (Ashgate, 2003). In addition, he has written a number of articles on the philosophy of Jonathan Edwards and on various philosophical influences on him.

Peter Jauhiainen is professor of religion at Kirkwood Community College in Cedar Rapids, Iowa. He has published several articles on Samuel Hopkins, including " 'Reasoning Out of the Scriptures': Samuel Hopkins, the Theological Enterprise, and the Deist Threat," *Journal of Presbyterian History* 79(2), Summer 2001. He is currently working on a book on Hopkins's theology to be titled *An Enlightenment Calvinist: Samuel Hopkins and the Pursuit of Benevolence.*

David W. Kling is professor of religious studies at the University of Miami, Florida. His publications include *A Field of Divine Wonders: The New Divinity and Village Revivals in Northwestern Connecticut, 1792–1822* (Penn State Press, 1993); *The Bible in History: How the Texts Have Shaped the Times* (Oxford University Press, 2004), and a variety of articles on the New Divinity. He is co-editor of *Jonathan Edwards at Home and Abroad: Historical Memories, Cultural Movements, Global Horizons* (University of South Carolina Press, 2003).

Michael McClymond is professor of modern Christianity at Saint Louis University, Missouri. He has written numerous essays on Edwards as well as *Encounters with God: An Approach to the Theology of Jonathan Edwards* (Oxford University

Press, 1998) and, with Gerald McDermott, *The Theology of Jonathan Edwards* (Oxford University Press, 2012).

Gerald R. McDermott is Jordan-Trexler Professor of Religion at Roanoke College. He is the editor, author, or coauthor of many articles and five books on Edwards, including (with Michael McClymond) *The Theology of Jonathan Edwards* (Oxford University Press, 2012), *Jonathan Edwards Confronts the Gods* (Oxford, 2002), and *Understanding Jonathan Edwards* (Oxford, 2009). He has published seven other books on various theological subjects.

Kenneth P. Minkema is the executive editor of *The Works of Jonathan Edwards* and of the Jonathan Edwards Center and Online Archive at Yale University, and research scholar at Yale Divinity School. Besides publishing numerous articles on Edwards and topics in early American religious history in professional journals, he has edited volume 14 in the Edwards *Works*, *Sermons and Discourses: 1723–1729*, and co-edited *A Jonathan Edwards Reader*; *The Sermons of Jonathan Edwards: A Reader*; *Jonathan Edwards at 300: Essays on the Tercentennial of His Birth*; and *Jonathan Edwards's "Sinners in the Hands of an Angry God": A Casebook*. He has also co-edited *The Sermon Notebook of Samuel Parris, 1689–1694*, dealing with the Salem Witchcraft crisis; and *The Colonial Church Records of Reading and Rumney Marsh, Massachusetts*. He is also currently part of a team that is preparing Cotton Mather's "Biblia Americana" for publication.

Anri Morimoto is professor of religion and philosophy at International Christian University, Tokyo. He has written *Jonathan Edwards and the Catholic Vision of Salvation* (Penn State University Press, 1995) and has contributed chapters to *Building New Pathways to Peace* (University of Washington Press, 2011), *Jonathan Edwards as Contemporary* (Peter Lang, 2010), *A Grand Design for Peace and Reconciliation* (Edward Elgar, 2008), as well as articles in *Studies in World Christianity* (2009), *The Princeton Seminary Bulletin* (1999 and 2008), and *International Journal for Philosophy of Religion* (2003). He has also co-edited *Asian and Oceanic Christianities in Conversation* (Editions Rodopi, 2011).

Mark Noll is the Francis A. McAnaney Professor of History at the University of Notre Dame. He has written *America's God: From Jonathan Edwards to Abraham Lincoln* (Oxford University Press, 2002); "Jonathan Edwards's Freedom of the Will Abroad," in *Jonathan Edwards at 300: Essays on the Tercentenary of His Birth* (University Press of America, 2005); "Edwards' Theology After Edwards," in *The Princeton Companion to Jonathan Edwards* (Princeton University Press, 2005); "Charles Hodge as Expositor of the Spiritual Life," in *Charles Hodge Revisited* (Eerdmans, 2002); and "Revival, Enlightenment, Civic Humanism, and the Evolution of Calvinism in Scotland and America, 1735–1843," in *Amazing Grace: Evangelicalism in Australia, Britain, Canada, and the United States* (Baker and McGill-Queen's University Press, 1994).

Charles Phillips is the senior analyst and national program officer at the Maclellan Foundation in Chattanooga, Tennessee.

Douglas A. Sweeney is professor of church history and the history of Christian thought and director of the Jonathan Edwards Center at Trinity Evangelical Divinity School in Deerfield, Illinois. He has published numerous books and articles on Edwards, his legacies, and various other aspects of the history of Christianity, including *Nathaniel Taylor, New Haven Theology, and the Legacy of Jonathan Edwards* (Oxford University Press, 2003); with David W. Kling (co-editor), *Jonathan Edwards at Home and Abroad: Historical Memories, Cultural Movements, Global Horizons* (University of South Carolina Press, 2003); with Allen C. Guelzo (co-editor), *The New England Theology: From Jonathan Edwards to Edwards Amasa Park* (Baker Academic, 2006); and *Jonathan Edwards and the Ministry of the Word* (IVP Academic, 2009).

Mark Valeri is the E. T. Thompson Professor of Church History at Union Seminary in Richmond, Virginia. Interested in the relationship between religious thought and social issues, he has written, among other works, *Law and Providence in Joseph Bellamy's New England: The Origins of the New Divinity in Revolutionary America* (Oxford, 1994) and *Heavenly Merchandize: How Religion Shaped Commerce in Puritan America* (Princeton University Press, 2010). He also edited volume 17 in *The Works of Jonathan Edwards: Sermons and Discourses, 1730–1733* (Yale University Press, 1999).

Abbreviations

All references to the works of Jonathan Edwards are to the letterpress edition published by Yale University Press (1957–2006). References are given by the designation *YE*, volume number, colon, and then pagination; for example, YE1: 21. When reference is made to the online version of the Yale Edition (located at http://edwards.yale.edu), it is given as *WJEO*, followed by volume number and pagination or section. Here is a complete list of the Yale letterpress volumes, given according to the abbreviations used in this volume:

YE1   Jonathan Edwards, *Freedom of the Will: The Works of Jonathan Edwards, Vol. 1*, ed. Paul Ramsey (New Haven: Yale University Press, 1957)

YE2   —— *Religious Affections: The Works of Jonathan Edwards, Vol. 2*, ed. John E. Smith (New Haven: Yale University Press, 1959)

YE3   —— *Original Sin: The Works of Jonathan Edwards, Vol. 3*, ed. Clyde A. Holbrook (New Haven: Yale University Press, 1970)

YE4   —— *The Great Awakening: The Works of Jonathan Edwards, Vol. 4*, ed. C. C. Goen (New Haven: Yale University Press, 1972)

YE5   —— *Apocalyptic Writings: The Works of Jonathan Edwards, Vol. 5*, ed. Stephen J. Stein (New Haven: Yale University Press, 1977)

YE6   —— *Scientific and Philosophical Writings: The Works of Jonathan Edwards, Vol. 6*, ed Wallace E. Anderson (New Haven: Yale University Press, 1980)

YE7   —— *The Life of David Brainerd: The Works of Jonathan Edwards, Vol. 7*, ed. Norman Pettit (New Haven: Yale University Press, 1984)

YE8   —— *Ethical Writings: The Works of Jonathan Edwards, Vol. 8*, ed. Paul Ramsey (New Haven: Yale University Press, 1989)

YE9   —— *A History of the Work of Redemption: The Works of Jonathan Edwards, Vol. 9*, ed. John F. Wilson (New Haven: Yale University Press, 1989)

YE10   —— *Sermons and Discourses, 1720–1723: The Works of Jonathan Edwards, Vol. 10*, ed. Wilson H. Kimnach (New Haven: Yale University Press, 1992)

YE11   —————— *Typological Writings: The Works of Jonathan Edwards*, Vol. 11, ed. Wallace E. Anderson and David Watters (New Haven: Yale University Press, 1993)

YE12   —————— *Ecclesiastical Writings: The Works of Jonathan Edwards*, Vol. 12, ed. David D. Hall (New Haven: Yale University Press, 1994)

YE13   —————— *The "Miscellanies": Nos. a–z, aa–zz, 1–500: The Works of Jonathan Edwards*, Vol. 13, ed. Thomas A. Schafer (New Haven: Yale University Press, 1994)

YE14   —————— *Sermons and Discourses, 1723–1729: The Works of Jonathan Edwards*, Vol. 14, ed. Kenneth P. Minkema (New Haven: Yale University Press, 1997)

YE15   —————— *Notes on Scripture: The Works of Jonathan Edwards*, Vol. 15, ed. Stephen J. Stein (New Haven: Yale University Press, 1998)

YE16   —————— *Letters and Personal Writings: The Works of Jonathan Edwards*, Vol. 16, ed. George S. Claghorn (New Haven: Yale University Press, 1998)

YE17   —————— *Sermons and Discourses, 1730–1733: The Works of Jonathan Edwards*, Vol. 17, ed. Mark Valeri (New Haven: Yale University Press, 1999)

YE18   —————— *The "Miscellanies": Nos. 501–832: The Works of Jonathan Edwards*, Vol. 18, ed. Ava Chamberlain (New Haven: Yale University Press, 2000)

YE19   —————— *Sermons and Discourses, 1734–1738: The Works of Jonathan Edwards*, Vol. 19, ed. M. X. Lesser (New Haven: Yale University Press, 2001)

YE20   —————— *The "Miscellanies": Nos. 833–1152: The Works of Jonathan Edwards*, Vol. 20, ed. Amy Plantinga Pauw (New Haven: Yale University Press, 2002)

YE21   —————— *Writings on the Trinity, Grace and Faith: The Works of Jonathan Edwards*, Vol. 21, ed. Sang Hyun Lee (New Haven: Yale University Press, 2002)

YE22   —————— *Sermons and Discourses, 1739–1742: The Works of Jonathan Edwards*, Vol. 22, ed. Harry S. Stout and Nathan O. Hatch (New Haven: Yale University Press, 2003)

YE23   —————— *The "Miscellanies": Nos. 1153–1360: The Works of Jonathan Edwards*, Vol. 23, ed. Douglas A. Sweeney (New Haven: Yale University Press, 2004)

YE24   —————— *The Blank Bible: The Works of Jonathan Edwards*, Vol. 24, ed. Stephen J. Stein (New Haven: Yale University Press, 2006)

YE25   —————— *Sermons and Discourses, 1743–1758: The Works of Jonathan Edwards*, Vol. 25, ed. Wilson H. Kimnach (New Haven: Yale University Press, 2006)

YE26   —————— *Catalogue of Books: The Works of Jonathan Edwards*, Vol. 26, ed. Peter J. Theusen (New Haven: Yale University Press, 2008)

After Jonathan Edwards

Introduction

Oliver D. Crisp and Douglas A. Sweeney

IN THE COURSE of a spirited and polemical defense of the New England Theology, its last great defender, Edwards Amasa Park, then Abbot Professor of Theology at Andover Theological Seminary, "begged leave" to explain the term "New England Theology" in these words:

> It signifies the formal creed which a majority of the most eminent theologians in New England have explicitly or implicitly sanctioned, during and since the time of [Jonathan] Edwards [Senior]. It denotes the spirit and genius of the system openly avowed or logically involved in their writings. It includes not the peculiarities in which Edwards differed, as he is known to have differed, from the larger part of his most eminent followers, nor the peculiarities in which any one of his followers differed, as some of them did, from the larger part of the others; but it comprehends the principles, with their logical sequences, which the greater number of our most celebrated divines have approved expressly or by implication.[1]

The New England Theology was a theological school of thought characterized by a number of ideas, a shared set of intellectual concerns, similar approaches to a range of central theological questions, and a common core of doctrine that is understood to be representative of this movement, even though not every individual theologian allied to this school would own every aspect of this conceptual deposit.[2] In other words, the New England Theology connotes a particular theological *tradition*. Its advocates looked to Jonathan Edwards (1703–1758) as *fons et origo*, the aboriginal intellect from which it sprang. But later developers of the New England Theology were, in some respects, as important as its founder for the ways in which they took and shaped particular ideas they found among Edwards's literary remains, before passing them on to their intellectual progeny.[3]

One important instance of this in the New England Theology is how Edwards's distinction between human natural ability to do a thing and a moral inability to do a thing was taken up and developed systematically by his immediate disciples, Joseph Bellamy and Samuel Hopkins. Edwards deployed it in order to show that fallen human beings could not claim they were without moral responsibility for their sinful actions. He reasoned that although a person may be morally unable to do a particular thing, he could remain naturally able to do it. Thus, if only a moral impediment prevents a person from asking for forgiveness, then even though this is a real impediment it is one for which he is responsible, since there is no natural thing preventing him from acting differently. His incapacity is at root a moral, not a natural, one.[4]

Bellamy and Hopkins fashioned from this distinction a theological reason for holding human beings responsible for failing to acquire faith. Although morally incapable of forming such faith thanks to the effects of sin, no natural impediment stood in the way of salvation for fallen human beings. As Park puts it with respect to later transmission of these ideas, "It is the common remark of the Edwardean school, that men have no inability to repent except their unwillingness, and this unwillingness is a sin, and sin is a voluntary act."[5] This was then set to work in the doctrine of atonement, which became a hallmark of this emerging "New Divinity" as the first phase of the New England Theology became known. The result was the New England version of the governmental account of the atonement. This, in turn, was passed on to the next generation of theologians and was developed in slightly different ways by them. Although some New Divinity men distanced themselves from this new atonement doctrine (John Smalley is perhaps the best known example of this), others honed it into a careful, cogent doctrine. The apogee of this doctrinal development can be found in the sermons of Jonathan Edwards, Jr., the son and intellectual heir to his father's theological legacy.[6]

In the course of its development, the New England Theology was transformed from the theological predilection of a few disciples clustered around their master into a powerful lobby within New England Congregational, and latterly, Baptist and Presbyterian circles that had international ramifications. Through training ministerial students, Bellamy put the New Divinity on the map. Meanwhile, in publishing his *System of Doctrines* (1793), Hopkins showed that this was no mere collection of ideas but a significant dogmatic force. It is a mark of the impression Hopkins's work made that thereafter the New Divinity was often referred to as "Hopkinsianism" or "Hopkintonianism."[7]

As it developed in numerical strength and intellectual weight, the movement began to look for institutional support. The colonial colleges were no longer places sympathetic to the evangelical zeal and Calvinistic concerns of these men. The establishment of Andover Seminary as the first and largest theological seminary in the country at the beginning of the nineteenth century, and in satellites such as Bangor and, more briefly, Union College in New York (founded in the late eighteenth century, but presided over by Edwards Jr. and Jonathan Maxcy in succession, between 1799 and 1804), was a moment of triumph for the New England Theology. Its theology was also influential in a number of other institutions of the period, among them Amherst, Dartmouth, Mount Holyoke, Williams, and the College of Rhode Island (later renamed Brown University). Its ideas were disseminated through these institutional organs to several generations of students and seminarians.

The New Divinity had become the New England Theology. Andover became identified with its later stages. But Yale also saw a return to Edwardsian thinking of a sort, in the teaching of Nathaniel W. Taylor, whose work at the fledgling Yale Divinity School generated another branch of the movement, namely, the New Haven Theology. These theologians all identified themselves as heirs of the Edwardsian project. But in the process of meeting new intellectual challenges, including the need to transmit a body of material to new generations of ministerial candidates as well as further theological refinements of particular points of doctrine and a changed social and political climate in the early decades of the nineteenth century, there were various ways in which key figures in these later phases of the movement ended up espousing views quite different from those of Edwards himself. Part of this change had to do with the philosophical climate in which later stages of New England Theology flourished. Whereas Edwards was a convinced idealist (albeit one ready to appeal to common sense in a number of important respects), later Edwardians drew on the Scottish commonsense realist tradition, which was imported to the colonies around the time of Edwards's demise. This meant that the theological notions with which the later Edwardsians wrestled were informed by different philosophical ideas as well as a changed political and intellectual situation.

It would be a mistake to identify the New England Theology with a purely intellectual set of concerns, however. The representatives of this movement were certainly doctrinally motivated, attempting to establish a distinctively Edwardsian brand of Reformed theology in the United States. But they also shared Edwards's desire for a vital spiritual life in the churches. Much of what is theologically distinctive about the movement stems from this experiential concern, a desire to see a change of heart among congregants and communities. It is no accident that the theologians of New England were actively involved in the Second Great Awakening, as Edwards was a leader in the first.

This New England Theology was a force to be reckoned with for almost a hundred years, finally passing from the American scene as the sun began to set on the nineteenth century. Its cultural impact can be seen in Harriet Beecher Stowe's New England novels, notably *The Minister's Wooing* (1859) and *Oldtown Folks* (1869), both of which place New Divinity theologians at the center of the narrative. She speaks of New England at the end of the eighteenth century as a society marked by a deep and abiding interest in theology: "Never was there a community where the roots of common life were shot down so deeply, and were so intensely grappled around things sublime and eternal."[8] The intricate metaphysical systems that divines such as Samuel Hopkins, Joseph Bellamy, and Jonathan Edwards, Jr., built in their studies and then preached from their pulpits were

> discussed by every farmer, in intervals of plough and hoe, by every woman and girl, at loom, spinning-wheel and washtub. New England was one vast sea, surging from depths to heights with thought and discussion on the most insoluble of mysteries. And it is to be added that no man or woman accepted any theory or speculation simply as a theory or speculation; all was profoundly real and vital—a foundation on which actual life was based with intensest earnestness.[9]

The New England theology remains the most significant and enduring Christian theological school of thought to have originated in the United States. Yet today little is known about it beyond the circle of those with a professional interest in the scholarship associated with this movement. Even in this select group, one seldom finds anything like a *complete* understanding of the phases of its life or the works of its main proponents. There has been scholarly work on the movement post mortem, but for much of the twentieth century that interest amounted to little more than a trickle of scholarly articles and several (important) monographs. It is only in the last quarter century that significant scholarly interest in these theologians has been rekindled. A clutch of significant studies and a collection of some of the most important writings from the movement have seen the light of day in this period, signaling a renewal of serious intellectual interest in the representatives of this movement.[10]

Yet this raises a question: What led to the eclipse of New England Theology in American theological literature? One reason is simply that it ceased to be a living force as liberal theology encroached on American institutions of higher learning in the second half of the nineteenth century. Once it had spent its capital, toward the end of the Victorian era, other theological interlocutors were sought. The early twentieth century was not a place especially hospitable to the Calvinism associated with the colonial period of American history.[11] Since the

New England theology stemmed from the work of Jonathan Edwards, it is not surprising that it too was regarded as something best left to die quietly.[12]

However, there are other reasons for this movement having been ignored. Perhaps the most important is the manner in which, in the middle third of the twentieth century, a narrative about the New England theology began to grow, one that regarded its development as the gradual departure from the grand metaphysical origins in Edwards's thought, coupled with a perceptible moralism and provincialism in later stages.[13] According to this story, the New England theology is a tale of ever more arid and abstruse metaphysical theorizing on the basis of an original, and intellectually dynamic, Edwardsian deposit. The somewhat paradoxical upshot of this is that the later generations of this species ended up repudiating central tenets of Edwards's theological vision, while simultaneously claiming him as their inspiration. One of the motivations for the present volume was to assist in dispatching this mistaken narrative.

Recent revisionist scholarship in post-Reformation Protestant theology has shown that successive generations of Reformed and Lutheran scholastic theologians did not contribute to the ossification of the doctrinal deposit handed on to them as was once thought. Nor were its Reformed proponents governed by a monomania about predestination and the divine decrees— the so-called central dogma of post-Reformation Protestantism that dominated later nineteenth-century historiographical work on this period. (A similarly mistaken *idée fixe* has been attributed to scholastic Lutheranism and its distinctive *sola fide* doctrine.) In like manner, this volume is offered as a contribution to the rehabilitation of New England Theology. Recent historical and theological work in this area has begun to show that the older "decline and fall" narrative often associated with the movement is, in fact, as mistaken as the central-dogma hermeneutic applied to the era of Protestant Orthodoxy. Far from moralizing on Edwardsian themes, or shutting up the metaphysical creativity of Edwards within the husk of an arid "scholasticism," the theologians of the New England school were creative contributors to a living American tradition of theological reflection. Although, like Edwards, many of these thinkers sought to "call no man father," they were a closely knit community of scholar-pastors whose principal aim was to fashion a viable strain of Reformed theology for North America. This drew deeply from the wells of Edwards, Bellamy, Hopkins, Edwards Jr., and other thinkers such as Nathanael Emmons, Nathaniel Taylor, and Edwards A. Park, yielding significant theological outputs.

As scholarship on Jonathan Edwards flourished and diversified over the last fifty years, a large and complex body of literature has been generated, which celebrates and critically engages with the work of the Northampton Sage. Today, there is an intellectual industry devoted to furtherance of Edwardsian scholarship, aided by completion of the Yale letterpress edition of Edwards's works, and its online, open-access counterpart. Given the maturation of this literature, a new examination of the reception of Edwards's ideas in the work of his intellectual progeny and successors seems an appropriate next step. How Edwards was "received," how his ideas were transmitted, changed, and developed in the process of dissemination and reception—these are important considerations that the essays in this collection seek to address. One of the important conclusions of a number of essays in this volume is that Edwards's legacy was broader, deeper, and further reaching than some previous scholarship has suggested. This is not intended to be the last word on the New England Theology. But it is a contribution to a new awareness of the importance of Edwardsian themes for subsequent theology, at home and abroad.

Overview of the Essays

With this in mind, we turn to a brief overview of the essays themselves. The volume is divided into three sections. In the first, some of the key concerns of the burgeoning New Divinity are set into a wider cultural and theological context.

Mark Valeri's chapter makes the case for the intellectual sophistication and culturally attuned nature of the emerging New Divinity. He argues that Edwards's manner of educating his first disciples emphasized the need for intellectual rigor and familiarity with, even emulation of, the emerging literature from the transatlantic republic of letters, as well as heartfelt religion understood in terms of Reformed theological sensibilities. What distinguishes the works of Bellamy and Hopkins as disciples of Edwards was this theological method, rooted in the print culture of the period. The need of the hour was that skeptical authors be rebutted. Bellamy and Hopkins met this challenge using "reason and moral sentiment" to address Calvinism's learned despisers. Far from being backwoods divines, Valeri argues that their devotion to all branches of polite learning demonstrated that the New Divinity was the intellectual equal of more cosmopolitan brands of theology.

Kenneth Minkema examines how Jonathan Edwards invested in educating the next generation of clergy, and how this in turn contributed to development and dissemination of the New Divinity movement. In the process, he draws attention to the New England Theology's introducing pedagogical innovations into ministerial formation and the impact this had on the movement and the wider culture. Of particular interest is the close manner in which Edwards and his epigones used a "familiar," elenchtic method of teaching, deploying questions and answers to draw out how much the student knew. The way in which they taught was, as Minkema puts it, "one of exchange, of allowing students to think for themselves but clarifying and refining that thought through a process of gradual correction and self-discovery." This method had remarkable effects: from ministerial "schools of the prophets" in the houses of pastors such as Joseph Bellamy, the New Divinity eventually became institutionalized in the early part of the nineteenth century, bringing Edwardsian pedagogical and theological sensibilities into the citadels of American higher education.

Allen Guelzo returns to the issues of original sin and human free will in his essay. These perennial dogmatic conundrums generate some of the most fundamental theological problems in the Christian tradition. They were also two signature doctrines of Edwards and the New England theologians. Focusing on the conceptual interrelationship between these two concepts in Edwards's thought, he traces out key Edwardsian ideas, including the distinction between moral and natural ability, and Edwardsian notions about imputation of Adam's sin—matters that were also of fundamental importance in the development of the New Divinity.

Taking up a related theme, James Byrd assesses how the New England doctrine of human freedom and moral responsibility was connected to benevolence and true virtue. He pays particular attention to the distinction between moral and natural ability, a matter we have already touched on. In showing how this was construed in terms of a doctrine of regeneration and the New Divinity understanding of benevolence, Byrd demonstrates that interpretation of Edwardsian ideas was part and parcel of a concerted effort to construct a coherent theological edifice on the part of his disciples, which would address nodal theological issues facing the movement as it developed, and which had important practical application in their opposition to slavery.

One of the puzzles attending this development is the departure of New Divinity theologians from Edwards's understanding of the nature of the atonement, in their distinctive brand of the governmental theory, according to which Christ acts as a penal example, not as a penal substitute. Edwards himself appears to have endorsed this view in the Preface to Joseph Bellamy's influential work *True Religion Delineated* (1750). Yet he seems to have favored a satisfaction or penal substitution account of the atonement elsewhere in his own work. Oliver Crisp takes up this theme, arguing that Edwards regarded Bellamy's work as a Reformed cousin of his own doctrine. Both theologians emphasized the same goals and similar conceptions of the divine motivation for atonement, but different models of the nature of atonement. If this is right, then it offers an answer to the question about Edwards's warmth toward

Bellamy's doctrine. It also provides an important reason for thinking that the New Divinity did not depart from the master in this central and defining doctrine in quite the way often alleged.

In the final essay in this section, Paul Helm compares the Edwardsian theology with older forms of Reformed doctrine to see whether, or to what extent, the New England divines departed from the tradition to which they claimed allegiance. He argues that there are important areas of development, even divergence. But there is also significant theological overlap, as one would expect from numerous representatives of broadly the same theological outlook. In the latter part of the paper he compares Edwards with Calvin on human freedom as a way of testing the scope of the theological differences between them on this fundamental theological issue. His chapter shows that although Edwards's theological method differed from that of his forebears because of the context in which he was writing, his theological sensibilities were similar to previous Reformed theologians, although his confidence in reason as a means of arbitrating theological and metaphysical disputes is distinct—a consequence of his immersion in the thought forms of the early Enlightenment.

In the second section, a number of the key thinkers of the New England Theology are discussed, covering the span of the movement and its several phases.

Peter Jauhiainen's essay considers the relationship between Samuel Hopkins's theology and that of the Hopkinsianism it spawned. Through careful examination of a number of key themes in Hopkins's thought, Jauhiainen shows that he was not guilty of some of the doctrinal excesses that have been attributed to him. In other cases where he does affirm the doctrine he is often thought to have held, a broader context throws a rather different light on the matter. Through his *System of Doctrines*, Hopkins's version of Edwardsian theology became arguably the most important influence on later New Divinity and New England Theology. Consequently, a right conception of the theology that underpinned these later phases of the movement requires correct understanding of the key tenets of Hopkins's theological project.

Gerald McDermott focuses on the important contribution of Nathanael Emmons, and the relationship of his thought to the decline of the New England Theology as a living force. Emmons was a singular figure, a sort of original, who influenced a generation of New Divinity ministers through his mentoring of them. He taught them to think for themselves and not to trust in tradition or received wisdom. His theology was, arguably, the most eccentric (even unorthodox) species of New England Theology. As McDermott reports it, Emmons "declared," among other things, "that God would be judged on the Day of Judgment, that Christ himself was in a state of trial during his incarnation, that God loves Lucifer as much today as before the Fall, and that it is easier to obey than to reject the commandments." He argued that regeneration was perfectly feasible as a *human* action because humanity is not subject to original sin as a consequence of Adam's fall. He also embraced the paradox that human beings are guilty of their own sin, although God is the efficient cause of such sin. As McDermott puts it, "this strange version of New Divinity showed signs of both hyper-Calvinism and anti-Calvinism at the same time."

Building on some of his earlier work in this area, David Kling looks at the New Divinity contributions of Edward Dorr Griffin and Asahel Nettleton to the Second Great Awakening. As revival was front and center in Edwards's affective theology, so it was a fundamental concern of many of his disciples. Griffin and Nettleton were, in many respects, of rather different temperaments and gifts. But both made a significant (and, until now, largely overlooked) contribution to the New Divinity through their revival preaching. Griffin was directly involved in the inception of the American foreign missionary movement that gained momentum in the early years of the nineteenth century, inspired by Jonathan Edwards's oft reprinted works on the revivals of the Great Awakening as well as works such as his *History of the Work of Redemption* and *Life of Brainerd*. Kling shows just how deeply Griffin was indebted to Edwards by comparing his most famous missionary sermon, "The Kingdom of Christ," with Edwards's published works. He also explains how Nettleton became the most successful New Divinity evangelist, a work that was cut short by ill health. At the end of their careers, both men were at pains to distance their own Edwards-inspired work from that of Charles Finney's "New Measures." But, as Kling points out, this only stoked the fires of controversy over which party (if either) represented this important aspect of Edwards's disputed legacy.

One of the significant and controversial phases of the New England Theology was that developed at Yale Divinity School by Nathaniel W. Taylor and dubbed the New Haven Theology. Douglas Sweeney spends time examining the controversy between the "Taylorites" and "Tylerites." The latter were followers of Bennet Tyler, who labored to set up a seminary in East Windsor, Connecticut, in 1834, in order to withstand the "innovations" Taylor was teaching at nearby New Haven. He argues that this acrimonious phase of one branch of the New England Theology shows two important things. First, the movement was a force to be reckoned with well into the nineteenth century, as it developed from the New Divinity of the first few generations of Edwardsians. A second, and related point, is that it was precisely because of the success of the movement in its expansion, especially in the northeastern seaboard of the United States in this period, that it ended up dividing along factional lines, which can be traced in the Taylorite-Tylerite controversy. Thus, in an important sense success proved to be its Achilles' heel, a weakness that eventually led to disintegration of the movement amid inroads being made in nineteenth-century American theology by exported German liberalism and the winds of change associated with Darwinian ideas.

The final essay of this section concerns the work of Edwards Amasa Park, the last of the New England Theologians. Charles Phillips considers his contribution to the movement and his intellectual legacy. Park has sometimes been written out of the story of New England Theology, or if not written out at least relegated to a footnote—a chronological appendage to the New Haven phase of the movement, and to Nathaniel W. Taylor in particular. Phillips argues that this is to traduce the important contribution to New England Theology made by Park. He was not a Taylorite, but a successor to the New Divinity theologians, especially of Hopkins (mediated via Emmons). But like many of his peers, he was also a devotee of the "Scotch Philosophy," that is, the commonsense realism of Thomas Reid, Dugald Stewart, and their disciples, which Park had imbibed as an undergraduate at Brown University. Park has also been regarded as a Romantic, or a crypto-Schleiermacherian, in substantial agreement with some of the views of "America's Coleridge," Horace Bushnell. But this too is mistaken, according to Phillips. Although he has an appreciation of German thought, his emphasis on religion of the heart was essentially Edwardsian in nature.

The third section considers Edwardsian theology's influence on particular denominations (e.g., Congregationalism, Presbyterianism, Baptists), as well as exploring the international reception of the movement. Some of the essays dealing with the impact of the New England Theology break new ground in their treatment of Edwardsian influences on British European thinkers, as well as the more recent Asian transmission of Edwards's thought and appropriation by the "Young, Restless, and Reformed" in North America.

In Chapter 12, Charles Hambrick-Stowe considers the primary site for reception of New England Theology, namely, the Congregationalism of New England itself, using publication of Hopkins's *System of Doctrines* as a means by which to trace out the organic development of the New Divinity. He begins with the original development of Edwardsian theology via Yale College, which provided the lion's share of New Divinity ministers in the first few generations of the movement. In fact, the New Divinity might be characterized, even in its later phases, as a "Connecticut diaspora." With publication of Hopkins's *System of Doctrines*, the movement found not only a comprehensive Congregationalist dogmatics in an Edwardsian key but a monument to the emerging influence of the movement. It was prefixed by an international list of 420 subscribers over eleven pages of close type—an advertisement, if any was needed, of the fact that this represented a significant theological event. Tracing out the connections between Hopkins's magnum opus and those who read and were influenced by it provides a fascinating window onto the close-knit brotherhood of ministers and sympathizers involved with the dispersal of this first phase of the New England Theology.

Mark Noll looks at how Edwards's intellectual legacy was fought over by New England Congregationalists and various branches of Presbyterianism in the nineteenth century. Although Edwards was appreciated and admired among the Presbyterians, it is from this quarter that the first indications of a declension narrative from Edwards to his Congregationalist successors in the New England Theology arose. This interpretation of the relationship between Edwards's work and that of his successors was complicated by the changing landscape in moral philosophy, appropriated by both Presbyterians and Congregationalists. As we have already noted, Edwards's idealism was succeeded by commonsense realism, and the Presbyterians were by and large unsympathetic to the former, and to Edwards's perceived theological and metaphysical eccentricities. But as Noll points out, some of their criticisms of Edwards's virtue theory were grounded in a relatively uncritical acceptance of the Scotch Philosophy. He ends his chapter with consideration of the reception of Edwardsian ideas in Scottish Presbyterianism. The Scottish admirers of Edwards were more interested in the man himself than Edwardsianism, and more concerned to use his ideas for their own constructive projects than to defend an Edwardsian tradition.

Michael Haykin offers an account of Edwards's influence on English Baptists. Although he appears not to have been read by the great John Gill, he was a considerable influence on Andrew Fuller and a number of other Baptists of the period. This interest was attended with some controversy: not everyone among the English Baptists was sympathetic to the "Transatlantic Divinity." But the distinction between moral and natural ability (and its releasing Fuller to preach the free call of the Gospel to all); the Hopkinsian notion of disinterested benevolence (itself a controversial notion that led Baptist John Ryland into correspondence with Hopkins); and the example of Edwards's *Life of Brainerd*, echoed in the life of the "Baptist Brainerd" Samuel Pearce, who became another exemplar of missionary zeal in the years in which the Baptist Missionary Society was in its infancy—these were important theological influences on the English Baptists. So too was the New Divinity doctrine of atonement, which was taken up by Fuller and American Baptists such as Jonathan Maxcy, who in turn influenced the "architect" of the Southern Baptist Convention, William B. Johnson. Fuller's adherence to many of the

New Divinity tenets became the main conduit by which such ideas influenced American Baptists in the first half of the nineteenth century.

Picking up where Haykin and Noll leave off, Michael McClymond considers Edwards's influence in several European theatres, focusing on reception of his metaphysics and his works on revival and eschatology, up to the middle of the twentieth century. He begins with Leslie Stephen, the father of Virginia Woolf, whose short essay on Edwards in his influential work *Hours in the Library* (1874–1879) was the first to regard Edwards as a figure of tragedy, someone fettered to an outmoded Calvinism, which robbed him of the means by which to express his genius. This was to become an important theme in the later-nineteenth- and twentieth-century literature on Edwards, from A. G. V. Allen's critical biography through to Perry Miller and Ola Winslow—the two authors whose work did so much to renew interest in Edwards's corpus. But Edwards was also revered as the author of *Freedom of the Will,* which, until publication of more of his philosophical works, was the means by which his philosophical acumen was judged. Interestingly, that judgment in British circles involved placing Edwards among the skeptics— Hume and Hobbes, as well as Collins—whose views seemed to be in sympathy with Edwardsian "necessitarianism." Although Edwards was largely ignored in German scholarship, McClymond shows that French Protestant writers were receptive to his work and found the Edwardsian emphasis on revival and spiritual theology most welcome. Nevertheless, it was as representatives of a "superior culture" that Europeans addressed themselves to Edwards, a singular intellect, or, as Stephens put it, "a German Professor dropped into the American forests." Trying to fit Edwards into the cultural taxonomies of Europe, he appeared to be something eccentric or extraordinary, rather than the progenitor of an American theology.

Chapter 16 is a bibliographical essay on the reception of Edwards in several parts of Asia. Anri Morimoto does this via a narrative commentary on the translation and publication history of Edwards's works in Japan and South Korea. His story begins in Princeton, where Edwards died. There as a graduate student, Morimoto discovered an aged copy of a Japanese translation of some of Edwards's sermons by Mamoru Iga, based on an English-language collection of Edwardsiana edited by Harry Norman Gardiner. Iga's Preface to his Japanese collection sketches out Edwards's social context in a way that mirrors aspects of his own postwar Japanese situation. Although there has been little subsequent original Japanese work on Edwards, aside from a translation of Morimoto's well-known monograph on Edwards's understanding of salvation,[14] there are signs that this is changing. A multivolume translation of parts of Edwards's *oeuvre* is now in the planning stage and an open-access online edition of much of Edwards's works is now available in Japanese. Morimoto also touches on the impact of Edwardsian studies in South Korea, where there is a small but thriving cottage industry devoted to translation of Edwards's writings, including several of the Yale letterpress editions of his works, as well as a number of secondary writings on Edwards's life and theology.

The final contribution to this volume brings Edwards's reception up to date. D. G. Hart looks at the revival of Calvinism in modern American evangelicalism via the "Young, Restless, and Reformed" movement. He considers a catena of scholars and pastors whose work has fed into this current popular interest in Calvinism, notably John H. Gerstner and Richard Lovelace at the beginning of the academic renewal of interest in Edwards in the 1960s; Iain Murray's hagiographical study of Edwards's life and reissue of the Hickman edition of *The Works of Jonathan Edwards* (1834) via the Banner of Truth Trust; and John Piper's republication of Edwards's *End of Creation* in a popular edition, as well as his advocacy for a species of Christian eudemonism that draws heavily on Edwards's spiritual writings. In recent times, there has also been a spate of edited collections on matters Edwardsian, led in large measure by academic historians. Of particular note here are the works of Mark Noll and George Marsden. Noll's interpretation of Edwards against the larger backdrop of the growth and change of American culture, including the changes entailed by the New Divinity, has proved influential. Marsden's magisterial biography, *Jonathan Edwards, A Life* (2003), is rightly regarded as a landmark work in Edwards studies. The contributions of Noll, Marsden, and other historians such as Nathan Hatch and Harry Stout was to make Edwards "the standard by which to judge subsequent evangelical developments." Hart rounds out his chapter with some remarks on Collin Hanson's book *Young, Restless, and Reformed: A Journalist's Journey with the New Calvinists* (2008) and the observation that many modern evangelicals, unlike Edwards, find the life of the mind a much more forbidding challenge than the piety that warmed Edwards's heart.

Summing up

Toward the end of his essay on the New England Theology, Park remarks that "the Theology of New England is the only system of speculative orthodoxy which will endure examination; it is, therefore, destined to prevail."[15] These words are salutary, given the subsequent disintegration of the movement. Nevertheless, as the essays in this volume testify, the New England Theology fructified American churches for a century and produced some of the most remarkable and original Reformed theology to appear on that continent. The time is ripe for reassessment of the relationship between Edwards and the theological school his thought spawned. It is hoped that the essays contained in this volume may contribute to redressing the balance in favor of a more measured, careful, and appreciative interpretation of this, the first and (to date) most influential species of American theology.

PART 1

New Light in the New World

Jonathan Edwards, the New Divinity, and Cosmopolitan Calvinism

Mark Valeri

IN 1765 SAMUEL Hopkins, a leader of the so-called New Divinity movement
and pastor in the Berkshire village of Great Barrington, Massachusetts, authored the first substantial biography of Jonathan Edwards. Hopkins had plenty of material from which to choose. As a literary executor for Edwards, he
could have probed Edwards's manuscripts for any number of personal traits
to define his subject: the great man's intense piety, devotion to the Bible, or
dogged promotion of Calvinist doctrine. Although he addressed these issues,
Hopkins chose another thread to weave through his account. As Hopkins put
it at the very beginning, Edwards was "of remarkable strength of mind, clear-
ness of thought, and depth of penetration," and "universally esteemed . . . to
be a *bright christian* and eminently *good man*." That is, Edwards had earned a
public reputation for learning and moral virtue.[1]

Hopkins returned to these traits throughout his account. Edwards "had an
uncommon thirst for Knowledge," "read all the Books" that "he could come at,"
entertained the ideas of his critics, and was "always free to give his Sentiments
on any Subject proposed to him." He was quick to engage in religious conversation with all comers, unfailingly honest, and friendly; he displayed "a
sociable Disposition, Humility, and Benevolence." He defended Calvinism—
pushing against the opposite errors of Arminianism and antinomianism—yet
Edwards always modeled a theology grounded on free exchange and intellectual discipline rather than sheer dogmatic assertion. He "judg'd that nothing
was wanting" but for Calvinists to make their case in a public sphere marked
by reason and politeness. In Hopkins's estimation, Edwards taught his followers "to have Doctrines properly stated and judiciously and well-defended,

in order to their appearing most agreeable to Reason and common Sense." Free conversation, reasonable methods, commonsense thought, wide reading, social sentiment, benevolence, and generosity: these were the virtues of an Edwardsian theologian according to Hopkins. They also were the virtues of the culture of gentility that defined the rules of Anglo-American social discourse during the second half of the eighteenth century.[2]

Along with Joseph Bellamy, a pastor in the Litchfield County town of Bethlehem, Connecticut, Hopkins created a theological movement that transmitted the inheritance of Edwards to New England congregational churches during the second half of the eighteenth century and first decades of the nineteenth. Bellamy and Hopkins formed the first cohort of this movement, which became known as the New Divinity. They taught Jonathan Edwards the Younger of New Haven and a host of western New England pastors such as John Smalley of New Britain, Connecticut. Smalley and his contemporaries, in turn, schooled yet another generation of so-called Edwardsians such as Nathanael Emmons of rural Franklin, Massachusetts. By the turn of the nineteenth century, New Divinity pastors were exercising considerable influence over the churches of western New England and some sectors of American Calvinism beyond New England. They were widely published, influential in debates about public and political issues, and noisy provocateurs at colleges such as Yale and the College of New Jersey. They claimed to carry the seminal insights of Edwards—the theology known as experimental or evangelical Calvinism—into the new nation.[3]

During the past century and a half, various scholars have used the New Divinity to ponder the relationship among three of the most powerful religious traditions in America: Calvinism, evangelicalism, and the moderate Protestant liberalism that characterized especially New England Congregationalism during the nineteenth century. Several historians have analyzed the extent to which New Divinity men maintained Edwards's revivalist agenda. Others have assessed how the Edwardsians applied Edwards's moral categories to political and social reform.[4] Most often, however, the arguments have plotted doctrinal disputes from Edwards to his students and their successors: permutations of ideas about human moral freedom, for example, or the meaning of sin and Christ's redemptive work. That history has raised several questions. Did Edwards's heirs isolate Calvinism in the arcane precincts of dogmatic precision? Did they compromise Edwards's theological system, leading to a breakdown of Calvinism?[5] Answers to these questions depend on tracing a line of innovation from Edwards through the New Divinity to a peculiarly American version of Calvinism in the nineteenth century, sometimes called the New England theology.[6]

Hopkins's biography of Edwards suggests a different approach to Edwards and his successors. His idealistic portrait indicates that Edwards influenced his first students not chiefly by handing down a set of doctrinal propositions but by showing them how to transpose Reformed tenets into contemporary cultural discourses. He urged them to present evangelical and Calvinist theology as reasonable and civil. "Reasonable" did not mean "rational" in the sense of rational religion, or a program such as deism, which eschewed traditionally orthodox Protestant doctrine in favor of natural morality and religious knowledge gained apart from divine revelation. It meant intelligible, logical, and philosophically defensible: accountable to the common dictates of public discourse. The earliest link between Edwards and his successors, that is, concerned a theological method. This helps to explain how Edwardsians distinguished themselves from more radical revivalists, making for an enduring difference between Calvinist and non-Calvinist evangelicals in America. More important, perhaps, it accounts for the instinct among American Calvinists to regard theology as a learned discipline—to reformulate doctrine in a structured system that reflected dominant intellectual discourses. The habits of Edwardsian theologians to make creed logical and precise expressed one of the very first impulses of what came to be known as evangelical Calvinism.

When Bellamy and Hopkins first met Edwards, they did not identify themselves as evangelical Calvinists per se: members of a religious party with clearly defined ideas that distinguished them from other orthodox ministers. Bellamy came to Edwards to study for a postcollegiate year of ministerial training in 1736. Through the next three years, Edwards and Bellamy were engaged in a broad-based movement, supported by nearly all of the New England clergy, to promote a vibrant piety that drew on traditionally Reformed precepts. It can be called evangelical in that it often stressed personal conversion in terms of union with Christ. They combined this emphasis on the New Birth with a conviction that God worked especially to convict many of the unregenerate at the same place and time—in other words, through revival.[7]

This evangelical agenda would become contentious after 1740, but Edwards had not yet drawn out its controversial implications when Bellamy arrived in Northampton. Like his urbane colleagues in Boston, Edwards fashioned his theology on commonly accepted standards of learning. He devoted himself to studying natural philosophy, ethics, and rational religion. He read from the transatlantic republic of letters, scouring serial publications and books written in England to find the meaning of religion held among his Protestant countrymen. He read latitudinarian divines such as Edward Stillingfleet and John Tillotson, rationalist philosophers such as John Locke and Samuel Clarke, natural theologians such as Gilbert Burnet and William

Whiston, deist moralists such as the Third Earl of Shaftesbury and Francis
Hutcheson, and social commentators such as Joseph Addison and Richard
Steele. He claimed that he had always been "in earnest to read public news-
letters" to "find some news favorable to the interest of religion in the world."
His reference to religion in such generic terms indicates that he thought a
conversion-oriented Calvinism could be the proper expression of what literate
Englishmen embraced as a common cultural mandate, even if they did not
draw the right (which is to say evangelical) conclusions.[8]

Edwards accordingly trained Bellamy to promote revival in concert with
Boston-area and other clergy who framed the evangelical message within a
tradition of respectable Protestant teaching. He had his students read a wide
range of publications that were steady fare for New England clergy. A solid,
erudite, and systematic theology formed the core of Bellamy's studies: the
Theologia Reformata of John Edwards, an English Anglican of Calvinist lean-
ings who marshaled dozens of sources to critique Anabaptists and enthusiasts
on one side, and skeptics on the other. Bellamy's student notebook from his
year in Northampton dutifully followed this method. His theological essays
conformed to a well-ordered script. He provided general definitions of God
and religion—those that befit a wide spectrum of Protestants—and the precepts even of natural religion. He constructed from them a rational apologetic
for Reformed theology and only then moved to its evangelical implications. It
was an exercise in religious reason: Calvinist in its conclusions, to be sure, but
nonetheless mindful of popular notions of religion, philosophical problems,
and public opinion.[9]

Edwards and Bellamy's interest in the dynamics of conversion mounted
through the next years, as the revivals spread. During the spring and summer of 1741, Edwards became so enamored of experimental piety that he
endorsed—indeed, promoted—spiritual experiences that fell outside the
customary lines of Reformed propriety. He appeared to sanction immediate
divine revelations, bodily convulsions or fits, and extreme emotionalism. He
frequently complained that New Englanders knew proper doctrine but did not
experience its life-changing power. His preached his famous "Sinners in the
Hands of an Angry God" to abet the spiritual agonies and ecstasies that had
spread throughout the Connecticut River Valley.[10]

During this period, Bellamy also joined the revivals in full force. After
a temporary pulpit assignment in Worcester, Massachusetts, he settled in
Bethlehem in 1738. He began a preaching ministry marked by modest and
sober conversions. Inspired especially by George Whitefield's stormy 1740
visit to New England, he overthrew the restraints of modesty and sobriety. He
itinerated frequently and became known for emotionally packed sermons that

drew fervent responses. He supported New Light preachers who had separated from the established church order and provoked legal quarrels over ordination and church property. He even welcomed the work of Moravians. He
focused his preaching on the dangers of religious formalism, decrying New
England's customary insistence on social morality and theological precision
as spiritually fatal. He criticized ministers who did not join the revival, especially those in Boston, as useless. He was something of a preaching celebrity,
known to be nearly as effective as Whitefield himself. During the summer of
1741, he and Edwards were part and parcel of a movement that burst the very
meaning of evangelical.[11]

From late 1741 to 1748, however, Edwards changed course and took Bellamy
and Hopkins with him. He gave one of the first indications of this shift in
his famous "Distinguishing Marks" sermon of 1741. Attempting to dissociate
heightened emotions, spiritual ecstasies, and disorderly behavior from genuine revival, he began to hedge spiritual experience with commonly accepted
Reformed rules for moral obligation and theological reflection. He came to
denounce what he deemed to be New Light radicalism under two rubrics.
First, he decried enthusiasm: the claim to immediate revelations from heaven
that displaced traditional interpretations of the Bible. He issued warnings
against calling other ministers godless, supporting unlicensed preachers, provoking church schism or separation, and behaving in an indecent or unseemly
manner. Second, he deplored antinomianism: any rejection of the Reformed
idea that individuals ought to pursue a moral life—obey the law of God—as
integral to the social order and development of religious sensibilities. He also
insisted that public institutions conform to scriptural standards for justice.[12]

In the spring of 1742, Edwards brought his new perspective to his congregation. He had been preaching in other pulpits for several weeks
and expressed some concern that the visiting preacher in Northampton,
Samuel Buell, encouraged the very excesses that so alarmed him. He
rushed to have the congregation sign a new covenant of faith. The document testified to their intention to deport themselves in a socially respectable manner. "In all our conversation, concerns, and dealings with our
neighbors," it proclaimed, "we will have a strict regard to rules of honesty,
justice, and uprightness . . . and will carefully endeavor in everything to
do to others as we should expect, or think reasonable, that they should do
to us." Edwards sent a copy of this covenant to Thomas Prince in Boston,
signifying his design to present a publicly respectable version of evangelical
religion.[13]

Hopkins witnessed these efforts firsthand. He resided in the Northampton
parsonage twice from 1741 through 1742, including the period in which the new

church covenant was instituted, to pursue his ministerial training. We have no record of the course of study that Edwards laid out for Hopkins, unlike for Bellamy. There are strong indications nonetheless that Edwards attempted to counsel Hopkins against a sort of hyperspirituality that washed away theological common sense. He instructed his pupil to read Protestant theologians who combined reason with the Spirit—who took seriously scholarly approaches to Scripture and moral duty. Later in life, Hopkins and Bellamy constructed their own manuals for ministerial training, which read very much like Bellamy's student notebook.[14]

Edwards alerted Bellamy and Hopkins to the threat that radicalism posed. Church separation and the excesses of revivals gave ammunition to rationalist ministers, such as Boston's Charles Chauncy and Jonathan Mayhew, who argued that all New Lights were disorderly, unreasonable, immoral, and scandalous. Edwards cast these so-called Old Lights as Arminians: crypto-enemies of Calvinism who misused reason and common moral sentiment to discredit even the theologically sound elements of revival. Yet he took his cue from the Old Light cynics. He realized that the whole evangelical cause might be portrayed as irrational and impolite—a disgrace to true religion. His most widely known work in the denouement of the Awakening, his *Treatise on Religious Affections*, amounted to an extended essay on the public evidence for genuine religious experience. Among those "signs" of true piety were social virtues such as genuine understanding, sincerity, honesty, modesty, deference, appreciation for excellence and beauty, and that most Enlightened of moral virtues, benevolence.[15]

Edwards urged Bellamy in particular to avoid any further association with separatists and to denounce radical evangelicals such as James Davenport and Andrew Croswell. He also advised Bellamy and Hopkins to read serious philosophical and theological works—everything from the moral philosophy of Hutcheson to respectable and highly systematic Calvinist theologians such as Geneva's Francis Turretin. Bellamy followed his mentor's advice. He stopped itinerating, broke relationships with separatists, and retreated into his study to read thinkers who made theology a matter of reasonableness and public concern. As Bellamy put it several years later, the "delusions which I saw take place in New Light times have engaged me, as well [has] the divided state of the Christian world in general, to devote my whole time for above twenty years to enquire into the nature of Christianity. I have conversed with all men of genius and have read all the books I could come at." Conversing with "men of genius," either in person or through their books: this was the mark of sociability and politeness, intellectual openness and theological deliberation.[16]

During the late 1740s, Edwards worked closely with Bellamy and Hopkins to ground evangelicalism in Calvinist theology and reconnect it to transatlantic learning. In so doing, they defined evangelical Calvinism.[17] It was evangelical yet distinguished from radicalism by its deference to learned culture, proper sensibility, and systematic theology. It reinforced the ideal of a piety that reformed from within rather than separated from the established church, ordained ministry, sacramental regimes, and civic order. It was polite, and politeness formed a hedge against irresponsible enthusiasm. It recognized a cosmopolitan culture that held all theologies accountable to reason and social morality. Politeness had its social expressions through proper greeting, expressions of deference to superiors and equals, and sentiments of kindness to inferiors. As a quality of intellectual activity, it included civility, urbanity, and cultivation of sensibility. Politeness implied a common understanding of the rules or reason that made for debate and exchange without rancor. It functioned as a mode of social credit, of trust between individuals based on language and deportment.[18]

Edwards, Bellamy, and Hopkins thus pursued a method designed to protect their position against enthusiasm and defend it against Arminianism. Edwards rededicated himself to Anglo-American letters that inculcated the virtues of politeness: cultural sophistication, familiarity with *belles lettres*, sincerity, and regard for social proprieties. He was not the first New England theologian to deploy politeness. His predecessors, such as the Boston pastor (and supporter of Edwards) Benjamin Colman, had long drawn on writers such as Shaftesbury and Tillotson to identify themselves with the cultured religiosity—and patriotism—of Britain's leading moralists. Edwards had read widely during the 1720s, and now he returned to his print collection, acquired other titles, and introduced his students to them. He immersed himself in London periodicals such as the *Guardian*, the *Gentleman's Library*, the *Spectator*, and *London Magazine*, which made suggestions on the latest fashions and social customs. He especially favored Steele's *The Ladies Library*, a serial advice book about manners; he copied passages from it and emulated the styles recommended in it. He lent his copies of *The Ladies Library* to Bellamy and Hopkins, along with issues of the *Monthly Review* and Daniel Defoe's *Family Instructor*. Edwards even came to like early English novels, such as Samuel Richardson's *Clarissa*, because they cultivated sensibility—the ability to perceive the moral states of other people (even if fictional).[19]

In their attempts to make evangelical religion sturdy, Calvinist, and morally reputable, Edwards and his students developed a theology that reflected the mid-eighteenth-century sensibilities of the Anglo-American Enlightenment. Edwards argued that New Englanders' aversion to the New Birth derived not from an overacquaintance with religious reason but from a misunderstanding of, even unfamiliarity with, the currents of cosmopolitan culture. So he used the latest epistemological treatises, moral philosophy, scientific works, latitudinarian sermons, and the irenic theologies of writers such as Philip Doddridge as vehicles for his message. He did not adopt all of their ideas, but he did believe that evangelical Calvinism could be accommodated to the universal knowledge accumulated throughout the Enlightened Anglo-American world.[20]

Edwards was eager to learn politeness and have his students do the same because it strengthened the appeal of evangelical theology. He signaled his approval of Bellamy's first lengthy publication, *True Religion Delineated*, in a preface that lauded the work in these very terms. Edwards described Bellamy's book in Tillotsonian cadences. It expounded a "Religion" that merited devotion because it provided "Knowledge" for "our enjoying the Benefits of God's Favour"—a benevolent deity. It also disclosed "the Connection and Reason of Things" in a way that "may be easily seen." As for the author, he was admirably modest, not motivated by "Vanity of Mind" or "Desire of Applause." Bellamy, Edwards admitted, did not bother with the "Ornaments of Stile and Language as might best suit the Gust of Men of polite Literature." Yet the very homespun nature of *True Religion Delineated* marked it as sophisticated nonetheless, "very entertaining and profitable to every serious and impartial Reader."[21]

During the final decade of Edwards's life (which ended in 1758), he, Bellamy, and Hopkins further developed their ideas in the forum of public debate. Opponents continued to attack evangelical Calvinism, but their criticisms did not concern the excesses of revivals, which had cooled considerably. They concerned the fundamental tenets of orthodox Calvinism: human depravity, divine election, and Christ's vicarious atonement in particular. This led to the "paper war" of the 1750s, when New England publishers produced, at a sometimes frenetic pace, dozens of works about free will, moral virtue, the deity of Christ, the process of salvation, divine sovereignty and the existence of evil, and the nature of eternal punishment. Those must have been heady days to be a theologian: New England presses issued eight publications on the doctrine of original sin in 1758 alone. The polemics involved Edwardsians from western New England, Boston's clergy, commentators from Scotland and England, and frequent references to English rationalists who deconstructed the whole platform of Reformed Protestantism.[22]

Edwards and his two students spent much of this period corresponding with each other, advising one another, and purchasing and reading books about reason, morality, and Calvinist theology. Edwards's son, Jonathan Edwards the Younger, a student of Bellamy's and a budding theologian in his own right, joined the epistolary conversation. They all conferred about how best to construct a rational apologetic for experimental Calvinism. Unlike their liberal theological opponents, who sacrificed much of Calvinist doctrine, they determined to present what they called consistent Calvinism—hard and fast evangelical Calvinism—as a theological system. At the same time, they intended to refute separatist or radical New Lights who refused to make intelligible theological arguments and isolated themselves in their unsociable ecstasies. As one rural Massachusetts pastor observed to Bellamy, the New Divinity gave evangelical-Calvinist sympathizers a "reason" and "a system." The Edwardsians operated in the polite precincts of social conversation and reading, and in the pubic sphere defined by print culture and appeal to universal standards of moral and philosophical validity.[23]

Other publications by a variety of popular authors informed Edwards's approach. He especially favored John Clarke's *An Essay upon Study*. Clarke advised readers to emulate learned writers of the modern age, such as Locke, so that they could make coherent arguments that took all relevant positions into account. Should they overcome ignorance with up-to-date knowledge, and bigotry with generosity, they could make their case while maintaining ties of sociability. According to Clarke, this method enhanced the true cause of religion, which was virtue. Edwards did not describe the cause of religion precisely in this way, but he nonetheless accepted Clarke's advice, especially because it was directed to dissenters in England who shared Edward's religious perspectives. They, Clarke suggested, would do well to write or speak in a public voice, to allow their critics "to see what they have to say" and "see" the "abundant Reason" behind their theologies. This "will lay a Foundation for Peace and mutual Forbearance, amongst such as prefer Virtue and true Religion before all Considerations." Edwards also consulted the *Youth's Friendly Monitor*, a London publication by James Burgh, a friend of Benjamin Franklin. Burgh gave his readers suggestions for their libraries—books that would make them learned and genteel, that would "qualify" them "for the Conversation of the greatest Men."[24]

Edwards also compelled Bellamy and Hopkins to borrow, collect, and lend books from all over the learned world, often provided by the Edinburgh bookseller John Erskine. Tellingly, Hopkins recounted how Edwards "had an uncommon thirst for Knowledge" and "read all the Books" that "he could come at." These were nearly the exact words that Bellamy used to describe his own theological studies during the late 1740s and early 1750s; by his account, he decided to "remain in my study" where he "read all the books I could come at."[25]

Edwards acquainted himself with a remarkable range of historical, scientific, philosophical, and religious works from the British Enlightenment.

He studied Ephraim Chambers's *Cyclopaedia* and an early version (in translation) of Diderot and D'Alembert's *Encyclopedia* to keep apace with current discoveries in the natural and human sciences. He collected histories and travel accounts. He quoted from rationalist theologians such as Chevalier Ramsay, Ralph Cudworth, and Joseph Butler; took a great interest in the Boyle Lectures (on natural philosophy and religion); and pondered the cosmologies of William Derham, John Ray, and Whiston. Bellamy was not as versed in natural philosophy, as was Edwards. He took the lead in reading the works of, and sharing thoughts with Edwards and Hopkins about, Continental theologians and British moralists. He informed Edwards that Swiss and German theologians such as Johan Friedrich Staupfer and Christian Wolff appeared to offer solutions to the problem of evil, even if they tended to a Leibnizian form of deism. He read the standard moral treatises by Hutcheson and Lord Kames. He also specialized in British critics who challenged the essential tenets of Protestantism: from the skeptic David Hume to deists and proto-Unitarians such as William Wollaston, William Sherlock and John Taylor.[26]

Such reading represented the attempts of the early Edwardsians to enter into transatlantic intellectual disputes. They staked their claim to reasonableness especially on the regnant moral philosophy of the British Enlightenment, which had come to fasten on benevolence as the definitive virtue. A reasonable theology in this sense promoted the belief that God designed the cosmos to reveal and enforce the virtues of benevolence. Contemporary British moralists and latitudinarian divines contended that the integration of the world into a moral system bound together by imperatives to benevolence had an aesthetic quality. It was beautiful, and therefore a sign that its Creator deserved worship. The Edwardsians determined to show that this system logically led to the tenets of evangelical Calvinism, from its assertions of divine sovereignty, human sin, and the doctrine of the atonement to its mandate for immediate conversion. Their definition of true religion, they maintained, not only encouraged benevolence but provided the most satisfying account of its origins, nature, and imperatives.[27]

Engaged in this task, they produced a burst of sophisticated theological works during the 1750s. Hopkins (to turn again to his biography of Edwards) recounted how Edwards wrote his most lengthy and formally argued treatises during this period: his *Freedom of the Will*; *Original Sin*; and *Two Dissertations, I. Concerning the End for Which God Created the World. II. The Nature of True Virtue*. By Hopkins's account, Edwards was "greatly helpful by his Direction and Assistance against the two opposite Extremes [Arminianism and antinomianism], both in Conversation, Preaching and Writing. His Publications on this Occasion" especially his treatises on the will and original sin, shed "the most clear and striking Light." Hopkins coded his understanding of Edwards's influence in the words "conversation" and "publications"; they implied the importance of a respectable, polite, and publicly intelligible theology.[28]

Hopkins followed suit with his first sustained theological work, *A Bold Push*, which offered a defense of the Calvinist proposition that divine sovereignty and human moral accountability were not incompatible but completely congruent truths. Hopkins's specific arguments are less important here than the mode of his argument. Constructing his piece in the form of a dialogue, he used subtle humor and the rhetoric of deference: popular literary devices employed by the most formidable and genteel thinkers. He contended that the Calvinist position was "most *reasonable*, and demonstrably evident from the Being and Perfections of God." Criticisms of Calvinism were filled with "Absurdity" and were "contradictory to the *common Sense* and *Reason* of Mankind." Hopkins appealed to the "common Sense of Mankind" throughout his work, using straightforward logic and commonplace stories to make his point. He did not appeal to creed and Scripture as authorities that trumped civil notions of good argument. Bellamy as well often wrote in dialogue form, sometimes through letters published in newspapers. He also deployed humor, sarcasm, anecdote, and common sense. In presenting their works in such fashion and venues, New Divinity thinkers located themselves in the public sphere, where decorous and widely accessible norms of truth counted for responsible debate.[29]

Edwards and his students also wrote more sustained theological publications—not without humorous jabs, but in the main dense and sober. They were not sermons that appealed to the faithful on the basis of dogmatic authority. They used reason and moral sentiment to address a skeptical audience. Bellamy perfectly followed Edwards's example—did theology in the fashion that Edwards taught him—when he began his first major work, *True Religion Delineated*. He conformed his apology for Calvinism to the moral philosophy emanating from Glasgow and London. "While *Arminians* are glossing their scheme, and appealing to reason and common sense, as though their principles were near or quite self-evident to all men of thought and candour; and while *enthusiasts* are going about as men inspired," he contended, he aimed to show the real meaning of "reason and common sense," "a compassionate sense, I say, of the exercises of mind." He meant to show that Calvinism "contains a scheme perfectly rational, divine, and glorious," "reasonable and fit, and a thing becoming and beautiful." His subsequent argument did not rush to proof-texting Reformed axioms. He built his case on "reasonable" definitions of God and religion—those confirmed by Tillotson, Shaftesbury, and Hutcheson. He meant to demonstrate that the God of Calvinism was hardly the monster that its critics portrayed. The Calvinist God, rather, was an "absolutely perfect" and morally "amiable BEING," wholly disposed to "virtue" as defined in common intellectual parlance. As Bellamy put it in a later treatise, "God's moral character" must "be ascertained" according to the nature of things in themselves, the moral world as civilized people saw it. He made a cultured if nonetheless rigorous claim for experimental Calvinism.[30]

The subsequent work of Bellamy and Hopkins, then, reflected Jonathan Edwards's influence most fundamentally in the very method they used to write theology. They attempted to produce writings that were polite, learned, and convincing. Like their mentor, they insisted that evangelical Calvinism be offered in the public sphere, to be deliberated along with the other ideas. This is not to suggest that they minimized the importance of essential Calvinist tenets. Indeed, it explains their devotion to a form of theological reason that moved from philosophically defensible principles to precise theological formulations all the way down the line to the most minute detail of doctrine. Their rigor, they believed, set them apart from Arminian and enthusiastic theologies that lapsed into quite contradictory but equally disastrous forms of theological unreason.

The New England theologians who followed Edwards, Bellamy, and Hopkins recognized as much. Jonathan Edwards the Younger claimed that the big, highly technical treatises of his father were his most important works because they were so powerfully and acutely persuasive. Edwards's *Freedom of the Will*, for example, showed "the absurdity, the manifold contradictions, the inconceivableness, and [as if those were not enough] the impossibility" of Arminian schemes resting on the fiction of a self-determining volition. "Now, therefore," Edwards the Younger claimed, "the Calvinists find themselves placed upon firm and high ground. They fear not the attacks of their opponents. They face them on the ground of reason, as well as of Scripture." *The Great Christian Doctrine of Original Sin Defended* likewise placed "the followers of Mr. Edwards" on "strong ground, ground upon which they are willing, at any time, to meet their opponents." Edwards instructed his followers "by resolving several complicated difficulties into one simple vindicable principle." He gave the Edwardsians a model of how to defend their theology in the swirl of polemics about God and reason.[31]

Nathanael Emmons described his own theological development to have included a growing appreciation for the method that Edwards inculcated in New England. Once again, print culture—the vehicle for knowledge in the public sphere—stood out. After reading Edwards, Emmons recounted, he "resolved to . . . furnish myself with a good collection of books" from all branches of knowledge. He kept his "eye upon the catalogues of book-sellers," used his church's considerable library, and spent his salary and occasional gifts on books. He read from all theological quarters, especially considering contrary opinions on theological controversies.

Like Edwards, Emmons also connected his books to a public culture constructed of polite letters and the intersections of diverse forms of knowledge. "The more I attended to theology," Emmons reflected, "the more I was convinced of the importance of acquainting myself with history, ethics, metaphysics, and civil polity. This led me to read freely upon those subjects, and to form my own opinions upon them." Emmons thought it a shame that so many pastors "so much disregarded general knowledge, and paid their whole attention to divinity." He even read "some authors for the sake of their beautiful style, their lively descriptions, and moral sentiments." The cultivation of sensibility enhanced sociability. Emmons respected polite "conversation," by which he "seldom failed of getting knowledge, by discoursing freely" with New Englanders of all religious conviction. He thought that Calvinists could persist in the public domain. Like Edwards and Bellamy, Emmons led his congregation into a revival. He was happy, however, that his people, unlike Edwards's, "never expressed any enthusiastic fervor or zeal, but manifested a sensible, rational, scriptural joy in God." Sensibility and rationality denoted the right kind of religious training.[32]

New Divinity men and their successors aspired all the more to cosmopolitanism for their social position. Rural parsons such as Bellamy, Smalley, and Emmons presented themselves as the intellectual equals of their urban interlocutors. Liberals in Boston and New Haven in turn ridiculed them as conservative rubes from the Berkshire backcountry. The Edwardsians, to be sure, carried their learnedness a bit too self-consciously, with a hint of provincial amateurism. Such judgments, however, merely reinforce this chapter's suggestion about the New Divinity. They took it upon themselves to rebuff Bostonian disdain with attempts at sophistication. Their relative isolation compelled them to claim cultural cachet all the more.[33]

It was an indication of the persistence of Jonathan Edwards's agenda that later Edwardsians, far into the nineteenth century, continued to shape the form of their theologies to cultural respectability even as they maintained the doctrines of evangelical Calvinism. They could have described God, creation, sin, and redemption in any number of terms. They chose the idioms of public moral deliberation. God was amiable and creation beautiful. Human nature was vicious and self-interested. The atonement was logically necessary. Those predicates were eminently respectable moral categories. They represented the mandate to proffer America a reasonable and systematic theology of Calvinism.

This admittedly quite general observation about formal rather than substantive matters—that Edwards bequeathed an intellectual method—might
serve as a way into reading the development of Edwards's religious ideas
through the New Divinity into the New England Theology. Edwards, Bellamy,
and Hopkins settled that tradition on cautious, careful, and systematic thought.
They did so because they feared something within the evangelical movement,
or more pointedly, perhaps within themselves: the temptation to remove spiritual experience from the realms of a publicly defensible Calvinism. If nothing
else, this observation at least explains why disputes over theological details
became so compelling. The reasonableness of doctrine became the whole
point of doing theology. Edwards, Hopkins, and Bellamy's insistence on that
created American evangelical Calvinism.

2

Jonathan Edwards on Education and His Educational Legacy

Kenneth P. Minkema

TODAY, WHEN YOU hear of "Edwardsian education," it more than likely involves downloading online curricula, or using mobile phones and social media—so ubiquitous, and so adapted to modern technology in a global age, have pedagogical tools on Edwards and his legacy become. But what are the roots of this educational legacy in texts and training? The topic of Jonathan Edwards as an educator is something that scholars and devotées often mention but have not discussed in anything like a concerted manner. Therefore, this essay examines some aspects of Edwards's educational thought and experience in his lifetime, and then it turns to some early figures within the Edwardsian tradition to show pedagogical changes and continuities over the late eighteenth and nineteenth centuries.[1]

Letter to Pepperrell

In regard to Edwards himself, we shall proceed not chronologically but by life course phase, from his education of children to that of young people in pastoral and collegiate settings, and then of the training of ministerial candidates. To begin with children, we must go nearly to the end of Edwards's career, when he took up the missionary post at Stockbridge and was responsible, among other things, for maintaining boarding schools for the Indian children there. "Children," incidentally, were for Edwards those younger than fifteen years of age.[2]

In November 1751, he wrote a key letter to Sir William Pepperrell, the hero of Louisburg and a supporter of the Indian mission. Edwards had visited Sir

William and his wife in the spring of the year, when the two discussed the prospects for the mission.[3] The letter is Edwards's most complete statement of his philosophy of education, which he sought to implement in his time at Stockbridge with teachers Timothy Woodbridge and Gideon Hawley.

As the schools for both the boys and girls were something of a blank slate, Edwards was particularly interested in establishing a system of instruction that would ensure the greatest efficacy.[4] Today, New England's public school system, founded in colonial times, is viewed by historians as one of the American puritans' chief legacies.[5] But if we were to judge it by Edwards's description, we might hesitate in this estimation. For his part, he defined a "successful" system largely as anything that schools among the English were not. The mission school, he felt, "should be free from the gross defects of the ordinary method of teaching among the English." Children in English schools were "habituated to learning without understanding," that is, they were taught to read only through the habit of "making such and such sounds, on the sight of such and such letters," and so without comprehension. "In like manner they are taught their catechism," Edwards opined, "saying over the words by rote, which they began to say, before they were capable of easily and readily comprehending them." Sounds, and the ideas that were associated with them, were not connected.

Edwards advocated a different kind of pedagogical episteme. Instead of implementing learning primarily by rote or memorization, he envisioned a dialogic, or what he called a "familiar," method that drew on new theories of learning from figures such as John Locke as well as on tried-and-true forms such as scholastic disputation.[6] "In these boarding schools, the children should never read a lesson," Edwards continued, "without the master or mistress taking a care, that the child be made to attend to, and understand, the meaning of the words and sentences which it reads." More important, "the child should be taught to understand *things*, as well as *words*." After reading something, the teacher should explain not only the words and phrases; "the things which the lesson treats of should be, in a familiar manner, opened to the child's understanding." This should in turn open a conversation between teacher and student, with "familiar questions" that encourage the child "to speak freely, and in his turn also to ask questions, for the resolution of his own doubts." So too when working with "printed catechisms," this principle of exchange, of encouraging inquiry on the part of the student, should prevail. "[Q]uestions should be asked them from time to time," Edwards asserted, "in the same familiar manner, as they are asked questions commonly about their ordinary affairs." Eventually, this would inculcate "the habit of conversation on divine things," and the child would be "divested of that shyness and backwardness discovered in children, to converse on such topics with their superiors." Though Edwards may have been no advocate of an open classroom, his idea of teaching was more open than the traditional relation between instructor and student.

Note, too, Edwards's stress on "understanding." In his treatises, particularly that on freedom of will, he identified understanding as the chief cognitive faculty over against will. Understanding for him was the faculty whereby a person judged, discerned, and speculated. He defined it in "a large sense, as including the whole faculty of perception or apprehension, and not merely what is called reason or judgment."[7] Knowledge is acquired, and thereby choices informed, through understanding. So, behind his theories about teaching Indian children lurked his anthropology.

Another way in which Edwards judged "the common methods of instruction in New England" to be "grossly defective" was that instructors did not give "a short general scheme of the scriptural history" to their charges. Here we see the centrality of *religious content* in Edwards's view of education and individual development, both intellectual and spiritual. From the general heads of this scriptural scheme, the teacher could "entertain them, in like familiar discourse, with the particular stories of the Scriptures, sometimes with one story, and then with another, before they can obtain the knowledge of them themselves, by reading." One of the chief components of Edwards's "familiar manner" of education was *telling stories*—the same shift we see in his sermonic delivery on coming to Stockbridge. In this way, the whole child was addressed: "informing of the child's understanding, influencing his heart, and directing its practice."

Once they had learned to read their Bibles with enough proficiency, children "might be set to read a particular story, sometimes one, and sometimes another, diligently observing it." After reading, the master or mistress could inquire "concerning the particulars of the story, to see that the child has taken good notice, and is able to give an account of it." Edwards became quite ambitious for his Stockbridge children. They were to be immersed in the connections between the Old and New Testaments, ecclesiastical history, chronology, and the geography of the Middle East.

Edwards was further innovative in arguing that these methods were to be taken with both boys *and* girls. This was going against custom, in which daughters were given only a minimal education, or if from an elite or upwardly mobile middle-class family then perhaps they attended a dame school for a time to learn domestic skills such as painting and embroidery. Edwards's inclusivism on this count was due in part to his own upbringing in his parents' home school with ten well-educated sisters, but it also seems to have reflected a commonly held, though little studied, view of coeducation within provincial gentry culture.[8]

However, having pleased modern readers with some hint of gender equality, Edwards goes on to show himself to a person of his times. He pointed out that these measures "would serve, the more speedily and effectually, to change the taste of Indians, and to bring them off from their barbarism and brutality, to a relish for those things which belong to civilization and refinement." Conventional European wisdom held that "Christian" meant "civilized," and "civilized" meant European in lifestyle, clothing, housing, manners, and especially speech. At Stockbridge, Indians were to be weaned from their native tongues and made to speak English.

> It is necessary that the children should be taught the English tongue; and indeed this is the most absolute necessity, on almost every account. Indian languages are extremely barbarous and barren, and very ill-fitted for communicating things moral and divine, or even things speculative and abstract. In short, they are wholly unfit for a people possessed of civilization, knowledge and refinement.

To this conventional end, Edwards again proposed an innovative step: mixing English and Indian students together.

Yet another intriguing aspect of Edwards's view of "Christian education" was his proposal to teach the students to sing. "Music, especially sacred music, has a powerful efficacy to soften the heart into tenderness, to harmonize the affections, and to give the mind a relish for objects of a superior character." His emphasis on the role of music was a carryover from his personal and his family life. In his private devotions, he sang and chanted his meditations.[9] Family devotions in his home included psalm and hymn singing, and there were instruments in the Edwards home as well.[10] Also, music points to Edwards's aesthetics, which was a central part of his philosophical theology. He portrayed the Trinity in musical terms and saw harmony as part of the excellency and beauty of the divine and of creation.[11]

Questions for Young People

Among Edwards's manuscripts is a little-referenced set of "Questions for Young People,"[12] which gives us a glimpse of how he functioned as a Bible instructor within his church at Northampton, Massachusetts. "Young people" Edwards defined as individuals from fifteen to twenty-five years old. This set of questions was for young men; a similar list for young women, if there ever was one, has not survived. In the list, a total of sixty-six names appear of individuals born between 1712 and 1728—in other words, those who joined the church during the Connecticut Valley revival of 1734–35.[13] These questions, some 150 of which survive, were drawn from Scripture to test the catechists' knowledge of the Scripture history, their power to relate one passage to another, and their reasoning ability.

Edwards constructed the list with a certain format. Here are a couple of random examples, showing how he stated the question, provided the scriptural reference that answered it, and appended the name of the person to whom it was assigned:

> 4. Where was the place where the tabernacle that Moses made in the wilderness was kept after the children of Israel were come up out [of] Egypt and settled in Canaan? Josh. 18:1. (Simeon Root)
> 48. How often did the children of Israel come to the Red Sea after they departed from Mt. Sinai before they came to Canaan? Num. 6:33, 35; Num. 6:14, 25; Deut. 2:1, I Kgs. 9:26. (Joseph Parsons)

These samples reflect a couple of things. First, Edwards set the bar pretty high for his catechists—though it's important to remember that biblical literacy was high at this time. Second, most of the questions relate to the Old Testament. More generally, however, Edwards could formulate a theme, such as "Questions that must be answered by the knowledge of the harmony of the evangelists." Still other items could relate explicitly to sermons that the examinees would have heard their pastor preach—perhaps to make sure they were listening attentively:

> 52. Questions concerning the circumstances of Christ's last sufferings, out of my discourse of the sufferings of Christ.[14]

An even more expansive approach is represented in an entry that appears at the very end of the list, where the manuscript is battered:

> [138. A]T ANOTHER TIME, put the [y]oung people upon giving [rea] sons of this or that, and proving such [and s]uch things by argument. [Also,] what arguments can you bring [for them], or how do you prove [them; wh]at can you mention that proves [them; what can] you give for this or that?

Even here, where students were to martial their reasons for "this or that," Edwards employed a variation of his open or "familiar" method.

Tutorship at Yale

From young people in a parish setting, we now move to Edwards as an instructor of baccalaureate students—still young people, to be sure, but at a more intensive and sophisticated level of instruction. For Edwards's first experience at this level, we must jump back in time to when he was still a young person himself, to the period from June 1724 to September 1726, when he was a tutor at Yale College.

We know that Edwards spent as much time as he could in the college library, but what did he teach? Though we have little direct knowledge, one source tells us something. In 1729, John Sargeant, who later would be Edwards's predecessor at the Stockbridge mission, gave the valedictorian oration at commencement. By this time Edwards was ensconced at Northampton; Sargeant and his classmates had been tutored as freshmen and possibly sophomores by Edwards, who attended the ceremony. Sargeant's language, in keeping with valedictories, is deliberately florid, but from it we learn that Edwards taught rhetoric ("the art of speaking"), mathematics ("the mysteries of number and mathematical quantity"), astronomy ("the magnitudes of the globes that compose our system"), and natural philosophy ("you have led us into the deepest recesses of nature, and disclosed her most intricate contrivances").[15] These topics reflect the college curriculum at the time, based on the medieval formula of the *trivium* (grammar, logic, and rhetoric) and *quadrivium* (algebra, geometry, astronomy, and music).

Edwards at Princeton

Next, we must fast-forward in time to the last months of Edwards's life. Perhaps the most famous document relating to his Princeton period is his lengthy and remarkably self-disclosing letter to the college trustees, in response to their offer of the presidency. Edwards demurred, giving them a wonderfully onomatopoeic description of his body's "constitution"—with its "flaccid solids, vapid, sizy and scarce fluids, and a low tide of spirits"—and a fulsome summary of his unfinished "great works." What is less frequently noticed in the letter is Edwards's self-estimation in scholarly terms. First, he confessed, "I am . . . deficient in some parts of learning, particularly in algebra, and the higher parts of mathematics, and in the Greek classics; my Greek learning having been chiefly in the New Testament." Next, he described his "method of study" as consisting "very much in writing."[16] Also, he was quite disingenuous—some might say he was negotiating terms—in setting limits to what would be expected of him as president. He would not "go through the same course of employ" as his late predecessor and son-in-law, Aaron Burr, Sr.—especially seeing that Burr's rigorous and rather hectic schedule had been the death of him. Rather, Edwards offered,

> I should be willing to take upon me the work of a president, so far as it consists in the general inspection of the whole society and sub-servient to the school, as to their order and methods of study and instruction, assisting myself in immediate instruction in the arts and sciences (as discretion should direct and occasion serve, and the state of things require), especially the senior class: and added to all, should be willing to do the whole work of a professor of divinity, in public and private lectures, proposing questions to be answered, and some to be discussed in writing and free conversation, in meet-ings of graduates and others, appointed in proper seasons for these ends. It would be now out of my way, to spend time, in a constant teaching of the languages; unless it be the Hebrew tongue, which I should be willing to improve myself in, by instructing others.[17]

From Samuel Hopkins, a student of Edwards's and his earliest biographer, we learn that Edwards "preached in the college hall Sabbath after Sabbath, to the great acceptance of his hearers."[18] In Edwards's extant sermon corpus, there are only two sermons that can be identified as having been preached at Princeton, in February 1758. The first was on II Peter 1:19, with the doctrine "Divine revelation is like a light that shines in a dark place."[19] For the students, Edwards emphasized the role of prophecy as the word of truth "in the midst of heretics and apostates." He engaged in a grand survey of world religions, from Deism to Catholicism to Islam, as instances of cultures that were devoid of divine revelation, or where it had been corrupted. Scripture, he concluded, was the "greatest and most important and most divine truth." The other sermon was on Jude 6, in which Edwards proclaimed that "the day of judgment will be a great day."[20] In a spectacular panoply, he described the final judgment from the manifestation of God's glory in its many aspects to the "grand assembly" that will be gathered before the judgment seat to the cessation of the earth. From comparative religions (albeit through the filter of protestant triumphal-ism) to the conflagration, Edwards, we can surmise, felt these sermons to be educational as much as inspirational, because of their basis in his reading of the Bible.

Theological Questions

Recounting Edwards's time at Princeton, Hopkins states that, besides preaching in the college hall, he gave out

> some questions in divinity to the senior class, to be answered before him; each one having opportunity to study and write what he thought proper upon them. When they came together to answer them, they found so much entertainment and profit by it, especially by the light and instruction Mr. Edwards communicated in what he said upon the questions, when they had delivered what they had to say, that they spoke of it with the greatest satisfaction and wonder.[21]

Two observations can be made about this recollection. First, we see Edwards employing what we have called here his open or "familiar" method, in which he had the young scholars write up their own thoughts first, and then engage with him in dialogue about them. Second, we can in all likelihood identify these "questions in divinity" that Edwards dispensed as coming from two extant lists. One is a manuscript entitled "Questions on Theological Subjects,"[22] which contains a total of fifty-three problems in doctrine and theology, set down in a notebook constructed in 1746 or later. These are a step up in complexity from the "Questions for Young People." At this point in his life, Edwards was attracting more ministerial candidates into his home, which may explain why he took the time to compose this document. These questions don't proceed in the order dictated by systematic theology but, much like the "Miscellanies," jump around from topic to topic, though with an emphasis on the nature of God (for example, "In what sense is God said to be necessarily existent?") and on aspects of soteriology, as represented by the query, "In what sense was faith in Jesus Christ necessary in order to salvation under the old testament"? The issues reflected his ongoing concerns about Arminianism, including divine foreknowledge, freedom of will, the end of creation, and original sin—all topics on which he was working in the 1740s and on which he eventually published.

The other list is in a pamphlet entitled "The Theological Questions of President Edwards, Senior, and Dr. Edwards, His Son."[23] A later reprinting of these questions in the prominent New Divinity journal Bibliotheca Sacra, in 1882, indicated they were for "their pupils in theology."[24] As opposed to the "Questions on Theological Subjects," Edwards's questions here were arranged systematically, starting with the nature of God and ending with the church.

1. How does it appear that something has existed from Eternity?
10. How do you prove that the persons in the Trinity are one God?
19. Why did God decree sin?
44. In what manner did Christ atone for sin?
83. What is the nature of the Christian Church?

Some of these questions reflect the "improvements" that Hopkins and the early Edwardsians gave to some of Edwards's teachings, such as:

65. What is the essence of true virtue, or holiness?
67. Is not self-love the root of all virtue?
68. Do not the unregenerate desire to be regenerated and can they not properly pray for regenerating grace?

Edwards's list amounts to ninety *quaero*. Although some questions by father and son deal with the same general topic (e.g., the nature of the Sabbath), none of them correlate exactly.

Edwards on Ministers' Education and as Teachers

The exact number of students Edwards took into his home is unknown. Joseph Bellamy and Samuel Hopkins were the first and the most famous. Other, less-known individuals, all Yale graduates, studied with Edwards or at least spent some time in his home. They included John Searl, Northampton native and pastor of churches in Connecticut, Massachusetts, and Vermont; Job Strong, another son of Northampton and pastor of Portsmouth, New Hampshire; Elihu Spencer, who with Strong spent the summer of 1749 at the Edwards parsonage, served as a missionary to the Oneidas, married Edwards's daughter Sarah, and served a variety of churches in New York, New Jersey, and Delaware; Daniel Brinsmade, pastor of Washington, Connecticut, for much of the latter half of the eighteenth century; and former Bellamy student Gideon Hawley, who after serving as teacher at Stockbridge under Edwards during the early 1750s was the missionary to the Mashpee Indians on Cape Cod for nearly half a century.

Beginning in the early 1740s, because of his prestigious position at Northampton and his reputation as a revivalist and theologian, Edwards was called on increasingly to preach at ordination services and on the nature of the ministry.[25] These sermons, as Wilson Kimnach characterizes them, conveyed a heroic sense of the minister's calling, emphasizing the sacrifices that must be made and the stand the minister must take for truth.[26] Some of them, too, touched on the issue of ministers as teachers. Here we find two senses of "teacher." In "One Great End in God's Appointing the Ministry," he used the term in the broadest sense of "guides" and "shepherds" who study the Scriptures.[27] So too in his "Farewell Sermon," when, in advising his former parishioners of Northampton on the kind of minister they should seek, he told them (with no small degree of self-justification) to keep in mind that

> Ministers are set as guides and teachers, and are represented in Scripture as lights set up in the churches; and in the present state meet their people from time to time in order to instruct and enlighten them, to correct their mistakes, and to be a voice behind them, when they turn aside to the right hand or the left, saying, "This is the way, walk in it"; to evince and confirm the truth by exhibiting the proper evidences of it, and to refute errors and corrupt opinions, to convince the erroneous and establish the doubting.[28]

More specifically, though, Edwards also described ministers as instructors of church members. In *The True Excellency of a Gospel Minister*, he stressed the learnedness of the minister:

> He must be one that is *able to teach*, not one that is raw, ignorant or unlearned, and but little versed in the things that he is to teach others; not a novice, or one that is unskillful in the word of righteousness; he must be one that is well studied in divinity, well acquainted with the written Word of God, mighty in the Scriptures, and able to instruct and convince gainsayers.[29]

Joseph Bellamy's Student Notebook

As was customary in colonial New England, after graduating from Yale College in 1736 Joseph Bellamy went to pursue individual study with an established minister. He eventually gravitated to Edwards. Like many who would become New Lights, Bellamy was from a rural, middling background and was attracted to the evangelical religion that Edwards dispensed. It's likely he came to Edwards because of his recent regional (soon to be international) fame due to the Connecticut Valley revivals, and because of Bellamy's ambition to be a preacher in the same vein.

In a ledger book over some twenty pages or so, Bellamy scrawled notes from readings assigned by Edwards, as well as what appear to be some incidental compositions of his own. Without the in-depth study that this notebook deserves, it is difficult to draw any direct correlations between Edwards's interests at this time and Bellamy's notes, but we can make some preliminary observations. Several entries correspond, not in exact wording but in subject matter, with Edwards's "Miscellanies" from this period, roughly entries 675–710. For example, Bellamy had an entry on the unpardonable sin—the sin against the Holy Ghost—and Edwards pursued this theme in "Miscellanies" 703 and 706.[30] The very next topic Bellamy took up was baptism, which Edwards likewise explored in number 694. Furthermore, Bellamy included a writing exercise on the theme, "Will there be employment in heaven?" Heaven was the topic of "Miscellanies" 681 and 701. Finally, as Mark Valeri has noted, some of Bellamy's reading notes are similar in tone to Edwards's developing vision of the history of the work of redemption.[31]

Bellamy either cited or directly quoted from several books, providing a view of what Edwards recommended to his first independent student—or what in Edwards's library caught Bellamy's eye. The primary text was by John Edwards, "the last of the English Calvinists," entitled *Theologia Reformata: or, the body and substance of the Christian religion, comprised in distinct discourses or treatises* (London, 1713). As the copious title page informs us, it was "Fram'd as to be useful not only to *Profess'd Students* in *Divinity*, but to all that are *Lovers* of *Divine Knowledge*, and desire to make farther *Proficiency* in it." Not only did it treat the Apostle's Creed, the Lord's Prayer, and the Ten Commandments but it provided an "Antidote" against "dangerous Opinions" ranging from Papists and Pelagians to Deists and libertines. Thus the work was a synopsis of the main points of Reformed religion and fodder against contrary views. This, as well as other less-cited titles in Bellamy's notebook, were also in Edwards's library or were referenced by him in his writings.[32]

Bellamy's notebook evolved organically. It began as brief statements of major doctrinal loci or theological topics, indexed to the discussion of them in *Theologia Reformata*. Later entries were short essays and longer quotes. In other words, it started as a traditional commonplace book and became a version of the "Miscellanies," writ small.

The postgraduate intensive was also to include a practical immersion in composing and delivering sermons. At this point in his career, what would Edwards have told Bellamy about preaching? In 1736, Edwards was trying to coax back the revival spirit while transitioning the congregation into a new meetinghouse, so Bellamy would have heard a considerable range of sermon types. Perhaps Edwards pointed Bellamy to Cotton Mather's *Manuductio ad Ministerium* (Boston, 1726), which he himself used, or to Solomon Stoddard's *Defects of Preachers Reproved* (Boston, 1724). Stoddard argued quite vehemently that good preachers were not afraid to preach terror, and they did not rely on notes in the pulpit to do so. For his part, Edwards retained his reliance on a manuscript in the pulpit, even if, by the end of his life, the sermon had shrunk to an outline of only several pages.

Or perhaps Edwards would have impressed on Bellamy his thoughts on preaching as summarized in his preface to the *Five Discourses*, a collection of sermons from the recent revival that would be published in 1738. There, Edwards observed that sermons with power often appeared in "very plain and unpolished dress," and so ministers should "despise such ornaments as politeness, and modishness of style and method, when coming as a messenger from God to souls, deeply impressed with a sense of their danger of God's everlasting wrath, to treat with them about their eternal salvation." "However unable I am to preach or write politely," Edwards continued,

> God has showed us he does not need such talents in men to carry on his own work, and that he has been pleased to smile upon and bless a very plain, unfashionable way of preaching. And have we not reason to think that it ever has been, and ever will be, God's manner to bless the foolishness of preaching to save them that believe, let the elegance of language, and excellency of style, be carried to never so great a height, by the learning and wit of the present and future ages?[33]

Edwards's claim to unstudied prose may be a bit overstated, but his mastery of the plain style would have been clear to someone like Bellamy.

Edwards influenced many generations of ministers, theologians, and missionaries, no less in his teaching than in his writings. We cannot pretend to survey the entire Edwards tradition here, but we will look at three figures from the first generation of Edwards's disciples to detect the nature of his educational legacy.

Joseph Bellamy as Teacher

Joseph Bellamy's "school of the prophets," or parsonage seminary, in Bethlehem, Connecticut (which today is a museum), where he spent his career, is reputed to be the earliest formally established one of its kind in New England.[34] For better than three decades beginning in 1750, he housed and educated more than sixty college graduates for the ministry and other professions. Bellamy's pedagogical procedure was first to take his protégés through a course of study on subjects dealing with

> the existence, attributes, and the moral government of God; our moral agency, and the law under which we are placed; the sinful state and

character of mankind; the need of a divine revelation; and the fact that one had been given; the great doctrines of revelation, especially of the gospel; the character, offices and work of Christ; the atonement, and regeneration through the truth, and by the Holy Spirit; justification by faith; the distinguishing nature and fruits of repentance, love, and other Christian grace; growth in grace; the perseverance of the saints; death, the resurrection, and final judgment; heaven and hell; the nature of the church; particular churches, their offices and ordinances; the nature, uses, and ends of church discipline, etc.[35]

Thus Bellamy guided the fledgling Edwardsian through an extended course on apologetics, starting with natural religion, moving on to revealed religion, and ending with the nature of the church.[36] He directed that his students use his library of some one hundred volumes and several hundred pamphlets to compose answers, which Bellamy would then critique. In addition to the Reformed theologians he read at Edwards's recommendation—including Peter van Mastricht and Francis Turretin—Bellamy plunged his students directly into the English philosophical current by reading authors such as Shaftesbury, Hutcheson, and Hume, on the principle that it was important to know one's opponents, particularly if they gave some "light."

Once a student had satisfactorily answered all or perhaps most of the questions—a process that could take months—Bellamy had him write and deliver sermons in his own pulpit and in surrounding New Divinity churches, of which, because of Bellamy's local influence, there were a goodly number.[37] They would sit under Bellamy's preaching, which, by all accounts, would have provided an impressive model. Edwards himself stated that Bellamy had "extraordinary gifts for the pulpit." With a large frame, he had a resonant voice and preached extemporaneously—a "son of thunder." "When the law was his theme," a hearer recalled, "Mt. Sinai was all in smoke; the thunder and the lightning issued from his lips, and all was solemn as the grave."[38] An aspiring awakening preacher could not do much better than to learn to sermonize at Bellamy's feet.

Samuel Hopkins as Teacher

Samuel Hopkins, pastor of churches in Massachusetts and Rhode Island, is known as the great systematizer and disseminator of Edwards's thought through his many publications. Yet, to complicate this characterization, we are going to present Hopkins first as a young seeker, trying to come to some sort of assurance that he was indeed converted. As a Yale student, Hopkins had as his classmates zealous New Lights such as David Brainerd and Samuel

Buell. He heard powerful awakening preachers such as George Whitefield and Gilbert Tennent, and, although he experienced raised affections, he could not be sure they had culminated in regeneration. He considered himself "a sinful lost creature." So when Hopkins heard Edwards deliver "The Distinguishing Marks of a Work of the Spirit of God" at Yale's commencement in September 1741, he found a spiritual as well as an intellectual guide and resolved to study with him.

It was not study only for which he came to Edwards, but for spiritual counseling and guidance. Hopkins, who we might think of as a mild-mannered bookworm and who described himself as "of a sober and steady make," was emotionally crippled by uncertainty about the state of his soul. His diary is a constant revisiting of the question of his salvation, since he would not be qualified for his chosen profession as minister if he were not a true saint. Therefore, we can use Hopkins as an example of another function of the schools of the prophets: spiritual formation. In the context of the Great Awakening, when the New Birth was the great byword and an unconverted ministry heralded as the great danger, Hopkins's concerns typified a whole cadre of would-be shepherds of souls.

Interestingly, it was first through the ministrations of Sarah Pierpont Edwards that Hopkins began to have some hope, a circumstance that highlights how the student would also be molded by exposure to his teacher's familial and congregational culture. After living as a recluse for several months following graduation, Hopkins came to Northampton; finding Edwards gone on a preaching tour, he spent days alone in his room, gloomy and listless. She noticed this, and drew him out of his shell. For the first time he gave vent to his feelings. "I was in a Christless, graceless state," he confided to her, but she encouraged him, saying that the family (who later came to call him "Old Benevolence") expected great things from him. Also, he would have witnessed some or all of her ecstatic and prolonged religious experiences in January 1742. After his return from a preaching tour with Buell, Hopkins was finally able to open up to Edwards himself, who asked his pupil why he had not told him these things before, and, as Hopkins recalled, "entertained a hope that I was a Christian."[39] From that point, Hopkins considered himself fit to be a minister. After spending another period of study with Edwards in the summer of 1742, and again briefly as Northampton's schoolmaster in June 1743, he embarked on a long career as a minister and theologian.

Publication was another important component of New Divinity education and polemics, and Hopkins provides an entrée into the education and dissemination of the Edwardsian Way through print culture in treatises, tracts, journals, and newspapers. If we look only at the posthumous publications of Edwards as an example, Hopkins himself oversaw the printing of *Two Dissertations* and a biography that included a number of previously unpublished sermons (1765). He also helped to create networks, for example introducing Edwards's son, Jonathan Jr., to John Erskine. Out of this partnership, in which Edwards Jr. sent transcripts of his father's work to Scotland, came *A History of the Work of Redemption*, collections of sermons and two volumes of selections from Edwards Sr.'s notebooks.[40]

New Divinity leaders such as Hopkins worked cooperatively with others to create several important reform movements, including advocating abolition of slavery. Hopkins published a *Dialogue* (1776) against slavery and helped to organize other Edwardsians to contribute sermons and newspaper articles to the cause, among them Ebenezer Baldwin, Levi Hart, and particularly Edwards Jr. Together, this group became the earliest organized party for immediate abolitionism in American history. Their influence extended into African Calvinist circles, and Hopkins's works were formative for the African American preacher Lemuel Haynes.[41]

At his church in Newport, Hopkins also encouraged female lay teachers. Sarah Osborn and Susanna Anthony, two members of his congregation, held theological and prayer groups for women and preached to blacks, building up a small community of free and enslaved black Edwardsians in town. A collection of their correspondence was printed in 1807, and Hopkins published a memoir of Anthony after her death.[42] Osborn and Anthony attest to the continuing importance of female educators, missionaries, reformers, and writers in Edwardsian circles.[43]

The Education of Jonathan Edwards, Jr.

After both of his parents died in 1758, Edwards Jr. attended the College of New Jersey, finishing in 1765. During the following winter, he went to Hopkins's home at Great Barrington, Massachusetts. Here Edwards Jr. reunited the bulk of his father's manuscripts with those that Hopkins had been perusing and transcribing.[44] Hopkins offered to pick up where the elder Edwards had left off in the young man's theological instruction. Hopkins's biographer described the encounter:

> Mr. Hopkins soon put into his hands a manuscript of his father's, maintaining a doctrine which he [Edwards Jr.] had controverted. When he had read it he brought forward objections which he appeared to think conclusive. But Mr. Hopkins attempted to correct this misapprehension, and to explain and strengthen by additional proof the arguments

of his father. Young Mr. Edwards was not convinced though his zeal was in some measure abated. He retired for reflection and the adjustment of his ideas, expecting to bring new force in the morning. But in the conversation he became more embarrassed, and found that the subject required a deeper investigation than he had ever paid to it.[45]

The method for Hopkins, as with Edwards Sr., was one of exchange, of allowing students to think for themselves but clarifying and refining that thought through a process of gradual correction and self-discovery.

In the spring of 1766, Edwards Jr. went for further training under Bellamy. Compared to the learned and retiring Hopkins, Bellamy was rustic and charismatic. Though temperamentally more like Hopkins, the younger Edwards kept up a closer relationship with Bellamy for the rest of his life. Under Bellamy's preaching instruction, he composed stern sermons, much like what his father had learned under Stoddard. In his time with Bellamy, he also came to emphasize doctrines that were to figure in his life's work, such as the nature of God's moral government and divine decrees, and the necessity and justice of eternal punishment.

Jonathan Edwards, Jr., as an Educator

Following Bellamy and Hopkins's examples, Edwards Jr. maintained a parsonage school where he trained prospective clergy. The small number of students he trained, compared to Bellamy, was compensated by the illustrious careers they enjoyed. His students included his nephew, Timothy Dwight, pastor of Greenfield Farms and member of the literary circle known as the Connecticut Wits; Samuel Austin, pastor of Fair Haven in New Haven; Jedidiah Morse, pastor and geographer, a founding member of Andover Seminary, and a conspiracy theorist who wrote about the "Illuminati";[46] Edward Dorr Griffin, pastor of Park Street Church in Boston and Andover Seminary faculty member; and Samuel Nott, pastor of Franklin, Connecticut, who in his pastoral tenure of seventy-four years trained several hundred seminarians and later directed the Connecticut Missionary Society, established in 1798 with Edwards Jr. as one of the founding members.[47]

We have seen that Edwards Sr. drew up a list of theological questions for his students. Bellamy and Hopkins also intended something similar with their unpublished "Philosophems." An important source for understanding the nature of the training that aspiring Edwardsians received under Edwards Jr. was his own list of questions, as preserved in the 1822 imprint.[48] Where Edwards Sr. had 90 questions, his son's tally rose to 313, incorporating many questions from his father's list but adding others that pertained to late-eighteenth-century controversies and issues dear to the New Divinity. For example, questions on Manichaeism and pagan polytheism in Jonathan Sr.'s list appeared as numbers 11 and 12, but they were 79 and 80 in his son's. Unique to Edwards Jr.'s list were these examples:

131. Is a damning God the proper object of love?
243. Is God to be loved disinterestedly?
262. What is the immediate duty of the unregenerate? and to what are they to be exhorted?
300. Is Universalism a just matter of excommunication?

Where the elder Edwards had only one question directly on justification (no. 57), the younger incorporated no less than sixteen (201–213, 224–226). Jonathan Jr. posed several questions on Leviratical laws of matrimony (302–305), such as on the legality of polygamy, that were absent in his father's agenda. And where Edwards Sr. included only one question on atonement (44), his son had at least four directed to the issue, reflecting the shift made by the New Divinity from a penal to a governmental theory of atonement.[49]

Mercifully, Edwards Jr. did not assign all 300-some questions to each student. Samuel Nott did postgraduate training with Edwards Jr. after graduating from Yale in 1780. He copied into his autobiography the 90 questions that he was assigned during his "regular study of divinity under Dr. Edwards." Nott attested to the usefulness and effectiveness of this mode of teaching:

The attention which I paid to the foregoing questions and the remarks made by Dr. Edwards when I read to him what I had written was of very special service to me. I became, of a consequence, more fully confirmed *in many sentiments* that I had previously embraced as well as established in the belief of some, the correctness which I had doubted.[50]

Another pedagogical device that Edwards Jr. composed, this one for homiletics, was "Miscellaneous Observations on Preaching." Several of them seem directed at his father's preaching habits, some of which he considered uncouth:

1. Avoid an argumentative strain of preaching and a frequent use of particles *thereof, so then, consequently*, etc.
11. It is a great fault in preaching to speak so as not to give to the audience an idea of tender concern in the preacher for their good. Some

men preach as if they were angry at 'em, and delighted to tease 'em, with horrible descriptions of their sins and ill desert, which I have heard called a *fancy way of preaching*. They seem to domineer and lord it over their hearers, treating 'em very roughly and to appearance proudly.

Others addressed the homiletical trends of the late eighteenth century:

5. It is very popular frequently to use the words *conviction, conversion, spirit of God, light, feeling, experience*. Other words perfectly tantamount, will not be agreeable.

8. It is also popular to give a particular description of the exercises of a sinner under awakening, and of his voracious temptations hesitations, difficulties, resolutions, promises, breaches of 'em, etc., etc., as also of the exercises, joys, temptations, deliverances, backslidings, quickenings, etc., of saints.

9. The Antinomians are the most devout and zealous preachers in the country and in the world. The Edwardseans almost all fail through want of zeal and devotion. Therefore the zeal of the former is worthy being imitated by the latter.

10. The Edwardseans are too apt to run into an argumentative and what is commonly called a metaphysical way of preaching.[51]

Besides training students in his home, Edwards Jr. was associated with Yale College. In a diplomatic gesture, but also in recognition of a fellow scholar, the decidedly anti-Edwardsian president of Yale, Ezra Stiles, appointed Edwards Jr. as an examiner of graduating students. He was notorious in this role and earned the title of "Old Haute Recte," due to his habit of shouting "Not Correct!" to a wrong answer. As one of his colleagues later recalled, "In scholarship . . . he was distinguished by the utmost exactness and preciseness. Of poor scholarship he was, as might be expected, invincibly impatient."[52] Edwards the Younger's name was placed in consideration for a position as professor of divinity in 1781, and as a fellow of the college the following year, but that was going too far for Stiles, who was wary of allowing the New Divinity any official inroads into Yale.

One of the several eerie parallels in the careers of Edwards Sr. and Jr.—including dismissal from a longstanding prestigious post to a backwoods church—is that both ended their lives as college presidents. In Jonathan Jr.'s case, he served for the last two years of his life as president of Union College, in Schenectady, New York, an institution that, as the name implies, brought together students from several Protestant denominations. Here, Edwards Jr.

taught rhetoric, using as his text Hugh Blair's popular *Lectures on Rhetoric and Belles-Lettres* (Edinburgh, 1783), which presented discussions of parts of speech, perspicuity and style, harmony and structure, metaphor, hyperbole, apostrophe, comparison, and other aspects, in the process reviewing the styles of some of the most respected rhetoricians of the day, such as the Archbishop of Canterbury John Tillotson, Sir William Temple, Joseph Addison, and the Third Earl of Shaftesbury. Edwards Jr. agreed with Blair's assessment that "sublime writing" was achieved through "conciseness and simplicity."[53]

Among his copious manuscripts, the younger Edwards left some items that give a flavor of him as president: an "Order of Commencement" and an "Address to the Graduates," from May 6, 1801. The commencement exercises, starting at ten o'clock in the morning, consisted of "forensic disputes" on issues ranging from the morality and policy of dueling, on whether "the planets be embriolated,"[54] on whether domestic slavery was justifiable—a topic close to Jonathan Jr.'s heart—and, finally, on "the most advantageous employment of time by a student in college."[55] Following these disputations, he gave his address, urging them to apply themselves, choose a profession without delay, and be on guard against vice and infidelity. President Edwards closed with a final word of adieu:

> Dear young gentlemen, lately my affectionate pupils, permit me to express a parental affection towards you, now that you [are] about to be dispersed in a turbulent and tempestuous world, a world full of temptations and dangers. May that great and good God, on whom you and we all are constantly dependent, extend his kind providence to preserve you, to protect you, to prosper you in our pursuits, and finally to receive you to himself. My dear young friends I bid you, a most affectionate farewell![56]

Institutionalized New Divinity Education

Over the succeeding generations, New Divinity pastors continued to run parsonage schools. Respected preachers and teachers such as John Smalley and Nathanael Emmons took scores of recently minted college graduates and continued their training, turning them into agents of the New Divinity. Meanwhile, other adherents of Edwards, such as Edwards Jr. at Union, or Timothy Dwight at Yale College, Edward Dorr Griffin at Williams College, Samuel Austin at the University of Vermont, and, later, Moses Stuart and Edwards Amasa Park at Andover Seminary and Nathaniel William Taylor at Yale, became faculty members and leaders of venerable educational centers. Thus, from its beginnings in informal apprenticeships, to the parsonage seminary, and finally achieving a presence in public and private colleges and universities, the New Divinity became institutionalized and mainstreamed.

Through the late eighteenth and into the nineteenth centuries, adherents of the New Divinity tradition also established new institutions specifically for the inculcating of Edwardsian principles and priorities such as revivalism and missions. Scholars such as Joseph Conforti, Amanda Porterfield, David Kling, and Charles Phillips have shown the centrality of New Divinity men and women such as Mary Lyons at Mt. Holyoke Seminary for Women, Samuel Mills at Williams College, and Edwards Amasa Park at Andover Seminary.[57] We can also point to other institutions, such as Amherst College, Dartmouth College, East Windsor Seminary, Hamilton College, and Hartford Seminary for Women, as having significant New Divinity origins, influences, and connections. With the rise of these institutions came new waves of revivals in the early nineteenth century, and the coalescence of missionary movements to domestic and foreign fields, emanating from deep within Edwardsian and neo-Edwardsian circles.

3

After Edwards: Original Sin and Freedom of the Will

Allen Guelzo

IT WAS THE fondest hope of Jonathan Edwards that the Great Awakening of the 1740s was simply the overture to the Day of Judgment and the thousand-year reign of God directly on earth, the Millennium, when "religion shall in every respect be uppermost in the world." But instead of the dawning of a general revival of the Christian church that would cause to "bow the heavens and come down and erect his glorious kingdom through the earth," what Edwards got was a controversy with his own congregation in Northampton over church membership, followed by the humiliation of dismissal by that congregation, and self-imposed demotion to management of a mission to a tribe of Indians whose language he did not speak as well as oversight of an English congregation whose attention span was, in Edwards's judgment, not up to what it should have been. It was a tenure punctuated by the onset of the French and Indian War, and wracked by still more stiff-necked controversies over pastoral issues, although, unlike his situation in Northampton, he had the powerful sponsorship of the provincial governor, Sir William Pepperell, to protect him. But his attention never wandered far from the possibility of a renewed visitation of divine grace. "I hope to humble his church in New England, and purify it, and so fit it for yet greater comfort." Only now, his intellectual enthusiasm turned to the rebuke of the spirit that he considered the most lethal to revival, the lukewarm wraith of "Arminianism"—not the literal teachings of the seventeenth-century Dutch anti-Calvinist, Jacobus Arminius, but the pallid, free-will, "natural" religion of theologians desperate to placate the spirit of the Enlightenment. "If some great men that have appeared in our nation had been as eminent in divinity as they were in philosophy," Edwards complained, "they would have conquered all Christendom and turned the world upside down." The temporizing strategy of bargaining away the pure principles of Christianity, which Edwards never doubted comprehended the pure principles of Calvinism, was aimed only at appeasing the wolf of Enlightenment unbelief, and it had no power at all to receive the grace of a renewed Awakening, much less the Millennium; only the unblinking proclamation of Calvinist orthodoxy had any real strength in its loins. "I think I have found that no discourses have been more remarkably blessed, than those in which the doctrine of God's absolute sovereignty with regard to the salvation of sinners, and his just liberty with regard to answered the prayers, or succeeding the pains of natural men, continuing such, have been insisted on." So, between 1750 and 1757, he managed composition of two landmark treatises in moral philosophy, *Original Sin* and *Freedom of the Will*, which few other eighteenth-century thinkers could have managed even in the placid Enlightenment confines of Oxford or Potsdam.[1]

Edwards had always seen himself as a restorer rather than an innovator. Much as he applied himself as a college student to the Cartesian-style new logic and the study of Mr. Locke and Sir Isaac Newton, he was "mightily pleased with the study of the old logic"—in other words, with the unsullied Calvinist scholasticism of Adrian Heereboord, Francis Burgersdyck, Peter van Maastricht (whose *Theoretic-Practico Theologica* was ranked by Edwards as "much better" than "any other book in the world, excepting the Bible in my opinion"), and Francis Turretin (whose sure-footedness on "polemical divinity" makes him ideal "for one that desires only to be thoroughly versed in controversies").[2] When he cast his eye back to his period of late-adolescent rebelliousness, it was not wine, women, or song that constituted the stuff of his wickedness, but a risqué repudiation of Calvinist predestination and "objections against the doctrine of God's sovereignty." And by the same token, he had not experienced any satisfactory sense of spiritual renewal until he received "quite another kind of sense of God's sovereignty than I had then," so that it became "my delight to approach God, and adore him as a Sovereign God, and ask sovereign mercy of him."[3] What earned him the fury of the Northampton church was his single-minded attempt to restore the original terms of communicant membership that were established by the founding generation of Massachusetts, and that his grandfather, Solomon Stoddard, had loosened during his long tenure as Northampton's pastor. And what most enchanted him about the brief successes of the Great Awakening was not any of the ways they pointed toward a new configuration for religion in American societies, but the hope they held out for turning the clock back a century to the era of New England's first love.

The Awakening had been a sign "for Arminians to change their principles" and "relinquish their scheme," and "come and Join with us, and be on our side."[4]

Yet, if Edwards's aim was repristination, he was more than perceptive enough to see that the old wine of Calvinism could no longer be poured into the wineskins of seventeenth-century scholasticism. It is the irony of so many efforts at intellectual repristination that the greatest and most successful succeed because they deploy, more skillfully than the innovators against whom they are struggling, the weapons, arguments, strategies, and methods of their own corrupted day. So it was with Edwards and the great treatises on God's unconditional election and man's total depravity. Edwards might have chosen, as his contemporary Jonathan Dickinson did, simply to hurl scholastic syllogisms built on biblical authorities at the many heads of Enlightenment unbelief and indeterminism.[5] But anyone who takes up *Freedom of the Will* or *Original Sin* in the expectation of following just another tedious exposition of Calvinism's favorite biblical proofs (on the assumption that a biblical proof carries its own authority) is in for more than a mild surprise. The argument of *Freedom of the Will* is based on psychology and analysis of language, not exegesis; the argument of *Original Sin* is based on observation and analysis of nature. And the result, produced in the interest of restoring Calvinism, may have ended up producing something significantly different from the restoration Edwards imagined.

The Enlightenment posed difficulties for Calvinism in other ways, since it was a movement that simultaneously embraced freedom of action, reason, and optimism, as well as cynicism, fanaticism, and the most iron-gloved forms of determinism. It was hatched from the struggle to replace a universe governed by animation and providence with one governed by predictable physical laws, but only at the risk of making those laws as inexorable as the rule of providence it wanted to leave behind. Julien de la Mettrie insisted that "the human body is a machine which winds its own spring." The fact that it does its own winding does not make it free: "We think we are, and in fact are, good men, only as we are gay or brave; everything depends on the way our machine is running. . . . In vain you fall back on the power of the will, since for one order that the will gives, it bows a hundred times to the yoke." Even Benjamin Franklin could at once extol rank determinism and then conclude, not that it was wrong, but that it was a subject inconvenient to drag into polite conversation. There was no greater mistake than to "suppose ourselves to be, in the common sense of the Word, *Free Agents*," but the practical effect of telling this to people, especially in front of the servants, "appeared abominable."[6]

What this division of mind testified to was the need to reconcile the natural regularity of observed physical laws with the ethical need to hold human

beings personally accountable for their actions, even as it was to acknowledge that human beings are not exempt from universal application of those
laws. Those who imagined that, by freeing themselves from the arbitrariness
of an intelligent Providence, they were delivering themselves into a kind of
self-starting, self-acting liberty could assert as much as they liked that they
now stood on a separate and higher plane of indeterminism and free action
than those poor deluded souls who still toiled under the "soft determinism"
of inability, depravity, and divine manipulation of all events. The uncomfort-
able question that sat beside this newly won self-possession was whether indeterminism's overconfident promoters had unwittingly sold themselves into a
more rigid and exacting form of control in which either (1) a faceless physical
mechanism made all ethical restraints disappear like a mirage or (2) a rudder-
less indeterminism made all ethical restraints meaningless. These latter-day
"Arminians" had, in effect, used their supposed free will to dig themselves into
a trench that they could not think how to escape. And so it became Edwards's
task to show them that Calvinism, or at least Calvinism's form of providential determinism, did not abolish moral accountability and restraint but was
in fact the only guarantor of it. He did not offer Calvinism as a rebuke to the
Enlightenment's optimism (which, by contrast, is what Dickinson was prepared to do) but as a solution to its ethical despair.

Edwards seems to have regarded this as a double-barreled opportunity,
since it so nicely tied together the ambition of a provincial intellectual to speak
to a significant thought problem, and in a way that the metropolitan centers
of the British empire would have to notice, with his concern to refound New
England on the unsullied principles of its founding. This was, in the largest sense, the project of his life; ideas and arguments on both original sin
and free will show up in Edwards's notebooks as early as 1729.[7] By the mid-
1730s, he had already worked out his fundamental critique of the "meaning of
the words *freedom* or *liberty*." But the actual beginnings of *Freedom of the Will*
and *Original Sin* probably date from 1748, when he simultaneously hatched
the plan "of publishing something against some of the Arminian tenets" and
acquired a copy for himself of John Taylor's *Scripture-Doctrine of Original Sin
Proposed to Free and Candid Examination* (1740), which would become the target of convenience for his own study of that name in 1758. A little more than a
year later, in a letter to his prize pupil, Joseph Bellamy, Edwards sketched out
the kernel of what became the central arguments of *Freedom of the Will*. But
his determination to move his edition of David Brainerd's journal into print,
along with the tempest of his dismissal from Northampton in 1750, pushed
work on these projects to a far corner of his mind, and it was not until 1754
that Edwards was at last ready with a manuscript for his Boston publisher,

Samuel Kneeland, to have "printed in . . . new types" which would be "better than any he now has." [8]

Edwards began his *Inquiry into the Modern Prevailing Notions of the Freedom of the Will which is Supposed to be Essential to Moral Agency, Virtue and Vice, Reward and Punishment, Praise and Blame* by adopting an unexpectedly secular definition of "the will." Rather than speak of it as a separate "faculty" within the mind, as the Protestant scholastics of the seventeenth century did, Edwards identified the will in the fashion of Locke's *Essay Concerning Human Understanding* (1690), as "that by which the mind chooses anything" or "that by which the soul either chooses or refuses." He did not intend by this to suggest that the mind ruled the will, in the manner beloved of Thomistic intellectualists; there was no complicated transaction in the mind, ending with a rational conclusion that the will then executes. Minds, after all, cannot deliberate between perceived alternatives without willing or choosing actually getting mixed up in the process of what intellectualists mistake for a purely intellectual sequence. Thinking itself is a ceaseless interaction between preferences and perceptions. Let the mind perceive something it prefers—something that acts as a "motive"—and the will at once reaches out for it. "And God has so made and established the human nature, the soul being united to a body in proper state, that the soul preferring or choosing such an immediate exertion or alteration of the body, such an alteration instantaneously follows." The connection between perception and volition is in fact so close and so instantaneous that one might as well give up all hope of finding a line between the two, and admit that "the will always is as the greatest apparent good is." Not the "good" in some rational, abstract understanding of the word, but "of the same import with 'agreeable.' "[9]

This definition chalked out the operating boundaries for Edwards's notion of willing. Minds perceive objects, which they either desire or do not desire, the desiring being a part of the perceiving; wills are a means toward putting the man in possession of that desired object. The will does not deliberate between willing and not willing that desire; the will *is* the desire. The question of free will is therefore not whether wills have an independent review power over minds, but whether wills have an unobstructed path to realizing the mind's preferences. Hence, the real problem involved in free will or determinism is not whether the will is hindered from choosing—this it does automatically—but merely whether it has the physical liberty to acquire the object of the mind's desiring. "Liberty" is only "that power and opportunity for one to do and conduct as he will . . . according to his choice." What made a person free was not a matter of how he or she came to "prefer" one thing rather than another, because he will do this as soon as he perceives that thing, but whether the person is restrained from acquiring what he is willing. "Let the person come by his volition or choice how he will, yet, if he is able, and there is nothing in the way to hinder his pursuing and executing his will, the man is fully and perfectly free. . . . "[10]

But if this was the case, on what ground does the modern "Arminian" complain against a sovereign God who ordains every event that comes to pass? Indeterminists would like to have the will free to determine itself, but this is not what wills do: "The advocates for this notion of the freedom of the will speak of a certain sovereignty in the will, whereby it has power to determine its own volitions." This is to mistake what the will actually is. Wills do not *choose* to will, because that would be a tautology, and "every free act of choice" would have to be "determined by a preceding act of choice, choosing that act." Wills reach out spontaneously as the mind responds to certain motives, and it is no diminution of the will's real freedom to say that it is ruled *by* those motives. That's what the will is there for. And so the trap closes, because if something outside the will *does* legitimately determine the will, then the "Arminian" withers, since it is no diminution of the will's scope of activity if God plants "motives" in the path of minds that minds prefer and which then instruct the will to apprehend. And the Calvinist, by the same reasoning, flourishes, since the connection between mental perception and willing is so immediate that no one ever wills against what he desires, or "chooses one thing before another, when at the very same instant it is perfectly indifferent with respect to each!" Hence, there is no reason the perceiving individual should not consider that he chooses freely, or is not morally accountable for the choice, since it proceeds from his own desires.[11]

Of course, one could object that this means Calvinists have exchanged an idea of God as a master who rigidly manipulates his creatures like puppets for an idea of God as gamester who dangles meat in front of starving dogs. The dogs might be technically free, but it did nothing to diminish the necessity of the result. But as far as Edwards was concerned, the problem was not in the necessity of the result, but in the *kind* of necessity involved when minds apprehended motives and moved at once to act on them, because not all versions of necessity were hostile to moral freedom and accountability. When God decrees a certain action, the action becomes necessary. But actions can become necessary in one of two very different ways: God actually could manipulate someone into doing what he wants, with the person all the while kicking and screaming in protest because of wanting to do something else. This is the concept of necessity most commonly used "from our childhood." But it is by no means the only one, or even the most comprehensive. An act, after all, can become *necessary* if someone already has a certain psychological inclination toward it. There is, after all, a measure of predictability in human behavior; we do not live randomly, and the more intense our inclination toward a sort of behavior, the more likely we will act on it.[12]

Edwards called the necessity that involves force *natural necessity*, and he cheerfully admitted that those who are compelled to act under the force of natural necessity cannot be held morally accountable for what they do: "By 'natural necessity' . . . I mean such necessity as men are under through the force of natural causes." The other necessity, which arises from our own inclinations, Edwards called *moral necessity*. Nobody is actually forcing anyone to do things by moral necessity. So, when someone wills to do something it is morally necessary to do, the person is not actually having a string pulled. But "moral necessity may be as absolute as natural necessity," since it consists "in the opposition or want of inclination . . . through a defect of motives, or prevalence of contrary motives." People are then acting on the basis of what they really want and thus can be held morally liable for the consequences of choice. In fact, the *greater* the force of an evil inclination on someone's actions, the *more* accountable the person is, precisely for having all the physical power needed to do otherwise. If what we possess are sinful inclinations, they will incline us to sin all the time, without God having to force anything to happen. Under the self-imposed sway of *moral* necessity, there is a *moral inability* to do anything other than sin. Yet, none of this happens from God forcing us to sin; that would be a natural necessity and would give us an excuse. We actually possess all the *natural ability* we could ever want *not* to sin:

> In the strictest propriety of speech, a man has a thing in his power, if he has it in his choice. . . . It can't be truly said, according to the ordinary use of language, that a malicious man, let him be never so malicious, can't hold his hand from striking, or that he is not able to shew his neighbor kindness.

The probability of the "malicious man" *not* behaving in a malicious manner takes unlikelihood to the vanishing point, and that is necessity enough to please whatever Calvinists might want from necessity; but it also places the blame and origin for the malice squarely on the malicious man himself.[13]

Translated into practical terms, what this meant was that people could not shelter themselves from the call to repentance and conversion (as they had for generations in New England) behind such pious fig leaves as the Half-Way Covenant or the plea that they were gradually working their way through their depravity by the means of grace (prayer, using the sacraments, reading the Bible, listening to sermons, coming under conviction of sin, and so forth, in slow order). Human beings were depraved, totally, and this ensured that they lacked the moral ability to do anything but sin; but they also had arms and legs and lips and a brain—*natural* ability—and could use them all *if they chose* to bow down in the dust and abase themselves before God, and they should do so at once; if they did not, they had no one to blame but themselves when they came to Judgment. Edwards had thus created not only a justification of the ways of Calvin to the eighteenth century but a psychology of crisis in which people were encouraged at once to decide, decide, decide.

It was necessary to the overall strategy of a religious Awakening to insist that the ultimate problem was not the will itself, since the will reached out for only what the perceiving mind desired anyway. That the will performed according to a predictable—and actually foreordained—pattern satisfied only the demand of Calvinism that all events be seen as a divinely ordered sequence that nevertheless allowed the human subject more than enough "freedom" to be held morally accountable. But there would be no impetus in favor of an Awakening unless what the human subject was being held accountable *for* was deeply, morally culpable in the eyes of God. Standing by itself, *Freedom of the Will* might end up proving little more than Thomas Hobbes, Lord Kames, or Anthony Collins had proven about the will: that it was not self-originating, self-sovereign, or "free." It was because human nature was profoundly and horribly depraved that the need to understand how the will operated suddenly became an urgent problem. And this was the task Edwards took upon himself in the waning months of his tenure at the Stockbridge mission, in *The Great Christian Doctrine of Original Sin Defended*.

Edwards actually had two problems to work out in *Original Sin*, one of them fairly easy in practical terms and the other hard enough to have broken the heads of centuries' worth of Christian theologians. In the first case, even in the sunny reasonableness of the eighteenth century it was not difficult to convince people that the human race teemed with moral turpitude. What Edwards had to prove, however, was that this turpitude was not the accidental result of a free will that might otherwise, with a little more education or encouragement, have been avoided, but an irremediable corruption of human nature itself. When he spoke of original sin, he meant "the *innate sinful depravity of the heart* . . . that the heart of man is naturally of a corrupt and evil disposition." What was more of a challenge was, in the second case, showing how God was as much a sovereign in the beginnings and continuance of that depravity without at the same time being responsible for it himself. He had to explain and justify, in theological parlance, "not only the depravity of nature, but the imputation of Adam's first sin" by God to all of his "posterity." Enlightenment optimists might want to get rid of original sin; Enlightenment theists were less likely to deny that humanity was sinful, but they were more anxious to shift the blame for it from God's decree to human free will.[14]

Original Sin devotes much more of its substance to biblical explanation and an appeal to human experience than *Freedom of the Will*, in large measure because this was not difficult to do. "The Scriptures are so very express," argued Edwards, in asserting there was little question that "all mankind, all flesh, all the world, every man living, are guilty of sin." If sin was not "a thing belonging to the race of mankind, as if it were a property of the species," then why do we have "such descriptions, all over the Bible, or man, and the sons of men! Why should man be so continually spoken of as evil, carnal, perverse, deceitful, and desperately wicked, if all men are by nature as perfectly innocent, and free from any propensity to evil, as Adam was the first moment of his creation"? The historical record was equally clear on the pervasiveness of human folly, since "if we consider the various successive parts and period of the duration of the world, it will, if possible, be yet more evident, that vastly the greater part of mankind have in all ages been of a wicked character." Even the "great advances in learning and philosophic knowledge" in his own day merely turned people more to "profaneness, sensuality and debauchery." But Edwards was not content to assert that human beings make moral mistakes; he thought it was necessary to prove not just that people sin but that there is "a prevailing propensity to that issue . . . that all fail of keeping the law perfectly . . . to such an imperfection of obedience, as always without fail comes to pass." It was true—and irrelevant—that human behavior is a mix of good and bad; the fundamental problem was with the set of the saw itself, and whether "he preponderates to, in the frame of his heart, and state of his nature . . . a state of sin, guiltiness and abhorrence in the sight of God." The clincher of Edwards's insistence on the root-and-branch origins of evil was the fact of death: "Death is spoken of in Scripture as the chief of calamities, the most extreme and terrible of all those natural evils which come on mankind in this world." Only the existence of "a perverse and vile disposition" was in any way commensurate with God's decision to "chastise them with great severity, and even to kill them, to keep them in order."[15]

But Edwards's relentless pushing on the biblical and historical reality of evil in human nature only pressed the discussion in another direction, and that was the question of how this evil came to take up residence in human hearts, and who was responsible for the calamity. Neither Edwards nor his opponents in the eighteenth century had much hesitation in fingering Adam, the original parent of the human race, with having begun the slide into the moral abyss. What they could not be reconciled on was what influence

Adam's transgression exerted on his subsequent progeny's instinct for evil. "Arminians" were likely to insist that Adam's sin in the Garden of Eden was certainly reprehensible; but what did it have to do with anyone else? Was it fair to suppose that Adam, in an exercise of moral genetics, passed on to his help-less descendents a "depravity gene"? It was now Edwards's turn to be hoisted on his own petard, since if Adam's fall was responsible for "*implanting* any bad principle, or *infusing* any corrupt taint" into the human race, it would consti-tute precisely the sort of natural necessity that, in *Freedom of the Will*, Edwards explained would cancel out moral accountability. Edwards's solution was not elegant: "Adam's nature became corrupt, without God's implanting or infus-ing any evil thing into his nature." God stepped back from Adam, allowing him to fall of his own moral weight; thereafter, God proceeds to deal "with Adam as the head of his posterity . . . and treating them as one . . . as having *all sinned in him*." Adam, in short, acts as a representative, or federal head, of the human race, and when he falls, then just as God "withdrew his spiritual communion and his vital gracious influence from the common head, so he withholds the same from all the members, as they come into existence . . . and so become wholly corrupt, as Adam did." This means that "the derivation of the pollution and guilt of past sins . . . depends on an arbitrary divine con-stitution," rather than an infected spiritual organism. Not some "oneness in created beings, whence qualities and relations are derived from past experi-ence," but God's "divine constitution"—his determination to treat the universe as a government, and his relations to his creatures as legal ones—was what prompted God to regard all the heirs of Adam as depraved. And they confirm God's rightness in so treating them, not "merely because God *imputes* it to them," but because they actually proceed to act sinfully, so that Adam's sin becomes "*truly* and *properly* theirs."[16]

This last argument was a surprise, coming from someone as focused on restoration of pure Calvinism as was Edwards, since Calvinism in its purest seventeenth-century expressions in the Synod of Dordt and the Westminster Assembly had laid down that inheritance of a depraved substance was pre-cisely what made people sin, and that redemption from that sin came through the compensatory imputation of the merits and righteousness of Jesus Christ. But Edwards's yearning to restart the Awakenings of the 1730s and 1740s, and his eagerness to rinse away any suggestion that sinners suffered under a natu-ral necessity to sin that prevented repentance and renewal, overcame whatever hesitations he might have felt about tampering with the strict formularies of the Calvinist fathers. Still, it would not be Edwards, but Edwards's disciples of the 1760s—Joseph Bellamy and Samuel Hopkins—who would develop this departure into a full-blown embrace of a governmental view of atonement and the jettisoning of the classic Protestant understanding of redemption through an imputed righteousness.[17]

Measuring the long-term "impact" of *Original Sin* and "Edwards on the Will" is somewhat like measuring the impact of a meteorite, in that the significance of the event overshadows the strictly measurable evidence. The great nineteenth-century Scottish divine Thomas Chalmers studied "Jonathan Edwards' Treatise on Free Will . . . with such ardour that he seemed to regard nothing else, and would scarcely talk of anything else," since it induced in Chalmers's mind "the sublime conception of the Godhead as that eternal, all-pervading energy by which this vast and firmly-knit succession was originated and sustained, and into a very rapture of admiration and delight." Sir James Mackintosh, another nineteenth-century Scot and a prominent jurist, lauded Edwards as "the metaphysician of America," whose "power of subtile argument" was "perhaps unmatched, certainly unsurpassed among men"; Mackintosh devoted the most "disputatious" part of his university education at Aberdeen in the 1780s to "the perusal of Jonathan Edwards' book on Free-Will." Mackintosh's classmate, the Leicester-born dissenter Robert Hall, "celebrated Jonathan Edwards, in his treatise on the Will, and the distinction [of natural and moral necessity] defended with all the depth and precision peculiar to that amazing genius." Samuel Lorenzo Knapp, the pioneer critic of American literature, thought that *Freedom of the Will* set Edwards's "reputation to an equality with the first metaphysicians of his age in this country and in Europe." Even Edwards's most vehement American critic, Rowland G. Hazard, conceded that "the work of Edwards 'On the Will,' marks it as . . . the great bulwark of . . . the necessarians." As to their creed, "the severest scrutiny of their opponents has discovered in it no vulnerable point. The soundness of the premises, and the cogency of the logic, by which he reaches his conclusions, seem indeed to be very generally admitted, so that, almost by common consent, his positions are deemed impregnable, and the hope of subverting them by direct attack abandoned."[18]

But if Edwardsian-style revivalism was an important means for firing up interest in the renewal of Calvinism, it was also a poor instrument for sustaining it. The demand for immediate repentance was supposed to infuse new virtue back into public life through renewed individuals; unhappily, it might just as easily convince renewed individuals to have nothing further to do with the sinfulness of their surrounding neighbors. Edwardsian revivalism was, at the end of the day, a reflection of the old Puritan weakness for separatism: the revivals called people to repentance, but they also called them out of society, out of their normal relations, out of their everyday moral lives, to participate in an intensely demanding but quite other-worldly version of

Protestant Christianity. The very fact that a revival was judged necessary at all was a judgment on the failures of the regular churches and the impurities of conventional society; its logical end was to turn people into come-outers of various sorts and inflate a radical individualism. To maintain momentum and influence, and to maintain it broadly in society, there had to be a second answer to the problem of religion's role in leading American life, and that would come from the nineteenth-century academic moral philosophers and John Witherspoon's Scottish philosophy of common sense.[19]

4

We Can If We Will

REGENERATION AND BENEVOLENCE

James P. Byrd

HARPERS FERRY, VIRGINIA, was a long way from Northampton, Massachusetts, and much more than place and time separated John Brown, the vigilante abolitionist, from Jonathan Edwards. But in spearheading his attack on slavery, Brown owed something of his zeal to the Edwardsian tradition. Brown admitted as much, often noting his admiration for Edwards, especially his preaching on judgment and hell, apt subjects for Brown's self-administered judgment of slavery. Brown's abolitionism—and his interest in Edwards—both developed in part through the influence of his father, Owen Brown. In the summer of 1790, Owen Brown heard a persuasive case against slavery made by Rev. Samuel Hopkins, a student of Edwards and perhaps the most influential Edwardsian theologian. Hopkins had traveled from Newport, Rhode Island, to West Simsbury, Connecticut, where Brown heard him speak. Later that summer, Owen Brown found an antislavery sermon written by Edwards's son, Jonathan Edwards, Jr. After reading it, Brown became a dedicated abolitionist. "From this time I was antislavery," he remarked.[1] The ramifications of this decision to oppose slavery were obviously momentous for the history of abolitionism in the United States. Moreover, this episode reveals just one among many facets of the Edwardsian influence on moral activism.

There was nothing typical about John Brown. Reports of his terrorist attack on slavery in 1859 reverberated through both North and South, dramatically affecting the abolitionist cause. Understandably, therefore, his appropriation of the Edwardsian tradition was far from typical. More often, Edwardian ideas inspired more peaceful advocates of social reform, whether the cause was antislavery or missions. But the fact that Edwardsians influenced Brown at all demonstrated the pervasiveness of the Edwardsian influence.

This chapter reveals how this influence developed with Edwards and his followers, specifically in their advocacy of a virtuous society. Edwardsians were hardly the only intellectuals concerned with virtue in the eighteenth century. In fact, they often perceived that there was too much fruitless talk about virtue in their day—too much talk, that is, but not enough virtuous activity. Most disturbing to Edwardsians was the tendency of both ministers and philosophers to herald the moral goodness of humanity without acknowledging that true virtue, often specified as benevolence, was impossible without divine influence. In response to this modern tendency to tear morality from its theological foundations, Edwardsians protested that true virtue, authentic benevolence, resulted from regeneration, which was possible only through the converting power of God. This chapter examines how Edwardsians shaped this pivotal relationship between regeneration and benevolence. The crisis over slavery provides a fitting framework for this chapter's theological analysis. Several of Edwards's most influential followers asserted that slavery was a horrific evil; more ominously, they recognized that slavery was, for many, an acceptable social reality, even a virtuous institution. For these Edwardsians, slavery revealed the disastrous consequences of an age obsessed with virtue that had, ironically, lost the true essence of virtue.

Holy Affections and True Virtue: Jonathan Edwards on Regeneration and Benevolence

Edwards shaped his unique connection between regeneration and benevolence through a theory of moral agency in *Freedom of the Will*, a concept of regeneration best expressed in *Religious Affections*, and a defense of benevolence as the essence of the virtuous life in *The Nature of True Virtue*.

Agency

As defenders of Calvinism against liberals (or more specifically, Arminians), Edwardsians engaged a problem that plagued Calvinism: How could people be free to make choices in a world in which God determined all actions? If human choices were determined and necessary, was not freedom meaningless? As Samuel West, a minister from New Bedford, stated it succinctly, "Wherever necessity begins, liberty ends." To the contrary, Edwardsians replied, necessity did not deny liberty, rightly understood, and Edwards defended this proper understanding in *Freedom of the Will*. The full title of this work revealed his central points: *A careful and strict enquiry into The modern prevailing Notions of that Freedom of Will, Which is supposed to be essential To Moral Agency, Vertue and*

Vice, Reward and Punishment, Praise and Blame. The title implied that the cherished modern idea of freedom was indeed at stake, but so was morality itself. If the will was not free, modern critics argued, then people could neither be praised for virtue nor blamed for sin. No freedom, no moral accountability.[2]

Edwards agreed—up to a point. Moral agency implied freedom, but what did it mean to be free? Edwards asserted that humans were free even though their choices were determined. Individuals were free to choose what they wanted even though their motives and inclinations made some choices necessary and others impossible. Though Arminians insisted that if choices were necessary then the will was not free, Edwards answered that it all depended on what one meant by "necessary." There were two kinds of "necessity," Edwards argued: "natural" and "moral." Natural necessity related to the natural world, and it included physical limitations. For example, by natural necessity humans had to live on the earth; they had no natural ability to fly. Natural necessity limited freedom, restricting one's ability to do what one may want to do.

"Moral necessity" worked in a similar way. Natural forces limited human choices, but so did moral forces such as motives and inclinations. Edwards illustrated the point with several scenarios. "A woman of great honor and chastity" may be morally unable to become a prostitute, for example, or a "malicious man may be unable to" love his enemies. In these scenarios, both the chaste woman and the malicious man were free because they were able to do as they wanted; they had natural ability, the very definition of freedom. But their choices were also determined; their motives and inclinations guided and limited their decisions. This limitation was powerful. An individual's "dispositions may be as strong and immovable as the bars of a castle," Edwards asserted. But it was incorrect to claim that those who lacked the moral ability to be virtuous were not free. Sinners were *able* to do the right thing; the problem was that they were not *willing* to do it. So Edwards argued that freedom was consistent with determination of the will.[3]

Regeneration

The problem for humanity, therefore, was not lack of freedom—lack of natural ability. It was lack of moral ability. Sinners were free to do what they wanted, but they wanted evil. Their minds were set against God and against virtue, and the only correction came through regeneration. In *Nature of True Virtue*, Edwards assessed this connection between regeneration and ethics that he had also addressed in his analysis of revival, *Treatise Concerning Religious Affections.* As Edwards assessed authentic religious experience, he asserted that truly holy affections came from God; they were "spiritual, supernatural and divine"—and the truly converted had the Holy Spirit within them, empowering their affections as a "supernatural spring of life and action." He called this indwelling of the Spirit "a new inward perception." Edwards famously illustrated this point with the sense of taste: knowing that honey is sweet was not the same as tasting the honey and experiencing the sweetness. Likewise, before regeneration individuals may know that God is holy and beautiful, but after regeneration they experience the holiness and beauty of God firsthand.[4]

This new ability to experience God's holiness was, primarily, a new moral sense. This moral ability was part of the divine image in Adam and Eve that "was lost by the fall" and was restored in regeneration. Before the fall, Edwards reasoned, there was "a twofold image of God" within humanity. The first was this "image of God's moral excellency," which humanity lost in the fall. The second was "God's natural image," which consisted in "reason and understanding," a "natural ability" that the fall did not extinguish. Regeneration therefore restored the moral ability of humanity, which consisted in "a love to divine things for the beauty of their moral excellency," and it was this view of moral excellency that was "the beginning and spring of all holy affections."[5]

Edwards's *Religious Affections* called for introspection; however, the primary ground of all truly religious affections was discoverable not by contemplation but by action. "Gracious and holy affections," he said, "have their exercise and fruit in Christian practice." This was Edwards's twelfth and final sign that he used to identify holy affections, and it underscored an essential point of his later dissertation on *True Virtue*: that true religion and true virtue prioritized the glory of God above any personal benefit. True religious affections flowed directly from love of "divine things, as they are in themselves, and not [from any] conceived relation they bear to self, or self-interest." Moreover, "This shows why holy affections will cause men to be holy in their practice universally." Just as true religious affections could not be primarily self-interested, neither could true virtue, and the two were connected; holy affections led to holy actions. One should not judge people "by their talk," or by their testimonies of devotion. In evaluating the sincerity of religious experience, one finds actions more reliable than words: "Hypocrites may much more easily be brought to talk like saints, than to act like saints."[6]

Virtue and Benevolence

To "act like saints," for Edwards, was to live a virtuous life, which he analyzed in his *Nature of True Virtue*. It was only through regeneration that people could truly glorify God by living truly virtuous lives, lives that reflected the beauty of God's moral excellence. Edwards's *True Virtue* opposed modern moral philosophy, which Edwards believed threatened to undermine traditional Christian morality. Edwards's famous contemporary Benjamin Franklin exemplified the problem. He separated the virtuous life from religious convictions, believing that anyone could be virtuous, regardless of regeneration, or any spiritual experience. "A virtuous Heretic shall be saved before a wicked Christian," Franklin quipped. *The Nature of True Virtue*, therefore, was Edwards's response to the idea that the highest form of virtue was possible for anyone regardless of whether the person had any concept of God.[7]

A representative of the "schemes of morality" that Edwards opposed was Francis Hutcheson, a Scottish thinker whose concept of a natural moral sense influenced many intellectuals.[8] Like Hutcheson, Edwards began his description of virtue with a discussion of beauty. Virtue, Edwards observed, was the highest form of beauty—not physical beauty, but "the beauty of the qualities and exercises of the heart," a beauty reflected in a virtuous life.[9] But not all forms of virtue were equally beautiful, and Edwards made the case for *true* virtue, which he defined as "benevolence to Being in general," a love that was "exercised in a general good will."[10] That is, true virtue was directed outwardly toward all that existed (or "being in general"). And since true virtue was a love of "being in general," it focused primarily on the great majority of "being," namely God, "the Being of beings, infinitely the greatest and best of beings."[11] But most modern moral philosophy neglected this central truth, Edwards believed. For all of their constant talk of virtue as beauty and excellence, modern schemes of morality focused on "self love"—centered on the self rather than on God.[12]

Edwards acknowledged that self-love was not bad. One of the chief benefits of self-love was the conscience, which enabled individuals to distinguish between good and evil. For all its great benefits, however, the conscience fell short of true virtue. That is, even though the conscience revealed the difference between good and evil, the conscience did not cause individuals to *love* good and *hate* evil. Through the conscience, individuals could understand that they were sinning, but that awareness did not necessarily cause them to hate sin and to repent. The problem, however, was that moral philosophers commonly did not distinguish between the natural moral sense—including the conscience—and the divinely inspired moral taste for true virtue.[13]

Old Calvinism and New Divinity on Regeneration and Benevolence

This connection between regeneration and benevolence, so critical to Edwards's theology, also influenced theological debates after Edwards. The most intentional heirs of his theology were ministers belonging to what came to be known as the New Divinity movement. The operative description was "new"—and this was not complementary. True Divinity could not be *new* divinity, most Calvinists believed, but old—ancient and biblical. And even though Edwardsian ministers believed that their theology was biblically faithful, they met opposition from a group of ministers known as "Old Calvinists," who claimed to defend the "old" faith against what they saw as the "new" divinity. In fact the "Old Calvinists" hardly constituted a unified theological movement; what united them most was their opposition to the Edwardsians.[14]

In contrast, the New Divinity ministers, who preferred the term "consistent Calvinists," found much to unite them. Several were Yale-educated, and all viewed themselves as followers of Edwards. Two of the leading New Divinity ministers, Samuel Hopkins and Joseph Bellamy, studied in Edwards's home. Others among the New Divinity were united by family as well as by theology; Jonathan Edwards, Jr., was his son, and Timothy Dwight was his grandson. Hopkins's brother and brother-in-law were New Divinity ministers, as was Bellamy's son-in-law.[15] Theologically, the New Divinity ministers strove to defend Calvinism against both liberal Arminianism and overzealous Antinomianism.[16] Old Calvinists also viewed themselves as defenders of Calvinism, but they and the New Divinity disagreed on the nature of Calvinism, just as they disagreed on how best to defend it. Despite their avowed loyalty to Edwards, New Divinity theologians adapted his thought; some even said they distorted his thought. Regardless, New Divinity ministers shared Edwards's zeal for revival—not merely as a religious experience, but as an impetus to regeneration and true virtue.[17]

The Edwardsians' interest in virtue stemmed from his *Nature of True Virtue*, and several related concerns. First, like Edwards, they sought to defend Calvinism from liberal attacks. Calvinism was most vulnerable, many believed, in areas of moral agency and accountability. Accordingly, defenders of Calvinism had to respond decisively to these challenges. Second, Edwardsians felt the pressing tide of social change, with the increasing commercialization and growth of markets that rewarded self-interest and punished self-sacrifice. One of the greatest dangers of the age was selfish religion, a counterfeit faith that was no more than selfishness disguised as piety.[18]

Old Calvinists believed that the New Divinity's so-called defense of Calvinism actually betrayed the tradition. Six years after posthumous publication of Edwards's *True Virtue*, William Hart responded from the Old Calvinist perspective.[19] Hart, who pastored in Saybrook, Connecticut, called the New Divinity a "chaos of divinity," labeling it "a hard-hearted, arbitrary, cruel tyrant, a tormentor of souls" that "scandalously represents the character and conduct of

God," among other criticisms.[20] Hart also asserted "that Mr. Edwards' notions" on virtue were "wrong, imaginary, and fatally destructive of the foundations of morality and true religion." His response to Edwards's *True Virtue* was, accordingly, an attempt to lay "the ax to the root of the tree," decisively refuting the ethical theories of Edwards and his followers, especially Hopkins.[21]

Hart attacked Edwardsian views of virtue on several grounds. First, he rejected Edwards's definition of true virtue as "benevolence to being simply considered," an abstract concept that Hart believed was idolatrous because it prioritized love to "being in general" over love to God. Such misplaced devotion made an "idol" out of "being" and made "virtue itself idolatrous." Second, Edwards demoted the natural moral sense to a status below true virtue. Even the conscience, "the natural guide of life," was for Edwards no more than "a blundering, blind leader," a pale reflection of true virtue. In Hart's view, the unhappy result was that "natural conscience and the moral sense can't taste and approve" true "virtue any more than the white of an egg." Such "a notion of virtue" had a "destructive influence," Hart believed, "on virtue itself." It reduced all natural duties, all obligations of justice in social relations as taught in scripture, and all obligations to God to a secondary kind of "beauty" comparable to "a square or a cube, and no more virtuous than they."[22]

Edwards's idea of virtue, though metaphysically abstract and complicated, was—ironically—too simplistic, Hart reasoned. "Virtue is a complex thing," Hart argued; "it does not primarily consist in one single disposition, tendency, or affection of the mind." Instead, virtue "includes various affections." Not all truly virtuous acts flowed from truly benevolent love to God. Even the unregenerate could desire virtue, strive for and achieve virtue, and be condemned if they did not.[23] True virtue needed to be accessible, therefore, within the domain of natural morality. Edwards and his followers threatened the accessibility of true virtue, Hart and his Old Calvinist colleagues feared, and they worried that Edwardsian ethics would make a moral society impossible. If true virtue were achievable only for the regenerate, then how could the unregenerate (obviously the majority of the population in even the best societies), be called on to be truly virtuous?

The response to Hart came from Samuel Hopkins, who published *Inquiry into the Nature of True Holiness* to defend Edwards's stance on true virtue.[24] Any theories about holiness and benevolence, sin and self-love were useless without a convincing argument for human agency against Hart's attacks, as Hopkins knew. So Hopkins rejected Hart's claim that Edwards rendered natural morality, including the conscience, useless. To the contrary, Edwards declared that the conscience informed all individuals of goodness and virtue, even the beauty of true virtue. This information for the reason was immensely valuable; it was natural knowledge to all people about true virtue, benevolence, its goodness and justice. Because all people had this natural understanding of true virtue, all people could be held responsible for acting on it.

The basis for this response was the distinction Edwards drew between natural and moral ability.[25] Against Hart's claim that Edwardsians made it impossible to expect the unregenerate to be virtuous, Hopkins responded that all people had the natural ability to repent and to live virtuous lives. Here the New Divinity followed Edwards in arguing that the fall of humanity affected only the will or the heart, the moral faculty of the soul, and not the understanding and the conscience, the natural faculties.[26] If the fall had damaged the natural abilities of the soul—the understanding and the conscience—New Divinity ministers feared that critics could rightly claim that Calvinists unfairly blamed sinners for not doing what they were unable to do. If the understanding and the conscience had been damaged, people would have been naturally handicapped in the same way that a blind person had a physical inability to see. If people had the natural inability to understand what God required, then they had a valid excuse for not doing it. Accordingly, Hopkins asserted that all of humanity were "capable of seeing and tasting the beauty of moral things, and of being perfectly holy." They lacked "nothing but an inclination to this, a heart to improve the faculties" they had "in order to see and taste this beauty, and be truly virtuous."[27]

A problem with Hart's argument, Hopkins reasoned, was that he did not make the common distinction "between the dictates of the judgment and conscience, and the relish and approbation of the heart." So even though all people, through the natural power of conscience, knew in their minds what true virtue was, and knew that it was what they should strive for, their hearts were still sinful, and they did not have the "relish" for true virtue. So the Edwardsians recognized the great distance between the right knowledge of true virtue that the mind granted and the love for true virtue that came only from the heart of the regenerate.[28]

With the Edwardsian idea of natural ability, therefore, the New Divinity could argue that all people were able to be holy, and it was inexcusable if they did not exercise benevolence. And yet with the Edwardsian idea of moral inability, the New Divinity could assert that people would choose to be holy only if they were regenerate, with their hearts transformed to God's purposes. Sinners were therefore caught in an excruciating dilemma. They had the natural ability to repent, so they were responsible for their sin. This natural ability, however, could not overcome the moral inability of their evil hearts; they were able to repent, but unwilling to do so. Their only hope was to strive and to pray for regeneration. What was needed, as Hopkins asserted, was a "new heart, the

circumcised, benevolent heart, and not the old, uncircumcised, selfish heart";
only such "a new heart . . . sees the divine character and loves it." This "new
heart" was a gift of grace, an unearned, "unpromised favor" through which
God created a new ability to understand "the truths, of the gospel in their real
beauty and excellency," and a new ability to exercise true holiness.[29]

Regeneration

Regeneration, as Hopkins described it, was distinct from conversion. In regeneration, God was active and sinners were passive; God regenerated individuals
by giving them new hearts, and God produced this transformation "immediately," without assistance from "any medium or means whatsoever." No
human works contributed to regeneration. "God said, 'Let it be,' and it was,"
Hopkins wrote.[30] Regeneration made conversion possible, and only the regenerate could be converted. In conversion, the regenerate took an active role
because God enabled them to repent, have faith in Christ, and receive forgiveness from sin. Only the regenerate could repent because only the regenerate
would want true conversion.[31] In Hopkins's view, any yearning the unregenerate had for conversion was really a selfish desire to save themselves from
hell. They did not love God for God's sake; they loved God for their own sake.
For the unregenerate, any use of traditional means of grace—such as praying,
reading scripture, and attending sermons—was merely self-interested works.
No matter how "engaged and diligent" the unregenerate were in practicing the
means of grace, their efforts did them more harm than good. The "impenitent
sinner," Hopkins asserted, was even "more vicious and guilty in God's sight,
the more instruction and knowledge he gets in attendance on the means of
grace." This was an outrageous statement, in the view of Old Calvinists who,
following Puritan tradition, encouraged sinners to rely on the means of grace
to lead them through the conversion process. No statement by Hopkins gave
Old Calvinists more evidence that he had espoused a "new" and untrue divinity. But Hopkins insisted that only the regenerate could desire conversion for
the right reason: to love and glorify God for God's sake.[32]

Benevolence and Self-Love

The holiness that God made possible for the regenerate, was, as Hopkins
described it, "universal benevolence or love to being in general." This universal benevolence, as Hopkins asserted in the thesis of his *Inquiry*, "is the
whole of holiness, and, on the other hand, all sin consists in self-love." In
response to Hart, who criticized as idolatrous Edwards's definition of virtue

as "benevolence to being in general," Hopkins stated that all Edwards meant by "being in general" was that "true love to God is a disposition to love being in general." That is, love to God was expansive, universal, and not a limited love, which centered on "any particular sort or circle of beings." It was not wrong for individuals to love themselves, their families, and their societies, but the love of self should not take precedence over devotion to God. Most often, however, "self-love" was really "selfish love" whereby individuals loved themselves above all and only loved others as an extension of self-interest. Whereas benevolence was "disinterested" and selfless, most forms of self-love were "interested" and selfish.[33]

The essence of holiness, therefore, was benevolence, and benevolence was both reasonable and scriptural. Although only the regenerate could be truly benevolent, with their hearts oriented around love to God and extending to love of all anyone could see the reasonableness of benevolence as the highest moral good. Who could doubt the virtue of self-sacrifice, the idea that "personal interest" should give way to the good of all? What was apparent through reason was even more obvious in revelation, however, as scripture was the clearest guide to the holiness of universal benevolence. How could one defend the virtue of selfish love in light of Jesus' command, "If ye love them which love you, what reward have you? Do not even the publicans the same?" (Matt. 5:46) Even the lowest of sinners loved those who loved them. In his rejection of this selfish love, Jesus commanded a higher form of virtue in his radical command, "Love your enemies" (Matt. 5:43–48). Love of the enemy was the ultimate form of disinterested love. Hopkins called on all to examine their piety and practice by this standard: "True religion consists in disinterested affection, and 'seeketh not her own'; false religion wholly consists in selfish affections and exercises. The former is holiness; the latter is nothing but sin."[34]

Hopkins pushed this idea to its ultimate conclusion, claiming that true disinterested benevolence would require people to be willing to accept their own damnation if it increased God's glory. Though Hopkins was not the first Calvinist to make this radical claim, he became infamous for it. But this statement of radical disinterestedness aptly demonstrated his concern that even religious practice, even obedience to God's commands, could be motivated by self-love.[35] Nothing concerned Hopkins more than the extent to which self-love dominated so-called Christian, even Calvinist, theology and piety in the eighteenth century. In a society that he believed was increasingly driven by selfish pursuit of personal gain, true religion needed to be a prophetic voice of disinterested benevolence. More often than not, however, selfish religion allied with selfish society. "How common it is to hear the preacher speak of religion as if it consisted altogether in selfishness!" Hopkins proclaimed. Even more distressing was the ecumenical pervasiveness of selfishness. No matter what their other disagreements, "Arminians, Neonominians, professed Calvinists, Antinomians," and even more groups sadly find common ground in preaching a selfish gospel.[36]

Edwardsian Benevolence Asserted: The Case Against Slavery

Old Calvinists claimed that Edwardsian theology would imperil efforts toward a moral society. Edwardsians responded by defying critics in the most tangible way: by advocating social morality in the strongest terms. New Divinity ministers synthesized convictions that Old Calvinists feared would conflict: a zeal for revival, firmly convinced that true virtue required regeneration, and a broad appeal for all people to strive for true virtue. Because they believed that true virtue required authentic regeneration, Edwardsians believed that the answers to many moral problems would come with revival. New hearts, redeemed by Christ, would create new societies, reformed by benevolence. Accordingly, the Edwardsians were zealous revivalists and advocates for missionary societies and publications.[37]

Without diminishing the importance of missions, one may assert that the most serious moral problem of the day (and arguably the most troubling moral crisis in American history), was slavery. Moreover, the New Divinity arguments against slavery, even more than their support of missions, revealed most clearly how they understood the relationship between individual regeneration and social morality, including how self-interest should relate to disinterested benevolence.

In opposing slavery, Edwards's students followed the implications of his thought to conclusions he never anticipated. Edwards owned slaves, and he never supported emancipation, though he did oppose the slave trade. In contrast, several of Edwards's followers opposed both the slave trade, and slavery itself.[38] Of the Edwardsians who published against slavery, Hopkins received the most attention. His opposition to slavery arose after he moved from a frontier pastorate at Great Barrington, Massachusetts, to Newport, Rhode Island. For a time during the pastorate, Hopkins tolerated slavery and, like his mentor, even had a slave in his home. After moving to Newport, however, he encountered firsthand the barbarity of the slave trade, once declaring that "this town is the most guilty respecting the slave trade, of any" in America. Newport was literally "built up by the blood of the poor Africans," Hopkins wrote.[39] Slavery was, he believed, not only sinful but a diabolical evil that many Christians accepted as respectable, virtuous, and biblical. It was true that slavery was in the Bible, but that ancient form of servitude bore little resemblance to the modern slave trade, which Hopkins argued was "contrary to the whole tenor of divine revelation" and was "a gross violation of every divine precept" contained in the scriptures.[40] Yet Hopkins recognized that he met formidable opposition from Christians who supported slavery on biblical and ethical grounds. This broad acceptance of slavery was one of the clearest signs for Hopkins of how depraved society had become. Virtue, though often discussed and apparently respected, had lost much of its meaningful content.[41]

Hopkins made this case in *A Dialogue concerning the Slavery of the Africans*, published in 1776—an appropriate year considering the Revolutionary arguments for freedom in the *Dialogue*. Moreover, Hopkins dedicated the *Dialogue* to the Continental Congress, which had just adopted a resolution against the slave trade in 1774. Buoyed by this stance taken by the Continental Congress, tentative though it was, Hopkins advocated an attack on slavery itself, the entire institution, beyond the slave trade alone.[42]

Theologically, Hopkins opposed slavery because it contradicted disinterested benevolence. Practically, he recognized that arguments on behalf of disinterested benevolence could be more convincing if combined with a zealous case against slavery on behalf of self-interest. This appeal to self-interest did not contradict the Edwardsian zeal for benevolence. Not all forms of self-interest were sinful, Hopkins argued, and he distinguished selfishness, which was the essence of all sin, from a healthy self-regard, described as "the love a person has for himself as part of the whole, which is implied in universal benevolence." So universal benevolence implied a healthy love of self and promoted a fitting concern for the happiness of society.[43] This dual-focused opposition to slavery, arguing on behalf of benevolence and self-interest, was typically Edwardsian. Jonathan Edwards, Jr. made a similar appeal in *Injustice and Impolicy of the Slave Trade, and of the Slavery of the Africans*, published fifteen years after Hopkins's *Dialogue*. As the younger Edwards indicated in the title of this sermon, slavery was not only morally wrong; it was self-defeating. That is, slavery was an "injustice," a violation of virtuous concerns for righteousness, and also an "impolicy," which was "exceedingly hurtful to the state" in several ways. Accordingly, to perpetuate slavery and the slave trade "is not only to be guilty of injustice, robbery and cruelty toward our fellow-men; but it is to injure ourselves and our country."[44]

Both Hopkins and Edwards cited examples of how slavery was morally wrong and practically disastrous. One of the pragmatic questions Hopkins addressed concerned timing: Even if slavery were wrong, was wartime a good time to address the issue? Many colonists argued that they were busy enough fighting the British, and everything else had to wait, including slavery.

Distraction, even to correct a gross injustice, could lead to defeat. To the contrary, Hopkins argued, wartime was precisely the right time to oppose slavery. He reasoned that if slavery was "a very great and public sin," and God punished sinful nations with multiple calamities, including war, then the colonies should reject slavery before they incited the wrath of God against them. For colonists to condone slavery was not just morally reprehensible and "unspeakably criminal," it was "awfully dangerous," Hopkins warned.[45]

It was especially perilous to support slavery in revolutionary times, both Hopkins and Jonathan Edwards, Jr. argued, as they cited the hypocritical inconsistency between republican cries for freedom and the American support of slavery. Patriots took up arms to fight British tyranny, lashing out in righteous indignation against a British government that they claimed treated them like slaves. And yet these same patriots ignored the much more devastating, actual slavery that they inflicted on the Africans. Hopkins remarked that the slaves saw the revolutionary "cry and struggle for liberty" but also "behold the sons of liberty oppressing and tyrannizing over many thousands of poor blacks who have as good a claim to liberty as" anyone. This obvious contradiction rightfully "shocked" the slaves, while white patriots seemed unaware that the tyranny they feared was "lighter than a feather compared to" the "heavy doom" inflicted on the slaves. In this contemptible hypocrisy, Hopkins blamed ministers who either supported slavery or stood silent, refusing to condemn it outright. True republicanism, and true Christian benevolence, cried out for liberty against slavery.[46]

Slavery was anti-revolutionary and anti-benevolent, just as it was anti-revival. Hopkins recognized, however, that supporters of slavery made the opposite claim, asserting that slavery was a benevolent institution. After all, said the pro-slavery contingent, slavery brought the "heathen" Africans to a Christian land where they could encounter the gospel. Arguments such as this horrified Hopkins. He found it reprehensible that apologists for slavery perverted Christianity so disgracefully, blatantly distorting the gospel into a tool for selfish gain. This claim for the evangelical benefits of slavery was both ideologically flawed and practically false. The slave system was hardly an evangelistic tool; most slaveholders refused to instruct slaves in the gospel. What Christianity slaves learned, they gathered from example—and what a bad example it was. Slaves encountered Christianity through cruel whites who enslaved them, which was hardly a good witness; such information about Christianity did more to prejudice slaves against the gospel than to draw them toward it. But even if slavery were the greatest system ever invented to evangelize the Africans, and even if all slaves converted, that good result would not justify the gross evil of the slave trade. The horrid truth was that slave trading was much higher on the agenda of both Americans and Europeans than evangelism. If only "Europeans and Americans had been as much engaged to Christianize the Africans as they have been to enslave them," the result would have been not enslavement and devastation but "the salvation of millions of millions" throughout the world. Because of slavery, however, the opposite occurred, with millions of Africans prejudiced against the gospel by Christianity's alliance with the vilest of institutions.[47]

Hopkins's call for immediate emancipation was radical, but he denied that it was either impractical or impossible. In terms drawn from the Edwardsian distinction between natural and moral ability, there was no natural hindrance to ending slavery; society was under no necessity to keep this oppressive institution in place. The problem was not natural ability—immediate emancipation was an open possibility—but moral ability: "there is no insurmountable difficulty" in ending slavery other than "that which lies in your own heart." White colonists acted out of self-love, rooted in prejudice against the Africans, a prejudice that allowed whites to prefer their own agendas to any benevolent concern for the slaves. As Hopkins claimed, white colonists typically did not oppose slavery because they believed that slaves "are Negros, and fit for nothing but slaves . . . and our education has filled us with strong prejudices against them," leading us to believe that they are not "brethren" but "animals" of servitude. This view, even though dominant and respectable, was hardly virtuous, hardly an exercise in disinterested benevolence. Consequently, what was needed was for colonists to replace prejudice with benevolence, viewing the slaves "as by nature and by right on a level with our brethren and children," loving slaves as colonists loved themselves.[48]

Conclusion

Slavery, to a greater extent than any other issue, galvanized Edwardsian convictions for regeneration and benevolence. Slavery incarnated much that Edwardsians reviled. Bondage of not only the will but also the body, slavery was unjustly imposed natural inability, a repulsive concept for ministers so committed to the natural ability of everyone to reject evil.[49] Moreover, slavery not only damaged the slave; it perverted both church and society. Slavery was a form of bondage that stifled the gospel and any free response to it, just as it destroyed any chance of a virtuous life. Slavery contradicted the spirit of benevolence, and it inculcated vice and sin into the fabric of society. Imposed servitude and injustice, all presumed by the slave trade to be virtuous, made virtue impossible to practice and even difficult to recognize.

In their abolitionism, the Edwardsians revealed that even if they could occasionally proclaim their willingness to be damned for the sake of God's glory, they opposed any threat to damn society for the sake of human glory and selfish gain. True benevolence was both biblically faithful and practically beneficial. A social policy of benevolence worked; it promoted justice and allowed the gospel to thrive. In contrast, a social policy of selfishness brought certain disaster; it promoted division and prejudice, and it squelched any hope for national revival. It is no wonder that abolitionists, even the radical John Brown, found in the Edwardsians a revivalist zeal that was well equipped for the abolitionist cause.

5

The Moral Government of God

JONATHAN EDWARDS AND JOSEPH BELLAMY ON THE ATONEMENT

Oliver D. Crisp

WHAT IS THE relationship between the doctrine of atonement owned by Jonathan Edwards and that developed by his disciples in the New Divinity? This question is not as straightforward as it might first appear. Edwards never completed a sustained account of the atonement, and the scattered remarks he did write on the subject appear to pull in rather different directions. For instance, he wrote an enthusiastic preface to *True Religion Delineated*, the work of his protégé, Joseph Bellamy, which offered the first complete account of the New England version of the governmental model of atonement, one of the hallmarks of New England theology. Yet it appears that Edwards's most reflective work on this subject in his notebooks stays within the bounds of satisfaction and penal substitution versions of the doctrine.

Behind this puzzle lies a question of doctrinal development. Was the New Divinity governmental theory of atonement a legitimate extrapolation of basically Edwardsian themes, a kind of Calvinized version of the doctrine in keeping with the New England attempt to reenvision Reformed theology for an American context? Or was it an important departure from the thinking of Edwards, a sign that his theological progeny were not content to pass on his theology but were at least as concerned to put their own imprimatur on the burgeoning movement?

The evidence suggests that the seeds of the New England governmental view of the atonement were sown by Edwards himself. But he did not have the opportunity, or perhaps the inclination, to develop this in his own work.[1] So the views expressed by Bellamy, Samuel Hopkins, and Jonathan

Edwards, Jr., to name the three most important exponents of the doctrine among the theologians of the New Divinity, were, one might think, a doctrinal innovation in one respect. But they were building on some ideas latent in the work of Edwards Senior, and they did, it appears, have his sanction for doing so.[2] Here, then, is an instance of theological development that, though complex, does not bespeak some sort of declension, or departure from the teaching of the master—the "decline and fall" narrative often associated with historiography of the New England Theology.[3] I suggest that this indicates one important way in which the relationship between the work of Edwards and that of his theological progeny (at least, in the first phase of the New England theology, that is, the New Divinity) is more complex than might be thought at first sight and merits further research.

The chapter is divided into five sections. The first offers some theological context on the doctrine of the atonement relevant to this historical discussion. The second section focuses on some key ideas in Edwards's soteriology. Then, in a third section, this is compared with the work of Joseph Bellamy, Edwards's principle disciple, whose work on the subject became the benchmark for later perorations on the New England doctrine of atonement. A fourth part rounds out the whole by offering some reflections on the relationship between the doctrines of Edwards and Bellamy. I close with some remarks about the implications this has for the broader canvas of New England theology.

The aim throughout is to show that the New Divinity men, here represented by Bellamy, were Reformed theologians developing basically Edwardsian insights in a changing intellectual context, which required them to think creatively about how atonement should be understood.[4] Using ideas Edwards Senior developed elsewhere in his metaphysics, these divines sought to remedy a lacuna in Edwards's theology, by formulating a version of the doctrine of atonement that made sense of central Reformed convictions while also reflecting some of the emerging themes of the New Divinity—themes that were essentially Edwardsian in character. The result was a creative and important contribution to the Reformed tradition, which has been overlooked or sidelined in subsequent systematic theology.

Diversity Within the Reformed Tradition on the Atonement

In their recent reader in the New England Theology, Douglas Sweeney and Allen Guelzo introduce the New Divinity doctrine of the work of Christ by pointing out that it departed from the standard, Reformed doctrine of a definite, limited atonement: "The judicial model of justification had immediate connections to the nature of the atonement, since a justification accomplished by the merits of Christ could be applied only to those whom Christ consciously intended them for; the elect." This "structured the atonement as a transaction in which the believer had no real role." For this reason, "many of the evangelical movements of the eighteenth century either softened or abandoned the limited atonement model."[5] But this is not quite right. Although many in the Reformed tradition did subscribe to the doctrine of a definite, limited atonement understood in terms of a penal substitutionary model, this was not universally the case. There were a number of Reformed theologians who were much less enamored of the idea that the atonement was limited, in effectiveness, to the elect alone. Before the Synod of Dordt, several accounts of the scope of the atonement were tolerated within the bounds of Reformed theology. Subsequent to this great conclave of Calvinist divines, there remained divergence within certain confessional boundaries.

To take just one example of this, Bishop John Davenant, who led the British delegation to the Synod, held to a species of hypothetical universalism.[6] This doctrine distinguishes between an initial divine intention to bring about an atoning work of unlimited scope and a consequent decree, which ensured that this work of Christ was applied only to the elect. Although the distinction may seem like a nice one, it has important theological implications, relevant to discussion of the Reformed credentials of the New Divinity. For if God's antecedent intention was to bring about a state of affairs whereby all humans could be saved via the atonement of Christ, then the scope of the atonement is not necessarily such that, as Sweeney and Guelzo put it, "justification accomplished by the merits of Christ could be applied only to those whom Christ consciously intended them for; the elect." Nor is it true of such hypothetical universalist theology that it "structured the atonement as a transaction in which the believer had no real role." The consequent decree to bring about the salvation of the elect only obtains precisely because God's initial or antecedent decree is ineffective, on this way of thinking; God foresees that fallen human beings will not choose the salvation his initial decree proffers. The response of faith is a key constituent of this consequent, effective decree.

But matters are more complicated than even this divergence suggests. Recent work on Hugo Grotius's doctrine of atonement suggests that he is not necessarily a Grotian. That is, his doctrine is not obviously the governmental view of the atonement often touted in the literature, though there may be the seeds of such a doctrine in his work.[7]

This is important because it means that the New England "softening" of a limited atonement doctrine into its distinctive version of the governmental theory need not have been quite the deviation from a Reformed consensus it is often thought to be. There are, I suggest, a range of possible options on the divine intention in the atonement, its nature, and its scope, consistent with the confessionalism of Reformed theology.[8] Sometimes commentators like to distinguish between what is called the "traditional five-point Calvinist" position, which includes commitment to a doctrine of limited atonement, and "four-point Calvinism," that is, Reformed theology that adopts an unlimited scope to the atonement, as the hypothetical universalists do. The four-point position is, on this view, something doctrinally inferior, a compromise for those unable to stomach the full five points. This is an unfortunate way of characterizing matters. There may be good theological reasons for embracing five-point Calvinism and its commitment to limited atonement, but there is nothing *un-Reformed* in the four-point Calvinism of someone like Davenant, or, indeed, Moise Amyraut or John Cameron.

By parity of reasoning, adoption by the New Divinity theologians of the idea that the atonement is unlimited in scope does not in and of itself tell against the Reformed credentials of its exponents. Consistent Calvinism (as the New England theology was sometimes called) is not necessarily *inconsis-tent* with the wider Reformed community on this matter. To claim otherwise at the outset is to beg the question at issue by assuming that the only position on the scope of atonement permissible in the Reformed tradition is that of a definite, limited atonement. But this is simply mistaken.

There is a polemical history behind this claim that is not inconsequential. In the midnineteenth century, when Princetonian Calvinists were fighting the representatives of the New England theology for theological supremacy, Charles Hodge (and later, Benjamin Warfield) sought to outmaneuver their opponents by claiming the high Calvinistic ground.[9] Theirs was the formula-tion of Westminster Calvinism that was truly representative of the tradition; the New England doctrine was a genetic spur that needed to be excised. Today, it is their version of events that is remembered because the Princetonian the-ology outlived that of New England, and had intellectual heirs to receive and transmit it. But although history may be written by the victors, this does not guarantee that the whole story is told. So it appears there is reason to think that the New England doctrine of the atonement is not necessarily beyond the bounds of Reformed theology on the scope of the atonement. The historiog-raphy of this work is fraught because this was a doctrine that caused consid-erable consternation among so-called Old Light Calvinists (i.e. those, like the Princetonians, committed to a traditional, Westminster Calvinism).

However, even if this is right, there is still the matter of the nature of the atonement, and the divine intention in bringing it about. Is the Consistent Calvinist position in this matter also consistently Reformed? There is a related concern that overlaps with this one to some extent. This is whether the New

England doctrine of atonement is a development of properly Edwardsian themes. If the answer to this latter query is in the affirmative, then the answer to the former question becomes even more important. For Edwards is claimed by both theological progressives, that is, the "New Lights" of New England theology, such as Park, as well as the "Old Lights" of traditional Calvinism, such as the Princetonians. In this way, the connection between Edwards and his erstwhile disciples in this central theological matter of the atonement has important implications for the theological "orthodoxy" of Edwards himself. These are not incidental concerns. Their theological resolution takes us to the heart of the New England theology, and by implication to the taproot of that tradition: Edwards himself.

But we begin to get ahead of ourselves. To provide some answers to these two nodal questions, let us turn in the first instance to consider the shape of Edwards's doctrine of the atonement. We will then be in a position to ascertain whether his immediate theological heirs departed from, or developed, basically Edwardsian themes on the work of Christ.

Jonathan Edwards on the Atonement

Robert Jenson reports that Edwards's doctrine of atonement has a different tenor from that of many defenders of penal substitution. For Edwards, God's rejection of sin is his own problem because he is "antecedently determined to be merciful." Indeed, "Christ's atoning suffering is God's own anguish suffered in the historically actual achieving of mercy."[10] The emphasis is on God's bringing about union with humanity via the work of Christ as an expression of divine love.

Of the many references to the work of Christ that can be found in the works of Jonathan Edwards (and especially in his notebooks[11]), one of the most sustained and carefully drawn is that found in Miscellany 779. There, Edwards speaks in language that seems to straddle aspects of traditional satisfaction doctrines of atonement alongside rectoral notions of God's moral governance of the world:

> Seeing therefore 'tis requisite that sin should be punished, as punishment is deserved and just, therefore the justice of God obliges him to punish sin: for it belongs to God as the supreme Rector of the universality of things, to maintain order and decorum in his kingdom, and to see to it that decency and right takes place at all times, and in all cases. That perfection of his nature whereby he is disposed to this is his justice; and therefore, his justice naturally disposes him to punish sin, as it deserves.[12]

Elsewhere, he makes plain his adherence to a traditional doctrine of penal substitution. Thus, for example, his discussion in his *Controversies* Notebook:

> What I think we may rationally and truly suppose concerning this matter, is this: that as of old God was long preparing his church to receive the doctrine of an atonement for sin by the sufferings of Jesus Christ, the second Adam, and imputing his sufferings to the sinner as one that in that matter stood for the sinner and was his representative, by representing himself as appeased and pardoning the sinner on the account of the sacrifices and vicarious sufferings and death of brute animals, and so long using his church and accustoming the world of mankind to the notion of an atonement by vicarious sufferings.[13]

Both aspects of Edwards's work were picked up by Edwards Amasa Park in his introductory essay on the New England doctrine prefacing his work, *The Atonement*. Somewhat reluctantly, he acknowledged that Edwards "adopted, in general, both the views and the phrases of the older Calvinists, with regard to the atonement. But like those Calvinists, he made various remarks that have suggested the more modern theory."[14]

A summary of these issues in Edwards's work can be given as follows. God is the moral governor of the cosmos against whom humans have sinned. His honor cannot be besmirched by human wickedness. Indeed, sin against such a being is sin against a being of infinite worth. The status of the person against whom one sins plays an important role in determining the seriousness of the crime and the suitability of punishment required. To sin against a being of infinite worth is to commit an act of heinousness corresponding to the status of the person concerned, in this case the Triune God. Since God is infinitely worthy, the demerit generated by sinning against him must be infinite, because (according to Edwards) the merit or demerit of an action corresponds to the worth of the person at whom the action concerned is aimed. Assume that humans normally commit at least one such sin.[15] Then, all such humans possess an infinite demerit, which they are incapable of remitting. To discharge his duty as moral governor of the cosmos, God must ensure that sin is punished; he cannot waive it, or forgive it.[16] Were he to do so, sin would go unpunished and his moral governance (and nature) would be called into question. (Behind this lies the assumption that justice is inexorable and must be served.) Moreover, for any theater of creation, the full panoply of divine attributes must be displayed so that both his justice and his mercy are manifest, thereby vindicating God's nature before his creatures. Thus sin must be punished in one of two possible ways: in the person of the sinner in hell, in an infinite punishment; or in the person of a suitable vicarious substitute to whom the infinite penal consequences of the demerit can be transferred. God ensures that Christ is the vicar for the elect; he alone is able to take on this task because he alone is both fully human (and therefore able to act on behalf of other humans) and also fully divine (and therefore able to offer up a merit of infinite value that may offset any infinite disvalue generated by human sin).

The act of atonement is a vicarious substitution. It is a provision that, although infinite in value and therefore in principle sufficient to remit the sin of all humanity, is in fact applied only to the sins of the elect. Nevertheless, all human beings are without excuse before God because all human beings are naturally able to turn to Christ and be saved. The reason all humans do not act on this natural ability is that they are morally incapable of doing so, because of the deformity of sin. It is like a man in prison whose jailer comes and unlocks the prison door, but who refuses to leave the prison because of his moral indignation at being incarcerated in the first place. Though there is no natural impediment to his leaving the cell, he is morally incapable of doing so because of his indignation.[7] In a similar manner, humans are able to come to faith in Christ but refuse to do so (although, for Edwards, this moral inability is as certain as any natural or metaphysical necessity—there is no sense in which the sinner will relent given time or inducement).

From this synthetic account of Edwards's doctrine, we can see six things relevant to the question of his relationship to the New Divinity conception of atonement. First, God is understood as a moral governor, and this plays an important role in how Edwards conceives the issues at stake. Second, justice demands that sin be punished; God is essentially just, so sin must be punished. Edwards upholds a strong, Anselmian account of the moral imperative for the punishment of sin. Third (echoing Anselm once again), Edwards provides a reason for thinking that human sin generates an infinite demerit for which only the God-man can atone. Fourth, although the scope of atonement is limited in intention to the salvation of some fraction of fallen humanity, in keeping with western catholicism Edwards affirms that it is sufficient in principle to save all humanity. Nevertheless, and fifthly, it is effectual only for the elect, who are made morally capable of receiving faith through the suasions of the Holy Spirit. Sixthly and finally, Edwards deploys his distinction between human moral and natural ability to argue that even the reprobate have no reason for thinking this action unjust because they are naturally (though not morally) able to come to faith if they so wish. It is just that they are morally incapable of so wishing because of their sinful condition.

This brings us to two important points of contention between Edwards and the New Divinity theologians. The first is that Edwards conceives of the atonement as definite and limited in scope. That is, God's intention in providing atonement for sin is that it is effectual only for the elect; it is not effectual for the reprobate. The reprobate individual does not have his sin atoned for by Christ only to then suffer an infinite punishment for that sin in hell. This would be an unjust double payment for sin. Edwards can avoid this objection by saying that Christ's work is limited to the elect only, though it has the power to atone for all human sin, just as a vaccine stockpile may be sufficient for an entire population although it is not administered to the whole population. The sinner in hell does not have the "vaccine" of Christ's atonement applied to him or her; hence he or she suffers the penal consequences of his or her sin. Second, and following on from this, Edwards clearly endorses the doctrine of penal substitution as the mechanism by which atonement is brought about. It is this core idea that is abandoned by the representatives of the New Divinity.

Joseph Bellamy on the Atonement

We are now in a position to turn to the work of Joseph Bellamy, Edwards's closest disciple. His *True Religion Delineated and Distinguished from All Counterfeits*, published in 1750, became one of the most influential works by any New Divinity author. This is evident in Harriet Beecher Stowe's "local color" novel of the period, *Oldtown Folks*, where she writes, "Its dissemination was deemed an act of religious ministry, and there is not the slightest doubt that it was heedfully and earnestly read in every good family of New England; and its propositions were discussed everywhere and by everybody."[18] This is important anecdotal evidence of the reception of Bellamy's work, which contains the first treatment of the New Divinity version of the governmental theory of atonement—what I have characterized elsewhere as the doctrine of penal nonsubstitution.[19] On this view, Christ's work is a penal example that vindicates God's moral governance by showing that the consequences of sin must be dealt with, in order that he may pardon (some) human beings.

Edwards's preface to Bellamy's *True Religion Delineated* states unequivocally that from his own perusal of the discourse he found it contains "the proper essence and distinguishing nature of saving religion," which is "deduced from the first principles of the oracles of God, in a manner tending to a great increase of light in this infinitely important subject; discovering truth, and at the same time shewing the grounds of it."[20] He had read and commented on a manuscript version of the book and was fulsome in praise of it in private correspondence with his Scottish friend John Erskine.[21] This has caused not a little puzzlement among scholars. For, plainly, Edwards's doctrine of atonement is quite different from the governmental view Bellamy's work sets forth. How could he endorse it? An answer to this question can be had if we pay attention to the logical form of Bellamy's doctrine and compare it to what Edwards himself says. As with the previous section, we shall have to provide a synthesis of Bellamy's views. We shall then be in a position to compare it with Edwards's doctrine. An examination of the two suggests a plausible explanation of this conundrum.

Bellamy's doctrine is as follows. Like his mentor, Bellamy thinks sin is infinitely heinous and worthy of an infinite punishment in hell. Fallen human beings have the natural ability to avail themselves of such faith in order to be saved. But they are morally incapable of doing so, because of the effects of sin. Nevertheless, because there is no natural impediment to closing with Christ, fallen humans who fail to ask for faith are culpable, and punishable in hell for their sin. Unlike Edwards, Bellamy thinks the atonement is, in one respect, unlimited in scope: Christ's work purchases all of humanity. He says, "All [of mankind] were purchased by him, none of these things could have been granted to mankind but for him."[22] Nevertheless, the net result is particular: God gives the elect faith, and it is his intention that the elect are those for whom the work of Christ is effectual through faith.

Hence, there are important parallels between Edwards's doctrine and that of Bellamy, centered around the intention of God in atonement and in the means by which this is applied to the believer (by faith), as well as the explanation as to why this is a just arrangement despite the fact that the reprobate are not given faith (via the moral-natural ability distinction). But there is a difference, having to do with the scope of the atonement. This is tied to Bellamy's understanding of the nature of atonement.

Unlike Edwards, Bellamy believed that Christ's work is merely a penal example, not a penal substitution. In a later summary statement of his views on the atonement, he says,

> The design of the incarnation, life and death of the Son of God, was to give a practical declaration, in the most public manner, even in the sight of the whole intellectual system, that God was worthy of all that love, honor, and obedience, which his law required, and that sin was as great an evil as the punishment threatened supposed; and so to declare God's righteousness, and condemn the sins of an apostate world, to the end God might be just, and yet a justifier of the believer. And this he did by dying in our room and stead.[23]

Being moral governor of the creation, God cannot wink at sin. Were he to do so, his moral governance would unravel because it would be manifestly unjust for God to fail to treat sin with the moral seriousness it deserves. It is impossible for God to fail in such a duty because he is essentially just. Nevertheless, how he goes about discharging this duty is not quite as Edwards conceives it. Christ's work serves to vindicate God's moral governance by showing through example what the moral law demands of those who transgress it, namely, an infinite punishment. Christ's suffering is not infinite in duration, but his is a suitably equivalent suffering, because as the God-man his suffering has an infinite value, generating an infinite merit that he does not need, because he is impeccable and therefore does not require salvation.

On the basis of this work, God is able to forgive human sinners. It is penal in nature, because it demonstrates what the consequences attending sin are, being a suitably equivalent punishment to what would be meted out to sinners in hell. But it is not a vicarious substitution whereby Christ stands in the place of the sinner, taking upon himself the penal consequences of the sinner's wrongdoing, and suffering in place of the sinner. Although there is a sense in which he stands "in our room and stead," he does so by virtue of offering a suitably equivalent act of atonement that demonstrates the heinousness of sin by his becoming an example of what would happen to human sinners if they were punished for their sins.[24] Because Christ does this, God is able to forgive sinners. His moral governance is vindicated, and Christ's work generates a merit sufficient in principle for the salvation of all humanity. More than that, as we have already seen, according to Bellamy Christ's work actually purchases all humanity. It is on the basis of this purchase that God may forgive sinners. All humans are naturally able to turn to God for salvation. But they are morally unable to do so without the secret work of the Holy Spirit. It is to the elect alone that God gives the gift of faith that enables them to appropriate the benefits of Christ's atonement.

However, this does seem to generate a problem of double payment for sin. If Christ's work purchases all humanity, yet the reprobate still suffer in hell for their sin, this seems unjust. To this Bellamy replies, "Christ did not die with a design to release them from their deserved punishment, but only upon condition of faith; and so they have no right to release, but upon that condition: it is just, therefore, [that] they should be punished as if Christ had never died, since they continue obstinate to the last."[25]

In other words, without faith the benefits of Christ's work cannot be applied to a sinner. Bellamy thinks that by appropriating Edwards's distinction between moral and natural ability he can have his cake and eat it. For then Christ can be said to purchase all humanity acting as penal exemplar. But effectual application of the benefits of this purchase is, in some sense, conditional on the exercise of faith. In a similar way, it might be that the government purchases sufficient stores of vaccine for the whole populace but distributes it only to those citizens who ask to be inoculated.[26] In this way, Bellamy thinks he can do justice to those biblical passages where Christ's work is said to be for the whole world. But he can also make sense of those passages where Christ's work is said to apply only to an elect, by invoking the moral-natural ability distinction: though all sinners have been purchased by Christ's work, not all sinners will avail themselves of this work because not all have been chosen by God to do so. They are still culpable because they are naturally able to avail themselves of Christ's work. But they will never desire to do so because they are morally incapable of doing so as a consequence of their morally vitiated condition. As Bellamy puts it, "God never *designed* to bring the non-elect to glory, when he gave his Son to die for the world. He designed to declare himself *reconcilable* to them through Christ."[27]

Why Edwards Endorsed Bellamy

We are now in a position to offer some explanation as to why it was that Edwards felt able to endorse Bellamy's doctrine, despite their disagreeing about the nature of the atonement. My contention is this: although Edwards could not have failed to see that Bellamy's doctrine provided a different mechanism for atonement than his own view, it yielded equivalent outcomes using several key distinctions he favored in order to do so. Although he does not say so, it seems plausible to think that Edwards was willing to allow latitude on the means by which atonement is brought about, provided the product shared his own Reformed sensibilities about restricting application of Christ's work to the elect alone. He certainly would have been aware of the latitude within his own tradition on this matter, through reading standard works of divinity, such as Turretin's *Institutes* (in which Turretin discusses the Amyraldian alternative to his own doctrine of satisfaction in detail). I suggest that, allowing for difference over the mechanism of atonement, Edwards was satisfied that Bellamy captured what was nonnegotiable in his battle against theological "Arminianism," that is, that the atonement is designed to be effectual only for the elect.[28]

Imagine two jazz saxophonists playing Charles Mingus's classic *Moanin'*. Both interpretations of the music contain similar leitmotifs, riffs, and the same recurring melody. But they are different in important respects, because each musician freely adapts the basic structure of Mingus's work to the set he is playing. Nevertheless, both are playing what are recognizably versions of the same piece of music.[29]

I am suggesting that something analogous applies to the differences between Edwards and Bellamy. They differ concerning their understandings of the mechanism by means of which Christ's work is said to atone for sin. According to Edwards, this is penal substitution; for Bellamy, it is penal nonsubstitution (his governmental theory). They differ as to the scope of the atonement. According to Edwards, God intends the salvation of the elect and brings about an atonement that is effectual only for the elect.[30] For Bellamy, the atonement is unlimited in scope because Christ purchases all humanity. But his work is made effectual via faith, and God provides such faith only for the elect. So somehow God intends the atonement to be universal in scope, though he also intends it to be limited in effectiveness.[31] As Guelzo observes, "for all its un-limitedness," Bellamy's doctrine in *True Religion Delineated* is "as particular and definite as the more classical constructions of the doctrine, since God in the end always has the final say in who shall be forgiven."[32] Edwards and Bellamy agree that God is a moral governor of the cosmos and that punishment of sin is intimately connected to that role. They agree on the heinousness of sin and the necessity for the God-man in order to atone for it. And they agree on the vital role played by the distinction between moral and natural ability in appropriation of Christ's work, and in explaining why those who are reprobate remain culpable for their lack of faith.

It would appear that Edwards thought there was sufficient similarity or family resemblance between his doctrine and Bellamy's that he was willing to endorse Bellamy's work. It may even have been that Edwards thought Bellamy's conception of atonement had certain virtues worth stating. At the very least, it appears that what separated them was less important to Edwards than what united them. Both were concerned to articulate Reformed doctrines of atonement that would erect a theological bulwark against the encroaching tide of "Arminianism" and freethinking, which favored Socinian critiques of traditional atonement theories.

This, I submit, offers a plausible explanation for why Edwards read and understood Bellamy's work and was willing to endorse it despite the differences between them. He was willing to do so because he saw that Bellamy's work was a Reformed cousin of his own, which had the same aims and equivalent outputs, but different accounts of the mechanism by which atonement obtains.

Coda

This particular point about the relationship between the doctrines of Edwards and Bellamy leads me to make a wider (and bolder) claim, one for which I cannot offer an argument here but which might be usefully followed up in further work. In formulating their account of the work of Christ, the theologians of the New Divinity may well have departed from the atonement theory expressed by Edwards, which seems to have been a species of penal substitution. But from one perspective, in developing their own position they did not deviate from Edwardsian theology as such. Rather, they fused certain elements within a basically Edwardsian scheme, particularly emphasis on the moral government of God in creation, to forge a novel and robust account of the work of Christ.[33] In other words, they innovated *within* an emerging theological tradition, developing a distinctively American strand of Reformed theology. The resulting account of the work of Christ is worthy of much more serious consideration in the academic literature than it has hitherto enjoyed.[34]

6

A Different Kind of Calvinism? Edwardsianism Compared with Older Forms of Reformed Thought

Paul Helm

THE STRUCTURE OF this chapter is as follows. In the first half or so, I consider a number of circumstantial facts that indicate some of the factors making it reasonable to suppose that Jonathan Edwards's thinking was along some importantly different lines from those of his Reformed forbears. In the second half, there follows a discussion of one important issue, freedom of the will, as this is treated by Edwards as well as by Calvin and by Reformed Orthodoxy before him. We shall note some striking differences in method and style and emphasis, even though the general theological outlook remains the same.

Some Circumstantials

In the course of his great work *The Freedom of the Will*, Jonathan Edwards had this to say about one of his notable theological predecessors:

> However the term 'Calvinist' is in these days, among most, a term of greater reproach than the term 'Arminian'; yet I should not take it at all amiss, to be called a Calvinist, for distinction's sake: though I utterly disclaim a dependence on Calvin, or believing the doctrines which I hold, because he believed and taught them; and cannot justly be charged with believing everything just as he taught.[1]

Some years earlier, writing to Joseph Bellamy, he advised:

> But take Mastricht for divinity in general, doctrine, practice and con-
> troversy; or as an universal system of divinity; and it is much better
> than Turretin or any other book in the world, excepting the Bible, in
> my opinion.[2]

This is a reference to Petrus Van Mastricht (1630–1706), professor of theology at the University of Utrecht from 1677 until his death. He was the author
of a number of works, but Edwards undoubtedly refers to *Theoretico-practica
Theologia*, published in two volumes in 1682 and 1687, and reprinted a number of times.[3]

I think it is fair to say that the tone of Edwards is somewhat different in
these two extracts, each of which has become well known. Writing about John
Calvin, and in public, he seems to be rather tetchy and grudging, expressing
both puzzlement and indignation that anyone should think he (of all people!)
takes Calvin to be a human authority, despite being willing, for the sake of a
label, to be called a Calvinist. He is not in thrall to Calvin, asserting his theological autonomy or independence at this point.

In the case of his letter to Bellamy, his words are for his eyes only, and
he is more relaxed, even fulsome. Of all the theological books he has ever
read, when one is looking for an all-round theological authority and guide,
van Mastricht's lengthy scholastic treatment is the best of the bunch, coming
second only to the Bible itself!

Edwards exhibits some historical awareness in delivering these two ver-
dicts. When he wrote to Bellamy, Edwards was preoccupied with the Arminian
issue, a concern that was to lead to the *Freedom of the Will* in 1754. Calvin
could not be of much direct help to him there. To pitch John Calvin into the
middle of the Arminian controversy would have been to court the charge of
anachronism. Van Mastricht could be of more direct help, since in the post-
Synod of Dordt world of the late seventeenth century, he was a leading anti-
Arminian theologian. However, it seems it was not his ability in handling the
Arminian controversy, but in his comprehensiveness, that Edwards thought
Van Mastricht's strength lay. And in any case, advising his student on which
textbook to use was a rather different undertaking from disclosing to the world
those theologians whose name he was willing to take.

In making comparisons between Edwards and these two earlier Reformed
theologians that he mentioned, it should be borne in mind that although they
each wrote a major systematic work of theology as a magnum opus Edwards
never did. Even here the hints that he provides of how he might have tackled

such a challenge reveal an approach that differs from those of Calvin and Van Mastricht. In a part of another letter that has also become well known, this time written to the trustees of Princeton toward the end of his life, Edwards told them he intended to write a "great work called *A History of the Work of Redemption*," which would be "a body of divinity in an entire new method, being thrown into the form of a history."[4]

It seems to be clear from this proposal, and what he left to us in his *History of the Work of Redemption*, a series of sermons posthumously published in 1772, that what Edwards intended was what is nowadays called a "redemptive-historical" theology, currently regarded as biblical theology rather than as systematic theology. Yet in the covenant theology in the Reformed tradition there was already such a treatment, and Edwards must have been very familiar with it: in the writings of Johannes Cocceius and of Herman Witsius. From what he wrote, he seemed to be proposing something rather in the historical vein of the covenant theologians, yet with its own unique method. This is another example of Edwards's boldness and his willingness to innovate, while at the same time keeping within, even touching, the limits of the boundaries of Reformed orthodox theology.

Besides that, Edwards's writing style does not correspond to Calvin's or Van Mastricht's. Like much that he gave his hand to, he was very self-conscious about what he was doing. He was self-conscious of his writing style and deliberately sought to cultivate it by reading widely, and no doubt, disciplining himself in the characteristically Edwardsian way. What emerges is sharply different from the rhetorical style of *persuasio* that Calvin exhibits in the *Institutes*, and of course he avoids the formalities of scholasticism. But these stylistic differences need not be altogether exclusive of each other. The Baptist theologian John Gill, a contemporary of Edwards some of whose writings were known and used by him, combined a rather orotund, stately eighteenth-century prose style with observance of scholastic distinctions, as is evident in his *Body of Divinity*.[5] In Edwards's case, the style is certainly that of the eighteenth century. Yet unlike Gill he employs scholastic distinctions in a minimal way, as we shall see later on.

When all is said and done, the fact is that Edwards's writings show little direct influence of either theologian. Although he occasionally quotes from Calvin, there is little if anything from Van Mastricht, despite Edwards's high praise of him. However, what has to be borne in mind is that Edwards sees himself writing for diverse readerships. Of his three great works, the *Freedom of the Will* (1754) is written for his fellow theologians of a Reformed stamp in New England and beyond, and their Arminian opponents; the *Great Christian Doctrine of Original Sin* (posthumously published in 1758) was intended to outflank the Arminian threat to New England by mounting a root-and-branch attack on what Edwards regarded as the ultimate enemy, European Deism. It is only his *Religious Affections*, the first of these three renowned books to be published (1746), that was designed for the domestic New England market.

But how is it possible to make these distinctions about different audiences with any confidence? Partly, of course, by their subject matter and provenance. The *Affections* arises directly out of the New England revivals and their abuses, a matter of acute concern both to the supporters of the revivals and to their critics. The book had its origins in courses of sermons to Edwards's Northampton congregation. The other two works are concerned with two fundamental topics in Christian dogmatics, and in particular in theological anthropology. In writing these books, Edwards focused his attention on the Colleges of New England and their alumni, and on Europe, whose latest radical ideas were beginning to reach the ears of those on the other side of the Atlantic.

There is another sign that Edwards had different audiences in mind: the footnotes he employed, and the figures whom he engaged in intellectual combat, or from whom Edwards garnered support, those who appear in the main text. So, for example, the footnotes in the *Religious Affections* are references to, and citations from, a whole range of Puritan writers from old England and New England—such as his grandfather Solomon Stoddard, Thomas Shepherd, William Ames, John Flavel, William Perkins, John Preston, John Owen, Samuel Rutherford, Anthony Burgess, and Theophilus Gale. In addition he cites Francis Turretin, John Calvin, and Martin Luther. The only exception to this roll call appears to be John Smith, the Cambridge Platonist; and Jeremiah Jones, who wrote on the canon of Scripture. He mentions John Locke, but only *en passant* along with Cicero, Addison, and others, though there is reason to think he silently relied on Locke in developing his comments on the human self in the *Affections*.

These lengthy citations from his Puritan forebears were partly a matter of presentation and partly of theological politics. Those chiefly cited were the New England theologians Shepherd and Stoddard, the first a theologian of considerable authority in that community, the second Edwards's grandfather, but more importantly his predecessor in the Northampton pulpit. Edwards clearly wanted it to be known that he had their endorsement for his teaching on the revival, particularly the careful discriminations he makes about the signs of genuine faith on the one hand and of hypocritical or self-deceiving faith on the other. So here, in the *Religious Affections*, his grandfather and Thomas Shepherd and the other Puritans were still speaking. He invites his readers to draw the obvious implication that each would have approved of the revivals and of Edwards's role in them.

But was the value placed on these writers a sign of their persisting influence? For such Puritan writers, the scholastic methods of distinction and disputation were a dominant intellectual influence. Theologians such as Owen and Turretin and Rutherford were in the front rank, men who were able to turn out scholastic Latin disputations at will. Owen and Rutherford locked horns over standard issues in scholastic theology, such as the necessity of the atonement. Rutherford was highly regarded by Gisbertus Voetius, Peter Van Mastricht's forerunner in theology at Utrecht. The scholastic Latin works of the Scottish theologian were published in Holland as well is in Edinburgh. Had he wished, Rutherford could have occupied a chair in theology there. Ames and Preston were similarly influential.

Despite this roll call of scholastically minded Reformed thinkers, I do not think this is very good evidence that Edwards was nothing more than an eighteenth-century exponent of Reformed Orthodoxy. The reason he cited all these theologians was not on account of their scholastic skills, but for a rather different skill. All of them were, in Edwards's eyes and in the eyes of the ministers of New England, masters of practical and especially of "experimental" divinity. That is, they were practiced in the testing of the soul, and in providing written guides for others to test their own souls, over the grand questions: Is my conversion real or counterfeit? Do I exhibit the signs of grace? What are these signs? As part of their general outlook on religion, such divines held that first thoughts are not always best thoughts, nor first feelings best feelings. Many who were religious will be barred when they reach the gates of heaven. Of the ten virgins, five of them were wise, but five foolish. When the coming of the bridegroom was announced, five had no oil in their lamps. The *Religious Affections* is a work of such divinity on a grand scale, with an orderliness and a penetration that surpassed Edwards's teachers, a response called forth by the expressions of heightened feeling as well as the bodily contortions of those affected by the revival.

It is true that in pursuit of such practical divinity fine discriminations were called for. In a work from which Edwards quoted, *Pneumatologia, or a Discourse Concerning the Holy Spirit* (1674), John Owen had agonized over the distinction between an account of regeneration that was the outcome merely of moral persuasion, and one that is truly spiritual, the direct renewing of the Holy Spirit. In making such a discrimination, Owen certainly exhibited scholastic skills. But the scholastic apparatus was fragmentary, and its language incidental. This was not controversial divinity against the Jesuits or Socinians. These practical preachers used their analytic skills like skilled physicians, to deal with the spiritual problems of the pew, cases of conscience. It was for this reason that Edwards appealed to them, not because they set out their grand theological vision in scholastic terms or seek to overturn errant divinity (though some of them, such as Owen, were certainly scholastic theologians in both those senses as well).

So a sign of Edwards's orientation is through this litany of familiar Puritan preachers and practical divines, and frequent citations of Scripture. Yet, in addition to this, another voice can be heard, the voice of John Locke, as evident in his *An Essay Concerning Human Understanding*. As is well known, this philosophical work bowled over the young Edwards when he first read it, and it continued to influence him until his dying day. The last of his great works, *The Great Christian Doctrine of Original Sin*, makes significant use of Locke.[6] But in the *Religious Affections* Locke appears incognito. For Edwards to have cited him, to have footnoted the *Essay* for his readers, would have been a distraction. It may even have aroused their suspicions. In the *Affections* Edwards was seeking to analyze the character of a "new simple idea," a new sensation, not a phantom, nor a mere image, but a new reality, like none experienced before. And the question was, What are the characteristics of the presence of this new simple idea, so that a person will know either that he has experienced it or that he has not? This is the Puritan doctrine of the Spirit's regeneration, dressed in new verbal clothing.

So, having in the first part of the *Religious Affections* shown the importance of the affections, and in the second part delineated a series of signs that are neither here nor here, in the third part, which Edwards calls "the trial of religious affections," he sketches no less than twelve signs "Shewing What Are Distinguishing Signs of Truly Gracious and Holy Affections." And what is the character of such affections? "Here is, as it were, a new spiritual sense that the mind has, or a principle of [a?] new kind of perception or spiritual sensation, which is in its whole nature different from any former kinds of sensation of the mind" (205–206). It is "the giving of a new sense," a "spiritual sense" (206). It is not a new faculty of the soul or a natural habit but "a new foundation laid in the nature of the soul" (206), giving rise to "sensations of a new spiritual sense" (271), a sense of the "supreme beauty and excellency of the nature of divine things, as they are in themselves" (271). Edwards's point is stark: regeneration is not the raising or exalting of what is already present in fallen human nature; this is, at best, mere imagination or moral reformation. Nor is it merely religious excitement of one kind or another. It is a novel intrusion, a new idea, a new sense, a "sense of the heart" (272).

Intriguing as its presence is to modern students of Edwards, the influence of Locke at this point ought not to be exaggerated. For here at least the influence of John Locke is confined to the reexpressing in Lockean terms of what was the common coin of Puritan practical divinity. Puritans such as John

Owen used the image of "light" and "illumination," keeping fairly close to the language of the New Testament, to convey the supernatural character of Christian conversion. In his work on the Holy Spirit mentioned earlier, which Edwards quotes, Owen wrote of a "new, spiritual, supernatural, vital principle or habit of grace, infused into the soul, the mind, will, and affections . . . a new principle of spiritual life."[7] "There is, therefore, an effectual, powerful, creating act of the Holy Spirit put forth in the minds of men in their conversion unto God, enabling them spiritually to discern spiritual things" (332). God "communicates a light unto our minds, and that so as that we shall see by it, or perceive by it, the things proposed unto us in the gospel usefully and savingly" (333). This is not quite the Lockean language of sense or sensation. Owen retains the scholastic terminology of habits, while using language that made the transition to the Lockean terminology of "new sense," "sensation," a "new simple idea" fairly easy to make. My own view is that Locke's influence here is merely terminological. Using Locke's terms, Edwards sharpened and renewed the standard teaching on regeneration and its call signs.

So far we have looked at what I call circumstantial evidence for the claim that Edwards was a new kind of Calvinist. In the remainder of the chapter, I attempt to offer a more detailed case for the novelty of some of Edwards's thought drawn from his *The Freedom of the Will*.

A *Test Case:* The Freedom of the Will

To begin with, it is worth noting that in the *Freedom of the Will*, which is of course a highly polemical work on a grand scale, on a central issue in theological anthropology the footnoting is altogether different. We may observe on one side his antagonists, Thomas Chubb the deist, Daniel Whitby the Arminian, and Isaac Watts the dissenter whom Edwards had a connection with, and who, perhaps for that reason, was treated anonymously in the text.[8] Who else does Edwards cite? Well, Locke, of course, and Samuel Clarke, and lesser philosophers, such as George Turnbull, and eminent Arminians, such as Episcopius, and John Taylor of Norwich, who was to be his chief antagonist in *The Great Christian Doctrine of Original Sin*. Thomas Hobbes, and lesser figures such as John Gill, a fellow opponent of Whitby, and Andrew Baxter, and Philip Doddridge. The European market, in other words.

The Freedom the Will, more than others of Edwards's writings, is in a significant Reformed tradition of writing about the will, its metaphysical character, its bondage to sin, and its liberation. Edwards follows in the line both of Martin Luther, *The Bondage of the Will*, and of John Calvin, *The Bondage and Liberation of the Will*, whose treatments (especially Calvin's) informed the growing Reformed dogmatic output. So Calvin's work gives us a significant point of comparison between Edwards and the earlier Reformed dogmatic outlook, on a crucial anthropological *locus*.

So, what of Calvin and Edwards? The first thing to say is that the New England divine cut the cake rather differently from Calvin and from the tradition. For Calvin, the dominant question, what makes the freedom of the will a vital issue, is the loss of moral and spiritual freedom as a result of the Fall. He argued at length against the semi-Pelagian divinity of the Roman theologian Albertus Pighius. Such a loss resulted in spiritual death, and restoration to life required operation of the effective (or "effectual") grace of God, which immediately brings new life to the soul. We have already seen Edwards in his *Religious Affections*, with the help of his band of Puritan practical divines, contending for this radical view of conversion involving the imparting of a new spiritual sense. We might, for clarity, call this the moral or spiritual sense of freedom.

Calvin takes for granted that the Fall left the will of mankind intact, in the sense that fallen human beings were still able freely to exercise their choices between such alternatives as did not involve any spiritual issue. Though dead in sin, a person might choose to wear either a red tie or a blue one, and whether to marry Nancy or Natalie. I believe it is plausible to suppose that Calvin had a broadly compatibilist view of such freedom, such as Edwards espoused, but he does not advise his readers of this in so many words. This is because the terms "determinist" or "compatibilist" are anachronistic in reference to the thought of the sixteenth century. The issues were not contested in these terms. Rather, the student of Calvin has to infer his position for what he regards as the criteria for human responsibility, in which the power to choose with the freedom of indifference is not mentioned, not affirmed but scarcely ever denied; but voluntariness, awareness of alternatives, and the absence of external compulsion are stressed as conditions of responsibility. These signs are clear evidence for what later came to be called a compatibilistic outlook.[9] There is some evidence of reliance on Aristotle, but otherwise the amount of explicit reasoning is small.

> When Aristotle distinguishes what is voluntary from its opposite, he defines the latter as *to bia e di agnoian gignomenon* that is, what happens by force or through ignorance. There he defines as forced what has its beginning elsewhere, something to which he who acts or is acted upon makes no contribution.[10]

Only very occasionally does Calvin express an explicitly compatibilist belief by denying libertarianism. For instance, in one place he argues against the idea that a person may possess the power to turn himself "in this direction or that, according to the mere freedom of his own will."[11] This implicit compatibilism is of course supported from another direction by Calvin's convictions about predestination and particular providence.

The contrast with Edwards's method at this point is rather stark. Edwards begins with a Lockean account of freedom, according to which freedom is choice that is the outcome of desire. This is drawn from the English philosopher's chapter "Of Power" in *An Essay Concerning Human Understanding*, which Edwards modifies somewhat. Equally significant is his commitment to Locke's unified account of the self, according to which the question is not whether the will is free (the faculty of the will in its relation to the faculty of the intellect), but whether the person is free: "For the will or the will itself is not an agent that has a will; the power of choosing, itself, has not a power of choosing. That which has the power of volition or choice is the man or the soul, and not the power of volition itself."[12]

So Edwards bids farewell to the faculty psychology that was characteristic of the Reformed Orthodox. He then proceeds to argue, throughout part II, on purely philosophical grounds, that the Arminian *concept* of the human will as essentially possessing the freedom of indifference between alternatives, and as being opposed to causal necessity, is not possible. In part III, he claims that such a view is in any case not necessary for moral agency and responsibility, and in part IV he considers the arguments given in support of the Arminian views of liberty. Each thesis is argued for in a purely philosophical manner, examining the cogency of the idea of indifference and offering definitions, and then arguing against its being necessary for praise and blame, and considering the Arminian arguments given in support of it. In a sense *The Freedom of the Will* is an exercise in overkill. Establishing the thesis of part I, that there can be no sense of freedom of the will such as is claimed by Arminians, is logically sufficient to establish Edwards's position. But with characteristic relentlessness, in the next part Edwards argues that even if there were such a viable concept of freedom, it is not necessary for ascription of praise and blame; in part IV he shows that the arguments used by the Arminians to support their view are insubstantial. So three times over Edwards offers a different, decisive attack on the Arminians, not the Arminians of the era of the Synod of Dordt, but contemporary, up-to-the minute Arminians, such as Thomas Chubb and Daniel Whitby.[13]

Only in the conclusion of the work does Edwards briefly consider the consequences of his philosophically argued conclusions for certain theological topics, including "The Total Depravity and Corruption of Man's Nature, Efficacious Grace," to which he devotes precisely two pages. Why this brevity? It is not because he does not have strong views on the topic, as can be seen from his teaching about the new spiritual sense in the *Affections*. It is rather that the *Freedom of the Will* is dominated by one metaphysical thesis Edwards deploys and defends in the different ways noted. He makes conceptual distinctions, presents arguments, and considers objections. This thesis is that, necessarily, every event, including every human action, has a cause, a thesis defended obliquely in part II by showing that the contrary thesis—that there are causeless events, namely actions of a libertarian free will, acts exhibiting the freedom of indifference—is impossible.

To Edwards's way of thinking, human choice between alternatives is an instance of a more pervasive truth: that every event has a cause. Human choices cannot be uncaused, or self-caused, because nothing can be uncaused or self-caused.

> It has been already shown, that nothing can ever come to pass without a cause, or reason why it exists in this manner rather than another; and the evidence of this has been particularly applied to acts of the will. Now if this be so, it will demonstrably follow, that the acts of the will are never contingent, or without necessity, in the sense spoken of, inasmuch as those things which have a cause, or reason of their existence, must be connected with their cause.[14]

I think it is fair to say that no claims as explicit as this are to found in Reformed thought before Edwards. For Edwards, operating in a world increasingly influenced by the emerging natural science, and by the empiricist philosophy of John Locke, human action is the result of one sort of cause, a "volition," which is in turn the outcome of certain beliefs and desires. Such causal links, of different kinds, necessarily pervade the entire creation. Edwards's stress is on this all-encompassing metaphysical principle.[15]

By contrast, the tendency of scholastic Reformed thought, even the thought of Calvin, is marked by recognition of a hierarchical arrangement of orders of created existence in which mankind is positioned above brute creation and beneath the orders of angels. Transcending these orders is God, the first cause. So Calvin can write:

> How may we attribute the same work to God, to Satan and to man as author, without either excusing Satan is associated with God, or making God the author of evil? Easily, if we consider first the end, and then the manner of acting. The Lord's purpose is to exercise the patience of His servant by calamity; Satan endeavours to drive him to desperation; the Chaldeans strive to acquire gain from another's property contrary to

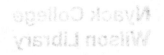

law and right. So great is the diversity of purpose that already strongly marks the deed. There is no less difference in the manner. The Lord permits Satan to afflict His servant; he hands the Chaldeans over to be impelled by Satan, having chosen them as His ministers for this task, Satan with his poison darts arouses the wicked minds of the Chaldeans to execute that vile deed. They dash madly into injustice, and they render all their members guilty and befoul them by the crime. Satan is properly said, therefore, to act in the reprobate over whom he exercises his reign, that, the reign of the wickedness, God is also said to act in His own manner, in that Satan himself, since he is the instrument of God's wrath, bends himself hither and thither at His beck and command to execute His just judgments.[16]

Calvin's world is one that does not tend to be "flattened," as Edwards's world does, by the pervasive operation of one uniform metaphysical principle. For Calvin, God acts in his own manner, Satan in his, the Chaldeans in theirs, and animate and inanimate causes in theirs. This difference is revealed in another way. Calvin readily employs the scholastic distinction between primary and secondary causality.[17] By contrast, as far as I can judge there is no instance of Edwards using this language in *The Freedom of the Will*. This is not surprising, given that his understanding of causation, at the creaturely level, is occasionalistic.

In the case of the distinction between the necessity of the consequence and the necessity of the consequent (used widely in scholastic discussions of necessity and contingency, and used by Calvin), Edwards is even more radical.[18] Calvin employed the two necessities in connection with general properties, not specific events. Human bones have the property of being breakable, necessarily so. However, if it is infallibly decreed that some human bones will not be broken (as in the example of Christ's bones that Calvin cites), then they cannot be broken. This is an instance of the necessity of the consequence. And for Calvin, every event that occurs is necessitated by the decree of God.[19]

Edwards's emphasis is different. His thesis, so dominant in *The Freedom of the Will*, is that metaphysical necessity pervades the creation. Everything that occurs is a necessary consequence of something else that occurs, the whole order being brought into being by the Creator, himself a necessary being. In his discussion of necessity in part I section III, Edwards reserves the necessity of the consequence for such "metaphysical or philosophical necessity." The idea that such necessity might be the outcome of metaphysically contingent events or actions is left undiscussed. The necessity of the consequent is what might be called psychological necessity, when something happens despite our resistance to it. Whereas

> The subject and predicate of a proposition which affirms something to be, may have a real and certain connection *consequentially*; and so the existence of the thing may be consequentially necessary; as it may be surely and firmly connected with something else, that is necessary in one of the former respects as it is either fully and thoroughly connected with that which absolutely necessary in its own nature, or with something which has already received and made sure of existence. This necessity lies in, or may be explained by the connection of two or more propositions one with another. Things which are perfectly connected with other things that are necessary, are necessary themselves, by a necessity of consequence.[20]

So even though here is a rare case where Edwards takes on some of the scholastic conceptuality of Van Mastricht and of others of the company of the Reformed Orthodox, he treats it in a novel way, with a boldness and authoritativeness characteristic of his mature philosophical and theological style.

Conclusion

What I have tried to do, in the first place, is to show there is strong circumstantial evidence that Edwards deviated from the scholasticism of his forebears, going back as far as Calvin himself. Despite his lauding of van Mastricht and his willingness to be called a "Calvinist" for distinction's sake, his projects, and his methods of working, were for the most part sharply different from theirs. For unlike Calvin and the Reformed Orthodox, Edwards does not look back to the ancient world, Christian and pagan, for precedent and inspiration. Instead his outlook marks a transition into the agenda of the modern world. Besides this, he wrote for distinct readerships, for the pastors of New England as well as (he hoped) for the *literati* of Europe. His projects were different, as was his use of the latest ideas to defend the old theology, and the display of a relentlessly polemical spirit.

From his youth, Edwards came under the influence of sharply different philosophical influences than his forebears, notably those of Locke and the Newtonians. In his anthropology these affected his attitude to the faculty psychology of the medievals and the Reformed Orthodox, as well as their distinction between practical and theoretical reasoning. His thought in *The Freedom of the Will* is dominated by the metaphysics of universal causality, which he argues for on grounds that any Enlightenment philosopher would recognize and approve: an appeal to human reason, and reasoning about the lawful orderliness of the creation. Though he regards the conclusions of his reasoning as theologically congenial, in these works he does not argue for them theologically, except, occasionally, in an *ad hominem* manner.

Of course, Edwards would have agreed with Calvin and Reformed Orthodoxy that God decrees everything that comes to pass. His detailed and explicit compatibilism fits snugly with such an outlook. So it would be incorrect to see doctrinal divergence at this point between Edwards and the Calvinist tradition. It is simply that he had much greater confidence in the powers of unaided human reason to establish the incoherence of libertarianism. The Reformed Orthodox tradition did not express an opinion on the question of the coherence or otherwise of libertarianism but was more inclined to regard Arminianism as false just because it was unscriptural.

Had spaced allowed, it would have been possible to extend our study to embrace not only Edwards's anthropology but his theology proper. For in his last great work, *The Great Christian Doctrine of Original Sin*, particularly in his answers to objections, for the first time in his published works (as opposed to his notebooks and private miscellanies) he avows the full theological consequences of his metaphysical outlook, his panentheism and occasionalism.[21] Nevertheless, perhaps enough has been said to make plausible the idea that Jonathan Edwards was certainly a Calvinist, though one of a rather different kind.[22]

PART 2

Carrying the Torch

7

Samuel Hopkins and Hopkinsianism

Peter Jauhiainen

SAMUEL HOPKINS (1721–1803) was a leading disciple of Jonathan Edwards and the preeminent formulator of the New Divinity, an innovative extension of Edwardsian Calvinism that dominated the New England theological landscape into the early nineteenth century. His bold reformulations of Edwards's ideas were disparaged as "new divinity" or "Hopkinsianism," although proponents preferred the terms "Consistent Calvinism" or "Edwardsianism." The New Divinity attracted many of the brightest minds of Yale College, quickly spread throughout New England, and became a major force in Congregationalism into the midnineteenth century. Hopkins's monumental, eleven-hundred-page *System of Doctrines*, published in 1793, codified New Divinity teachings and was the first comprehensive, systematic theological work published in New England since Samuel Willard's *Compleat Body of Divinity* in 1726. Unlike Willard, Hopkins pressed beyond the creedal confines of the Westminster Confession of 1636 to create a truly indigenous American Calvinist theology. His *System* provided the foundation for the theological training of future Edwardsian ministers and set the intellectual agenda for "almost all theological development in New England for more than half a century."[1]

Hopkins's theological project adjusted Calvinism to Enlightenment intellectual discourse; countered Arminian, antinomian, and universalist concepts; defended the rationality and moral accountability of the Reformed tradition; and redirected Edwards's ethical teachings in a more socially constructive, activist way. He appropriated a key Enlightenment idea—universal or disinterested benevolence—and made it the centerpiece of his theology. If Calvinism were to remain viable, it must confront charges that its central affirmations violated rational notions of divine goodness. Hopkins furthermore recast essential doctrines in republican, constitutional language—amplifying the rule of law and moral government—that became a hallmark of Hopkinsianism. His apologetic and constructive efforts produced a complex, painstakingly reasoned theological edifice that pushed some Reformed doctrines to their logical extremes while modifying others in an attempt to respond to modern sensibilities without being co-opted by them.

Given the preoccupation with divine benevolence and a growing challenge to Reformed notions of providence and original sin, Hopkins treated the problem of theodicy in his first major publication. Edwards had addressed this issue toward the end of the *Freedom of the Will* (1754), as had Joseph Bellamy in *The Wisdom of God in the Permission of Sin* (1758). Hopkins joined the debate in 1759 with the provocatively titled *Sin, through Divine Interposition, an Advantage to the Universe.* Starting from the premise that benevolence was God's decisive attribute, he affirmed that God always acted to promote the greatest good and happiness of the whole. Thus God not only *permitted* but *willed* the existence of sin in creating the best possible world. Hopkins insisted, drawing on Edwards, that the world was a *much better* place than it would have been had not sin entered into it. This became a central theme of Hopkinsianism. The world was better because sin occasioned full display of God's redemptive love and grace in salvation and allowed God's "power and wrath" to be manifested in the judgment and eternal punishment of sinners.[2]

Hopkins's argument epitomized the penchant of Edwardsians to justify the ways of God to humanity and to contend for the rational coherence of Calvinism. Yet his position on divine decrees and human sin was neither original nor a radical extension of the Reformed tradition. He did state more decisively the case for God's dominion over sin than Bellamy, who argued that God had permitted sin by merely "not hindering" it. For Hopkins, if everything that happened in the world was an expression of God's eternal decree, then God must have *willed* the existence of sin. This did not mean that "God 'willingly brought sin into creation,' " as if God produced it by being the positive agency or efficient cause of sin. Rather, God willed or determined to permit sin, creating the conditions whereby sin would necessarily result.[3]

Hopkins developed his views on divine benevolence most fully in his *System of Doctrines.* Since "the infinite excellence, beauty, and glory of God" consisted entirely "in his moral perfections and character," God could not act arbitrarily, like "an almighty despot and tyrant." God's absolute sovereignty meant "benevolence doing whatever it pleases."[4] Thus Hopkins and other Edwardsians made a typical Enlightenment move—limiting divine power by benevolence—in order to rebut an extreme view or caricature of Calvinism that emphasized divine arbitrariness. This move had already been taken by late-seventeenth-century Reformed dogmaticians such as Petrus van

Mastricht, Johann Heidegger, and Francis Turretin in response to the same forces that were shaping latitudinarian theology in England. To them, placing such restrictions on divine sovereignty did not diminish it but confirmed its moral perfection.[5]

Hopkins affirmed that God's "moral character and perfection" consisted of holiness or "universal benevolence"—a disposition to "promote the greatest possible general good and happiness." Such benevolence was "perfectly disinterested, in opposition to self-love or selfishness." This notion of "disinterested benevolence" was first articulated by Hopkins in his *An Inquiry into the Nature of True Holiness*, published in 1773. Since God's love had universal being as its object, it excluded all that could "be properly called self-love, all selfish, partial, interested affection."[6] Like Edwards, Hopkins insisted that God was "the chief and supreme object of his own love and regard" since God was "the infinite fountain and sum of all being and perfection." An impartial, disinterested benevolence necessarily paid the greatest regard to that Being which comprehended all other being.[7]

In appropriating the language of benevolence, Hopkins tried to harmonize the Calvinist emphasis on divine glory with an Enlightenment stress on human happiness, while avoiding universalism. Since the highest happiness was equal to the "good of the whole" or God's own glory,[8] this entailed demonstrating divine justice, honor, and hatred of sin. Hopkins defended the orthodox doctrine of hell to combat a growing liberal tendency that viewed it as incompatible with humane notions of God and optimistic views of human nature. The reprobate deserved infinite or eternal punishment because all sins were infinite crimes committed against an infinite deity.

Yet to Hopkins everlasting torment was not an outgrowth of retributive justice alone but an expression of divine benevolence. First, it preserved the authority of divine law and moral government and deterred criminal behavior. And although it had no deterrent value in the afterlife for the damned, it helped to ensure the righteousness of the blessed, since the smoke of endless punishment would "rise up" in their sight "forever and ever." Second, eternal punishment enabled the fullest display of the divine character, which included terrible wrath and "infinite hatred of sin." Third, it would advance the greatest good and happiness of the blessed since the perpetual view of the wicked in their misery would provide a striking contrast to the beauty and delight of holiness, remind the blessed of "the infinite guilt and misery from which they have been redeemed," and help them see the power, dignity, and love of Christ.[9]

The Reformed doctrine of rewards and punishments presumed that far more souls would be damned than saved in the end. Did this not impugn divine goodness? Not according to Hopkins. First, the punishment of the wicked would produce "millions of millions of degrees of good and happiness" to God's kingdom so that there would be infinitely greater good overall than if it were to cease. Second, in a significant departure from traditional Calvinism he even contended that many more people might be saved than damned. Perhaps drawing from Bellamy, Hopkins alleged that during the millennium humankind would propagate so remarkably that the redeemed inhabitants at this time would easily outnumber the preceding six thousand years of humanity, so that there would be many more "saved than lost," perhaps even "many thousands to one."[10] But by resorting to such calculations to bridge the gap between the divine glory and human happiness, Hopkins ceded important ground to the universalists. He invited the retort, "Why, then, did not God save even more?"

Hopkins's defense of eternal punishment presumed that humans were morally accountable; nevertheless Arminian critics charged that the Reformed doctrines of original sin, unconditional election, and irresistible grace robbed humans of their freedom and made salvation arbitrary. In a 1761 publication, Jonathan Mayhew argued that the door to salvation was open to all who, having received divine grace, strived earnestly to reach that goal. God's Spirit awakened the wicked to a sense of sin and guilt, prompting them to sincere use of the means of grace (prayer, Bible study, Sabbath observation, etc.) and obedient living prior to regeneration. Genuine striving did not presuppose a "new heart" already irresistibly transformed by grace, as the Calvinists believed, but rather willingness on the part of the sinner to cooperate with divine grace in desiring to obtain a regenerate heart.[11]

Hopkins responded to Mayhew's work in his *An Inquiry Concerning the Promises of the Gospel* (1765). He denied the spiritual goodness of unregenerate endeavors in order to preserve the doctrine of sovereign grace. Unregeneracy, by definition, implied a "reigning wickedness of heart" that ruled out appropriate striving and a hearty desire of the things promised in the gospel. The unregenerate may yearn for salvation for purely selfish reasons, out of their desire to escape "natural evil" or to secure their own "safety and happiness." But this did not exclude continuous hatred of Christ's character and rejection of his offer of salvation. If they were truly sincere, they would repent *immediately*. In Hopkins's view, genuine striving entailed a regenerate, holy desire that relished salvation for its own sake—heartily approving the good things entailed in it, the character of Christ, and the means of salvation provided by him. Regeneration was an act of sovereign divine grace wrought "immediately" and "imperceptibly" on "wholly passive" human subjects. It implanted a "right taste" or "disposition" in the mind for "holy exercises"—"for hungering and thirsting after righteousness," for enjoying "spiritual objects," and for discerning "the truths of the gospel in their real beauty and excellency."[12]

In a provocative move, Hopkins turned Mayhew's argument on its head. Awakened sinners who, having used the means of grace, stubbornly continued to reject the gospel became "not less, but more vicious and guilty in God's sight, the more instruction and knowledge" they received. With increased "light" came greater awareness of one's own sinfulness, the terrible price of dying unrepentant, and one's need of a Savior. Continued impenitence then revealed a deepening obstinacy that aggravated one's criminality.[13] Hopkins's bold conclusion shocked many of New England's clergy as theologically extreme, socially dangerous, and a threat to the Puritan founders' ideal of a covenanted society. Old Calvinists such as Jedidiah Mills and William Hart accused him of preaching "new divinity." Hart complained that Hopkins's "laboured metaphysical reasonings" or "chaos of divinity" had become a tool of the devil "to discourage sinners from seeking salvation." His "new system" was "a hard-hearted, arbitrary, cruel tyrant, a tormentor of souls."[14] Thus the terminology of Hopkinsianism and New Divinity developed in particular reference to a single doctrine: "the greater guilt of the awakened sinner."

Yet contrary to such outcries of "new divinity," dispute over this doctrine had been ongoing. Edwards, Bellamy, and Hopkins all found scriptural precedent for it in Jesus' condemnation of the cities of Chorazin, Bethsaida, and Capernaum for remaining impenitent in spite of all the mighty works he did in them (Matt. 11:20–24).[15] Furthermore, Edwards applied this principle in his revival preaching, warning those who continued to reject "the glorious gospel" that they "sinned more, and provoked God far more" and had "greater guilt" upon them "than the inhabitants of Sodom" (Matt. 10:15).[16] Years earlier, Turretin argued that inability to embrace salvation did not excuse sinners but rather aggravated and increased their guilt because their impotence consisted of unwillingness to believe. Beyond Reformed circles, the eminent Anglican divine Samuel Clarke espoused a similar position. Thus contrary to a leading work on Hopkins, he was not "original" in this regard at all.[17]

The New Divinity refusal to acknowledge the moral or spiritual value of an intermediate, unregenerate state of striving undercut the preparationist views of the Old Calvinists as well as the basis for the Half-way Covenant. A flurry of publications in the late 1760s and early 1770s further stoked the flames of controversy. The debate with Old Calvinists provided the theological stimulus for Hopkins to develop fully his own ideas about self-love and the nature of holiness or benevolence. Like other New Divinity ministers, Hopkins equated holiness with obedience to the divine law.[18] In 1768, he explained that the law was "the eternal rule of righteousness" declaring to moral agents their duty and "the rule of God's conduct towards them, as their moral Governor." Those sinners who came to Christ for salvation without first submitting to and delighting in the law and experiencing remorse for sin lacked genuine religious conviction.[19]

The New Divinity stressed the necessity of holy exercises—i.e. repentance, love of God and the moral law—prior to faith in order to combat selfish religion, maintain the power of divine law, and rebut Arminian accusations that Calvinism undercut moral accountability. In their view, regeneration immediately changed the fundamental orientation of the heart from sin to holiness. Since regeneration preceded justification, some holy volition was prerequisite to forgiveness.[20] As Hopkins argued, virtue alone enabled sinners' hearts to "be so united to the Mediator" that God would treat them as being one with Christ, imputing to them "his merit and righteousness" so that they might receive "pardon and justification."[21]

Hopkinsians charged that the Old Calvinist morphology of conversion weakened the authority of the moral law and promoted a selfish view of religion. If faith (belief in God's saving mercy through Jesus Christ) preceded and formed the basis of holy love of God, as the Old Calvinists taught, then it appeared as if salvation presupposed no change of heart or repentance. The unregenerate could be saved while continuing to love sin. They did not have to surrender their selfishness to love a God who promised to save them in return for their faith. The Old Calvinists countered that natural self-love was a perfectly acceptable basis for seeking salvation since the gospel message was addressed to people's natural desire for happiness. Moreover, the unregenerate, building on this natural principle, could perform some acts that were acceptable to God and at least begin to draw near to salvation. To Hopkins and the New Divinity, no act performed from natural self-love was virtuous in any degree since it lacked a "true disinterested regard" for God and others.[22]

In 1773 Hopkins published a more complete account of his views in *An Inquiry into the Nature of True Holiness*. This work was written partly to address criticisms leveled by William Hart against Edwards's theory of virtue. Edwards had built his theory of virtue on an ontological foundation that viewed all intelligent beings as part of an immense interconnected system of being. The truly virtuous person would recognize his or her place in this comprehensive system and cordially consent to "the great whole." True virtue, then, was "benevolence to Being in general," or "that consent, propensity and union of heart to Being in general, that is immediately exercised in a general good will." Since God comprised the entirety of intelligent Being, or was "Being, simply considered," he was the primary object of virtue. The love of particular, intelligent beings was included in true virtue, but only as they were related to "Being in general," as they formed "part of the universal system of existence." Therefore virtuous benevolence "will seek the good of every *individual* being" unless it conflicts with "the highest good of Being in general."[23]

Hart ridiculed Edwards's views as too abstract, metaphysical, aesthetic, and cryptic to be an effective spur to moral living. Moreover, he charged that Edwards's substitution of "being simply considered" and "being in general" for the biblical God was idolatrous. Hart furthermore objected to Edwards's reduction of true virtue to a single disposition—"benevolence to being in general"—which required a supernatural operation of the Holy Spirit on the human heart. To him, this scheme oversimplified the complexity of virtue, denigrated the natural "moral sense," and represented "virtue as an unnatural thing." The effect was to confound the understanding of "simple" people and "involve practical religion . . . in a cloud." [24]

In the *Inquiry*, Hopkins reacted to criticisms that his mentor's treatise was too abstract and metaphysical by substituting biblical terminology for much of Edwards's philosophical language. "Virtue" and "Being in general" were often replaced with "holiness" and "God and neighbor." Edwards's aesthetic vision was echoed by Hopkins's identification of holiness with "true moral beauty," or the "beauty, excellence, brightness, glory, and perfection of God," and by his image of a harmonious ordering of love that reflected the grand symmetry of the universe.

> Holiness is that by which intelligent beings are united together in the highest, perfect, and beautiful union. It consists in that harmony of affection and union of heart by which the intelligent system becomes *one* . . . which fixes every being, by his own inclination and choice, in his proper place, so as in the best manner to promote the good of the whole.[25]

Put in simpler, biblical terms, holiness was none other than "love to God and our neighbor, including ourselves." Here Hopkins hoped to "improve" on Edwards's abstract treatise by trying to state more clearly and concretely the nature of holiness. He did not begin, as Edwards had done, with a theory of beauty or a philosophy of being (although traces of Edwards's aesthetic and ontological perspectives are found in Hopkins's opening remarks). Rather, he turned almost immediately to Scripture and to the divine law. To be holy was to obey the law.[26]

Hopkins's legalistic conception of virtue differed in tone from Edwards's aesthetic vision and typified the legalism of Hopkinsianism. The law of God,

Hopkins declared in opposition to Hart, reduced holiness to a single principle: love, universal or disinterested benevolence, or "friendly affection to all intelligent beings." Yet he did not completely shy away from Edwards's abstract language. True benevolence was a "holy love" that united "the heart to universal existence." Its object was "universal being, including God and all intelligent creatures" and "the highest good of the whole."[27]

From a cosmic perspective, human disinterested benevolence was none other than God loving the divine self, for both the source and object of benevolence was God. In *The End of Creation*, Edwards had spoken of virtue or holiness in the creature as part of a divine process of *"emanation* and *remanation"* of the divine fullness. God communicates the divine love to human beings, who then, in their exercise of virtue, reflect that love back to God. Hopkins argued similarly that humans participate in God's love by receiving from the divine "fountain of love" that emanates toward creation. [28]

Since disinterested benevolence was exercised toward the entire system of existence, it included proper love of self. Hopkins even allowed that this love may be exercised with greater energy and awareness concerning one's own benefit than that of one's neighbor, since God entrusted to each individual the responsibility for his or her own welfare. Hopkins has been misinterpreted here partly because he defined "self-love" as selfishness rather than as that proper self-regard implied in universal benevolence or that morally neutral, "natural capacity" in willing agents who desired good or pleasure and disliked evil or pain. Self-love by nature was opposed to universal benevolence since it sought only those things that suit one's personal interest.[29]

Hopkins castigated self-love to counter what he perceived to be a dangerous appropriation of Enlightenment thinking by Old Calvinists and Arminians. Their endorsement of natural self-love as a legitimate starting point for religious striving exposed to him a naïve confidence in human nature and an alarming concession to selfishness. They did not fully appreciate the insidious, constrictive, and obsessive nature of self-love or private affection, unregulated by a temper of disinterested benevolence. Self-love was not, as Hemmenway suggested, an "innocent, useful, and good principle," bereft of any positive sin in itself. Nor was it true that the sinfulness of self-love consisted only of its *inordinateness*. Self-love was like "a devouring beast of prey" that, "when confined in a cage, may not be so mischievous, or appear so dreadful, as when let loose and destroying all before him."[30]

Another reason Hopkins's views on self-love have been misrepresented is because they are interpreted through the grid of his controversial theory of conversion, involving "willingness to be damned for the glory of God." Although this teaching became associated specifically with "Hopkinsianism" in late-eighteenth and nineteenth-century America, it has had a lengthy history within Christianity, particularly within the mystical tradition of the church. Edwards explicitly rejected this doctrine as being too extreme a form of disinterestedness since he thought it was "impossible for any person to be willing to be perfectly and finally miserable for God's sake." This would violate the general sense of self-love as "a capacity of enjoyment or suffering." A person "may be willing to be deprived of all his own proper, separate good for God's sake," he conceded. "But then he is not perfectly miserable, but happy in the delight that he hath in God's good."[31] Although Edwards repudiated this teaching, he did teach that true believers consented to God's justice in damning sinners prior to believing themselves to have been pardoned. And his theory of true virtue required an individual to sacrifice "the good of a particular being, or some beings" if it conflicted with "the highest good of Being in general."[32] It remained for Hopkins to exploit this qualification and extend Edwards's ideas to their logical extreme.

Drawing on the Apostle Paul ("For I could wish that myself were accursed from Christ, for my brethren, my kinsmen according to the flesh"; Rom. 9:3), Hopkins asserted that Paul was willing to sacrifice his own interest in Christ if this would bring about salvation for his brethren. "This is the genuine expression of disinterested benevolence," he commented, "which always gives up a less good for a greater, and the private good of individuals for the sake of the public good, or the salvation of many." This did not mean that Paul was willing to be entirely miserable for all eternity, "for he would be so gratified in their salvation" by means of his self-sacrifice that he would be far happier "than he could be in any possible enjoyment which he should have at the expense of their salvation." Here Hopkins circumvented the objection that willingness to be damned violated a basic principle of human nature: to seek happiness in our choices. A benevolent person might enjoy greater happiness by submitting to hell's torments than he would enjoy in heaven if he knew that others were saved by his self-renunciation.[33]

This point was reiterated in Hopkins's *A Dialogue Between a Calvinist and a Semi-Calvinist*, published posthumously in 1805. A Christian ought to be willing to suffer damnation "*if it be necessary* in order to avoid a greater evil, or to obtain an overbalancing good, *if* such a case can be supposed." Hopkins set up a hypothetical situation to illustrate dramatically that the truly benevolent person would "prefer a greater good to a less, and a less evil to a greater."[34] It served a rhetorical function of challenging Christians to examine the sincerity of their benevolence. True holiness entailed an *unreserved* surrender to the divine will. But until one did so, one could not know whether promotion of God's glory—which included the damnation of some sinners—necessitated one's own damnation. The irony then was that those who displayed willingness to be damned would in fact be saved. Such a disposition was a sign that grace had transformed the temper of their hearts from selfish to disinterested love.[35]

In his *System of Doctrines*, Hopkins articulated two additional doctrines that deserve mention, both reflecting the constitutionalism of the New Divinity. First, in addressing the objection that Calvinist teaching on original sin undercut human freedom and moral responsibility, he stressed humanity's corporate solidarity with Adam. God treated Adam "as comprehending all mankind; and he was the real and constituted head of the whole race, so that his obedience or transgression should affect all mankind as it affected him." Hopkins repeatedly used Edwards's language of "divine constitution" to emphasize the point that Adam and his posterity were seen by God to be a unity. As the sin of Adam was the sin of all, and as all humanity fully consented to it, so then was the guilt or condemnation shared by all. The offense of Adam was not imputed to innocent persons; nor were they "guilty of the sin of their first father, antecedent to their own sinfulness." Rather, when Adam sinned "the character and state of all his posterity were fixed . . . before they had actual existence." God made certain "that all mankind should sin as Adam had done, and fully consent to his transgression, and join in the rebellion which he began."[36] Thus Hopkins affirmed, "This sin, which takes place in the posterity of Adam, is not properly distinguished into original and actual sin, because it is all really actual, and there is, strictly speaking, no other sin but actual sin."[37] By this he meant that "the sin of the heart" or "total moral depravity" (i.e., original sin) was really as actual as the "acting out" of "sinful disposition."[38] Humans were rightly condemned for the evil inclinations or exercises of their hearts prior to their actions. One should not conclude, therefore, that Hopkins so downplayed the sense of corporate solidarity with Adam and so neglected Edwards's "treatment of the inherited and imputed character of sin" that he "innovated by arguing that human sinfulness was the result only of the sins of individuals." Hopkins had not yet taken the step chosen by later New England theologians toward defining "sin as preeminently the result of human action."[39]

Constitutional language also shaped the New Divinity's governmental theory of atonement, one of its more significant departures from traditional Calvinism. It replaced a limited substitutionary model wherein Christ paid a debt for the elect with an unlimited one that emphasized the role of Christ's death in upholding the authority of divine law. Hopkins explained that Christ suffered "the penalty or curse of the law" so that sinners could "be pardoned consistent with the law" and "moral government." Christ, the Second Adam, was "constituted by God a public head and representative" for all humanity, laying "the foundation for a treaty with mankind" in which redemption was applied to "those who embrace the offer" and accept Christ in faith. The atonement was "sufficient to expiate for the sins of the whole world," but it would remain effectual only for those who were united to Christ "by a peculiar union" brought about by the Holy Spirit.[40]

To conclude, Hopkins's theology centered on a benevolent sovereign deity who promoted the highest good by upholding the rule of law and moral government. The human quest for benevolence began with loving and earnest submission to divine law. Hopkins relished the divine law because it expressed the moral beauty and excellence of God's character and provided a dependable blueprint for the welfare of society. It furthermore supplied a moral and spiritual anchor amid the religious, political, economic, and social upheavals of late-eighteenth-century America. The context of slave-trading Newport, Rhode Island, where Hopkins became a leading abolitionist, gave him a momentous opportunity to develop and implement the social and political implications of disinterested benevolence. His summons to radical, self-denying service in promoting the common good inspired a host of evangelical missionaries, religious reformers, and social activists of the early nineteenth century as they sought to construct a benevolent empire.

Hopkinsianism continued to spread until the mid-1800s, establishing an institutional foothold at Andover and Bangor seminaries, and for a time Hopkins's *System* was standard reading at Yale, Williams College, and numerous New Divinity "schools of the prophets." In 1808, the liberal Calvinist William Bentley estimated that there were 170 Hopkinsian ministers in Massachusetts alone, and five years later he confessed grudgingly that Hopkins's *System of Doctrines* had become "the basis of the popular theology of New England."[41] Theologians such as Stephen West, Nathanael Emmons, Enoch Pond, and Edwards Amasa Park developed and promoted Hopkins's ideas, and a magazine bearing his name—*The Hopkinsian Magazine*—was published from 1824 to 1832. By midcentury three memoirs of his life, his collected works, and a separate collection of his antislavery essays had been published. And Edwardsian and Hopkinsian doctrines were vehemently debated in Congregational and Presbyterian seminaries through the 1860s, attesting to the longevity of this theological tradition, even if by this time its popularity among New England Congregationalists was already in steady decline.[42]

8

Nathanael Emmons and the Decline of Edwardsian Theology

Gerald R. McDermott

NATHANAEL EMMONS (1745–1840) was one of the most peculiar but influential theologians of the New England Theology. He declared that God would be judged on the Day of Judgment, that Christ himself was in a state of trial during his incarnation, that God loves Lucifer as much today as before the Fall, and that it is easier to obey the commandments than reject them.[1] Although his influence on abolitionism and democratic liberalism was important to American social and political history,[2] this chapter focuses on his eccentric theology. It will show how this tobacco-chewing thinker, "the most extraordinary specimen of the Calvinist personality ever developed in the historic seedbed,"[3] used a radically individualist hermeneutic that eventually undermined the Calvinism of his own tradition.

I

In the early Republic, Nathanael Emmons was the best-known theologian of the New Divinity, the school of Edwardsian disciples that was both America's first indigenous theology and, according to Bruce Kuklick, "the most sustained, systematic, and creative intellectual tradition produced in this country."[4] By his teaching, preaching, and writing, Emmons shaped several generations of American religious leaders. While pastoring a Franklin, Massachusetts, congregation for fifty-four years, Emmons trained more men in his home (about ninety) than any other teacher in the history of the Congregational church. These pastors went on to spread his theological ideas across New England. Both Bangor and Andover seminaries were founded by his students. One hundred of his sermons were published in pamphlets and journals, and then in two editions of his collected works, one totaling more than four thousand pages.[5]

Emmons was read by leaders as diverse as Lyman Beecher and William Ellery Channing, who were drawn to his theological daring and crystal-clear logic. These traits made him a legendary preacher. A traveler wrote of his reward for spending a Sabbath in Franklin:

> I felt an emotion of the moral sublime, when I saw one old man after another, who had grown gray under the patriarch's ministrations, bending forward in breathless silence, rising at length from their seats, and gazing with eagerness to catch every word that fell from the lips of their teacher. The several parts of the discourses were kept so distinct, were arranged with so much skill, and announced in so uncompromising a style, that curiosity was kept on the alert, to see what would come next; and we all looked forward with growing interest for the catastrophe of the whole plan.[6]

Harriet Beecher Stowe reported that his sermons on Judas, Jeroboam, and Pharaoh—diatribes against Thomas Jefferson—were heard all over New England. "Everybody went to hear him. . . . [He] shook and swayed his audience like a field of grain under a high wind . . . for he dealt in assertions that would have made the very dead turn in their graves."[7] His appearance alone was enough to draw some. In the last decades of his seventy-one years as a minister, he sported white locks that flowed down past his shoulders and wore the then-antiquated costume of the Revolutionary era: knee breeches, bright silver buckles on his shoes and knees, and a black three-cornered hat. His personal habits were no less arresting. He studied so intently for seventy-eight years, ten to sixteen hours a day, that he wore four holes in the floor where the legs of his chair rested. He married for the third time at the age of eighty-six and lived in full vigor to the age of ninety-five. But it was Emmons's fearless and uncompromising thinking that made his theology so compelling. According to Stowe, "He reminded one of some ancient prophet, freighted with a mission of woe and wrath, which he must always speak, whether people would hear or whether they would forbear."[8]

Ironically, it was this unswerving commitment to what he thought to be intellectual consistency that caused this Calvinist theologian to dissolve traditional Calvinism. By his lights, reason forced him to reject the eternal generation of the Son as "eternal nonsense," deny imputation of Adam's sin and Christ's righteousness, and replace Calvinist inability with natural ability capable of frustrating the divine decrees.[9]

II

Emmons's most fundamental principle was his notion of "God's efficiency," which means God's positive agency in producing everything that comes to pass, even moral choices. Emmons declared that God does not merely give permission for moral creatures to act, but produces their acts "by a positive agency."[10] This meant God makes human beings sin. He produces both their right and wrong volitions, even the first sin of Adam: "There is but one true and satisfactory answer to be given to the question which has been agitated for ages, *Whence came evil?*—and that is, *it came from the great First Cause of all things.*" God is "the efficient cause of sin."[11] Not only does he exhibit motives before the minds of the wicked, but he "dispose[s] their minds to comply with the motives exhibited."[12] For Emmons, this scheme was neither incoherent nor unjust. For it seemed clear to him that Scripture taught both divine efficiency and human freedom: "It is repeatedly said that God hardened [Pharaoh's] heart, and repeatedly said that he hardened his heart." Reason, he wrote, teaches the same. We know from our own consciousness that we are dependent and that we nevertheless act freely.[13]

This also meant, among other things, that "original sin is a lie."[14] Emmons believed that Jonathan Edwards, in his treatise on original sin, made the mistake of taking his first principle on trust rather than thinking for himself and so "became a great horse foundering in mire." Contra Edwards, Emmons said that Adam fell by "the immediate interposition of the Deity," and we had "no agency" in the sin.[15] Therefore God did not transfer Adam's guilt or corruption to us because Adam was the only person guilty of original sin. We act as freely in committing sin as if Adam had never sinned. We have no corrupt nature or principle requiring us to sin.[16]

Emmons became famous for his flamboyant ways of overturning traditional Calvinist inability. For example, he said sinners are fully able by their own natural powers to understand and accept the gospel.[17] They are capable of regenerating themselves and are in fact commanded to do so.[18] Contradicting both Calvin and Edwards, Emmons declared that "regeneration is not a miraculous or supernatural work."[19] Once regenerated by their own determination to exercise benevolence, they can just as easily do right as wrong.[20] According to Emmons, it was as easy to repent as to walk or eat.[21]

In another departure from Edwards—whom Emmons regarded with reverence—the antebellum theologian denied the existence of affections existing independently of choices. He repeatedly argued that holiness was neither a nature nor principle nor taste nor relish—all of which terms Edwards used for the disposition of the saints—but a series of benevolent exercises. Emmons transmuted Edwards's "affections" by redefining them as "exercises".[22] Hence they did not consist of a taste or principle that directs the will but were simply a train of discrete choices of the will. Nor could they be inherited or transferred from one person to another. Just as we inherit no moral stain, pollution, or depravity from Adam, so (he said) we inherit no taste or disposition from Christ.[23] Every volition we exercise is an instantaneous creation of God. We are both active and passive at the same time.[24]

This strange version of New Divinity showed signs of both hyper-Calvinism and anti-Calvinism at the same time. On the one hand, Emmons said the doctrine of the divine decrees (that God has predetermined the final states of all his creatures) is the foundational principle of the gospel, so "to deny or disprove this doctrine is to deny or disprove the whole gospel."[25] Luther famously said that on the doctrine of justification the whole church stands or falls, but Emmons insisted it is on the divine decrees that "the whole system of divine truth must stand or fall."[26] He also taught that "it is absolutely necessary to approve of the doctrine of reprobation in order to be saved." Those who cannot sing the song of Moses and the Lamb (Rev. 15:3), praising God for the torments of the damned, "must be excluded from the abodes of the blessed, and sink speechless into the bottomless pit of despair."[27]

Yet Emmons also rejected doctrines that previous Calvinists, including Edwards, thought integral to the gospel: the covenants of works and redemption, the merit of Christ's obedience to win eternal life for the elect, justification as a thick doctrine centered in union with Christ, and regeneration as intimately connected with Christ's life and death. Emmons fairly ignored the covenantal system, contended that Christ's obedience was not meritorious for sinners, argued that justification won pardon and nothing else, and insisted that regeneration was an act of sheer sovereignty having nothing to do with the cross of Christ. The saints are rewarded with eternal life, Emmons proclaimed, not because of Christ but "for all their virtuous actions entirely on their own account."[28]

This odd marginalization of Christology was perhaps the most surprising feature of Emmons's theology. In his system, Christ's cross was not necessary for salvation itself but was decreed for the purpose of showing the principalities and powers the riches of God's grace and his vindictive justice. The atonement did not transfer Christ's righteousness to anyone but simply provided "moral ground" for God's pardoning some and not others. Therefore Christ did not pay our debt or suffer our punishment or bear the legal penalty for our sins. All the biblical language about Christ purchasing, buying, ransoming, and redeeming men by his suffering and death was figurative, not literal. Christ's death "laid a foundation for the pardon and salvation of all mankind," but it did not merit eternal life for anyone. His atonement is "a remote, but not an immediate, cause" of the saints' sanctification. Not unlike later Jehovah's Witnesses, Emmons preached an atonement that did not merit anything for anyone, but by its declaration of justice made it "consistent" for God to save those whose own obedience merited eternal life.[29]

Emmons had come a long way from Edwards, whose Christology was central to his soteriology. For the eighteenth-century theologian, Christ's earthly obedience merited for sinners their title to eternal life, and his death saved them from eternal death. Christ's righteousness was not only imputed to the elect but also infused into them. Sanctification was only by union with Christ, so that the perseverance of the saints was meritorious by virtue of the righteousness of Christ. Edwards accepted what Emmons rejected: the distinction between Christ's active and passive obedience, and imputation of not only the death but also the righteousness of Christ.[30]

Edwards fully affirmed Calvinist inability. Although for Emmons the sinner is under no moral necessity to sin and is able to understand and accept the gospel, for Edwards the unregenerate are "totally blind, deaf and senseless, yea dead."[31] According to Edwards the unregenerate sin by moral necessity, and only by a work of supernatural regeneration can they understand the gospel and accept it. Emmons denied the centrality of the affections in religion, adopting a faculty psychology that separated the mind from the will. Edwards in contrast believed that true religion consists chiefly in the affections, and he held to a unitary self in which the mind and will are determined by the affections. Emmons denied any connection between Adam's sin and ours, while Edwards believed we shared in Adam's sin and therefore his guilt was transferred to us. For Emmons, God's benevolence is his beauty and can be rationally comprehended by the natural mind; no mystery is required or expected.[32] For Edwards, on the other hand, God's beauty is his ineffable holiness, and mysteries are expected when dealing with an infinite being.[33]

III

How could Emmons have wandered so far from his own Calvinist tradition and from the theological teacher he revered? The answer begins with his apologetic concerns. He believed the greatest threats to orthodoxy were Arminianism, antinomianism, and universalism. To defend Calvinism against the perception of what he called "Mohammedan fatalism," he taught "the natural ability of man to do all that is required of him." This, he felt, would rob sinners of the excuse that they cannot accept the gospel until God does a miracle in their hearts.[34] He denied imputation of our sins to Christ and Christ's righteousness to us, for fear that they would lead logically to universalist conclusions.³⁵ To forestall both universalist and antinomian inclinations, Emmons rejected taste and disposition as abiding entities and taught that all sin and virtue are various exercises—lest people presume that because they have a sinful disposition they cannot accept the gospel (thus yielding to despairing passivity), or that because they have a saving taste they need not strive to exercise it (succumbing to universalist antinomianism).³⁶ Against Arminian synergism, he taught divine efficiency to produce all of our choices. Ironically, his affirmation of natural ability and rejection of imputation suggested the same sense of a neutral human nature that lay at the foundation of what he fought bitterly: Arminian soteriology.

But if apologetics was the final cause of Emmons's departures from the Edwardsian vision, the efficient cause was his theological hermeneutic, which was both rationalistic and experientialist. He placed extraordinary confidence in the ability of natural reason to understand abstruse doctrine, in part because of his assumption that the Fall did not affect the understanding. He taught that "loose and abandoned wretches" with seared consciences can reason just as clearly about divine things as those with settled virtue.³⁷ Therefore the Word of God and doctrines such as divine decrees and atonement were sufficiently intelligible to people of every moral and intellectual capacity.³⁸ Furthermore, reason was the principal instrument of spiritual transformation: "It is the *reasonableness* of this revealed religion that has convinced ninety-nine in a hundred, if not nine hundred and ninety-nine in a thousand, of those who in all ages have embraced it, either in speculation or practice." Hence he was convinced that "if we can only make men understand the gospel, we may be sure we have gained their everlasting belief."³⁹ This rationalistic approach was due in part to the influence of John Locke and his *Reasonableness of Christianity* (1696); Emmons praised Locke as one of the two great metaphysicians in history (the other was Thomas Reid).⁴⁰

Reason, he contended, should be the judge of doctrinal truth. Emmons taught that if any doctrine is "contrary to sound reason" and in light of the "common sense of mankind" appears to be "absurd," then it ought to be "exploded." Therefore if we could perceive "that there is a real absurdity in the doctrine of the Trinity, we ought not to believe it."⁴¹ This is why Emmons rejected the eternal generation of the Son and the eternal procession of the Holy Spirit. These doctrines suggest "an infinite inequality" among the divine Persons, which contradicts "the true doctrine of three equally divine persons in one God."⁴² This is also why Emmons could not accept the cross as payment of debt for sin. Reason tells us "it is impossible for one divine person to bring another divine person under obligation, while both are absolutely independent." Thus Christ could not have purchased our salvation from the Father by paying a debt of suffering or obedience that we owed to God.[43]

If Emmons's reason was enough to explode traditional doctrine, so too was the wind blowing from Scotland in the form of commonsense philosophy. This was an indirect result of eighteenth-century battles against deism. As Brooks Holifield has observed, deism influenced American thought far out of proportion to its numbers. By attacking Christian orthodoxy for lacking "reasonable" evidence, deists inspired eighteenth-century Christian intellectuals to a renewed search for evidences that would pass muster among skeptics. The rising prestige of science further encouraged theology to emulate the scientific demand for rational "proofs." Deists derided mystery and claimed that "common sense"—open to all and not just the regenerate—was the foundation of true religion and philosophy. Scotsman Thomas Reid and his philosophy of common sense seemed just what was needed. Like Kant, he appealed to first principles of the mind. But in an effort to undermine Locke's epistemology and Hume's skepticism, Reid asserted that the human mind perceives objects directly, not merely images of those objects. The mind also has immediate access to commonsense principles that, if universal and not self-contradictory, are self-evident axioms. This new "Scottish Realism," strengthened by Dugald Stewart and Sir William Hamilton, discouraged metaphysical speculation and advocated reliance instead on inferences from "facts of consciousness."[44]

Steeped in this new outlook, Emmons often appealed not to Scripture, as was Edwards's wont, but to "the moral sense" and "the operation of our own minds." For example, Emmons argued that Hume was wrong on causation because his conclusion ran contrary to "common sense."[45] Hume and Kames failed to consult the operation of their own minds, he averred, when they suggested that things can exist without a cause. We know we are worthy of praise and blame even if our actions are caused by God, because of what we "intuitively know."[46] It was a dictate of common sense that even when we are under special grace we are still free. Emmons thought people knew this because they "felt" it.[47] The human conscience existing in the heart was "infallible" in distinguishing holy affections from sinful exercises.[48] Ironically, it was its development of Edwards's theory of moral agency, distinguishing between moral and natural ability, that "was undoubtedly the most important mark of the New Divinity."[49] But by the time Emmons was finished with this distinction, it had been turned inside out. Reid had so impressed Emmons that when the latter spoke of natural ability it contained the very moral ability that Edwards emphatically denied to the unregenerate, natural person. Edwards would not have recognized his theory in Emmons's hands, even though Emmons used much the same language.

Reason and common sense were especially persuasive to Emmons because of his conviction that Christians should be independent in their thinking. "Do let every man think for himself" was his motto.[50] Not only was autonomous thinking an imperative, it was also a right. "The right of private judgment" was "the right of forming our opinions according to the best light we can." Churches too had the right of autonomous theology. They could write their own creeds, "independently of any superior ecclesiastical power on earth."[51] The result of these convictions was a fierce self-confidence. His student Leonard Woods observed that Emmons made little use of books but "relied with unusual confidence upon the results of his own reasonings." He believed others should have this same trust in their own reasoning power, since "God has made men capable of judging for themselves in matters of religion." All they needed were the Bible and "their own noble, rational powers."[52]

What they did *not* need was tradition. They should make it a habit to examine the evidence for theological doctrines "without trusting to education, former opinion, or the assertion of others."[53] He warned of the "undue influence of tradition" and declared that "God has forbidden men to take their religious sentiments from others upon trust." His biographer, Edwards Amasa Park, reported that Emmons "did not appeal to the harmony of the church fathers, but to the mutual harmony of biblical doctrines."[54] He told his auditors that Catholics teach "implicit faith" in their own tradition, but God had forbidden this sort of misplaced trust. We were to listen to our teachers but then judge for ourselves the truth of tradition.[55] On rare occasions, Emmons conceded that confessions and creeds such as the Thirty-Nine Articles and the Westminster Catechism had helped protect Christians against "gross and fatal errors" and indeed were necessary because Scripture could not always interpret itself, especially when there were "seeming contradictions."[56] But far more often he insisted on the ability of the lone Christian with her Bible and reason to decide for herself what was true and right.[57] His own practice was to prefer his own reason and common sense to received traditions.

IV

Emmons's theological method was a highbrow version of a cultural current that pulsed through countless revivalist and restorationist sects in the early Republic. These sects, documented by Nathan Hatch, were generally united in the conviction that the common sense of the people was more reliable, even in theology, than the judgment of an educated few.[58] Restorationist leaders such as Alexander Campbell joined Emmons in calling it the principle of "private judgment." Of course, this principle had been a staple of Protestantism since its beginning. Religious liberals used it in the eighteenth century to attack the awakenings. One of their number, Charles Chauncy, used it to argue for universal salvation.[59] But it was in the age of Jackson that evangelicals took it up with a vengeance. They used it as Emmons did: not as another guide alongside tradition, but as the ultimate tribunal. As Campbell said of himself, "I have endeavored to read the scriptures as though no one had read them before me."[60]

In his survey of the creeds of fifty-three American denominations, Mercersburg theologian John W. Nevin called this hermeneutic the principle of "no creed but the Bible," and concluded it had become the distinctive feature of American religion.[61] Theological tradition was seen as human distortion of a transparent divine word needing no interpretation. Therefore the common Christian with the Bible in his hand had as much access to divine truth as the minister with his theological diploma. Emmons, of course, had his own kind of theological diploma, having been trained by John Smalley, who was a student of Jonathan Edwards's student Joseph Bellamy. But his hermeneutic was essentially the same. Radically individualist, formally divorced from previous theological tradition, it drove Emmons, in an age of multiplying evangelical associations, to oppose national religious societies, statewide general associations of ministers, and the Congregationalist-Presbyterian Plan of Union of 1801.[62] It also moved him to knock out the legs on which Edwardsian theology stood.

V

One way to measure the importance of Nathanael Emmons for American theology is to look at the Beecher tribe, among the most celebrated and influential families in nineteenth-century New England. Lyman Beecher (1775–1863), the forceful revivalist pastor and social reformer, was converted at Yale College under Timothy Dwight, Edwards's grandson. His eleven children included Catharine Beecher, who championed female higher education, and Edward Beecher, a pastor and important abolitionist. Better known, however, were two of Lyman's other children, Harriet and Henry. The latter was admired by Walt Whitman and Mark Twain; Abraham Lincoln said no one in America had "so productive a mind." Henry Ward Beecher (1813–1887) was an influential writer and preacher. His Plymouth Heights Church in Brooklyn was one of America's first megachurches, regularly squeezing three thousand souls into its Sunday services. Beecher subscribed to "Progressive Orthodoxy," which retained orthodox language but stressed God's love rather than divine wrath, and experience instead of doctrine.[63] Harriet Beecher Stowe (1811–1896) took a similar turn away from traditional Calvinism. Most famous for *Uncle Tom's Cabin* and President Lincoln's 1862 remark that she was "the little woman who wrote the book that started this great war," Stowe wrestled with New England's Calvinist and Edwardsian heritage in her *Oldtown Folks* (1869), another bestselling novel. Stowe's own sensibilities can be seen in her depiction of Emily, a protagonist who rejected the god of Nathanael Emmons ("Dr. Stern" in the novel) because of his depiction of heaven rejoicing in the torments of the damned. For solace, Emily turned to Rosseau's *Èmile*, where she found a statement that summed up her own theology: "J'aimerais mieux croire la Bible falsifée ou unintelligible, que Dieu injuste ou malfaisant" (I would rather believe in a Bible that is false or unintelligible than in a God who is unjust or does evil).[64] Stowe noted that although Emily cast off Dr. Stern's God, she retained his "utter self-reliance and fearlessness of consequences in pursuit of what she believed to be true."[65] Of her fictional town of Adams (Franklin), Stowe wrote, "There is no other region in Massachusetts where all sorts of hardy free-thinking are so rife at the present day as in the region formerly controlled by Dr. Stern." The effect of his preaching on children and teens "was to make them consider religion and everything connected with it, as the most disagreeable of all subjects, and to seek practically to have as little to do with it as possible."[66]

May writes that the entire Beecher family was "haunted" by Emmons.[67] His church was not theirs, but he preached the funeral sermon for Catharine Beecher's beau, who was lost at sea. The death somehow became "an epoch in the history of the Beecher family." Because it was associated with Emmons and his portrait of what they thought to be Edwards's God, it served as their final break with most things Calvinist and Edwardsian.[68]

The Beechers' break with New England's earlier theological tradition was in some ways similar to nineteenth-century America's departure from Edwardsian theology generally. Many Americans in the antebellum and post–Civil War periods detested what they heard from Emmons and his disciples: God as the author of sin, heavenly celebration of the sufferings of the damned, and the perception of divine determinism. At first they were persuaded by Scottish common sense that they had the ability to know right and wrong and choose accordingly. Nathaniel William Taylor (1786–1858) provided an elegant way to retrieve the best of Emmons's thinking without its most noxious element: the Yale theologian taught that we have the power of contrary choice and that God himself might not be able to prevent sin.[69] The New Theologians agreed with Emmons on the elements of earlier Calvinism that were no longer necessary—covenants, imputation, inability, limited atonement—and that pardon for sin came not by Christ's work but by God's free decision. They could not stomach Emmons's decrees but followed up on his implication that trinity and incarnation were not central to salvation by dropping them altogether.

By the last third of the nineteenth century, Edwards had become an "anachronism." He was typically cited as an "important" thinker, but few intellectuals paid serious attention to his work. The New England Theology had vanished with little protest. As historian Frank Hugh Foster put it, "In a night, it perished off the face of the earth." Its questions were no longer the questions of the New Theology or Progressive Orthodoxy, whose thinkers asked not how each of us is responsible, but how the few who are responsible can fulfill their obligations to the many who are not.[70] They emphasized human freedom and rejected traditional thinking about original sin; replaced the millennium with the Kingdom of God, which highlighted its human agents; and stressed the historical Jesus rather than historic creeds. With the exception of Methodists and Baptists, the mainline Protestant churches had long since disengaged from revivalism. Emerson's suspicion of doctrine and new hope in the promise of science helped shift the locus of value from the supernatural to the natural, and as a result philosophers began getting the money and talent once devoted to theology.[71]

Historians have offered a range of explanations for this near-disappearance of interest in Edwards and his epigones. Some have blamed self-absorption and inattention to larger cultural movements such as urbanism, German idealism, romanticism, and evolution. David Bebbington, for example, has shown how nineteenth-century thinkers tended to turn from exalting reason to emphasizing will, spirit, and emotion. They stressed knowledge that comes by imagination and intuition, and they considered a certain imprecision of expression as a strength. Others have focused on the sudden absence of great theologians and major syntheses—and the way in which Darwin's materialist determinism "made untenable commitments to a Christian philosophy based on Scottish thought." American slavery, at least for a moment, undermined commonsense philosophy, since both abolitionists and slavery supporters appealed to supposed laws of consciousness.[72]

Whatever the reasons, in the last few decades of the nineteenth century Emmons's system had long since been dismissed as repulsive, and Edwards's theology appeared to be unrealistic or irrelevant for leading American thinkers and the few British intellectuals who knew of him. Both Stowe and Oliver Wendell Holmes, for example, admired Edwards's noble life but thought he set the bar too high in *Religious Affections*; they concluded that his God was cruel.[73] Leslie Stephen, the British agnostic intellectual and father of novelist Virginia Woolf, puzzled over Edwards's combination of mysticism and stern theology, concluding he was "formed by nature to be a German professor, and accidentally dropped into the American forests."[74] Perhaps the most representative portrait of Edwards in this period was the full-length biography by Alexander V. G. Allen published in 1889. Allen regarded Edwards's great treatises on the will, original sin, true virtue, and the end of creation as confused and based on false premises. His proposed history of redemption showed an inattentiveness to "second causes." Allen conceded that "there was in him something of the seer or prophet who beholds by direct vision what others know only by report" but then alleged that much of the "revelation" received by this prophet was simply "untrue." Edwards's basic mistake was to highlight the divine rather than human nature: "The great wrong which Edwards did which haunts us as an evil dream throughout his writings, was to assert God at the expense of humanity." As a result he neglected to see "the divineness of human nature."[75]

Not all of Edwards's heirs in the nineteenth and twentieth centuries followed Emmons's methodological path or reached Allen's lugubrious conclusion.[76] But the story of theological decline from Edwards's obsession in large swaths of American theology can be better understood by Nathanael Emmons's role in this history. In his system, reason—which had been theology's handmaid for Edwards—was promoted to queen. Faith seeking understanding became rationalistic intuition judging faith. The preeminent question was no longer how to see God's mysteries but how to explain human agency. The focus shifted from God's beautiful being to man's able willing. Edwards's language turned up from time to time, but with wholly different meaning. As Henry Boynton Smith put it, "The same phrases may be used, but there is another sense; there may be, to outward seeming, the same eyeball, but another soul looks out; the hands feel like the hands of Jacob, but the voice is the voice of Esau."[77] Americans like Stowe and Allen used familiar theological language to repudiate Emmons's and Edwards's theologies. But they could reassure themselves they were being faithful to Emmons's admonition to think for themselves, not trusting what previous tradition had passed down.

9

Edwards in the Second Great Awakening

THE NEW DIVINITY CONTRIBUTIONS OF EDWARD DORR GRIFFIN AND ASAHEL NETTLETON

David W. Kling

THE PULSATING HEART of Edwards's theology was God's great work of redemption, in which revival was the lifeblood. In his lifetime Edwards experienced, promoted, and wrote extensively about revival. The core of his writings from 1734 to 1746 concerned revival. In letters, treatises, and sermons, Edwards explained, defended, promoted, and tracked revivals. He viewed revivals as the means to corporate renewal and moral reform—indeed, the means by which the millennium would come. Edwards conceded that the events of history "might appear like confusion," but if viewed through the lens of providential design, if alert to the work of the Holy Spirit, the divine pattern was discernible.[1] God's work of redemption, "the great subject of the whole Bible" and subsequent history, would not be accomplished "by authority of princes, nor by the wisdom of learned men, but by the Holy Spirit" that "shall be gloriously poured out for the wonderful revival and propagation of religion."[2] The key to human history, then, was "glorious," "wonderful," "blessed," "great," "remarkable," and "happy" revivals.[3] And the key to personal human destiny was conversion—"the most important thing in the world."[4]

If Edwards lived and breathed revival, and if by his estimation revivals were the center stage of God's work of redemption, then any consideration of "after Edwards" must take into account his influence on the revivalist tradition.[5] Indeed, as Avihu Zakai and others have pointed out, "By placing revival at the center of salvation history, Edwards conditioned many generations of

Protestants in America to see religious awakenings as the essence of sacred, providential history."[6] In the past three decades a growing body of scholarship has addressed this very legacy. Of particular interest and the focus of this essay is the way in which Edwards was appropriated in promoting revival (and by extension, missions) by his third generation New Divinity disciples associated with the Second Great Awakening.

Edwards's immediate disciples certainly shared his vision for God's work of redemption being accomplished through revivals, and in a number of cases (e.g., in Joseph Bellamy's Bethlehem, Connecticut, congregation) that vision became a local reality, though not until the post-Revolutionary era did another "great" revival take place. Harry Stout has observed that thanks to the influence of Edwards's father Timothy and his maternal grandfather Solomon Stoddard, "revivals were in [his] genes."[7] What Jonathan passed on to his Edwardsian progeny, however, was a recessive gene, for not until a third generation of Edwardsians (which included Edwards's grandson, Timothy Dwight) did revival erupt in any numerically significant and widespread way.

The circumstances surrounding the origins and duration of the Edwardsian Second Great Awakening have been examined elsewhere, although a synthesis of New Divinity revivals in New England, the Middle Atlantic States, and the frontier awaits historical investigation.[8] Suffice it to say that by the 1790s the New Divinity was in a position to push its agenda for an outpouring of divine grace. This they did by recourse to Edwards, who, in his extensive writings on revival, recommended preparatory "concerts of prayer" or "praying societies," conference meetings or lectures, clerical visitation teams, evangelistic preaching aimed at the heart, and circulation of published accounts of revival.

Theologically, the New Divinity uplifted two of Edwards's fundamental convictions. First, they defended his distinction between natural and moral ability to obey God. In *Freedom of the Will* (1754), Edwards claimed that original sin did not obliterate the human capacity to obey divine commands; it only disoriented the human will and affections so that the sinner no longer desired what is right. Humans had freedom, but that freedom always led to wrong choices and sinful behavior. Second, the New Divinity echoed Edwards's insistence on immediate repentance. No one, of course, could pass through heaven's portals except by grace alone, but God nonetheless called sinners to forsake spiritual passivity posthaste and "take the kingdom by violence" (Matt. 11:12). Working from these dual theological concerns, Edwards and his disciples defended revivals and heartfelt, "affectionate," or "experimental" religion as an authentic expression of the Spirit and insisted that only the regenerate or truly saved qualified for church membership. These "pure church" principles prompted the Edwardsians to repudiate the

Half-way Covenant and to conceive of the church as a radical new kind of community at odds with the world.

The New Divinity also embraced Edwards's view of providential history. In *A History of the Work of Redemption* (1782 in America) and *A Humble Attempt to Promote . . . Union Among God's People* (1747), Edwards proposed that the eighteenth-century revivals in Europe, England, Scotland, Wales, America, and elsewhere signaled the dawn of the millennium.[9] According to Edwards, this new age would not come through cataclysmic means (as earlier interpreters had suggested) but through natural means, interposed by the outpouring of God's Spirit manifested in Christian teaching, preaching, and religious activity. Because the world was gradually, though haltingly, improving in anticipation of Christ's return, guarded optimism attended this view. Christian activity was a precondition of the coming new age, for Christians who engaged in benevolent activities, social reform, and missionary outreach actually played a divinely ordained role in ushering in the Kingdom of Christ. Edwards's millennialism thus joined revivalism and missions in a providential scheme.[10]

Two New Divinity Revivalists

It is these two areas—revivals in established congregations and missions to the unchurched frontier regions, Native Americans, and non-Christian "pagans" abroad—that captured the imagination of the New Divinity.[11] And it is in the work and writings of two of the New Divinity's premier revivalists, Edward Dorr Griffin (1770–1837) and Asahel Nettleton (1783–1844), that these developments are most clearly embodied. Both confirmed Edwards's conviction that "the deliverance of the Christian church will be preceded by God's raising up a number of eminent ministers that shall more plainly and fervently and effectually preach the gospel than it had been before."[12] Both expressed their fidelity to Edwards by promoting revivals as the means of God's great work of redemption. Their success vindicated Edwards's view of salvation history and substantiated his conviction that "there is *yet remaining* a great advancement of . . . the kingdom of Christ in this world, by an abundant outpouring of the Spirit of God, far greater and more extensive than ever yet had been."[13]

Neither Griffin nor Nettleton achieved the status of a great theologian or revivalist comparable to an Edwards, a Whitefield, or a Finney. Considered minor figures by scholars of the Second Great Awakening, neither has been the subject of a scholarly article or monograph.[14] However, both were well-known figures within the New Divinity movement and hailed as outstanding revivalists in their day. One of Griffin's eulogists called him "unequal as a preacher" and elevated him to the rank of a Great Awakener: "I doubt whether the minister can be named since the days of Edwards and Whitfield [sic]," wrote Gardiner Spring, "to whom God has given more seals of his ministry. God had eminently fitted him for usefulness in revivals."[15] Nettleton, by far the more successful revivalist, was accorded Wesley-like status by Lyman Beecher, who concluded that Nettleton had "been the means of plucking thousands as brands from the burning and bringing them into the kingdom of God."[16]

Both Griffin and Nettleton remained firmly tethered to New Divinity theology yet exhibited an ecumenical Reformed evangelicalism insofar as they, like Edwards, developed mutual and lasting relationships with other Reformed pastor-theologians. Both ministered beyond the New Divinity stronghold of New England, including in New York among the Dutch Reformed community and in the mid-Atlantic region among Presbyterians. In this respect, both (especially Griffin) were part of the larger "united evangelical front," a coalition of evangelicals bent on advancing the gospel, defeating the forces of godlessness, and promoting a "republic of righteousness."[17]

Griffin and Nettleton offer an instructive contrast in career paths and preaching styles, illustrating the variety within the New Divinity movement as well as the overlapping connection of people, places, and events that gave the movement its particular character. Griffin could be confrontational, exceedingly formal, and autocratic (as president of Williams College, he insisted that students doff their hats to him when passing).[18] Nettleton was reserved, somewhat enigmatic, and publicly irenic (his private correspondence reveals another side). Whereas Griffin excelled in rhetorical skills before large audiences, Nettleton mastered pastoral techniques of personal counsel in small groups. Griffin chased fame in the cities of Newark and Boston, whereas Nettleton itinerated in the villages of New England and New York. Griffin's ambition got him into salary troubles at Boston's Park Street Church, whereas Nettleton never demanded or accepted a salary.[19] Griffin spent the last years of life preserving his legacy by revising sermons for publication; Nettleton never published a sermon. Occasionally, their paths crossed, but not until later in their careers as both united in their opposition to Charles Finney's "new measures" in the 1820s and Nathaniel William Taylor's "improvements" to Edwards's theology in the 1830s.[20]

Edwards in *Griffin: Missions Abroad*

His sympathizers called him the greatest revivalist and missionary spokesman of his day; his detractors deemed him vain, pompous, a man of "great ambition." Edward Dorr Griffin was that and then some. A man whose ego matched his stature—no small feat considering he stood six feet three inches and weighed 260 pounds—he was, as a colleague put it, "one of the most eloquent, pungent, and useful preachers" he had ever heard.[21] Throughout Griffin's forty-year career, in all but one of his pastoral appointments, be they rural or urban settings in Connecticut, New Jersey, and Massachusetts, or as president of Williams College (1821–1836), numerous conversions followed. Nearing the end of his life he observed, "I wish to live long enough to promote revivals of religion by preaching and the kingdom of Christ by any other means in my power. These are the only two objects for which I wish to live."[22]

Griffin's revivalist successes have been documented elsewhere[23]; what has been overlooked is his crucial role in promoting "the kingdom of Christ" in foreign missions and his dependence on Edwards to that end. Although Edwards and his closest disciple, Samuel Hopkins, never provided an explicit theological rationale for foreign missions, their writings profoundly influenced the modern American missionary movement. Edwards proposed a metahistory of cosmic redemption and supplied the exemplary missionary model in *Life of Brainerd* (1749), his most popular and most frequently reprinted work. Hopkins then furnished the theological underpinnings for missions by revising Edwards's aesthetic concept of "disinterested benevolence" into a practical one of self-denial for the greater glory of God's kingdom and the betterment of human-kind.[24] Drawing from these concepts, proponents of the New Divinity such as Griffin made explicit what was implicit. Inspired by evangelicals in England, who themselves were influenced by Edwards's writings, New Divinity men promoted the cause of missions and became the dominant force in creating what would become the largest U.S. missionary society in the first half of the nineteenth century, the American Board of Commissioners for Foreign Missions.[25]

Influenced by Edwards and subsequent evangelicals, Griffin linked revival to the extension of God's kingdom throughout the world. Since the 1790s, continuous revivals and expanding missions raised expectations of the millennium to a fever pitch. In Edwards's view, the revivals of the 1730s and 1740s signaled the imminence of Christ's second coming and possibly the beginning of the new age; but with the Second Great Awakening millennial prognostications were validated in the minds of evangelicals by even greater empirical proof.[26] By the early nineteenth century, Americans had become, in Ernest Sandeen's notable phrase, "drunk on the Millennium."[27] Griffin was convinced the church lived in that period which "is to extend to the morning of the millennium."[28] In sermons and other writings, he identified the year 1792 as the *annus mirabilis*, not only marking the beginning of four decades of continuous revival in America but also the year in which "the grand era of Missions" was launched in Kettering, England, by William Carey, John Ryland, Andrew Fuller, and others.[29]

Griffin was personally and directly connected to the beginnings of the American missionary movement. During his first pastorate, in New Hartford, Connecticut (1795–1800), he developed a close relationship with the nearby New Divinity pastor in Torrington, Samuel Mills, and got to know his son, Samuel Jr. Some years later, when Griffin was serving in New Jersey, Samuel Jr., who by then knew of Griffin's keen interest in missions, briefly studied theology with him in order to gain an influential ally for his missionary cause. Samuel's awareness of Griffin's support for missions was largely due to Griffin's 1805 sermon "The Kingdom of Christ." Along with John H. Livingston's "The Everlasting Gospel" (1804), this sermon deeply influenced Mills and the Brethren at Williams College (a group dedicated to foreign missions) who reprinted the sermon in 1808. Its popularity reached other student missionary organizations such as the Society of Inquiry at Andover Seminary, who also reprinted it. Clearly, Griffin's sermon inspired the first generation of American foreign missionaries and has a rightful place in the canon of prominent missionary sermons.

While serving as assistant pastor to the aging Alexander McWhorter at the First Presbyterian Church in Newark, Griffin was invited by the Presbyterian General Assembly to deliver the annual missionary sermon in 1805. Presbyterians had a long history of home missions to new settlements and Native Americans, but not until Griffin's sermon was an explicit call made for foreign missions. The sermon was not only Griffin's first published sermon; it proved to be his best missionary sermon among those he delivered in the next three decades.[30] No other matched "The Kingdom of Christ" for its clarity of expression, biblically rooted rationale for foreign missions, and indebtedness to Edwards's vision of world redemption. Griffin sensed its importance (or perhaps his own self-importance), for he sent a copy to John Ryland in England, who acknowledged receipt and queried whether Griffin was the same person at whose ordination "his excellent Tutor" Jonathan Edwards, Jr., had delivered the sermon.[31]

Scholars have acknowledged that "The Kingdom of Christ" was an important contribution to the rising interest in foreign missions but typically give it passing notice without a full examination of its contents.[32] To be sure, it is not an original composition. In fact, "The Kingdom of Christ" is essentially a distillation of Edwards's salient themes in the *History of Redemption* and *Concerning the End for Which God Created the World* (1765). It is, of course, impossible to confirm that Griffin had these works in hand when he composed the sermon; nevertheless, it reveals the extent to which Edwards's ideas and vocabulary permeated nineteenth-century Protestant culture. As an English reviewer noted, the *History of Redemption* was "one of the most popular manuals of Calvinistic theology" in the nineteenth century.[33] To indicate Griffin's reliance on Edwards, I summarize Griffin's sermon and offer corresponding references to Edwards's works in the endnotes.[34]

By introducing his sermon with a view to the "amazing purposes which God is carrying into execution" (3), Griffin mirrored Edwards's grand theme in the *History of Redemption*. Similarly, Griffin followed Edwards's reasoning for divine creation. God created out of God's very nature: "We must conceive an eternal propensity in the fountain of love to overflow, and fill with happiness numberless vessels fitted to receive it" (4).[35] The end of creation, as any orthodox Reformed theologian would affirm and which Edwards uplifted, was "to enrich the universe with the knowledge of his glory, and to lay a foundation for a general confidence and delight in him. . . . The stupendous object which he contemplated was an immense and beautifully adjusted kingdom of holy and happy creatures, in which he should be acknowledged as the glorious head" (4).[36]

The fundamental significance Edwards attributed to God's redemption and his self-glorification was reiterated by Griffin, who, like Edwards, subordinated the doctrine of providence to that of redemption: "The whole plan of the world, including creation and providence, including every event from its beginning to the final judgment, was involved in the plan of redemption" (10).[37] The plan is one, yet its many parts *are all designed to promote the glory of God*, though the *manner* cannot be explained" (11).[38] The means that God ordained to bring this about was through Jesus Christ, God's "viceregent" who acted as the "grand connecting bond between finite and infinite natures" (4–5). "All the works which God designed to produce throughout the universe, he delegated Christ to accomplish" (6).[39] God in Christ created and redeemed the earth; "*for* Christ the earth is also governed" (11). Under his government, "all things work together for good" (Rom. 8:28); even "the revolution of empires, rebellions and wars, the councils of kings . . . are all pressed into the service of Christ" (12). All that humans do—"secular employment, their social duties"—is subordinated to the kingdom and God's redemptive work (13).

Griffin then warms to the missionary challenge by turning to millennial themes that Edwards uplifted in *Humble Attempt*. A new age is approaching when "the everlasting gospel [Rev. 14:6] shall be preached to every kindred, and tongue, and people. . . . Paradise will be restored" (16).[40] But to reach this blessed state requires human effort, for human activity is the "established method of grace."[41] Griffin exhorts his audience: "Awake, and generously expand your desire to encircle this benevolent and holy kingdom" (19). There is much to be done, for five-sixths of the world's population is dying in sin.

Griffin moves Edwards's timetable forward: unlike previous generations that were content to pray, the present generation has been chosen to play "a conspicuous part in this blessed work" (20). "Great events appear to be struggling in their birth. . . . Men, warmed with apostolic zeal, have abandoned the comforts of civilized life, and are gone to the ends of the earth" to preach the gospel. (20). To hasten the coming kingdom, more Christians should join their efforts and support the missionary cause (21).

Throughout "The Kingdom of Christ" Griffin's reliance on Edwards is unmistakable. In describing the unfolding of divine history in which human activity is crucial, he limns major themes in Edwards's works. Revivals and their extension into foreign missions are the glorious means by which God's work of redemption is accomplished.

Edwards in *Nettleton: Revivals at Home*

In 1812, Asahel Nettleton accepted a temporary appointment as an evangelist to the "waste places" (i.e., pastorless) of eastern Connecticut. In the ensuing decade, he would become the New Divinity's greatest revivalist. Bennet Tyler, Nettleton's longtime associate and laudatory biographer, claimed (though it cannot be substantiated) he was instrumental in the salvation of thirty thousand souls.[42]

Nettleton was a product of the early New Divinity village revivals in New England. His conversion followed the paradigmatic New Divinity conversion narrative drawn largely from two of Edwards's works, "Faithful Narrative of the Surprising Works of God" (1737)—a work reprinted more than sixty times by the early nineteenth century—and his "Personal Narrative," a brief account of his conversion written circa 1739, first published in 1765, and frequently reissued in the late eighteenth and early nineteenth centuries. Although Edwards was indebted to his Puritan forebears' preparationist schemes or morphologies of conversion, he was not indebted to them. As he put it, "some have gone too far towards directing the Spirit of the Lord, and marking out his footsteps for him, and limiting him to certain steps and methods."[43] Yet there were consistent themes to God's work of individual redemption, themes that reverberate throughout Nettleton's conversion narrative.[44]

As a farm boy in rural Killingworth, Connecticut, Nettleton sat under the preaching of the New Divinity pastor, Josiah Andrews. At age seventeen, amid the outbreak of revival in Killingworth and surrounding areas in 1800—when, as Griffin observed, "I could stand at my doorstep in New Hartford . . . and number fifty or sixty congregations laid down in one field of divine wonders"— Nettleton was brought to saving faith.[45] Like any anxious sinner, he appropriated the standard means of grace. For ten tortuous months he "mourned in secret," imploring God out in the field and in the "closet," and yet "God seemed to pay no regard to his prayers." His problem: "He had not hated sin because it was committed against God, but had merely dreaded its consequences." He read the Bible. He poured over Edwards's "Faithful Narrative of Revival" and the *Life of Brainerd*, yet he experienced no breakthrough. He questioned the doctrines of divine sovereignty and election.

Eventually, in true New Divinity fashion, he came to realize the futility and sinfulness of his unregenerate doings: "He had been prompted by selfish motives. He saw that in all which he had done, he had not love to God, and no regard to his glory; but that he had been influenced solely by a desire to promote his own personal interest and happiness." Finally, after being seized by "an unusual tremor" during which the "horrors of mind were inexpressible" and thinking he was about to die, Nettleton "felt a calmness for which he knew not how to account." He thought he had lost all conviction, but then "a sweet peace pervaded his soul. The objects which had given him so much distress, he now contemplated with delight." Even so, for several days he did not consider himself to be saved. Not until he discovered that his views and feelings corresponded to those of others who were converted to the Edwardsian way of salvation did he begin "to think it possible that he might have passed from death unto life." God had given Nettleton a new heart and a new taste for spiritual things. And so, first, "the character of God now appeared lovely." Then "the Saviour was exceedingly precious; and the doctrines of grace, towards which he had felt such bitter opposition, he contemplated with delight." The months of Nettleton's spiritual travail, culminating in regeneration and conversion, confirmed in his mind the truth of New Divinity theology and gave him, according to Tyler, "a knowledge of the human heart which few possess."

Following the standard New Divinity educational route—college at Yale and pastoral preparation under a New Divinity pastor—Nettleton accepted an interim position as itinerant evangelist to eastern Connecticut. After outpourings of revival under his ministrations, Nettleton abandoned his earlier plan of becoming a foreign missionary. He had found the "field white unto harvest" in his own backyard. In the ensuing decade (1812–1822), Nettleton experienced his greatest evangelistic success. Most of these years were spent in Connecticut, but he also visited New York (Saratoga County and Long Island), Rhode Island, and western Massachusetts—all regions with a significant orthodox Calvinist or New Divinity presence. In 1822, a severe bout with typhus forced Nettleton into semiretirement. Though used as an instrument of scattered awakenings for the remainder of his life, his career as a full-time evangelist was finished.

Nettleton's extraordinary success as an awakener was largely indebted to selective application of Edwards's methods and message of revival. The New Divinity in general, and Nettleton in particular, followed Edwards's later more cautionary writings (e.g., *Religious Affections*) in conducting revivals and assessing their spiritual phenomena. Indeed, Nettleton was something of a control freak. At conference or inquiry meetings, which he perfected as a catalyst of revival, he insisted on complete quiet. As he put it, "God does not always speak *by words*."[46] He decried excessive conversation as indicative of spiritual pride and an impediment to the Spirit's work. To know God was to be still before him (Ps. 46:10). "I love to talk to you," he told a group of inquirers, "you are so still. It looks as though the Spirit of God was here."[47] After counseling those under conviction, he advised them to leave the meeting quietly and deal with God alone. Crying out or bodily manifestations were met with removal from the meeting. On occasion, Nettleton preserved decorum by personally arranging placement of every chair in the conference room.

Behind this controlled environment were the hard lessons Edwards learned from the Great Awakening and that he addressed subsequently in the *Religious Affections*. These were lessons taken to heart by the New Divinity. By Griffin's reckoning, the "extravagances which took place in the days of Edwards and Whitefield put back revivals half a century."[48] No New Divinity minister would abide another James Davenport or other censorious itinerants whose rants and ravings during the Great Awakening both wreaked havoc with settled ministers and divided congregations. Davenport's and others' divide-and-conquer tactics, which Edwards attributed to the demise of the Great Awakening, were anathema to Nettleton, who, evangelizing in the very places Davenport had decimated, never conducted meetings without the express invitation and endorsement of the local pastor. Sane, sober, still, and orderly revivals: the Spirit worked within these New Divinity constraints.

Nettleton perceptively applied Edwards's insights to the dynamics of revival. He would typically visit established congregations where no extraordinary spiritual seriousness existed before his arrival, and then urge weekly congregational concerts of prayer as a necessary prelude to the outpouring of divine showers, knowing that God "revives His work in the hearts of his own people" before "He awakens and converts sinners." Just as Edwards posited that the work of the Spirit ebbs and flows throughout history, so Nettleton claimed that "there is as really a season of harvest in the moral as in the natural world." At such propitious moments,

the conversion of one sinner is often the means of awakening every member of the family, and the impulse is again felt through every kindred branch, and through the village and town, so one town may be the means of a revival in another, and that in another. . . . There is a crisis in the feelings of a people, which, if not improved [i.e., acted upon], the souls of that generation will not be gathered. In the season of a revival, more *may* be done—more *is* often done to secure the salvation of souls, in a few days, or weeks, than in years spent in preaching at other times.[49]

Indeed, what happens in the large canvas of history also happens in the details of individual lives. The Spirit is poured out briefly for a sinner's eternal benefit and is then withdrawn: "The awakened sinner will not remain long in his present condition." Hence the need to repent immediately and respond to God's gracious offer of salvation. For some, however, "the sun has already passed the meridian." There are those who "have lost their day of grace." Once the Spirit has departed, they are lost for eternity.[50]

Nettleton was no match for the eloquence of Griffin, yet his simple, clear, and occasionally emotion-charged delivery had its desired effect. He preached the "hard sayings" of Calvinism (total depravity, human dependence, God's sovereignty, personal election, reprobation, divine grace, etc.), though modified by New Divinity "improvements"—doctrines that "did not *paralyze*, but greatly *promoted* the good work."[51] Nettleton emphasized "the duty of every sinner immediately to repent," yet he recognized that true repentance follows God's act of regeneration.[52] To assure the sinner that she was still responsible for her condition, he distinguished between natural and moral ability ("The reason you will not come to Christ is not because you cannot, but because you will not").[53] To further cut out the props of excuses, Nettleton softened the "L" in the Calvinist "TULIP" (L = limited atonement). He stressed the unlimited sufficiency of the atonement and portrayed God as moral governor who "is disposed to do every thing in the best possible manner."[54] He did not dwell on this significant departure from traditional Calvinism but simply reiterated a view of the atonement that had become a New Divinity trademark.

Conclusion: Edwards in a Contested Second Great Awakening

Whether championing the cause of overseas missions, conducting a revival, or narrating the divine workings of God in the soul, the New Divinity stood tall in the long shadow of Edwards. From Edwards's corpus, the New Divinity appropriated a vocabulary and theological framework to describe God's redemptive work in the grand scheme of history made evident by outpourings of revival at home and abroad. Griffin and Nettleton were emblematic of hundreds of New Divinity pastors and laypeople whose religious consciousness was shaped by Edwards, including the evangelist Charles Finney and revivalist-theologian Nathaniel Taylor. To Nettleton and Griffin, however, Finney and Taylor betrayed Edwards's legacy. From the mid-1820s until his death, Nettleton spent much of his time and energy castigating the revival methods of Finney, the theological revisions of Taylor, and the New School Presbyterianism of his former revivalist colleague, Lyman Beecher. Nettleton's correspondence reveals an indignant, defensive, and intransigent personality who likened his situation to that of Edwards and Brainerd. Just as they were "denounced in their day" for blowing "the trumpet of alarm," he too he had been denounced for defending "true" revivals of religion.[55] Reacting to what he considered Finney's out-of-control revivals, Nettleton sounded Edwards's alarm: "*False affections often rise far higher than those that are genuine.* . . . Feelings which are not founded on *correct* theology cannot be *right*; they must *necessarily* be spurious, or merely animal."[56] As for Taylor and Beecher, they had become "the guilty cause of all the present divisions in the New England & Presbyterian churches."[57]

For his part, Griffin joined in the publication fray by turning out works against Finney's new measures and Taylor's New Haven theology. Taylor mistakenly maintained "a liberty of will" and "everywhere denies divine efficiency" by telling sinners "they may and can succeed."[58] Finney besmirched "the honour of revivals and the salvation of men" by introducing the anxious seat and allowing "vulgar expressions" of converts and public prayers by females in "promiscuous assemblies."[59] The new measures and new theology were bedfellows; they placed their adherents "within the pale of another denomination, . . . between us and them as intervenes between Presbyterians and Methodists."[60]

"*If genuine religion is not found in revivals,*" wrote Nettleton, "*I have no evidence that it exists in the world.*"[61] All Edwardsians would heartily agree. However, the other side to "after Edwards" was contention over the correct means to and theological understanding of genuine religion. Edwards was *in* the Second Great Awakening of Griffin, Nettleton, and other like-minded New Divinity adherents. But Edwards was also *in* the revivals of their Edwardsian foes—proof enough that God's work of redemption in revivals of religion would remain at the core of Edwards's disputed legacy.

Taylorites and Tylerites

Douglas A. Sweeney

YALE'S NATHANIEL WILLIAM Taylor and the Taylorite-Tylerite controversy have long served as benchmarks for the study of American religious history. Planted firmly in historical memory by classic texts in the field, they are used to measure all manner of historical developments, from the diminution of what Perry Miller depicted as America's "Augustinian strain of piety" to the spread of what Nathan Hatch called "the democratization of American Christianity." But nowhere have the Taylorites and the Tylerites loomed as large as in discussions of what Joseph Haroutunian decried as "the passing of the New England Theology," the rich tradition of religious reflection that stemmed from the thought of Jonathan Edwards and later foliated in the work of his Edwardsian successors. Indeed, despite their claims to Edwardsian paternity, New Haven's Taylorites especially have symbolized for decades a declension in New England away from Edwards's bold theocentric vision. Though unfavorable, this symbolism has granted them a historical stature larger than life and guaranteed them a lasting, though awkward, place in the American historical canon.[1]

Although the Taylorites and the Tylerites are legends of American religion, few of us know very much about them. What we "know," moreover, we have usually learned second- or thirdhand, and the significance of their dispute is easily misconstrued. Even when theological controversies constituted the most important episodes in many histories of American religion, leading neo-orthodox church historians (with the support of their secular sympathizers) dismissed the Taylorites out of hand as important but lamentable Protestant moralists, un-Edwardsian theological pragmatists, and anthropocentric accommodators to the modern spirit of liberal democracy. Most others classify the Taylorites as part of a nearly comatose "Old Calvinism," as latter-day leaders of a coalition formed originally to oppose the (Edwardsian) "New Divinity" but kept on life support in the nineteenth century by the mere force of cultural inertia. The Tylerites, for their part, are portrayed rather perfunctorily as antagonists, archrivals of the Taylorites typecast as crotchety obscurantists (after the manner of their best-known theologian, Bennet Tyler). In recent years, as WASP elites proved uninteresting to most scholars, historians have bypassed both groups on the highway of social history.[2]

Significantly, however, the American scholarly community has witnessed a minor renaissance of interest in "Edwardsian culture" during the past three decades, a renaissance located primarily among social and cultural historians of religion. Working in the train of Joseph Conforti, a cadre of specialists is beginning to unearth the remains of an Edwardsian civilization that apparently dominated New England Calvinism during and after the Second Great Awakening, co-opting virtually all its trinitarian Congregationalist institutions—from local churches and their policies to most of the region's colleges, from the "schools of the prophets" to the fledgling seminaries and parachurch societies of the region's benevolent empire. On the basis of this "discovery," these specialists call for a revision of traditional arguments for the demise of Edwardsian culture in the late eighteenth century. Rather than continue to suggest that the New England theology declined, devolved, or passed from the cultural scene during and after the difficult years of the American Revolution, these scholars point to the continued vitality of the Edwardsian religious tradition throughout much of the first half of the nineteenth century.[3]

Unfortunately, this new literature on Edwardsian culture in the nineteenth century includes little useful analysis of theological developments, and almost nothing on the dispute between the Taylorites and the Tylerites. I have addressed this problem elsewhere with an analysis of the Taylorites, their ties to Edwardsian culture, and modifications of Edwards's theology.[4] In what follows, then, I focus on the consequences of the Taylorite controversy for the subsequent history of the Edwardsian tradition. After summarizing the institutional history of the Taylorite-Tylerite split, I reassess its significance for the history of the New England theology. Building on earlier work that explains how both the Taylorites and the Tylerites proved central figures in what was by their day an immensely influential Edwardsian movement, I argue that their dispute is best interpreted in a new way: not as an *inter*mural battle between increasingly liberal accommodationists and retrograde hyper-Calvinists, all of whom ministered after the wane of the New England theology, but as an *intra*mural struggle waged in the thick of this tradition, though one that contributed in an ironic way to its ultimate dissolution.

Edwardsianism in New England on the Eve of the Taylorite-Tylerite Controversy

After a period of slow growth in the second half of the eighteenth century, Edwardsianism exploded during the first third of the nineteenth century. In fact, Edwardsian preaching, polity, institutions, and theology infiltrated New England to such an extent that it would not be inappropriate to speak of an Edwardsian enculturation of the region in this period. Contemporary accounts from observers all across the religious spectrum suggest that friends and foes alike recognized the strength of the Edwardsian tradition. The liberal William Bentley admitted with regret in 1813 that Samuel Hopkins's theology stood as "the basis of the popular theology of New England." Berkshire clergy-man Sylvester Burt agreed in 1829 that the main contours of Hopkinsianism, "waiving a few points," had become standards for "the orthodox and evangelical clergy of N. England at the present day." Princetonian Archibald Alexander testified in 1831 that "Edwards has done more to give complexion to the theological system of Calvinists in America, than all other persons together." His colleague Samuel Miller affirmed in 1837 that "for the last half century, it may be safely affirmed, that no other American writer on the subject of theology has been so frequently quoted, or had anything like such deference manifested to his opinions, as President Edwards." Bennet Tyler claimed in 1844 that the Edwardsians constituted the "standard theological writers of New England." Samuel Worcester echoed in 1852 that "within fifty years past" Edwardsianism had "pervaded the orthodoxy of New England." By 1853 the Edwardsian Mortimer Blake could boast that Edwardsianism had "modified the current theology of all New England, and given to it its harmony, consistency, and beauty, as it now appears in the creeds of the churches and the teaching of the ministry."[5]

Despite their controversial insistence that original sin was "in the sinning," that penitent sinners played an important role in their own regeneration, and that God's grace was not coercive but worked in conjunction with human free will, Nathaniel Taylor and the Yale Divinity School participated fully in the Edwardsian culture, attracting many of its best and brightest ministers in training, and defending it against Unitarians, Old Calvinists, and Arminians. This comes as a surprise to those of us reared on traditional Reformed historiography. But Taylor and his companions always deemed New Haven theology Edwardsian. They perceived it as a modification of Edwards's own thought, whose repackaging was done according to Edwards's theo-logic for traditionally Edwardsian revivalistic reasons. Taylor's daughter, Rebecca Hatch, described her father as a proponent of what she called the "New Divinity" and distanced him quite clearly from "Old Calvinism."[6] His son-in-law and colleague, Noah Porter, noted that "the works of all the New England divines were the familiar hand-books of his reading." Taylor's successor at New Haven's Center Church, Leonard Bacon, called him "the last, as the elder Edwards was the first, of the great masters of the distinctive theology of New England. . . . The names in that succession . . . are few,—Hopkins, the younger Edwards, Smalley, Emmons, Taylor,—and the last, not least in the illustrious dynasty." Taylor's student and colleague George P. Fisher once referred to him as "the last of our New England schoolmen, . . . the compeer of Emmons and Hopkins, of Smalley and the Edwardses," noting that "probably none of his contemporaries was so well acquainted with the great divines of the New England school of theology. . . . The principal works of President Edwards, Dr. Taylor knew almost by heart." And Taylor himself, though less concerned with theological labels than his peers, confessed his own allegiance to the Edwardsian tradition, working almost exclusively with the Edwardsians as his authorities at hand, suffusing his writings and his lectures with Edwardsian concerns, and defending Edwardsians constantly from the criticisms of Unitarians, Methodists, and other Arminians.[7]

Tellingly, although the New Haven theology had been developing publicly throughout the 1820s, it was not until the end of that fateful decade that Taylorite views received much criticism. Indeed, before publication in 1828 of Taylor's *Concio ad Clerum*,[8] a controversial sermon on original sin that some thought supported Charles Finney's "new measures," New England's Congregationalists stood largely united on rather conservative Edwardsian principles. As noted in Lyman Beecher's *Autobiography*, "Time was when Taylor, and Stuart, and Beecher, and Nettleton, and Tyler, and Porter, and Hewitt, and Harvey were all together, not only in local proximity, but in the warmest unity of belief and feeling." This claim was not unfounded. In the middle years of the 1820s, these future rivals banded together to battle both Unitarianism back east and Finneyite methods in the west. For example, when Unitarians attempted to divide New England's trinitarian standing order by separating Beecher and New Haven (Beecher was Taylor's closest ally) from the region's historic Calvinism, none other than Asahel Nettleton, the fiery conservative soon to serve as the Tylerite party's leading activist, supported Beecher and the unity of the Edwardsian ranks in Connecticut. "I believe it to be a matter of fact," he claimed,

> that you and I are really a different kind of Calvinists from what Unitarians have imagined or been accustomed to manage. Probably [your Unitarian critic] thinks that you are in sentiment at war with

the orthodox at the present day, but he is grandly mistaken so far as Connecticut is concerned. . . . We feel no concern for old Calvinism. Let them dispute it as much as they please; we feel bound to make no defense.

When the Finneyites in upstate New York threatened to encroach on their region, moreover, these men joined hands again to keep the new measures out of New England. Beecher and Nettleton led the charge against Finneyite progressives in New Lebanon, New York, when the two sides met there in 1827 to discuss their differences. And though it was Nettleton who left this meeting to become Finney's worst New England nightmare (his zealous revivalistic itinerancy and public relations work for the Tylerites would make him the closest thing to Finney's archrival in New England), it was Beecher who promised to fight him every inch of the way to Boston.[9]

The Institutionalization of the Taylorite-Tylerite Split

Before long, however, things changed along New England's united front, and it was only a matter of time before the Edwardsians were divided. Nettleton's doctors urged him to move south soon after the end of the New Lebanon conference. His health had never been good, and Finney had worked him into a frenzy.[10] Nettleton obliged them the following winter, staying with Presbyterian colleagues in Virginia and remaining in the south until the spring of 1829. While there, one of his friends, the Presbyterian minister John H. Rice, received copies of Taylor's *Concio ad Clerum* as well as his views on regeneration, recently published in New Haven's *Quarterly Christian Spectator*. These items were covered in the mail by a letter from Yale's Chauncey Goodrich attributing Nettleton's own success as a gospel preacher to Taylorite views. Unfortunately, as it turned out, Nettleton's friends found Taylor heretical. Terribly embarrassed, Nettleton labored now to distance himself from New Haven.[11]

On his return to New England, Nettleton tried to quiet the Taylorites, hoping to avert any future embarrassments with Presbyterian friends. Failing this, he took up his pen and launched a letter-writing campaign, casting aspersions on Taylor's doctrine among his colleagues.[12] He proved somewhat persuasive at Andover Seminary, whose president, Ebenezer Porter, and leading theologian, Leonard Woods, soon joined the ranks of those who opposed New Haven theology. During Andover's anniversary celebration in September 1829, President Porter called a meeting of New England's minds in his study at home. All the region's luminaries were there—Taylor, Beecher, Goodrich,

Nettleton, Woods, Stuart, and others—and they engaged in a charitable airing of their differences. But after the meeting, Woods published a series of captious *Letters to Rev. Nathaniel W. Taylor* (1830), and the battle for control of New England's Calvinist institutions was joined.[13]

Before this meeting, Beecher had promised to remain a theological peacemaker, telling Porter, "With me it is a fundamental maxim not to expend my strength in contending with the friends of Christ, when so much effort is needed to turn back his enemies." But after the meeting, he spun around nearly 180 degrees, encouraging Taylor to respond to Woods with decisive force. "Attack," he wrote to his friend, so that Woods would "never . . . peep again or mutter. . . . I would have him exposed and pushed with great directness and power, and unsparingly, leaving of his temple not one stone upon another." Always more aggressive than the academicians in New Haven, Beecher now played the part of New Haven's battlefield commander. "We are not to be browbeaten," he exclaimed, "and driven off the ground of New England divinity—Bible divinity—by a feeble and ignorant philosophy."[14]

Making matters worse, by this time Beecher had already ruined his friendship with Nettleton, having tried to intimidate him during a conversation held, quite literally, in Beecher's woodshed. Though, as might have been expected, these men interpreted the encounter differently, both allowed that it took place in October 1829 after a meeting of Boston-area clergy held in Beecher's own home at which Nettleton publicized his opposition to Taylor's theology. After the meeting, Beecher and Nettleton spent time alone in Beecher's woodshed, Beecher chopping wood while the younger Nettleton looked on. At a memorable point in their conversation, Beecher shook his axe at Nettleton and said, "Taylor and I have made you what you are, and if you do not behave yourself we will hew you down." Beecher always remembered this as "a mere playful act of humor," claiming that Nettleton had understood it as such himself. But when word of it spread southward down the seaboard, Nettleton fumed in humiliation, and the story of their encounter generated discomfort wherever it went.[15]

Meanwhile, Taylor's views were stirring up strife in the religious periodicals and theological quarterlies, in which he was gaining notoriety that would soon catch up with him back home. In 1832 he engaged in a highly publicized exchange on his creedal commitments with friend and colleague Joel Hawes of Hartford's First Church. Published originally in the *Connecticut Observer*, this exchange was reprinted numerous times. Hawes intended it as an opportunity for Taylor to clarify his orthodoxy. It wound up provoking further dissension, though—not over the eleven articles Taylor laid out in a basic statement of his beliefs (which he phrased in fairly traditional Edwardsian terms) but over his annotations to the articles, which struck many as suspiciously elaborate and ambiguous.[16] Beecher took steps immediately to reclaim New Haven's reputation, soliciting Woods' "cordial" consent to a common statement of New England doctrine.[17] But by 1834, Taylor faced heresy charges at home, as Daniel Dow, a ten-year veteran of the Yale Corporation, complained of his failure to adhere literally to Connecticut's Saybrook Platform (1708). After an internal investigation, Yale's trustees acquitted Taylor, concluding that throughout the college's history, "excepting the period from 1753 to 1778, it has been an established principle, that the assent to the Confession of faith in question, is to be understood, as only an assent to 'the substance of doctrine therein contained.' " But Dow departed Yale determined to thwart its innovations, and New Haven acquired a reputation for doctrinal legerdemain.[18]

The Taylorites disowned this reputation whenever they had the chance, contesting the Tylerites' frequent claim to be New England's true Edwardsians. They contended that the spirit of the New England Theology had always been one of investigation, of creative advancement of the gospel, not a spirit of fearful clinging to the past. Though the Tylerites seemed to think "that the Congregational ministers of New England should never dream of making a single advance upon the views of Bellamy and Edwards—that nothing shall be deemed not heretical, except the exact phraseology adopted by these divines," this "was not the spirit of Edwards," they insisted—"Not at all." The Taylorites felt that they had been largely misunderstood and that New England's theologians held more in common than they knew. They pleaded for unity both in print and in their private correspondence "between those who agree in the cardinal points of Calvinism—decrees, election, total depravity by nature, regeneration by the special and direct influence of the spirit, and final perseverance of saints." They viewed the Tylerites as friends, as Taylor made unmistakably clear early in 1843 when he visited Nettleton on what everyone thought would be his deathbed. As remembered by Leonard Bacon, "There were no dry eyes in that chamber of suffering when Taylor fell weeping on the neck of Nettleton and kissed him." Taylor repeated on many occasions what all of his friends knew to be true: "Nothing could have been farther from my wishes than to be drawn into a theological controversy with the Rev. Dr. Tyler of Portland; a man for whom an intimate friendship, in early life, has made it impossible for me to entertain any sentiments but those of respect and affection."[19]

The Tylerites refused to accept New Haven's olive branch. Taylor had simply gone too far in his dilution of their Calvinism. The future of the churches was at stake. So while the Taylorites remained the most popular Christian group in the region,[20] the Tylerites laid plans for an ecclesiastical schism and associated more frequently with Old School Presbyterians than with their former colleagues in New England.[21] They disagreed among themselves over the extent to which they should separate, but they all believed they should "separate as soon as possible." As one anonymous Tylerite wrote, "By continued contact the evil [of Taylorism] will secretly spread, until the whole mass be corrupt. . . . Until we have a separate organization, and are united in our exertions to exclude false teachers from our churches, there will be no effectual barrier to their influx."[22]

After a secret meeting in Norwich in October 1831, at which they formed their own Doctrinal Tract Society, planned their own *Evangelical Magazine*, and developed a constitution that would govern the proceedings of their group, the Tylerites met in Hartford in January 1833 to work on a list of doctrinal articles of agreement. This process culminated in a larger meeting in September 1833, held symbolically in East Windsor, Jonathan Edwards's hometown. It was there that the Tylerites formally launched their separate Pastoral Union, electing George Calhoun as their founding president. About forty clergymen attended from all across the state of Connecticut, adopting the Tylerite constitution and Articles of Agreement and stipulating that future members had to be nominated from within and then approved by a two-thirds vote at the annual meeting. Most important, the union planned establishment of a seminary, the Theological Institute of Connecticut. They appointed a board of trustees and determined to build it in East Windsor, right down the street from Edwards's birthplace. On May 13 of the following year, they took the Edwards family doorstep and laid it ceremoniously as the cornerstone of their seminary. By October 1834, the Theological Institute was open for business, and Bennet Tyler was hard at work as the founding president and professor of theology.[23]

The Dissolution of the New England Theology

For all intents and purposes, the Taylorites and the Tylerites now moved in different clerical networks. The most acrimonious days of their dispute lay in the past. Leonard Bacon and George Calhoun would wage a paper war at decade's end,[24] and by midcentury the Tylerites would begin to squabble among themselves.[25] But by and large the smoke was clearing and the most perceptive members of both groups began to feel as though their differences were no longer as important as they once were. During the 1840s and 1850s, enrollments at both schools were low. In fact, by 1855 there was talk under way of a merger. Many regretted that the controversy had sapped their churches' strength, and this in a period of challenge to New England's Protestant Christians.[26]

Indeed, as urbanization and industrialization altered the region's landscape, and German idealism, biblical criticism, and Darwin altered theology, the Edwardsian culture proved to be weaker than it had been since the 1780s, and its leaders, now tired and aging, lacked the energy to respond. The next generation of Christians began to look elsewhere for guidance, seeking new and creative solutions to problems Edwardsians had not addressed. By the eve of the Civil War, even their teachers began to respond by paying homage to their ancestors but offering a more expansive, less parochially Edwardsian curriculum.

The New England theology did decline, then, but not at the end of the eighteenth century and not for the reasons usually suggested. Rather, it flourished in the northeast during the early nineteenth century, becoming America's first indigenous theological tradition—the most popular movement of indigenous theology in all of American evangelical history. Its great success was a two-edged sword, though, for the Edwardsians grew so large and diverse that they tore themselves apart, leaving their culture too weak to sustain a vital tradition of theological reflection.

Edwards Amasa Park

THE LAST EDWARDSIAN

Charles Phillips

IN THE MORNINGS on Andover Hill, before his death at the age of ninety-one, Edwards Amasa Park would take up a book "usually bearing upon the life of Jonathan Edwards," though when he tired in the afternoons Park would have read to him "Locke, Hamilton, Reid, Dugald Stewart, Dorner, McCosh . . . and Clarke on the Attributes."[1] If he felt well enough to receive visitors, some of his almost one thousand former students might call on their now nearly sightless professor. Dominating Andover with a "massive and striking personality,"[2] reigning as the consummate Congregationalist at the largest seminary in the land for more than forty-five years, the editor of the influential *Bibliotheca Sacra* for forty, a distinguished theologian in the prominent Abbot chair for almost thirty-five—few of these visitors at the time of his death in 1900 would have challenged Park's description by his eulogists as one who "since Edwards . . . has hardly been surpassed in acumen,"[3] who was "one of the greatest teachers of theology . . . this country has known."[4] Revivalist preacher, rhetorician, theologian, editor, author, historian, biographer, redactor, disputant: in the words of an Andover memoirist, Park's "fame was great in Zion."[5] Edwards Park was the last nineteenth-century American theologian of significance to identify deliberately with Jonathan Edwards. From his hilltop, Park creatively recast his inherited New England theology and so extended the influence of his beloved namesake from the midnineteenth century to the beginning of the next.

Even in Zion, however, fame must be fleeting, for as the next century's scholars erected monographs as monuments to Jonathan Edwards, Park himself merited no more than a footnote here or a brief notice there. Readers searching for an elaboration of Park's place in the complex story told in Mark

Noll's magisterial *America's God* (2002), for example, would have to seek else-where.[6] Park had fared no better in Joseph Haroutunian's earlier *Piety Versus Moralism: The Passing of the New England Theology* (1932).[7] The long decline Haroutunian described from Edwards's theocentric piety to a stultifying mor-alism in Yale's Nathaniel William Taylor relegated Park to a single citation, and that merely in the context of sharp criticism of Taylor and Frank Hugh Foster's *Genetic History of the New England Theology* (1907). Even Foster—a student and confidant of Park's at Andover—had diminished his old mentor by leaving the significance of Park's work finally dependent on the heroic Taylor, for Yale's great iconoclast had "captivated [Park's] imagination by boldness of specu-lation and led his judgment into substantial agreement."[8] Much contempo-rary scholarship follows this path in describing Park as essentially a Taylorite. Douglas A. Sweeney, in his admirable recent study of Taylor, describes Park as "won over to New Haven Theology" by the time he assumed the Abbot chair in 1847.[9] Whether the Edwardsian theological arc is interpreted as ascending or descending, Park is merely tangential to the climactic significance of Taylor.

A complete reappraisal of Park's historical significance is beyond the scope of this essay, though a few suggestions may nonetheless be useful. Edwards Park's own self-identification was securely with Jonathan Edwards and his New Divinity descendants, and particularly with the exercisers Samuel Hopkins and Nathanael Emmons. Park asserted in 1854, at the height of his ascendancy as a public churchman, that the "Edwardean definitions were introduced not to subvert the substance, but to *conserve the substance* of the old Calvinistic faith, and to *prolong its influence* over the minds of an intelligent community."[10] Park's own New England theology constituted a "Calvinism in an improved form" that shrugged off its former apologetic burdens in meeting contempo-rary tests of fairness and reasonableness.[11] In practice this meant a synthesis of Edwardsian natural ability, New Divinity moral government, and a Hopkinsian exercise scheme. This compound was the form of Edwardsianism best fitted to the world of midnineteenth-century evangelicalism, and its fitness was duly certified for all to see by its prolonged success in stimulating revival from the pulpit.

From his boyhood in Rhode Island, Edwards Park was able to ring deftly the New Divinity changes. Born in 1808, Park described himself as "at ten years of age somewhat of a theologian, and a rigid Calvinist" who "had a great reverence for Dr. Emmons and Dr. Hopkins."[12] Nathanael Emmons himself would regu-larly be received in the Park family parlor in Providence. According to Richard Salter Storrs (Park's lifelong friend), the Park household was as "intense a theological atmosphere as probably was encountered in the world," where the subjects "of God's sovereignty, of His decrees, and of . . . harmonizing with these the obligation of man, were the supreme, almost the sole, topics of reflection and talk."[13] Unsurprisingly, Edwards Park's specific theological inheritance was preeminently the New Divinity "improvements" on Jonathan Edwards, as interpreted by the work of the two men who dominated his youthful conversations at home: Hopkins and Emmons.[14] Park's lectures at Andover and his published articles and biographies consistently affirm the exercise system detailed by Hopkins and adumbrated by Emmons. If the traditional Calvinist view of innate depravity as a "taste" or "disposition" to sin seemed to compromise natural ability and so neutralize the moral demands of God's law, then it must be made absolutely clear that one's "exercises" were the entire basis of one's moral standing. Hopkins was categorical: "all sin consists in the nature and quality of the exercises which take place in a moral agent, and not in any thing that goes before."[15] Wobbly tasters like Leonard Woods (Park's predecessor in the Abbot chair) only weakened the defense of Calvinism. For Park, if "moral agency . . . does consist in the choice or refusal of that wh[ich] conscience approves or condemns," it "does not consist in the antecedents of choice."[16] Park affirmed for his Andover seminarians the Hopkinsian principle that "Holiness is a hatred of selfishness, or a preference for something else beside the highest good of the universe"[17]—this would limit for him the usefulness of New Haven theology and its rehabilitation of self-love. Edwards Amasa Park was by birth and training a Hopkinsian. It was natural, then, for Park to observe in 1859 that "I am more convinced that Hopkins was a great man, that he had great influence over Edwards, and that in many respects he is of more *historical* importance than any other American divine, unless Pres. Edwards himself be excepted."[18]

If Park's theological identity was well established in his family home, his epistemological foundation was also secured in his early days as an undergraduate at Brown, where sturdy axioms from Scotland joined reliable British natural philosophy. Like many of his contemporaries, Park was a lifelong devotee of Thomas Reid, Dugald Stewart, and Scottish commonsense realism. He described Reid's *Essays on the Intellectual and Moral Powers of Man* (1785) as "the classical standard of our intellectual philosophy."[19] Park is even willing to suggest that "so far as the theology of New England is a distinctive system . . . it is the theology of the Bible explained by common sense."[20] Additionally, in Park's senior year eighteenth-century works of apologetics and natural theology by Lord Kames, Samuel Clarke, Joseph Butler, and William Paley complemented the commonsense volumes from Scotland. Other Scots, Hugh Blair of Edinburgh and George Campbell of Aberdeen, made a significant contribution to the Brown curriculum as proponents of the "New Rhetoric": Park well appreciated the Scots' fundamental rejection of ornamentation in favor of persuasion. As a revivalist rhetorician *and* Hopkinsian, Park taught his own seminarians that "the great object is to move men to *immediate action*."[21]

Park never doubted that the Edwardsian theology of the great exercisers Hopkins and Emmons was the biblical "substance" required in his day; in this sense his life's work was first to conserve the tradition passed to him from boyhood. But if the basic matter was undoubted (because the "people, intent on having a creed that may be preached to them," have "required their ministers to make the Edwardean analyses"), the sacred rhetorician must then attend to the manner of its expression (to "portray fully and boldly the ancient faith in a form more consonant with . . . the idioms of our speech"): this dual action is "sound conservatism."[22] It was required that the preacher become concerned with presentation and proportion, with contemporary "idioms," in order to convict and persuade. Park's underappreciated early articles in Edward Robinson's *American Biblical Repository* in 1837 and 1839 balanced the importance of theology and rhetoric in the practice of preaching as established by the Scottish New Rhetoric.[23] For example, in "The Mode of Exhibiting Theological Truth" (1837) Park declared that if "theology is concerned with the essence of Christian doctrine . . . sacred rhetoric is concerned with the manner in which this doctrine should be presented." It was unfortunate that some preached divine sovereignty as "a hard and harsh truth." This "favourite doctrine . . . would appear far more amiable, and in its meaning far more correct, if it were blended more with God's love." In such an adjusted representation, the "matter of the doctrine is the same, yet it is more seemly."[24] Although these articles are among Park's first published works, he confidently asserts an essential connection between the substance of a doctrine and its mode of expression, because only in this way do the contemporary sensibilities of the congregation become the definitive context for persuasive speech. Park's rhetorical instincts were always linked to the imperatives of Edwardsian revival.

It is within this framework of Park's early rhetorical strategies that his great Convention sermon at the Brattle Street Church in Boston, "The Theology of the Intellect and That of the Feelings" (1850), can best be assessed. The *theology of the intellect* is the language of doctrine and of propositional or creedal statements—the "theology of reason." It is primarily "abstract," applying "deductive powers" to "evidence [and] trains of proof."[25] The theology of the intellect "comprehends the truth just as it is, unmodified by excitements of feeling." This "intellectual theology" is by definition "self-consistent." Alternatively, the *theology of the feelings* employs indefinite but expressive language to capture vital religious experience. Its aim is ultimately persuasive, "to arrest attention" by straining a word "to its utmost significancy." The two theologies do not operate in isolation but complement each other: if reason "amplifies . . . the affections," it is in turn "improved and enlarged" by them.[26] The essential craft of the preacher is to keep each theology in its proper sphere while promoting harmonious interaction.

If the Convention sermon was the apex of Park's public career as Abbot Professor of theology at Andover, he was in effect only restating for a larger audience the principles he had taught at the seminary more than a decade earlier as the Bartlet Professor of sacred rhetoric. Ebenezer Porter, Park's mentor and predecessor in the Bartlet chair, and an advocate of the New Rhetoric, had argued that "the end of eloquence . . . is to move men to *action* . . . by exhibiting light to convince their understanding and motives to influence the heart."[27] George Campbell asserted that the aim of a discourse is to "move the will" by "an artful mixture of that which proposes to convince the judgement and that which interests the passions."[28] Hugh Blair defined eloquence as "the Art . . . of speaking both to the understanding and the heart."[29] Park said no more than these when he proposed in 1850 that the "perfection of our faith is, that it combine in its favor the logic of the understanding with the rhetoric of the feelings."[30]

"The Theology of the Intellect and That of the Feelings" has been interpreted as Park's embrace of Romanticism and intuition in the spirit of Horace Bushnell. D. G. Hart's 1987 essay insists that the discourse was distinguished by "German ideas . . . rooted in its appropriation of Bushnell."[31] In 1848 (speaking before Andover's Porter Rhetorical Society, no less, with the Abbot Professor likely present), Bushnell proposed a radical revision of the uses of reason and language.[32] He argued that knowledge received by intuition was essentially superior to knowledge gained by dogmatic study. Moreover, in his influential "Preliminary Dissertation on the Nature of Language" (published as an accompaniment to the Andover address), Bushnell argued that truth was exclusively metaphorical, so that "language [is] an instrument wholly inadequate to the exact representation of thought."[33] In this light, Park's Convention sermon ought not to be viewed as a concession to Connecticut's home-grown Coleridge. Indeed, Park rejects Bushnell's entire Romantic project in describing the intellect as "the decisive standard of appeal," because "reason has an ultimate, rightful authority over the sensibilities"—the reverse of Bushnell's position at Andover.[34] Park's 1850 sermon is best viewed as the culmination of rhetorical strategies promoted formally as early as his inauguration to the Bartlet chair in 1836. The address at the Brattle Street Church provided apologists for orthodoxy with a specific rhetorical strategy, one that allowed vital biblical content to be appropriated by an audience requiring increased purchase for the affections within a newfound cultural mood.

It was primarily the affective element of Romanticism that proved useful to Park. When ideality bent toward immaterialism or pantheism, he resisted the shift. Park traveled extensively in Germany in 1842 and 1843, but he continued to judge German thought by his inherited principles, and not the reverse. For example, guarding his Scottish metaphysics, Park objected that Kant required that one should have "no innate idea of God." Since commonsense realism affirmed that the mind apprehended real knowledge of the world as it was, Park remained firmly with the Scots in dismissing Kant.[35] Park did not reject German scholarship out of hand; the exegetical model for Andover was Moses Stuart, Park's own professor. One of Park's earliest published works, *Selections from German Literature* (1839), provided swaths of translations from the German mediating theologians, including August Tholuck (with whom Park had studied at Halle).[36] Park did not swallow whole the antirationalist or pantheistic assumptions of full-bore German idealism when they were in conflict with his foundational epistemic premises, but he willingly appropriated German methodologies where *Wissenschaftlichkeit* or *Entwicklung* advanced evangelical piety. In the end, Bushnell's assertions are fundamentally at odds with Park's confidence in the ability of his British epistemological nexus to define truth propositionally. To read the Convention sermon as Park's own proto-liberal manifesto is to ignore the fact that Park disagreed with Bushnell at almost every important point, and to forget that the bimodal aspect of the Boston address was long an element of Park's rhetorical training.

Princeton's Charles Hodge, for one, believed that Park gave too much away to Bushnell in the sermon, and that Andover had moved into hazardous proximity to Schleiermacher's grounding of Christianity solely in religious experience. Without a substantive role, the intellect became "the mere interpreter" of the feelings.[37] Park and Hodge tortured each other's views in a series of journal articles over the next two years but accomplished little in the way of real communication, shooting great volumes of ink into increasingly opaque waters. But Hodge had certainly misjudged the significance of the superficial resemblance to Bushnell suggested by Park's affective strategy in the Convention sermon. Park's relatively minor accommodation to emotive Romanticism was a consequence of his attention to the requirements of the new tastes of his audience, while Bushnell's identification with Coleridge was an entire metaphysical sea change. Jonathan Edwards had spoken of the expressive "language of the heart"[38]; that was sufficient authority for Edwards Park.

One important aspect of the Convention sermon did not escape Hodge's concerned notice, however: Park's "intellect"-and-"feelings" distinction provided a hearty redactor's tool able to shape an Edwardsian tradition into a coherent narrative of his choosing. Two years after his lecture in Boston, Park was ready to describe in detail this representative "New England Theology" in a summary article in the *Bibliotheca Sacra*.[39] The "term, New England Theology . . . signifies the formal creed which a majority of the most eminent theologians in New England have explicitly or implicitly sanctioned, during and since the time of Edwards." The "comprehensiveness" of the "Edwardean scheme" consists of its balancing God's sovereignty with human liberty: it "unites a high, but not an ultra Calvinism, on the decrees and agency of God, with a philosophical, but not an Arminian theory, on the freedom and worth of the human soul." Park shows that the New England theology carefully retains human moral accountability (where Calvinism might otherwise be challenged), for the "truth which has been so clearly unfolded by the New England divines" is that "an entirely depraved man has a natural power to do all that is required of him." This is, of course, the "far-famed 'natural ability' of the Edwardean school." There is no room here for taste or disposition: Park the exerciser does not fail to remind that "sin is a voluntary act." Remarkably, the New England theology straightens the older, "crooked parts of Calvinism" with a new "self-consistency" supplied by the improvements embedded in "Edwardeanism and Hopkinsianism."[40] Park's historical *tour de force* used his unsurpassed knowledge of the sources, a genetic strategy of oral transmission within the exercise line, and his useful intellect-and-feelings editorial tool to level the sometimes eccentric contours of New England theology into an apologetically useful Calvinist tradition invigorated by Edwards and Hopkins.

For Park the historian, this tradition making was neither an antiquarian project of little immediate use nor a tactic to feign an imaginary consensus where none existed. It was an important conviction of centrist Congregationalists such as Park, Enoch Pond at Bangor, and Edward Dorr Griffin at Williams that a core Edwardsian theology could be found below the apparent verbal differences that divided honest churchmen. Indeed, it was the very function of "The Theology of the Intellect and That of the Feelings" to clear away the clutter of apparent differences in language in order to reveal an underlying agreement on orthodoxy. Park explained to Hodge that the "discrepancies so often lamented are not fundamental but superficial, and are easily harmonized by exposing the one self-consistent principle which lies at their base."[41] As late as 1873, in Pond's review in Park's *Bibliotheca Sacra* of Hodge's *Systematic Theology*, Pond concluded that Hodge "really differs from us of New England much less than he thinks he does . . . [the] difference between us is chiefly in words."[42] Park's 1850 Convention sermon intended to unify the parties of orthodoxy by revealing an underlying theological unity—and Park and Pond took for granted that the exposed granitic bedrock looked exactly like the "self-consistent" New England theology Park would detail in 1852.

In one sense, this irenic spirit of orthodox Congregationalism was built into Andover seminary from the first, and the Convention sermon can be seen as the methodological engine by which Park—the leading Congregationalist—drove the theological content of his New England theology toward a winsome synthesis. But there were times when the intellect-and-feelings tool in Park's editorial hand appeared to attempt too much and finally misrepresent the underlying source material. For example, pointed criticism of Park's method came a decade later when his lengthy *Memoir of Nathanael Emmons* (1861) was published as a separate volume.[43] One of Park's purposes in the biographical study was to draw Emmons into the mainstream of New England theology by declaring his most eccentric apothegms to be figurative speech used for emphatic purposes, consistent with the disproportion built into the theology of the feelings. Yale's George Park Fisher (a student of Park's at Andover) reviewed the *Memoir* for the *New Englander* with scarcely concealed disapproval for his former professor's bag of tricks: Park had cut "off the claws—if he will pardon the expression—of the author he has taken in hand."[44] Like Fisher, Union Seminary's Henry Boynton Smith did not believe that Nathanael Emmons ought to be softened by even as sinuous an editorial tool as the intellect-and-feelings distinction. In an important 1862 article on Emmons's *Works* and Park's *Memoir*, Smith protested that "just so far as the peculiarities of his system are explained away, Emmons himself is explained away."[45] In Smith's mind, Park's legerdemain had not done justice to his biographical subject.

By the midpoint of the nineteenth century, Edwards Park had established on Andover Hill a bulwark of improved Calvinism ready to take on all comers. Significantly, however, Park's Scottish realism failed to reinforce one critical section of his Edwardsian defenses. To Park, the intellectualist model of the will demanded by commonsense realism looked suspiciously like the self-determining power that Jonathan Edwards had roundly rejected in *Freedom of the Will*. Edwards had employed a simpler model than Thomas Reid's, where the will always corresponded to what appeared to be "the greatest apparent good."[46] By contrast, the commonsense intellectualist scheme inserted the will between the motive and the act. This central role for the will grew from the realists' intellectual debt to prior Scottish jurisprudence. The probative value of evidence at trial was measured by the degree of confidence in it established by a proficient judge, so that the matter of judicial competence became central to jurisprudence, and by extension to epistemology.[47] The faculty of judgment is presented with evidence, over which it pauses to apply axioms of commonly held truth in determining its validity. This suspended point of deliberation is precisely where the intellectualist model placed the human will in matters of salvation—in equipoise, weighing the truth claims of the gospel.

Park resisted following Reid's model to such a balancing point. He consistently taught his seminarians the older view of Edwards that "the will always is as the greatest apparent good." He argued that the position of "Arminius and Dr. Reid . . . that man does act without any influence of motives" ought to be "denied," because "Pres. Edwards and his followers rightly oppose the doct[rine] of the self-determining power." Park asserts that Jonathan Edwards's "design . . . was to prove the doctrine of total depravity . . . as against the Arminian notion that man's will was in equilibrium."[48] Importantly, Park's rejection of the intellectualist model is a patent dismissal of a characteristic feature of New Haven theology: the essential independence of the human will as it is poised on the brink of salvific choice. Frank Hugh Foster—no mere amateur, and always eager to connect Park with Taylor—was certainly correct when he observed that Park "maintained Edwards's theory of the will, not following Taylor's modifications."[49] Foster comments in the *Genetic History* that Park "manifested no interest in Taylor's eagerness to establish the existence in the soul of a neutral point to which the truth could appeal."[50] Out of loyalty to Jonathan Edwards, Park would not follow the logic of his own commonsense realism to its natural conclusions, and here he abandoned the field to a more determined and more consistent intellectualist in Nathaniel William Taylor—though perhaps also a less loyal innovator.

Park and Taylor shared much common ground, including a penchant for creatively adapting their New Divinity inheritance to the new conditions of the nineteenth century. Park's lectures illustrate a willingness to adopt features of Taylorism where they advance the collective defense of Calvinism. For example, Park found repeated use for Taylor's famed *certainty, with power to the contrary* when it aimed exactly where Park aimed, at preserving God's sovereignty without fatalism (*certainty*, not necessity) and validating human free will (*power to the contrary*) within limits. But when interpreters of Park see him employing at Andover such a signal feature of New Haven theology as this and go on to assume that he must have converted wholesale to Taylorism in 1835, they mistake a part for the whole. Park—loyal first to Jonathan Edwards—reminds his Andover seminarians that in "the improper sense, power to the contrary is the uncertainty how one will act—what one will choose. . . . In this sense, Pres[ident] Edwards believes we have no power to the contrary."[51] Park could not remain self-consciously Edwardsian and forsake Edwards's model of the will for New Haven's, even if such an intellectualist view was demanded by the commonsense realism he otherwise endorsed. In fact, Park rejected characteristic elements of Taylor's—a self-determined will, the use of means, the rehabilitation of selfishness, a rejection of Edwards's natural ability—wherever Taylor rejected characteristic elements of Hopkinsian New Divinity. Park's relation to Taylor was precisely the posture Nathanael Emmons described in a letter to Park in 1838: "I have not given up any of my doctrinal opinions, am no nearer Taylorism than ever I was. I do indeed go about half way with Taylorites, and then stop and turn against them with all my might."[52]

In just the last decade of Park's long career at Andover before his retirement in 1881, Park taught more than 250 graduates and resident licentiates. Most are recorded as actively pursuing careers as ministers, missionaries, and educators down to 1909, when the last Andover *General Catalogue* was published on the occasion of the seminary relocating to Cambridge.[53] It is true that control of the seminary had been wrested from Park by the "Andover liberals," whose theology evolved in the direction of organic, liberal Protestantism.[54] Nevertheless, the extension of his Edwardsian definitions at least to the First World War in the careers of Park's many students is striking; it may well be that the Civil War has been the wrong war to use in fixing the waning influence of Edwardsian culture. The work of Park's student Joseph Cook is perhaps the most remarkable evidence for the continued vitality of Park's personal influence. At the height of Cook's fame in 1882, copies of his Monday Lectures distributed in various newspapers reached an audience of almost one million people.[55] But Cook's public theology essentially replicated the system he had heard Park supply in class. The reformer Washington Gladden described the Monday Lectures as "theologically a reproduction, almost to the extent of plagiarism, of Professor Park's lectures at Andover."[56] Cook's expression of his professor's New England theology may have been in a more popular vein than Park's own lectures, and may have held little interest for the intellectual elite busy reordering the academy, but Cook's career suggests that Park's influence had been extended by proxy to a vast popular audience in the last years before Park's death.

The persistence of Edwardsian theology into the early years of the twentieth century in both mass culture and the worldwide ministry of Park's own students is significant evidence that Park largely fulfilled his commission as a steward of the tradition passed to him. Edwards Park's long tenure may imply that the relevance of Edwardsianism cannot be contained by the final years of Taylor's active career, and that Joseph Conforti is correct when he observes that Park was a pivotal figure in this extension of Edwardsian culture beyond the Civil War.[57] Princeton's Benjamin Warfield acknowledged at the close of his (largely critical) summary of New England theology that Park gave to Edwardsianism "a lease of life for another generation" after Taylor.[58] Before his death at the turn of the century, Park had prolonged the currency of his great namesake in the popular imagination; after all, for Park it was first "the people" who "required their ministers to make the Edwardean analyses." [59]

If such was (in one view) the nature of Park's success, it is also fair to ask how Park might have failed Jonathan Edwards. For some, Park's vast labor seemed little more than an intricately spun web of brilliant ruses. The Old Princetonians certainly thought Park adept at a magician's misdirection in abducting Edwards, though Princeton's views moderated later when worse evils than the theology of the feelings reared their heads from the swamp. It was easy to mistake Park's sincere hope for an irenic unity of core evangelical truth in the glare of his reflexive partisanship on behalf of Hopkinsianism. But Union's Smith, in his review of his friend Park's memoir of Emmons, showed that Andover's Abbot Professor labored under more profound limitations than simply an excess of editorial energy. Smith understood that Nathanael Emmons had built on Jonathan Edwards's principle of God's continuous creation a distinctive Calvinist ideality uniting divine sovereignty and human responsibility. This dynamic point of spiritual integration was now no longer accessible, for regnant commonsense realism required a new world in which human action proceeded not immediately from God's will but deliberatively from man's. In Smith's view, "The whole state of the case was entirely altered, when Berkeleianism was supplanted by the Scotch philosophy."[60] Hence, by extension, Park's grounded commonsense realism would forever be unable to apprehend—much less transmit—the incandescent ideality of Edwards's Trinitarian vision. In this sense, Edwards Park failed Jonathan Edwards. Yet, in echoing an earlier failed disciple's impulse at the Mount of Transfiguration, Park's willingness to build a structure to express his devotion in the face of unimagined radiance was sincere enough. For some, the Andover professor may have erected just a "dry, shingle palace of Hopkinsian theology"; but Edwards Amasa Park stood in the oldest tradition of discipleship in constructing a durable New England theology that honored his master.[61] At the very end of his days, he would be unashamed to take up in his familiar way a book bearing upon the life of Jonathan Edwards.

PART 3

Edwardsian Light Refracted

The New England Theology in New England Congregationalism

Charles Hambrick-Stowe

THE THEOLOGICAL RENEWAL movement that developed under the banners of Edwardsianism, New Divinity, Hopkinsianism, and Consistent Calvinism had to take root and flourish in New England if it were to hold any hope of achieving its broader aspirations of national revival and global mission. Large challenges loomed: creation of innovative missionary institutions to plant churches and schools in the American West and in Africa and Asia, abolition of slavery and other besetting social sins, securing the Protestant Christian character of the country as a whole. But the immediate issue facing pastors and lay leaders identified with the movement was the theological fidelity of the Congregational churches of New England. The problem persisted and became increasingly complex from the 1760s through the first decades of the nineteenth century. The movement's fundamental task was to place the stamp of evangelical Calvinism on the churches of the region to create a strong base for its wider goals. As its advocates knew, this had to become the *New England Theology*.

The cultural and spiritual upheaval known as the Great Awakening in the 1730s and 1740s broke up whatever was left of a Puritan New England synthesis, even as it revived and recontextualized Puritan spirituality.[1] Pro-revival New Lights, with Jonathan Edwards as the major theologian of religious experience, faced off against socially conservative but theologically liberal Old Lights, with Charles Chauncy the leading spokesperson for reason and decorum. Evangelicals could not maintain unity among themselves, however, and Separate New Lights split from established congregations to form new churches, some of which went further and became Baptist. The Awakening continued to reverberate in society through the 1750s and 1760s, with followers of Edwards seeking to develop his retooled Calvinism as the legitimate modern expression of the original New England Way. Allen Guelzo and Douglas Sweeney summarize the ecclesiastical situation:

> Gradually, the contours of New England religion, during the Revolution and into the nineteenth century, sorted themselves out into three broad categories: the genteel congregations of upper-crust Boston, who eventually went the distance in their embrace of the Enlightenment and turned Unitarian; the Old Calvinists, who struggled to preserve some traditional sense of Calvinist orthodoxy within a state-established parish system in which baptism and communion defined church membership more than conversion; and the Edwardseans, who set the bar of church life as high as Edwardsean revival could put it.[2]

Mark Noll argues that the image of Edwardsians such as Samuel Hopkins and Old Calvinist proponents of Congregational social order such as Timothy Dwight "moving in opposite directions . . . is too simple." Underlying their nuanced differences on the proper shape of Calvinist theology for the new era were shared understandings of church membership, the role of the church in society, and the mandate to oppose Unitarianism. Building on this common commitment, "institutional evidence of New Divinity and Old Calvinist confluence came in the founding of Andover Seminary in 1808." As E. Brooks Holifield points out, Andover's founding was the event that prompted and justified use of "the New England Theology" as a label.[3]

Before Andover, for the theological heirs of Jonathan Edwards the focal institution for their project was Yale College, the school from which most of them, like Edwards himself, had graduated. Congregational ministers serving primarily along the Connecticut River Valley had joined with Boston's famous Mathers, Increase and Cotton, and other evangelical Calvinists in eastern Massachusetts to found Yale in 1701. It was not merely that Connecticut needed its own college. With Harvard deemed less than reliably orthodox, the religious future of the region required a school that would carry into the eighteenth century the essence of New England's Puritan founders. But Yale College's first hundred years reflected the contentious nature of the times. In 1722 President Timothy Cutler converted to the Church of England, crossed the Atlantic for reordination, and returned as an Anglican missionary of the Society for the Propagation of the Gospel in Foreign Parts. Following evangelist George Whitefield's visit to Yale, President Thomas Clap in the early 1740s defended a conservative Congregationalism that opposed spiritual enthusiasm almost as strongly as it battled the rationalism of Boston's Congregational Arminians. Clap's expulsion of Edwardsian students David Brainerd and John and Ebenezer Cleaveland during those heated early days of the Awakening "earned the everlasting enmity of the New Divinity." To evangelicals, it appeared that Yale was bent on training well-behaved but "unconverted clergy" rather than fulfilling its calling as "a school of the prophets." Clap nevertheless invited evangelist Whitefield back to preach in 1755, and the college continued to produce candidates for the ministry who sought theological training with Edwardsian pastors after graduation. Clap's successor as president, Ezra Stiles, maintained this Old Calvinist wariness toward evangelical zeal during his tenure, from 1778 through the first half of the 1790s. Stiles complained about the dominance of New Divinity clergy in western New England and their proliferation throughout the region, but he was powerless to diminish the movement's popularity among young men aspiring to the ministry. Yale continued overwhelmingly to be their college of choice. According to David Kling, "Nearly all Connecticut New Divinity men whose careers fell between 1740 and 1820 graduated from Yale College." Moreover, Stiles's successor in 1795 was none other than a grandson of Jonathan Edwards, Timothy Dwight.[4]

The son of Mary Edwards Dwight, Timothy Dwight was born in Northampton, Massachusetts, in 1752, shortly after Edwards's famous dismissal by the congregation. He identified himself with the New Divinity as a student at Yale and trained for ministry under his uncle, the junior Jonathan Edwards. Dwight resigned his teaching position at Yale when the Old Calvinist Ezra Stiles assumed the presidency and wasted no time branding him as a leader of the acerbic evangelical movement within New England Congregationalism. Over the next two decades, serving as pastor in the village of Greenfield, Connecticut, Dwight moderated his views. He lost his taste for acrimonious debate and came to appreciate the Old Calvinist values of parish life. Installed as president of Yale College in 1795, like his predecessors Dwight displayed ambiguity with regard to the theological particularities of Edwards and disciples such as Hopkins and Joseph Bellamy. Nevertheless, he took up the evangelical cause of spiritual rebirth, moral reform, commitment to mission, and refutation of Enlightenment rationalism. His four-year cycle of chapel sermons on Christian doctrine sparked a revival on campus that led to the conversion of hundreds of students, many of whom enlisted as the next generation of ministers and missionaries in the evangelical Calvinist movement. Before his death in 1817, he envisioned a graduate divinity school at Yale, which, along with Andover Seminary north of Boston, would provide a higher level of professional training for nineteenth-century evangelical ministers.

In short, Timothy Dwight secured the place of Yale College as the epicenter of an evolving evangelical Calvinist New England Theology.[5]

Joseph A. Conforti, whose study *Samuel Hopkins and the New Divinity Movement* was instrumental three decades ago in launching the rescue of Edwards's disciples from academic and ecclesiastical obscurity, described the majority of these evangelicals as "small-town Connecticut boys" from modest family backgrounds who succeeded at Yale by dint of intelligence and religious commitment. Of the fifty-five "New Divinity Men" listed in an appendix of his book, forty-seven were Yale College alumni. The eight non-Yale graduates included six (among them Jonathan Edwards, Jr.) who attended the College of New Jersey, where Jonathan Edwards served as president before his untimely death. Two graduated from Dartmouth after it was founded by New Divinity pastor/missionary Eleazar Wheelock. Further, all but six were born or raised in Connecticut or Edwards's town of Northampton, Massachusetts.[6] Although Conforti's list is far from a complete roster of Edwardsian evangelical Calvinists, and a larger list might reveal greater variety of origins, it underscores the fact that the movement was spawned in the Connecticut River Valley. In his study of revivals in western Connecticut, David Kling appends a similar list with biographical sketches of twenty-six New Divinity clergy in Litchfield and Hartford Counties, only five of whom were listed by Conforti. All but three were Yale graduates, with the one Dartmouth graduate, Ebenezer Porter, going on to teach and serve as president of Andover Seminary. In fact, the New England Theology continued throughout its development as a project of a Connecticut Diaspora, against countervailing ideas centered in Boston, to define the religious identity of the whole region.[7]

The ambition of the Edwardsian movement and the geographical extent of its influence was displayed in the front matter of Samuel Hopkins's two-volume magnum opus, *The System of Doctrines, Contained in Divine Revelation, Explained and Defended* (1793). That the books were published in Boston, rather than at a regional press, made a statement in itself. Writing from his Newport, Rhode Island, parsonage, Hopkins intended for this systematic theology to harmonize the views of Edwards and his various disciples, to that point in their development, and to speak both to and for all of New England. In the preface, he exhibited a blend of dogmatic certitude and intellectual humility. Though there may be "many defects" in his presentation of some details of theology, Hopkins had "not the least doubt that the chief and leading doctrines here advanced are contained in the Bible, and are important and everlasting truths." Referring implicitly to the Arminian rationalism of liberal clergy, he argued that any "sentiments, and schemes of doctrine and religion, which are wholly inconsistent with these, and contrary to them, are not consistent with the Bible" and will ultimately lead to "the horrible darkness of atheism itself." On the other hand, acknowledging the dynamic nature of and nuanced differences within the New England Theology, Hopkins insisted that "the truth is great" and human understanding of it was constantly advancing. Hopkins designed his work as an irenic standard for evangelical Calvinists and a weapon against the current wave of the Arminian enemy that had engaged Edwards the generation before, the urban eastern clergy who espoused a reasonable Christianity in tune with the Enlightenment agenda.[8]

> There is no reason to doubt, that light will so increase in the church, and men will be raised up who will make such advances in opening the scripture, and in the knowledge of divine truth, that what is now done and written will be so far superseded as to appear imperfect and inconsiderable, compared with that superior light with which the church will be blessed.

In a demonstration of force, following the preface Hopkins printed the names of more than 1,200 subscribers, individuals who had paid to underwrite publication costs by preordering one or more copies. The list runs to eleven full pages of small type, with two columns per page, before the reader finally reaches the table of contents. The names, including each subscriber's town of residence, are organized by state: Hopkins's original home state of Connecticut produced 165 subscribers, 68 of them ministers and 10 candidates for the ministry. New Hampshire's list contains 60 subscribers, with 20 ministers (one of whom is President John Wheelock, son of Eleazar, of Dartmouth College), one licensed preacher, and four candidates. Vermont includes a total of 56 subscribers, 25 of them ministers and four candidates. Hopkins's current state of Rhode Island, where he served as pastor of the First Congregational Church of Newport, yielded a remarkable 61 subscribers, just seven of whom were clergy (plus one candidate)—and other distinguishing features to be discussed later. Most important of all the states, given the goal to win New England for evangelical Calvinism, was the list of Massachusetts names—a stunning total of 420 subscribers, with 82 clergy, two candidates, and three licensed preachers. Compared with other states (except the unique case of Rhode Island) where the proportion of clergy hovered between one-third to one-half the number of lay subscribers, in Massachusetts the list was weighted in favor of the laity. The number of subscribing ministers was a bit higher in Massachusetts than in Connecticut, but participation of lay subscribers in Massachusetts was much greater both in numbers and in their five-to-one ratio to clergy. Subscribers were also listed for New York, New Jersey, Pennsylvania, Delaware, Maryland,

Virginia, North Carolina, South Carolina, Georgia, Scotland, Ireland, England, and Jamaica. The effect is—and was intended to be—staggering.

The list is not a precise roster of adherents of the New England Theology, nor of a more limited Hopkinsianism. Among the Massachusetts ministers who preordered Hopkins's *System of Doctrines*—and found their names in print when their copies arrived—were at least three from the other side of the line of scrimmage, all Harvard graduates. The Rev. Dr. William Bentley, urbane pastor of the Second (East) Church in Salem, probably ordered a copy because he was genuinely interested in theological discussion and enjoyed remaining on good terms with evangelical colleagues at the Tabernacle Church, however much he might despise their zeal and debate their Trinitarian orthodoxy. Another Massachusetts liberal whose name appears as a subscriber was William Symmes of Andover, whose biographical sketch is included in the Unitarian volume of Sprague's *Annals of the American Pulpit*. He was remembered there for the fact that "subjects of controversy . . . he rarely brought into the pulpit" and for a theology that "accorded rather with Arminius than Calvin, and with Arius than Athanasius." Similarly, Zephaniah Willis of Kingston, according to a eulogy in the *Christian Examiner*, was known for avoiding conflict: "It would not be possible, perhaps, to state his precise religious views," but he was "Unitarian in sentiment" and more practical than doctrinal in his preaching.[9] But these were exceptions; generally speaking, subscribers can be identified as Edwardsian evangelical Calvinists who supported the theological agenda represented by publication of Samuel Hopkins's systematic theology.

William Bentley expressed alarm in a 1790 diary entry at being surrounded "by men called Hopkintonians." In 1808, fifteen years after publication of *The System of Doctrines* and the same year that Andover Seminary was founded, he complained that there existed "one hundred and seventy Hopkinsian ministers in Massachusetts." For more than thirty years, he and other opponents of the movement had watched with dismay as, growing in numbers, their geographical reach extended east from the Berkshires and the Connecticut River Valley. Conforti described the pattern of evangelical pastors serving churches in eastern Massachusetts as "an arc outside the Boston area extending from the old Plymouth Colony to the New Hampshire border."[10]

The clerical distribution noted by Conforti is borne out by the subscription list in Hopkins's systematic theology. Furthermore, as the number of lay subscribers indicates, fertile soil for evangelical Calvinism abounded throughout Massachusetts. Although it was natural in churches with evangelical pastors for leading members to order copies of such a work, the list also includes many members of churches without a pastor. In eastern Massachusetts, they range from churches with one or two (Cambridge, Dorchester, Danvers,

Ashburnham, Wilmington, Malden, Walpole, among others) to churches with three or more lay subscribers (Marblehead, Wenham, Scituate, Taunton, Ashby, and, at the arc's outer edge, Worcester). In the town of Boston, eleven laity (including one woman) supported publication, but apart from Joseph Eckley of Old South Church not a single minister subscribed. Evangelicals certainly occupied pulpits in the immediate Boston area, including Jedidiah Morse at Charlestown. Morse was born in Woodstock, Connecticut, in 1761, graduated from Yale in 1783, and studied theology with Jonathan Edwards, Jr., before ordination at Charlestown in 1789. He became famous for his pioneering work in the field of geography, founded the journal *Panoplist*, and was instrumental in establishing Andover Seminary. But his church was across the Charles River, not in Boston proper, where Old South Church stood as the lone outpost of evangelical Calvinism.[11]

Joseph Eckley was unusual among clergy of the time in that he was born in London, England, immigrating with his family at age seventeen to Morristown, New Jersey, in 1767. After graduation from the College of New Jersey in 1772, he began his ministerial studies with President John Witherspoon. But he was drawn to the Edwardsian expression of Calvinism that Witherspoon had worked to expunge from Princeton. Eckley moved to Bethlehem, Connecticut, as scores of other young men did for thirty years, to study under New Divinity pastor-theologian Joseph Bellamy. The parsonage-based theological curriculum developed by Bellamy and other New England pastors was modeled on the training Bellamy, Hopkins, David Brainerd, and others had received in the home of Jonathan and Sarah Edwards in Northampton. These "schools of the prophets" served at least three functions: professional theological training, generation of an Edwardsian legacy, and "social cohesiveness among the New Divinity men." By living and studying at the Bethlehem parsonage, Eckley grafted himself into the Edwardsian intellectual genealogy. He was licensed to preach by the Presbytery of New York in 1776 and responded two years later to the call from Boston's Old South. Their building was still in disrepair from British army occupation, so his ordination took place at the nearby Stone (King's) Chapel. From its founding as Third Church in 1676, Old South was a bastion of Puritan orthodoxy and, under Thomas Prince's pastorate (1718–1758), promoted the revivals of the Great Awakening. It is likely that the eleven Bostonians who supported *The System of Doctrines* were members of Old South.[12]

The pastor-theologian who most powerfully embodied the New Divinity's advance into eastern Massachusetts was Nathanael Emmons. Born in 1745 in East Haddam, Connecticut, Emmons graduated from Yale College in 1767 and studied theology with two Connecticut pastors, Nathan Strong (father of

Nathan Strong, Jr., just behind Emmons at Yale) in Coventry and John Smalley in New Britain. Licensed to preach in 1769, Emmons received a call to Massachusetts, where he was ordained in Franklin (Wrentham's second parish) in 1773. Franklin may have seemed like nothing but a rural village in southern Massachusetts, not far from eastern Connecticut. But it was also just over thirty miles from Boston, signifying the New Divinity's thrust toward the cultural hub of New England. Emmons exerted extraordinary influence on a new generation of Edwardsian evangelicals through his preaching and, like Bellamy and others, as a mentor of college graduates aspiring to the ministry. The fact that Emmons trained ninety candidates for the ministry, more than any other pastor-theologian, made his Franklin parsonage a center of evangelical Calvinism in eastern Massachusetts.[13]

The New Divinity as a theological movement thus became a web of interpersonal relationships, even a family tree. David Kling describes the clerical bond in western New England, quoting pastor Edward Dorr Griffin, as "the united brotherhood of ministers."[14] The intensity of fellowship may have attenuated somewhat as the movement spread, but the connections remained strong and close. The first three Massachusetts clergy on the list of those underwriting *The System of Doctrines* illustrate this fact, as each life intertwined with Emmons, Hopkins, Eleazar Wheelock, and the Edwards family. The first, David Avery, was born in Norwich, Connecticut, in 1746 and converted under the preaching of George Whitefield. Avery was a contemporary of Emmons at Yale, graduating two years after his friend in 1769. After studying theology with Wheelock at his Indian School in Lebanon, Connecticut (a project supported by Hopkins, building on his experience with Edwards at the Stockbridge mission), Avery served a church in Vermont and as a chaplain in the War for Independence. At age forty he became Emmons's neighbor as pastor of the Wrentham church. Emmons preached at his installation service there in 1786. The second minister, Solomon Aiken, was born in Harwick, Massachusetts, not Connecticut, but studied with Wheelock at newly founded Dartmouth College. After graduating in 1784, he settled as pastor in Dracut, Massachusetts. The third, Samuel Austin, was born in New Haven in 1760. After joining the army as a teenager, he practiced law before matriculating at Yale in 1781, graduating just two years later. He studied theology in the New Haven parsonage of Jonathan Edwards, Jr., who preached at his ordination service at Fair Haven. Austin married Samuel Hopkins's daughter Jerusha and, when he was called to the church in Worcester, Hopkins preached at his installation. Austin went on to edit the works of Jonathan Edwards, became the president of the University of Vermont, and closed his career at Hopkins's old church in Newport, Rhode Island.[15]

Personal roots in Connecticut were not required for membership in the "brotherhood." To the east of Emmons's Franklin church, Jacob Norton's thirty-seven-year ministry at Weymouth was shaped over time by the New Divinity. Norton was born in Abington in southeastern Massachusetts in 1764 and, unlike most of those who became evangelical pastors, graduated from Harvard College (1786). With no direct experience of the religious culture of Connecticut, he was nevertheless surrounded in his youth by the influence of the Connecticut Diaspora through Emmons and other pastors and churches in the New Divinity's arc south of Boston. Mary Kupiec Cayton has shown how, besides personal relationships with evangelical clergy, Norton came increasingly to embrace their doctrine through reading classic Puritan texts and the works of Edwardsian theologians, as "evangelicals produced a world of print that reinforced their common view and shared identity."[16]

The settlement of Connecticut-born and Yale-educated evangelical ministers in eastern Massachusetts was reinforced, in a way that has gone largely unnoticed, by the New Divinity's movement into northern New England. In 1767 Eleazar Wheelock succeeded in raising funds in England and Scotland and moved his Indian school from Lebanon, Connecticut, north to Hanover, New Hampshire, on the Connecticut River. Established as Dartmouth College, the school played a significant role in the spread and legitimization of the movement as it reached to the north. Solomon Aiken was not the only minister on the list of Massachusetts ministers subscribing to Hopkins's *System of Doctrines* to attend college there. Alvan Hyde, born in Norwich, Connecticut, in 1768, graduated from Dartmouth in 1788 and was ordained as pastor in Lee in 1792. Joseph McKeen was born in Londonderry, New Hampshire, and graduated from Dartmouth at age 17 in 1774. He was ordained in Beverly, Massachusetts, in 1785 and became president of Bowdoin College in 1802. Elijah Parish, born in Lebanon, Connecticut, in 1762, graduated from Dartmouth in 1785. He studied theology with Ephraim Judson at Taunton before settling as pastor in 1787 at Byfield, a parish of Newbury, Massachusetts, where he spent his entire career. In addition to his ministry, Judson collaborated with Jedidiah Morse in the publication of several of his geographical studies. Jonathan Strong was born in Bolton, Connecticut, in 1764 and moved to New Hampshire with his parents as a boy. After graduating from Dartmouth in 1786, like Parish he prepared for ordination at Ephraim Judson's Taunton parsonage. In 1789 the church in Randolph, Massachusetts, called Strong as minister and he served his whole career there. Pearson Thurston, a native of Lancaster, Massachusetts, also graduated from Dartmouth in the class of 1787 before studying with Emmons in Franklin and with Samuel Spring in Newburyport. Spring, another leader in the founding of Andover Seminary, was eulogized after his death in 1819 by Andover's Leonard Woods as having "harmonized in the main with Dr. Emmons, with whom he was united in the most intimate friendship."[17]

Emmons himself shared a Dartmouth connection, as the college granted him a Doctor of Divinity degree in 1798. This was an honor that Dartmouth bestowed on several other notable New Divinity pastors, including Chandler Robbins of Plymouth and Stephen West of Stockbridge, both of whom had experience with Native American educational efforts. Robbins, born in Branford, Connecticut, in 1738, graduated from Yale in 1756 and taught at Wheelock's Indian School at Lebanon before preparing for ordination with Bellamy. West was born in Tolland, Connecticut, in 1735, graduated from Yale in 1755, and three years later succeeded Jonathan Edwards at the Stockbridge Mission. Although he originally tilted theologically toward the Arminian position, long discussions with Samuel Hopkins, at that time pastor at nearby Great Barrington, led West to embrace the New Divinity. West became a close friend of Bellamy, Hopkins, and the younger Edwards and, like them, trained numerous candidates for the ministry. After his friend's death, he published *Sketches of the Life of Samuel Hopkins* (1808).[18]

As the Edwardsian family tree stretched its branches, therefore, influence flowed not only from the Connecticut trunk but also from the north and east. Ministers in eastern Massachusetts and at Dartmouth and other centers in northern New England inspired, instructed, and trained a new generation of evangelical Calvinists for the churches of the region and for the wider mission they were beginning to organize. Ebenezer Porter exemplifies this movement. Born in Cornwall, Connecticut, he graduated from Dartmouth in 1792 and trained for the ministry with Bellamy and Smalley. After 15 years as pastor in Washington, Connecticut, in 1812 he moved to Andover Seminary as professor of preaching, serving as president from 1828 to 1832.[19]

The *System of Doctrines* subscription list for the other northern New England state, sparsely-populated Vermont, was the only one in which the ratio of ministers to lay supporters was virtually one-to-one, with 25 clergy (plus four candidates for the ministry) and 26 laity. The congregation with the largest number of subscribers was at Bennington, with four lay members along with the church's pastor, Job Swift. Swift was born in Sandwich, Massachusetts, raised in Kent, Connecticut, and graduated from Yale College in 1756. Prepared for ministry by Joseph Bellamy in Bethlehem, Connecticut, Swift's New Divinity credentials were therefore solid. He served churches in Massachusetts and New York before his call to Bennington in 1786. Most Vermont ministers (20 out of the 25) were the sole subscriber from their congregation. Typical of these were Joseph Bullen of Athens (born in Brimfield, Massachusetts, in 1750; Yale College 1772), Asa Burton of Thetford (born in Stonington, Connecticut, in

1752; Dartmouth College 1777; said to have trained 60 ministers in his parson-age), and Chauncey Lee of Sunderland (born in Salisbury, Connecticut, in 1763; Yale 1784; studied with Stephen West at Stockbridge). The reverse was also true: Many churches without a minister supporting publication (12 out of the total 38 Vermont towns represented) had one or more members who insured that a copy of Hopkins's systematic theology was available in their town.[20]

The most noteworthy name among Vermont subscribers was Lemuel Haynes of Rutland's Second (West) Church. The first African American ordained in a Congregational church, Haynes was born in Hartford and, abandoned by his white mother, raised in a pious household in Granville, western Massachusetts. As a soldier in the Continental Army, in 1776 he wrote the remarkable sermon, "Liberty Further Extended: Or Free thoughts on the illegality of Slave-keeping." Licensed to preach in 1780 by the Litchfield Association, Haynes was ordained five years later in Torrington, Connecticut. Following an evangelistic tour of Vermont, the Rutland congregation called him as pastor in 1788. Haynes was known for his powerful preaching, defense of New Divinity orthodoxy, support of missionary societies, and acute rebuttal of Universalism. Nevertheless, like Hopkins and Edwards before him, in 1818 he suffered the indignity of dismissal by his congregation, after which he served other churches in Vermont and New York.[21]

If the establishment of Dartmouth College and dispersion of Connecticut-born and Yale-educated ministers enabled the movement to spread geographically, developments related to Samuel Hopkins's ministry in Newport, Rhode Island reveal another significant aspect of the evangelical movement. The percentage of lay to clerical subscribers for *The System of Doctrines* in Rhode Island was greater than anywhere else—53 laity to eight ministers (including one candidate). Newport itself skewed the figures, with 42 of the Rhode Island lay supporters located there. This would not be surprising, since Hopkins was pastor of the First Congregational Church, the smaller but more evangelical congregation in Newport. More remarkable is the gender and racial composition of the list of lay subscribers. The columns for Rhode Island posted a separate category of "Free Blacks," four of them residing in Providence and 13 in Newport. Of the African Americans, five were women (Mrs. Wishee Buckminster, Mrs. Jenny Gardner, Mrs. Priscilla Freeman, Mrs. Obour Tanner, and Mrs. Duchess Quamine), all members of Hopkins's church. Eight Newport African American men (Prince Amy, Lincoln Elliot, Newport Gardner, Robert Keith, Congo Jenkins, Adam Millar, Solmar Nubia, and Zingo Stevens) supported their pastor's publication. Four black supporters (Cato Coggeshall, Cato Mumford, Nimble Nightingale, and Bristol Yamma) lived in Providence. The pastors of both Congregational churches in Providence subscribed, but

Joseph Snow of Second Church aligned himself theologically with Hopkins while Enos Hitchcock was more moderate and in 1805 his successor carried First Church into Unitarianism.[22]

In the years leading up to the Revolution, New Divinity ministers started to connect their Edwardsian doctrine of disinterested benevolence with the full humanity of Africans who were shipped to America as slaves. Hopkins first recognized the sin of slavery when he moved from western Massachusetts to Newport in 1770 and witnessed the slave trade for himself. He welcomed blacks into his church, began planning a mission to Africa, worked together with slaves to purchase freedom from their owners, and trained some of these church members as future missionaries. In 1776—the same year that the young soldier Lemuel Haynes preached "Liberty Further Extended"—Hopkins published *A Dialogue Concerning the Slavery of the Africans*. He followed this with *A Discourse Upon the Slave Trade and the Slavery of the Africans* in 1793, coinciding with publication of his *System of Doctrines*.[23]

Hopkins's strongest support throughout his Newport ministry came from a group of women led by Sarah Osborn. Osborn conducted a school in her home where she taught both black and white youth and where an "astonishing" (as she described it) spiritual awakening occurred in 1766. Her Female Religious Society was the backbone of the congregation, was largely responsible for its calling Hopkins as pastor, and sustained him through turbulent times. Sarah Osborn was also a prolific author of biblical commentaries, devotional and theological works, a spiritual autobiography, poetry, diaries, and letters. She published a book, *Nature, Certainty, and Evidence of True Christianity* (Boston, 1755), at age 41, which exemplified the rise of a new evangelical generation after the death of Edwards. Hopkins edited material from her diaries and spiritual autobiography after her death as *Memoirs of the life of Mrs. Sarah Osborn* (Worcester, 1799). A decade later publication of *Familiar Letters, Written by Mrs. Sarah Osborn and Miss Susanna Anthony* (Newport, 1807) suggests her continued influence among New England evangelicals.[24] Fourteen Rhode Island women—nine white, five black—supported *The System of Doctrines*. Hopkins's Newport church was unique in this regard, as just one woman appears on the list for Connecticut, one for Vermont, and nine for Massachusetts (three of whom lived in Stockbridge). A few women's names appear among the states outside New England. While Hopkins was not known as a compelling preacher, and was continually frustrated at his failure to experience large-scale revival in his churches, the list of Newport subscribers testifies to his success in implementing several New Divinity priorities—substantial lay support, involvement of women in evangelistic ministry and theological discussion, and the liberation and evangelization of black Americans.

Publication of subscribers' names was intended not as a mere expression of appreciation but as a political demonstration of the extent of the movement's influence throughout New England and beyond. Most powerfully, then, the list for Rhode Island, with its number of women and prominent column of "Free Blacks," announced the missionary trajectory of evangelical Calvinism in the New Republic. Hopkins argued that the fullest expression of Edwardsian theology would come, not in the Connecticut Valley, Litchfield County, or the Berkshires, but from locations facing out into the world.

13

Jonathan Edwards, Edwardsian Theologies, and the Presbyterians

Mark Noll

IT WAS NO surprise that Presbyterians took a great interest in Jonathan Edwards and the theologians of New England who claimed Edwards as their progenitor. One reason for the interest came from the circumstances of Edwards's life. It was not just that as a young man he had ministered to a Presbyterian church in New York City and then as a mature pastor-theologian agreed to serve as president of the Presbyterian-dominated College of New Jersey (later Princeton University). Even more, after his dismissal from Northampton, Edwards corresponded with leading Scottish Presbyterians about the possibility of moving to Scotland and taking a pulpit in the Kirk. The prospect of Jonathan Edwards theologically active for fifteen or twenty years in the Scotland of David Hume, Thomas Reid, and a young Adam Smith leaves unrealized one of the great might-have-beens in the whole history of Christian theology. Documented as fact from that exchange, however, are the personal preferences that Edwards recorded in a letter from 1750 and that many later Presbyterians loved to quote. While conceding that some things about the Church of Scotland might be improved, Edwards also stated:

> As to my subscribing to the substance of the *Westminster Confession,* there would be no difficulty: and as to the Presbyterian government, I have long been perfectly out of conceit with our unsettled, independent, confused way of church government in this land. And the Presbyterian way has ever appeared to me most agreeable to the Word of God, and the reason and nature of things.[1]

Since Edwards did not embark for Scotland, where those professions about the Westminster Confession and Presbyterian church order would surely have been given a real workout, interested students are left with the history of Presbyterians and Edwards that did take place. The most contentious phase of that history unfolded over the first two-thirds of the nineteenth century as a by-product of intensely argued intramural debates within American Calvinism. But those American debates were also accompanied by ongoing engagement with Edwards from a number of Scottish Presbyterians, perhaps the only instance of sustained European attention to a nonpolitical American thinker before the twentieth century. Although Presbyterians continue to write on Edwards, the intense interest of the earlier period offers the most revealing insight into how Presbyterians assessed the theological significance of Edwards and his New England heirs.[2]

The impetus for founding Presbyterian churches in the American colonies was the desire of Scottish people, migrating directly from the mother country or with a stopover in the North of Ireland, for religion as they had known it at home. Beginning with establishment of the first Presbytery in 1707, American Presbyterians were marked by the standard practices and convictions of churches in the homeland. They were eager to employ well-educated ministers, committed to organization by congregation-presbytery-general assembly, and engaged actively with wider social and political concerns. Their theology was spelled out in the *Westminster Confession of Faith* and *Catechisms* that the General Assembly of the Church of Scotland had adopted in 1647 as its subordinate (after Scripture) confessional standards. Like Presbyterians of Scotland, the Americans also participated fully in many of the era's transnational movements. The history of Presbyterian involvement with Jonathan Edwards and later varieties of Edwardsian theology was largely set by the varied Presbyterian responses to those developments.

The most important were evangelical revival, oppositional (or republican) politics, the Scottish Enlightenment, and rising religious diversity.[3] Connections were straightforward between Presbyterian attitudes toward revivals and republicanism, on the one side, and opinions about Edwards and the later Edwardsians, on the other. In brief, the more directly Presbyterians promoted revival, the more they identified self-consciously with Edwards and his lineage. Likewise, the more fully Presbyterians internalized the republican (and then later the democratic) political culture of the new United States, the more closely they were aligned not so much with Edwards but with the theological line stretching in New England from Timothy Dwight to Lyman Beecher and Nathaniel W. Taylor.

The situation for religious diversity was more complicated since diversity was correlated with the need to address specific theological questions rather than with a theological stance as such. Thus, the more theological diversity Presbyterians encountered, the more pressure existed to spell out which particular aspects of theology from Edwards and later Edwardsians were acceptable and which were not. The pressure was much stronger in the mid-Atlantic states, where propinquity between Presbyterians and Congregationalists as the most self-conscious heirs of Edwards was a fact of life, than in the southern United States or in Scotland.

For the bearing of Scottish philosophy, there are still deeper complications. It is a judgment based on the materials cited below that where principles of eighteenth-century Scottish Philosophy abounded, there Jonathan Edwards's theology did not abound. But this judgment is too simple since it made a great difference whether Presbyterians adopted (or contested) the sentimental ethics of Francis Hutcheson or the challenges to orthodoxy from David Hume or the epistemological conclusions of Thomas Reid or the syntheses of Dugald Stewart. One of the main reasons for the length, bitterness, and confusion of the great battles over Edwards that nineteenth-century theologians at Princeton, Andover, and Yale sustained for more than thirty years was that all participants accepted in relatively simple terms some aspects of the new moral theology that Edwards had not known, or had developed to serve his own larger purposes, or had embraced only after the most rigorous criticism. Those who fought over his legacy most aggressively in the nineteenth century did not exercise such rigor; because their embrace of philosophical principles was more intuitive, their arguments were less compelling.

By contrast, where Presbyterians addressed the various principles of Scottish moral philosophy more self-consciously (as was the case in nineteenth-century Scotland) or when Presbyterians added elements of idealism to Scottish Common Sense (as Henry Boynton Smith did in the United States), then engagement with Edwards moved beyond turf battles to stimulating theological insight.[4]

EARLY PRESBYTERIAN ATTENTION to Edwards in America was laudatory and uncritical. The first professor at Princeton Seminary (the Presbyterians' first theological seminary) was Archibald Alexander; as a youth, he considered himself a "follower" of Edwards. He also seems to have been influenced directly by Edwards on the will, and he later quoted Edwards liberally in his widely circulated volume on religious experience.[5] As early as 1803, Samuel Miller, who later became Princeton Seminary's second professor, also praised Edwards for his book on "Liberty and Necessity . . . the greatest work which the century produced on this subject."[6] Yet when in this early assessment Miller paused to express regret at certain unspecified "extremes" to which Edwards's followers took his ideas, he outlined a position of praising Edwards and disparaging his New England heirs that later conservative Presbyterians developed into a full-scale judgment.[7]

Some twenty years after Miller's early commendation, the most active revivalist associated with the New School wing of American Presbyterianism joined the chorus, but with a different focus and result. When Charles Grandison Finney first perused "Edwards on Revivals and on the Affections" sometime in early 1827, the effect was dramatic. As reported by a witness, Finney "frequently" read Edward on these topics and also "other volumes of that great writer . . . [and] often spoke of them with rapture."[8] Finney was especially taken by the fact that Edwards's account of awakened religion included a defense of evangelistic innovation. By the time Finney published his Lectures on Revivals of Religion in 1835, he had been criticized sharply by Calvinists who regarded those innovations as theologically dangerous. Later, Finney in effect agreed with these critics by rendering a severe judgment on main points of Edwards's *Freedom of the Will*: the "notions of natural ability and inability have no connection with moral law or moral government, and, of course, with morals and religion."[9]

But against his critics on revival, Finney held firm. His defense cited many earlier believers who had also forsaken traditions in order to accomplish necessary spiritual tasks. Prominent in that list was "President Edwards," a "great man [who] was famous in his day for new measures." Finney specified in particular Edwards's refusal to baptize the children of unregenerate parents as a precedent for his own use of protracted meetings and the anxious bench. Just as an "Old School" had stood against the colonial "New Light," so now other petty-minded obscurantists opposed "seeking out ways to do good and save souls."[10]

Conservative Congregationalists were the first to rescue Edwards from Finney's clutches. As early as 1828, Asahel Nettleton and Lyman Beecher argued it was illegitimate to enlist Edwards as an indiscriminate champion of "new measures."[11] When Presbyterians joined the attack, they found even more cause for alarm. Soon after Beecher and Nettleton spoke out, Samuel Miller contrasted the "triumphs of gospel truth" exhibited in the revivals of Edwards's day (especially as set out with proper discrimination in "the fourth part of the venerable Edwards's treatise on that revival") with "the rapid multiplication of superficial, ignorant, untrained professors of religion" and "every species of disorder" associated with the revivals in Miller's own day.[12]

After Finney's lectures on revival were published in 1835, they were accorded a full-scale Presbyterian counterblast in the pages of the *Princeton*

Review. Albert Dod, professor of mathematics at the College of New Jersey, was peremptory: Finney's "use of the name of this great man [Edwards]" to defend his new measures was "to slander the dead." Finney might claim that Edwards sanctioned widespread use of "lay exhortation," but such a claim merely illustrated Finney's "ignorance of Edwards's opinions and writings."[13] Then Dod made a larger claim that broadened out Presbyterian consideration from Edwards to those who were presuming to develop the master's doctrines further for their own day. To Dod, instead, it seemed obvious that "the coarse, bustling fanaticism of [Finney's] New Measures" was "in entire keeping with the theology as well as the religion" then being expounded at New Haven and elsewhere in New England.[14] For some time, Presbyterian conservatives had been observing New England theological trends with concern. When in his criticism of new-measures revivalism Dod linked Finney to the new nation's major theological tradition, as it had developed from Samuel Hopkins and the younger Jonathan Edwards through Timothy Dwight to Lyman Beecher and N. W. Taylor, he made the Old School Presbyterian critique that would be repeated in great detail for a full generation.

It is significant that the first contentions about Edwards in nineteenth-century American Calvinist history concerned revival. Edwards's relationship to the colonial awakenings was a key to much of the controversy over his legacy. Finney and a few other New School Presbyterian revivalists of the Jacksonian era valued Edwards for his promotion of revival even though they repudiated the specific convictions of Edwards's theology. The leading New England Congregationalists and many other New School Presbyterians, by contrast, valued Edwards as a revivalist and contended that their own theological principles had developed from aspects of Edwards's thought coming from his revival experience. Some Old School Presbyterians, especially in the South, were inclined to agree with the Congregationalists and therefore to consider both Edwards and later Edwardsians grossly deviant. In further contrast, a few conservative Congregationalists and the cohort of Old School Presbyterians at Princeton applauded Edwards's specifically theological positions, but they worried that these positions were being compromised by stray remarks of Edwards that later New England theologians greatly distorted. In still another contrast, Scottish Presbyterians, though not agreeing with everything Edwards wrote, nonetheless felt he had been exemplary in combining the strictness of traditional Calvinism, the rigor of intellectual precision, and the experimental piety of revival.

In the United States, questions of theological orthodoxy were complicated by practicalities of ecclesiastical cooperation. Into the first years of the nineteenth century, New England Congregationalists and mid-Atlantic

Presbyterians seemed to share the same basic theological positions. But as the century wore on, the two were pulled in different directions. The course of differentiation was marked by the Plan of Union in 1801, which joined Presbyterians and Congregationalists for the Christianizing of the frontier but was dissolved in 1837 at the same time the Presbyterians broke into Old School and New School denominations.

The result was a tripartite division of American Calvinists: Old School Presbyterians who defined themselves by upholding Westminster theology, New School Presbyterians with some Congregationalists who attempted to uphold historical Calvinism as they made adjustments to American circumstances, and the main body of Congregationalists with some New School Presbyterians who deliberately modified Calvinist traditions in order to address contemporary American conditions. Within each division, there were also differences about how to read Jonathan Edwards. As representatives of these positions staked their claims, the landscape was arrayed for battle.

ONE OF THE era's most intense theological controversies addressed specifically the interpretation of Edwards's theology; it pitted the Old School Presbyterians of Princeton against a variety of New England Congregationalists. The counterpunching represented the most extensive Presbyterian commentary ever published on Edwards and the Edwardsians.

Four publications appearing around the time of the 1837 Presbyterian schism defined the interpretation. First was the appearance that year of Samuel Miller's *Life of Jonathan Edwards* in Jared Spark's Library of American Biography. This laudatory study, one of the first major biographies from outside New England, drew particular attention to Edwards's "majesty of Christian integrity and of Christian conscientiousness" and to his unusual possession of a united "intellectual and moral excellence."[15] The book's extensive praise for Edwards's discrimination and restraint during the first Great Awakening (39–40, 81, 193) drew attention to the revivalistic excesses Miller observed in his own day, excesses that Old School Presbyterians associated with the New School and their Congregationalist allies. Miller's discussion also maintained that Edwards's theology agreed with Old School Presbyterian positions and differed radically from theology as it was being presented by Miller's Congregationalist contemporaries. Thus Edwards's treatise on the will defended with "original . . . arguments" (228) the traditional convictions of Augustine, Luther, "and almost all the Calvinistic writers of Geneva and Holland, during the sixteenth and seventeenth centuries" (224), even though "some of the indiscreet friends of this great man have claimed for him the honor of more entire originality" (223) to support a sense of the will's self-determination that Edwards utterly rejected. Edwards's defense of the classical Augustinian position "has never yet received any thing that deserved to be called an answer" (229).

In like manner, Miller argued that Edwards's book *Original Sin* taught in essence what Princeton also held concerning the atonement: "the immediate imputation of Adam's sin to his posterity" (236).[16] Yet despite what Edwards had actually proposed, "many errorists take shelter under his wing, and are fond of claiming to agree with him" (237) when they deny the imputation of sin and the covenantal union with Adam. To be sure, Miller did feel Edwards was somewhat overly prone to "a spirit of abstruse, metaphysical speculation in discussing Christian doctrine" (247). And among all his works of surpassing greatness, Miller felt the posthumous dissertations on "God's Last End in the Creation of the World" and "The Nature of True Virtue," though harmless in themselves, had led to evil consequences—the first by encouraging a utilitarian conception of happiness and the second by its stress on "love to Being in general." The latter concept was what Miller identified as the root of Samuel Hopkins's misguided principles concerning "disinterested affection" and the professed willingness to be damned for the glory of God (241–244, also 136–140).

On balance, however, Miller concluded that Edwards distinguished himself in the "full and zealous maintenance of the old Calvinistic doctrines, particularly humankind's moral impotence without grace, the sovereignty of God in the dispensation of that grace, and justification solely by the imputed righteousness of Christ" (245–246). Not coincidentally, the doctrines Miller praised Edwards for maintaining were precisely the convictions that Old School Presbyterians felt New Haven and New School Presbyterians were subverting. Miller did not hesitate to make his meaning plain: "Not a few of [Edwards's] professed admirers are, insidiously, attempting to turn his heavy artillery against that very citadel which it was his honor to have long and successfully defended" (248–249). He concluded that if ever a great light of the past had upheld the doctrines of Old Calvinism, even with an occasional excess of metaphysical subtlety, it was Jonathan Edwards.

In the January 1839 number of the *Princeton* Review came the second publication, a hard-hitting attack on several varieties of nineteenth-century idealism. Under the general rubric "Transcendentalism," Albert Dod and one of Archibald Alexander's sons, James Waddell Alexander, excoriated Kant, Coleridge, Fichte, Schelling, Hegel, Victor Cousin, and Ralph Waldo Emerson, whose recent Divinity School address at Harvard had been filled with so much "nonsense and impiety" as to prove its author "an infidel and an atheist."[17] As the essay recited this litany of errors, it paused to reflect on the lineage of New England Congregationalism. Edwards, "this greatest of modern

Christian metaphysicians," had committed New England Calvinists to a speculative "sort of discourse" thanks to his fascination with John Locke (38). Yet he also "stands immeasurably above many who have followed in his steps, and attempted his methods" (38); he was able to achieve "noble" results by plying metaphysics with "a strong hand" (39). But after Edwards's passing, the preference for abstract speculation over patient "unfolding of scriptural argument" led to disaster. The errors arising among those who followed in Edwards's train cropped up everywhere—including the "gross absurdities" (39) of Nathaniel Emmons's hyper-Calvinism, the false views of virtue propounded first by Samuel Hopkins and then by N. W. Taylor, and a poisonous utilitarianism ascribed to Timothy Dwight (39–42). Albert Dod, who once again was identifying Congregationalist errors as the prime agent of theological problems among the Presbyterians, drew a closer link between Edwards and his descendents than had Miller. But along with Miller, Dod and his coauthor exempted Edwards from New Haven's errors, just as Dod had done with Finneyite fanaticism four years before.

The third publication was Charles Hodge's massive *Constitutional History of the Presbyterian Church*, rushed into print shortly after the 1837 schism. Hodge, the third professor at Princeton Seminary, never expressed admiration for Edwards as forthrightly as his older colleagues Archibald Alexander and Samuel Miller. The probable reason was that Hodge began writing about New England theology in the context of the Presbyterian division into New School and Old School. To be sure, Hodge never begrudged "the world-wide fame of President Edwards."[18] And on more than one occasion he held up Edwards's definition of justification by faith as a model.[19] Yet when Hodge turned to Edwards, he usually did so to point out areas either where he erred practically or where he gave theological inquiry a harmful impetus that led later New Englanders astray.

Hodge's *Constitutional History* offered a learned historical justification for Old School positions in the then-current Presbyterian division. The work spent considerable time discussing the colonial awakenings, for Hodge concluded that excesses in those revivals had twisted the entire course of New England divinity. According to Hodge, Edwards's major error was his tolerance for the excessive enthusiasm of the Awakening. Hodge did commend Edwards for what he had written in his *Treatise on Religious Affections* about the need to discriminate true religion from false (67). Still, at least in the revival's early stages, the Northampton pastor was not "sufficiently aware of the nature and effects of nervous disorders" (42); he overlooked the evil of "loud outcries, faintings, and bodily agitations" (66); he approved such exercises "during the time of public worship" (70–71); and he allowed his congregation to regard them "as probable tokens of the favour of God" (72). Significantly, these excesses of enthusiasm led to heightened views of natural human powers that, in turn, nurtured the Arminianism and Pelagianism "over which President Edwards lamented" (58). As he summed up the period, Hodge praised Edwards for coming to his senses and once again acknowledged the helpful strictures of *Religious Affections* (100). Yet even here, Hodge reversed the judgment that most later evangelicals would offer: he suggested that when the antirevivalist Charles Chauncy publicly chastised the radical revivalist James Davenport, and when Harvard and Yale published denunciations of George Whitefield, those critical voices anticipated what the mature Edwards would say (83, 90). According to Hodge, Presbyterian revivalists, such as his own teacher and mentor Archibald Alexander, had always kept their work within the bounds of orthodoxy. Indeed, to show he was not opposed to revival as such, Hodge described the colonial awakenings as "the commencement of a new life" among the Presbyterians, the "vigour of which is still felt in all her veins" (101).

From the pages of Hodge's history emerges an Edwards whom Hodge respected as a theologian, a proper "object of veneration to the Christian public" (61). Yet it was also an Edwards who tolerated enthusiasm. It was an Edwards who appropriated Locke's theory of ideas incautiously, without realizing their idolatrous potential (67–69). And it was an Edwards who encouraged a climate that damaged New England spirituality and eventually threatened the Presbyterian.

Princeton's fourth publication introduced a significant contributor to debates over Edwards. Lyman Hotchkiss Atwater was a New England Congregationalist who was born in New Haven, was baptized in N. W. Taylor's Center Church, and graduated from the Yale Divinity School after study under Taylor. Yet even though Atwater served as a Congregationalist pastor in Fairfield, Connecticut, from 1835 to 1854, his theology was much closer to Princeton than to New Haven. Indeed, as a perceptive student of the general story once put it, Atwater "practically made a career out of criticizing his former pastor's theology."[20] In 1840, shortly after the appearance of Hodge's *Constitutional History*, Atwater published an article in the *Princeton Review* entitled "The Power of Contrary Choice." It was the first of ten full-scale polemics Atwater would publish in the journal in an effort to uphold Westminster Calvinism against various New England alternatives. Atwater published the last of these articles after he moved from Connecticut to become the professor of moral philosophy at the College of New Jersey.

In the course of reviewing a new edition of *Freedom of the Will*, Atwater's 1840 essay refined the Princeton defense of Edwards against the "Edwardseans." Not only did Atwater uphold the traditional Calvinistic reading of this treatise, but he also attacked N. W. Taylor's famous formulation of self-determination, "power to the contrary" (though without mentioning his former teacher by name). This article set the tone for most of Princeton's later efforts: "Who more valiant for the truth, or mighty in counsel and set for its defense than" Edwards? And who more opposed to Edwards than his self-defined successors? "Shall we not heed his counsels as well as revere his name?"[21] Atwater, a product of New England, knew the works of Edwards better than Miller did and felt less concern about the excesses of the Great Awakening than did Hodge. But he nonetheless enjoyed the confidence of these senior colleagues as he set about vindicating traditional Calvinism as well as the reputation of Edwards.

From the late 1830s to the late 1860s, Princeton Presbyterians and New England Congregationalists regularly hurled literary thunderbolts at each other in an effort to claim Edwards as their own. Although this exchange was one of the most consequential debates in American theological history, a hasty survey must suffice here.[22]

Time and again, the Old School Presbyterians insisted that the entire drift of New England theology after Edwards had moved to embrace what Charles Hodge described as three "anti-Augustinian" principles: "First, that all 'sin consists in sinning' " (or, as Hodge interpreted New Englanders as saying, that morality came from action and had nothing to do with nature, either regenerate or redeemed), "secondly that the power to the contrary is essential to free agency" (or that true freedom required, as N. W. Taylor contended, the liberty of indifference that Edwards had attacked in his *Freedom of the Will*), and "thirdly, that ability limits responsibility" (or that human responsibility ended where people could choose freely, with freedom defined as the ability to act against character).[23]

New Englanders made two responses. The ablest Congregationalist to provide a detailed exposition of both Edwards's thought and the thought of later New England theologians was Edwards Amasa Park of Andover Seminary. He acknowledged that the New England line of theology beginning with Samuel Hopkins and Jonathan Edwards the Younger had developed Edwards's teaching on sin, freedom, and human responsibility. But he challenged Hodge's interpretations of the development, contending it was neither "anti-Augustinian" nor alien to Jonathan Edwards's central teachings. The response of theologians associated most closely with Yale's N. W. Taylor was indifferent about whether Hodge's three points were anti-Augustinian, but they contended that the three assertions were true and had come to New England via Edwards's authentic teaching.

The New Englanders were most convincing when they refuted Princeton's claim that Edwards's *The Nature of True Virtue* was superfluous to his theology and a prompt that sent New England off into error. In the dispute over this work, however, the limitations imposed by Scottish philosophy on all nineteenth-century disputants was at its most manifest. Edwards had himself taught that humans enjoyed a common moral sense capable of recognizing beauty in moral relations, responding to natural conscience, and experiencing instinctive affections like pity or love of family. He could write about the moralists of his day that "some of the arguments made use of by these writers do indeed prove that there is a moral sense or taste, universal among men, distinct from what rises from self-love."[24] But he was also fastidious, as almost no American in the nineteenth century was fastidious, discriminating between this natural moral sense and "true virtue"; the former was open to all humankind, the latter present only where hearts were turned in love to God as purest being.

Archibald Alexander laid the foundation for Princeton's position by following the Scottish philosophy and teaching that a universal common moral sense provided the basis for ethical judgment in every creature. As summarized by Lefferts Loetscher with quotations from Alexander, through "reason and experience" humans discovered the "dictates of conscience," or "the law of nature, written on the hearts of all men." Moreover, these "first principles or intuitive truths in morals" were "as certainly and as universally believed, as any mathematical axioms."[25] Furthermore, these universal moral intuitions revealed the moral qualities of actions in and of themselves, irrespective of the consequences of these acts. Alexander's convictions represented an extension of the moral philosophy that John Witherspoon had introduced at Princeton in the 1770s and that William Graham, a Witherspoon student, had passed on to Alexander in the 1780s. (Later Presbyterians never mentioned that when he came to Princeton from Scotland in 1768, Witherspoon replaced texts by Edwards and other Christian idealists with works reflecting the commonsense intuitive realism he brought with him from Scotland.[26]) Because Alexander was so deeply committed to ethical common (or universal) sense, he regarded Edwards's proposals in *The Nature of True Virtue*, and their extension in Hopkins, Dwight, and Taylor, as mistaken. Alexander read Edwards's stress on benevolence as referring to the happiness of humanity in the universe. And he interpreted this emphasis as a thoroughgoing utilitarianism: we should do good because it will increase the amount of moral happiness in the world.

In an article from 1852, Lyman Atwater upheld Alexander's criticisms of New England ethics, but he also tried to show that Edwards's mistakes in *True Virtue* did not justify later New England errors on the will and human nature. Immediately, an anonymous essayist in *Bibliotheca Sacra* responded convincingly that Edwards's theory of virtue was "the result of those remarkable intuitions of religious truth, with which God so wonderfully favored him, in the early stages of his Christian life, and [which] was in its mature form given to the world as a bulwark of the great fundamental doctrines of natural and total depravity, regeneration, etc."[27] But then the essayist posed an embarrassing question to Princeton: How was it that the Old School Presbyterians, who insisted so unbendingly on an original sinfulness that regarded humans as morally unable to seek salvation, postulated a universal moral sense that provided a natural foundation for virtue?[28]

In point of fact, repeated Princeton comments on *The Nature of True Virtue* failed to recognize that Edwards grounded his reasoning in the supernatural work of God among the elect. The Princeton theologians, though fervent defenders of original sin and divine election, were Scottish moral philosophers on virtue. As Atwater quoted Alexander, "Virtue is a peculiar quality of certain actions, which quality is perceived by the moral faculty with which every man is endued."[29] To Atwater, in fine Scottish phrases, "moral rectitude is as much a part of the nature of things, and as much an ultimate good, and a simple uncomprehended idea, as beauty, truth or happiness"; and "the power of perceiving what is . . . right or morally good, [God] has implanted in all moral agents, by enduing them with conscience, or the moral faculty."[30] To Princeton, true virtue was approached through universal human nature. On this basis, Edwards's conception was faulty, even though he devised his explanation precisely to keep real virtue within the framework offered by the doctrines of original sin and supernatural regeneration. A century after Edwards, his would-be heirs in New England gleefully pointed out Princeton's inconsistency. Princeton protested its desire to uphold the divine centrality in salvation and life that Edwards had also advocated, yet based its ethics on a system in which divine activity was not required.

New England's claim for Edwards was, however, compromised by its own application of Scottish thinking. In one of his long essays trying to rescue Edwards from the Old School Presbyterians, Park contended that New England theology grew from Edwards, as well as from "the philosophy of Reid, Oswald, Campbell, Beattie, Stewart . . . the philosophy of common sense." The Scottish contribution was "to develop 'the fundamental laws of human belief' . . . which so many fathers in the church have undervalued." The result was that "the metaphysics of New England theology . . . is the metaphysics of common sense." As a follower of this theology, Park could also be proud that "the New England system is not only scriptural, but is scriptural science."[31] By this he meant it used the insights of the Scots concerning moral axioms and Baconian theory construction to better interpret the Bible.

When Princeton continued to attack N. W. Taylor for deviating from Edwards's Calvinism, an exasperated response came from Noah Porter,

Taylor's son-in-law and a Congregationalist pastor, moral philosopher, and eventual president of Yale. In Porter's account, Taylor put the general principles of Scottish moral philosophy to use even more consistently than E. A. Park. Thus, Taylor taught "as first moral truths that are self-evident" the very convictions that Hodge labeled as anti-Augustinian: "that no man ought to be punished or incur penal evil except for his own sin—that neither the sin nor the holiness of one can be imputed to another—that the cause or condition of sin cannot be sinful—that an act, in order to be morally good or evil involves "the power to the contrary."[32] The final result, when Taylor "used conscience and common sense to assail traditionary and fantastic speculations," was an advance for the Christian cause that paralleled the advance under Edwards and that greatly benefited the church.[33] Progress with Taylor came when he escaped from "scholastic metaphysics" and relied on "the moral intuitions" to interpret Scripture in accord with "conscience and common sense."[34]

In sum, Princeton theologians rejected a position of Edwards because they were committed to the same philosophical principles New Englanders deployed even more comprehensively to modify Edwards in directions that Princeton considered heretical. "Axioms of the mind," "conscience," "common sense," and "moral intuition" built a hidden link between the antagonists but also masked the chasm that separated all of them from the careful distinctions of Jonathan Edwards.

IF PRESBYTERIAN VIEWS on Edwards and the Edwardsians received their fullest airing in the tussle between Princeton and New England, this exchange by no means exhausted Presbyterian commentary. A few Old School stalwarts, for example, agreed that nineteenth-century New England theology flowed directly from the eighteenth-century Edwards and, therefore, concluded that Edwards too was lacking. Samuel Baird, a prominent Old School minister, author, and ecclesiastical historian, held that Edwards's arguments in *Original Sin* concerning God's continuous creation of the universe not only violated "all our intuitive apprehensions" but were also "inconsistent with the teachings of consciousness." It rendered Edwards's theology pantheistic and caused Edwards to make God the author of evil. Moreover, this error was of a piece with Edwards's mistaken views on virtue and the happiness of the universe. Edwards, Baird concluded, "was led astray, by the subtlety of his own philosophy" and so bore responsibility for the heresies that had so thickly populated New England since his day. Because Baird shared Princeton's convictions about theology and New England's about its own history, Baird found nothing redeemable in Edwards.[35]

The South's leading Presbyterian theologian, James Henley Thornwell, could occasionally commend Edwards, as he did when reviewing one of Baird's books.[36] But mostly Thornwell thought Edwards was a fountain of mistakes: his theory of the will made God the author of sin and failed to explain "self-determination," his view of original sin still left God the author of evil, his theory of human unity in Adam "set at defiance the plainest intuitions of intelligence," and his definition of virtue as "being" turned sin into a "phantom."[37] An even stronger dismissal came from R. H. Dabney, who denounced Edwards completely as a fount of unnecessary and harmful innovations.[38]

For a very different perspective, the New School Presbyterian Henry Boynton Smith often expressed gratitude for Edwards from his post at Union Seminary in New York City. A mediator by temperament and conviction, Smith drew theological assistance from self-described New England Edwardsians, from Old School Calvinism, and from contemporary Europe. Although Smith had almost as many objections to N. W. Taylor's theology as did Princeton, his theology was unusual among his American contemporaries in trying to begin with the person and work of Christ. Princeton, by contrast, regularly moved from authority—whether creedal or scriptural—to Christ, while for New England the move was from consciousness to Christ.

Smith was a lifelong admirer of Edwards, with a particular fondness for the *History of the Work of Redemption*. In this exposition Smith appreciated especially Edwards's interpretation of all past and all future as an outworking of God's activity in Christ. As Smith read him, Edwards showed how "in this redemption, and here alone, is to be found the centre of unity to human history," with human kind viewed "in its two prime and fundamental relations to the first and to the second Adam, and all converges upon the idea of a redemption, prepared, purchased and applied, running through the whole of man's history, to its consummation in eternity."[39]

Smith also seems to have followed Edwards on the complicated questions of original sin, imputation, and atonement.[40] Princeton, which advocated immediate imputation (humanity became sinful because it stood in covenant relation with Adam), held that Edwards had erred with a doctrine that looked like mediate imputation (humanity was sinful because all humanity sinned in Adam). These Old School Presbyterians felt Edwards's position opened the way for New England's attack on imputation (human union with Adam and then the believers' union with Christ). New England, by contrast, moved beyond imputation of any sort to affirm that human guilt came from individual acts of sinning, an affirmation the Congregationalists traced to comments by Edwards in *Original Sin* and *The Nature of True Virtue*. In opposition to those contrasting positions, Smith was able to see what Princeton, with its fear of the supposed implications of immediate imputation, could not: in reality Edwards affirmed both immediate and mediate imputation.[41] Smith did the same. Moreover, his move seemed to come from his reading of Edwards. According to Smith, "his leading works may all be grounded around one idea: man in his relation to divine grace."[42] Because his reading of Edwards was not forced into the antitheses that marked the New England-Princeton dispute, Smith defended a more complex, and perhaps more satisfying, theory of original sin and the universal effects of sin and also the believer's union with Christ.

As much as Smith benefited from Edwards, he could still level gentle criticism. Although "we have not looked upon his like again," Edwards still slighted "the objective facts" of Christianity in favor of "the subjective aspects." In Smith's opinion, Edwards worked harder on questions relating to the effects of God's grace in the individual than on questions about the outworking of that grace itself. Because Smith self-consciously aimed for a Christocentric theology, he questioned the balance of Edwards's efforts.[43]

Yet as Smith set about constructing his own theology, he also praised Edwards for combining commitment to modern leaning and fidelity to historical Calvinism, the same commendation that Smith's Scottish Presbyterian contemporaries would also highlight. For Smith, modern learning meant the organicism of German idealism, especially as mediated through the *Vermittlungstheologen* F. G. A. Tholuck and Augustus Neander. In a landmark essay from 1849, Smith singled out Edwards as one who saw "the necessity of bringing the subtlest researches of human reason into harmony with the truths which lie at the basis of all piety. . . . Intellect and faith acted together in him, distinct, yet as consentaneous as are the principles of life and the organic structure of our animal economy."[44] In his efforts to make this same attempt, Smith followed where Edwards led. Neither philosophy without faith (which was Smith's harsh assessment of New Haven) nor faith without philosophy (his milder criticism of Princeton) provided for the nineteenth century what Edwards had offered to his.[45]

In Scotland, Edwards was well known before his death, and he continued to be read widely into the twentieth century. Scottish interest in Edwards was not a mystery since Scotland shared a common Calvinistic heritage rooted in the English Reformation. Edwards's personal ties with Scotland were also extensive. He gave serious, if not prolonged, consideration to Scottish offers for clerical employment after his dismissal from Northampton, and he also corresponded with several leaders in the Kirk, especially John Erskine, who later became a major figure in the Church of Scotland's evangelical party and a dedicated promoter of Edwards's writings.[46] Many Scots also remembered that Edwards's *Humble Attempt to Promote Explicit Agreement and Visible Union of God's People, in Extraordinary Prayer, for the Revival of Religion and the*

Advancement of Christ's Kingdom on Earth (1747) was a response to a memorial with the same goal from Scotland.

The three most conspicuous Scottish theologians who expressed indebtedness to Edwards were Thomas Chalmers (1780–1847), Scotland's leading divine during the first half of the nineteenth century; John McLeod Campbell (1800–1872), its most creative theologian of the era; and James Orr (1844–1913), its most responsible theological conservative at the end of the century. The three shared a common respect for Edwards, made a common criticism of his works, and yet developed his insights in very different ways.

Edwards's impact on Thomas Chalmers was especially profound. Chalmers had been a young ministerial student, with a predilection for the spirituality of the Moderate party and a susceptibility to the radical notions of William Godwin, when in 1796 he encountered Edwards's *Freedom of the Will*. The result was electric. A fellow student recorded that Chalmers "studied Edwards on Free Will with such ardour, that he seemed to regard nothing else, could scarcely talk of anything else, and one was almost afraid of his mind losing its balance."[47] As an old man, Chalmers recalled that there was

> no book of human composition which I more strenuously recommend than his Treatise on the Will,—read by me forty-seven years ago, with a conviction that has never since faltered and which has helped me more than any other uninspired book, to find my way through all that might otherwise have proved baffling and transcendental and mysterious in the peculiarities of Calvinism.[48]

Edwards's lasting bequest to Chalmers was twofold. He gave Chalmers a sense of how God's omnipotence was manifest in every aspect of creation. He also greatly impressed Chalmers by embodying both intellectual acuity and spiritual fervor. Chalmers eagerly took up the phraseology of an American correspondent when he wrote in 1821 that Edwards was "perhaps, the most wondrous example, in modern times, of one who stood richly gifted both in natural and spiritual discernment."[49]

Not as much is recorded about the effects when Campbell and Orr read Edwards. But they offered the same respect for his learned piety. Orr, speaking at the two hundredth anniversary of Edwards's birth, remembered that, "it is forty years and more since I first made my own serious acquaintance with Edwards in poring over his treatise on The Freedom of the Will . . . and I have no doubt that the trains of thought then set in motion have continued to vibrate in my conscious or subliminal self till the present hour." Yet to Orr as to Chalmers, the crucial thing was that "the intellectual and spiritual or mystical power in Edwards . . . exist [sic] in inseparable union, and even his speculative insight . . . cannot rightly be understood, if divorced from the spiritual perception from which a large part of the light arises."[50]

For all their respect, the Scottish Presbyterians made a common criticism of Edwards. Chalmers expressed it indirectly when writing about his adolescent encounter with *Freedom of the Will*:

> I spent nearly a twelve-month in a sort of mental Elysium, and the one idea which ministered to my soul all its rapture was the magnificence of the Godhead, and the universal subordination of all things to the one great purpose for which He evolved and was supporting creation. I should like to be so inspired over again, but with such a view of the Deity as coalesced and was in harmony with the doctrine of the New Testament.[51]

James Orr seconded this opinion with an even sharper comment: Edwards's piety, for him, possessed "a certain strain . . . as if he were bent on disciplining himself to live at a height of religious emotion which it does not lie in the weakness of human nature to sustain." In short, Edwards's zeal toward God limited "the range of his human sympathies."[52]

John McLeod Campbell also employed Edwards with great respect, but not slavish imitation. Campbell remains an important figure in the history of the Kirk because of a well-publicized theological trial in 1831, which led to his being dismissed from the ministry, and because of the creativity of his *The Nature of the Atonement* (1856), the book that summarized his heterodox proposals. A good part of Campbell's *Atonement* carried on a dialogue with Edwards, particularly in an effort to render Edwards's conception of Christ's redeeming work more human. Built into Campbell's constructive theology, therefore, was an answer to the gentle criticisms raised by Chalmers and Orr.[53]

For Campbell, following Edwards's course meant exchanging the older views of a legal, penal atonement for an ethical, subjective one. Campbell's move sprang from practical need. Several of his most faithful parishioners were trapped by the fear that they were not among the elect, and others seemed to pursue good works only in order to obtain divine favor. In response, Campbell proposed a new application for the meaning of Jesus' death for sinners. Was it true, as the *Westminster Confession* held, that Christ died only for the elect? Did his death not rather suggest possible reconciliation between God and all humanity? Could not believers think of Christ's sacrifice as a supererogation of suffering that opened the way to God?

In working out his positive answer to these questions, Campbell made specific use of a suggestion Edwards raised in a treatise entitled *The Necessity and Reasonableness of the Christian Doctrine of Satisfaction for Sin*, published with Edwards's collected works in the nineteenth century. There Edwards suggested that for the greatness of evil "either an equivalent punishment or an equivalent sorrow and repentance" must exist. Although Edwards did not follow up the second possibility, Campbell took it seriously and argued that the atonement was best explained by the infinite nature of Jesus' sorrow for sin. This solution pushed Edwards's Calvinism out of its own orbit, away from an objective to a subjective view of the atonement (not what God did for humanity directly, but indirectly by affecting human consciousness of God). Although Campbell's view took the enormity of sinfulness less seriously than had Edwards, Campbell still manifested a fruitful effort to put Edwards to use in a situation where the problem was not, as for Edwards, waking the unconcerned to their spiritual need, but assuring the faithful of the certainty of God's love.[54]

None of the Scottish Presbyterians felt the need manifest in the United States to vindicate, claim, condemn, or exonerate Edwards. None of them bothered much with the work of the later Edwardsians. Rather than competing for Edwards, they drew together piety, learning, and doctrine in a manner similar to how Edwards had worked. These Scottish Presbyterians did not master the Edwards canon as it was mastered for imitation and rebuttal in the United States. But for giving their version of Presbyterian theology a bracing example, Edwards's legacy was just as fruitful in Scotland as in America.

LOYALTY TO THE *Westminster Confession* kept all nineteenth-century Presbyterians, whether Scottish or American, relatively close to the main outlines of historical Calvinism. What they did with that historical Calvinism could of course vary enormously, as the distance between J. H. Thornwell and John McLeod Campbell attests. As more-or-less self-consciously traditional in their Calvinism, however, Presbyterians of all sorts were better prepared than most of Edwards's New England heirs to benefit from his theology. Some of the New Englanders, especially N. W. Taylor, and a few of the Presbyterians, especially Henry Boynton Smith, were inspired by Edwards's intellectual subtlety. Smith and the Scots appreciated and at least partly imitated Edwards's acute philosophical self-consciousness. Edwards's own comprehensive supernaturalism, his deep piety, his instinctive Augustinianism, and his intense scripturalism (a subject neglected in this chapter as it has been sadly neglected in much other work on Edwards) kept Edwards relatively close to a traditional Calvinism similar to the outline of the *Westminster Confession*. When any or all of these traits receded among later New Englanders, it was relatively easy for them to slide away from traditional Calvinism. Among American Presbyterians, instinctive

Augustinianism was their strongest link to Edwards.[55] As indicated by the titles cited in note 2, Presbyterian engagement with Jonathan Edwards continues to benefit those who make the effort. In the nineteenth century, no Presbyterian was worse off for taking Edwards seriously, and some were considerably better.

14

Great Admirers of the Transatlantic Divinity

SOME CHAPTERS IN THE STORY OF BAPTIST EDWARDSIANISM

Michael A. G. Haykin

It w[ould] be well if all Christians w[ould] labor earnestly after the investigation of truth, without being unduly influenced either by their attachment to old ideas and phrases on the one hand, or by the affectation of novelty on the other.

JOHN RYLAND, Jr.[1]

IT WAS AS an advocate of revival that Jonathan Edwards (1703–1758) was first read by English Baptists in the "long" eighteenth century. Representative in this regard was Benjamin Beddome (1717–1795), the Baptist minister of Bourton-on-the-Water in the Cotswolds. A local revival that took place under his ministry in the early months of 1741 was quite significant for the shape of his long ministry at this church, which lasted from 1740 till his death in 1795. Around forty individuals were converted, including John Collett Ryland (1723–1791), a leading, though eccentric, Baptist minister in the latter half of the eighteenth century.[2] It may well have been this taste of revival that helped make Beddome a cordial friend to those who were involved in the evangelical awakenings of the mid-eighteenth century—men such as George Whitefield (1714–1770) and the Mohegan Indian preacher Samson Occom (1723–1792)[3]— and gave him an ongoing hunger to read of revival throughout the English-speaking world. Certainly, within a year of the Bourton awakening Beddome purchased a copy of Edwards's *The Distinguishing Marks of a Work of the Spirit of God* (1741), which would have given him a sure foundation for thinking about and laboring for revival.[4]

Other English Baptist divines who read Edwards over the next thirty years included the Yorkshire Baptists John Fawcett (1740–1817) and Joshua Wood (1734–1794),[5] Caleb Evans (1737–1791), principal of Bristol Baptist College in the West Country during the 1780s and early 1790s, and Robert Hall, Sr. (1728–1791) of Arnesby, and his precocious son and namesake, Robert Hall, Jr. (1764–1831).[6] What is quite striking, however, is that there is no explicit evidence that the doyen of the English Baptists, John Gill (1697–1771), almost an exact contemporary of Edwards, ever read the American divine. Edwards did note his reading of Gill,[7] but it appears to have been a one-way street. An older Baptist historiography would have put this down to Gill's hostility to revival, but further study is really needed to ascertain why this was the case. If Gill, the leading Baptist theologian of the English Baptist community for a good portion of the eighteenth century, seems to have evinced little interest in Edwards, the same cannot be said of the next leading divine in this Baptist community, Andrew Fuller (1754–1815), whose thought dominated the late-eighteenth- and early-nineteenth-century Particular Baptists on both sides of the Atlantic and who began to read Edwards in the late 1770s.[8] For a good number of Baptists in Fuller's day, so intertwined was the Englishman's thought with that of his mentor, mention of the one inevitably led to the other. Joseph Belcher (1794–1859), the editor of Fuller's complete works, was confident that these works would "go down to posterity side by side with the immortal works of the elder president Edwards, a man truly like-minded with the English writer."[9]

"A Great Admirer of the Transatlantic Divinity"

An excellent vantage-point from which to see the range of influence that Edwards and his New Divinity disciples had on Fuller and his English Baptist contemporaries is a controversy that erupted in the Baptist congregation of Olney, Buckinghamshire, after the death of their pastor, John Sutcliff (1752–1814), one of Fuller's closest confidants and, like Fuller, an ardent Edwardsian. In January 1815, a certain William Hawkins (1790–1853), a graduate of Edinburgh University, came to Olney to supply the pulpit on the recommendation of Fuller.[10] By early April, though, Hawkins's preaching had caused considerable unrest in the congregation. As Hawkins admitted in a letter to Joseph Kinghorn (1766–1832), there were a number in the church who were quite displeased with his preaching.

These are they who worshipped Mr. Sutcliff and they object to me that I do not preach about the Law, only about the Gospel, and because I cannot enter into the absurd scheme of disinterested love and all the dogmas of the American school. Mr. Sutcliff was a great admirer of the Transatlantic divinity and drank deep into their theory. He was also very diligent in circulating their writings among his people and now the happy fruits begin to show themselves.[11]

Hawkins's criticism here was directed against Sutcliff's deep-seated commitment to the theology of Edwards and that of his New England heirs, in particular, Joseph Bellamy (1719–1790) and Samuel Hopkins (1721–1803). In mentioning what he called the "absurd scheme of disinterested love," however, Hawkins probably had in mind a focus more properly attributable to Hopkins and his immediate followers than to Edwards and the other divines who fall under the denotation of the New Divinity.[12]

In another letter Hawkins wrote to Kinghorn in the middle of April 1815, his criticism was even more biting.

Mr. Sutcliff . . . laboured to inculcate all the subtleties of the American school. He pointed out at great length the metaphysical distinction between moral and natural inability—dwelt much upon the Law of God as a transcript of the divine character as lovely, beautiful etc., etc., whereas Christ and his cross were but subordinate topics. . . . When persons under serious convictions went to Mr. Sutcliff to enquire of him about the way of salvation, the first question he put always was, "What do you think of the Law and of God as a lawgiver—is he not lovely, beautiful in this character? Have you read Bellamy and Hopkins and the rest? I'll lend you them." Not a word of encouragement or comfort to poor, cast-down, despairing sinners. This, of course, kept people back and I suppose for the last ten years not about a dozen people have been added to the church.[13]

What Hawkins stated in this text about Sutcliff's pastoral style obviously came from someone within the Olney congregation who was disgruntled with either Sutcliff himself or his theology. A number of Hawkins's assertions here are clearly wrong—for instance, the actual figure of new members between 1805 and Sutcliff's death in 1814 was forty-three[14]—yet in identifying Sutcliff as one profoundly influenced by the theology of Edwards and of his disciples Hawkins was spot on.[15]

Fuller was deeply disturbed by this turn of events. Hawkins's criticism of Sutcliff's theology was at once an attack on his theological views and his own Edwardsianism. By this time, though, Fuller was a dying man. In the last letter he ever sent to another friend, John Ryland, Jr. (1753–1825), which he dictated on April 28, 1815, only nine days before his death, he gave his answer to Hawkins and others of this man's persuasion.

> We have some, who have been giving out of late, that "If Sutcliff and some others had preached more of Christ, and less of Jonathan Edwards, they would have been more useful." If those who talk thus, preached Christ half as much as Jonathan Edwards did, and were half as useful as he was, their usefulness would be double what it is. It is very singular that the [Baptist] Mission to the east should have originated with men of these principles; and without pretending to be a prophet, I may say, if ever it falls into the hands of men who talk in this strain, it will soon come to nothing.[16]

In other words, to take Edwards as a theological mentor was to learn from a man whose writings were supremely Christ-centered, focused on the work of his cross and the glory of his person. Moreover, Fuller felt that the rectitude of Edwards's shaping of Sutcliff's principles lay in its tangible fruit, namely the Baptist Missionary Society, in which Sutcliff and Fuller had played major formative roles.

Eight days after Fuller's death on May 7, Ryland—who, like Sutcliff and Fuller, was an unrepentant Edwardsian—preached his friend's funeral sermon. In it he made a point of quoting the entirety of Fuller's last letter to him, and thus made public the Kettering Baptist's refutation of Hawkins's charges. When Ryland eventually published the funeral sermon, he added a postscript, in which he sought to provide a clear explanation of the important distinction between "those religious affections, which are founded on the transcendently excellent and amiable nature of divine things as they are in themselves, and those which are primarily founded on a conceived relation to self-interest," an Edwardsian sentiment if ever there was one. His two closest friends were gone, and the responsibility of defending their shared theological convictions—convictions by which they had lived and labored together, and which had been given shape and substance by the writings of Edwards and other New England authors—now wholly devolved upon him. Near the conclusion of the postscript, Ryland thus wrote: "If I knew I should be with Sutcliff and Fuller tomorrow, instead of regretting that I had endeavoured to promote that religion delineated by Jonathan Edwards in his treatise on *Religious Affections* and in his *Life of David Brainerd*, I would recommend his writings, and Dr. Bellamy's . . . with the last effort I could make to guide a pen."[17] As Hawkins had said of Sutcliff, Ryland was "a great admirer of the Transatlantic divinity."[18]

"All the Dogmas of the American School"

In this minor controversy we see a number of issues raised that reveal some of the main ways in which the thinking of Edwards and the New Divinity—the "dogmas of the American school," as Hawkins put it—had an impact on the English Baptists. There was Edwards's distinction between natural and moral inability, found especially in his *Freedom of the Will*, which enabled Fuller in *The Gospel Worthy of All Acceptation* (1785, 1801 2nd ed.) to argue with biblical reasoning for indiscriminate preaching to all and sundry, what came to be called the free offer of the gospel. With the aid of this distinction, Fuller also demonstrated that faith in Christ was the duty of all who heard the gospel.[19] The larger ambience of this entire discussion was undoubtedly the issue of human agency, given fresh urgency by various voices of the Enlightenment.

Then, the Olney controversy touched on the Edwardsian emphasis on the key place of the affections in the Christian life. Ryland singled out the spiritual classic *A Treatise Concerning Religious Affections* (1746) as being at the heart of the religion he and his Baptist friends wished to promote. Following Edwards and the New Divinity, the English Baptists argued that even as unbelief, the forthright rejection of the gospel, involves an aversion to the truth, faith in it must include love and receptive approbation of the truth.[20] "The very essence of Scriptural knowledge," Fuller wrote, "consists in the discernment of Divine beauties, or the *glory of God in the face of Jesus Christ*."[21] In perfect alignment with Edwards, these English Baptists were convinced that "faith as doctrine is incomplete without fruition in felt experience."[22]

It was in his book *Religious Affections* that Edwards touched on what became one of the most controversial aspects of his thinking and that of the New Divinity: true Christian spirituality, Edwards argued, loves God for who he is in himself rather than for what he does for the sinner. This is the notion of "disinterested love," and especially through its Hopkinsian expression it kindled a firestorm of controversy in England. Contrary to the impression of Hawkins that Sutcliff and his friends were totally undiscerning in their adoption of this view because it came from the mouths of their mentors, Ryland actually wrote to Samuel Hopkins in the year the latter died and disputed with him on this very point:

> What call have they [i.e. Christians] to be willing to be damned, when God assures them Christ is able & willing to save them? and can be glorify'd more in their Salv[ation] than in their Damnation? It also seems strange that a Man sh[ould] from *Love to God*, be willing for ever to *hate* God, & blaspheme him.—That a sinner ought to own the perfect

Equity of his Condemnat[ion], and to consider the very Sanction of the Law as an expression of divine Equity and Love of order, etc. I readily admit—But do we not puzzle people needlessly, to require them to be willing to be eternally *tormented*, & even eternally *wicked*, when Christ came on purpose to save them both from torment and sin?[23]

Ryland also mentioned Edwards's life of Brainerd as being central to the Edwardsian heritage he and his fellow Baptist treasured. For instance, when William Carey (1761–1834)—at the heart of the missionary movement Fuller mentioned in his final letter to Ryland and a close friend of the trio of Fuller, Ryland, and Sutcliff—drew up a bond of agreement for the missionary community at Serampore in 1805 with his co-workers, he specifically pointed to Brainerd as a model of piety:

That which, as a means, is to fit us for the discharge of . . . laborious and unutterably important labours, is the being instant in prayer, and the cultivation of personal religion. Let us ever have in remembrance the examples of those who have been most eminent in the work of God. Let us often look at Brainerd in the woods of America, pouring out his very soul before God for the perishing heathen, without whose salvation nothing could make him happy. Prayer, secret, fervent, believing prayer, lies at the root of all personal godliness.[24]

Brainerd, through the medium of Edwards's pen, became "the principal model of early British missionary spirituality."[25] In fact, the Baptists had their own Brainerd: Samuel Pearce (1766–1799), whose remarkable mission-minded piety led Fuller to tell his wife Sarah after her husband's death: "Memoirs of his life must be published: he is another Brainerd."[26] Fuller's prayer in this letter—"Oh, that we all may emulate him!"[27]— became a reality throughout the nineteenth century as his own memoir of Pearce went through numerous editions on both sides of the Atlantic.

One area of Edwardsian influence not mentioned in the Olney controversy had to do with the understanding of the atonement. Although Fuller used the language of penal substitution with regard to the atonement to the end of his life,[28] his preferred language about the cross grew to be that of the governmental theory. A version of this model was propounded by the Dutch jurist Hugo Grotius (1583–1645), and for this reason it is often denominated the Grotian version, though there are substantial questions about whether or not the model as it develops is fully in line with Grotius's thinking about the death of Christ. Moreover, as Oliver Crisp has handily shown, the governmental view of the death of Christ that received a warm welcome in New England among the New Divinity, cannot be regarded as identical to that passed down as the Grotian view. Both adhere to a penal, non-substitutionary view of the atonement, but that of the doctrine of the New Divinity—and Fuller—is developed within a specifically Calvinistic *mentalité*.²⁹ Edwards himself published nothing that promoted the governmental view, though some scholars, notably Allen Guelzo, have argued that the American divine laid the foundations for the New Divinity doctrine in his private notebooks and *Miscellanies*.³⁰ Benjamin B. Warfield and George Ella have vigorously disputed this particular link between Edwards and his New Divinity followers,³¹ though Guelzo points out that Edwards was quite willing to contribute a preface for *True Religion Delineated* (1750), written by Joseph Bellamy. In this standard exposition of New Divinity theology, Bellamy blazed the trail that other New Divinity thinkers such as Hopkins, John Smalley (1734–1820), Stephen West (1735–1819), and Jonathan Edwards, Jr. (1745–1801) would take with regard to the atonement. Whatever the elder Edwards's actual view of the atonement, that of his New Divinity followers is explicitly governmental. For them sin is regarded primarily as flouting the moral rule of God as the governor of the universe. In order to maintain the honor of his government, God therefore has to punish sin. However, since God is also a God of benevolence and mercy, he finds a way whereby sin can be punished and the honor and majesty of his government upheld: Christ lays down his life, displaying God's holy aversion to sin and his unalterable determination to punish it.

Fuller was avidly reading the New Divinity writers on the atonement from the mid-1790s onward.³² As a result, Fuller argued in *The Calvinistic and Socinian Systems Examined and Compared* for a view of the atonement that is unmistakably governmental:

> God had love enough in his heart to save sinners without the death of his Son, had it been consistent with righteousness; but that, as receiving them to favour without some public expression of his displeasure against their sin would have been a dishonour to his government, and have afforded an encouragement for others to follow their example, *the love of God wrought in a way of righteousness*; first giving his only begotten Son to become a sacrifice, and then pouring forth all the fulness of his heart through that appointed medium.³³

But the "pivotal doctrine" in Fuller's teaching about the cross was his argument that Christ's atoning death was sufficient for all, though truly efficacious only for the elect. As E. Brooks Holifield notes, this all-sufficiency of the cross further buttressed Fuller's argument that it was the duty of all to believe.³⁴

"Moderate Calvinists"

Not long after Benjamin Beddome read one of Edwards's treatises on revival in the early 1740s, the Massachusetts Baptist Isaac Backus (1724–1806) discovered his fellow American's writings. Though Backus's roots lay in the Congregationalist establishment of New England, he became a Baptist in 1751 after reading a well-known defense of believer's baptism by the English Baptist Samuel Wilson (1702–1750). The works of "our excellent Edwards," as Backus called him, helped him in crafting an argument for religious toleration in Massachusetts—a good number of Backus's treatises, the first substantial corpus of American Baptist thought, were devoted to this subject—as well as providing him with principles to respond to the twin threats of Arminianism and antinomianism.[35] However, Backus never accepted the governmental view of the atonement so beloved of Edwards's New England disciples.

Much more Edwardsian in this regard was another Massachusetts Baptist, Jonathan Maxcy (1768–1820), who was the youngest college president of the period when he was appointed at Rhode Island College (later Brown University) in 1791. Eleven years later he moved to New York State after being called to succeed Jonathan Edwards, Jr., a paradigmatic figure of the New Divinity, as president of Union College in Schenectady. His final move was in 1805 when he assumed the presidency of South Carolina College in Columbia (later the University of South Carolina), thereby importing Edwardsianism into Baptist circles in the south. One of Maxcy's most famous sermons was his two-part "A Discourse, Designed to Explain the Doctrine of Atonement" (1796), in which he referenced the younger Edwards and argued that Christ's death is an obligatory punishment by God on behalf of sinners primarily because "punishments are necessary in God's moral government of the universe." His atoning work thus satisfies public justice in that it "presented the law, the nature of sin, and the displeasure of God against it, in such a light, that no injury would accrue to the moral system, no imputation would be against the righteousness of the great Legislator, though he should forgive the sinner, and instate him in eternal felicity."[36]

Among the Southern Baptists, William B. Johnson (1782–1862), the first president of the Southern Baptist Convention and its "single most influential architect," was also an ardent advocate of this governmental view of the atonement, which he appears to have learned from Maxcy when Johnson lived in Columbia between 1809 and 1811.[37] In a sermon he preached before the Charleston Association in South Carolina on Monday, November 4, 1822, Johnson spoke of the death of Christ in unmistakable New Divinity terms. The cross, he told his hearers, contains "the strongest expression of Jehovah's abhorrence against sin, an irrefragable evidence of his immaculate holiness," and it must not be regarded as "the payment of the sinner's debt on the principles of pecuniary or commercial justice, but a satisfaction to moral justice, to open the way for the consistent exercise of mercy."[38] By 1848, Johnson was pleased to tell James S. Mims (1817–1855), professor of theology at Furman University, that most South Carolina Baptists were followers of the New Divinity, or, as he put it, "moderate Calvinists."[39] This remark came in the midst of one of the most serious controversies in the history of the South Carolina Baptists, involving a number of aspects ranging from student housing and personalities to New Divinity theology. The latter came into play when it became known that Mims rejected the doctrine of imputation of sin as well as imputation of Christ's righteousness to the believer—both marks of some New Divinity teachers—and Johnson sought to defend the Furman professor. The Baptist newspapers of Virginia and both North and South Carolina were filled with details of the controversy, with both Johnson and his main opponent, James L. Reynolds (1812–1877), a one-time colleague of Mims, claiming Andrew Fuller for support.[40] Reynolds deemed Mims heretical in his view of imputation but failed to secure his dismissal from Furman. Yet, as Gregory A. Wills has noted, the controversy did signal a substantial turning of the tide against the New Divinity among Southern Baptists. When Mims died in 1855, the trustees at Furman replaced him with James Petigru Boyce (1827–1888), who became the president of the Southern Baptist Theological Seminary a mere four years later.[41] Although Boyce admired an Edwardsian like Fuller as "a man of the clearest perceptions, and of remarkable power of precise statement,"[42] his own Calvinism was far more traditional. It was rooted in seventeenth-century categories of thought typified by the Second London Confession of Faith (1677/1688), which Boyce knew through the Charleston/Philadelphia Confession, and in the teaching of Charles Hodge (1797–1878), under whom Boyce studied at Princeton from 1849 to 1851.[43]

"Drinking out of Fuller's Spring"

Another, though earlier, controversy also played a role in raising concerns about Edwardsianism. In 1830 the Georgia Baptist Jesse Mercer (1769–1844) published a series of ten letters that were directed against views expressed by Cyrus White, the minister of Bethlehem Baptist Church in the Ocmulgee Association in Georgia, which had been made public in White's *A Scriptural View of the Atonement* (1830). White argued for universal application of the atonement and the fact that humanity, though fallen, possessed complete freedom to choose or not to choose to follow Christ. In reality, White's soteriology was a variant of evangelical Arminianism.[44] In describing Christ's death and its effects, White also employed the governmental theory of the atonement and appealed to the writings of Andrew Fuller. When some Georgia Baptists came to the conclusion that Mercer, a prominent Baptist leader in Georgia, had imbibed similar views and was "drinking out of Fuller's spring with White," Mercer decided to respond with a collection of letters that would both detail his own view of the atonement and demonstrate that "Mr. Fuller . . . [has] been grossly misrepresented."[45] With lengthy passages cited from Fuller's corpus—a body of writings that Mercer happily acknowledged were "prized as standard works of divinity, on both sides the Atlantic"[46]—Mercer ably demonstrated that, far from being among Fuller's faithful followers, White actually would have been considered by the British Baptist to be a theological opponent.[47] Mercer admitted that Fuller, like other Edwardsians, "contends for the atonement, as made to law and justice, as satisfaction for a crime, and not as payment of a debt," but he cogently showed that Fuller "never thought of denying imputation, or even substitution."[48] In fine, Mercer employed Fuller's Edwardsian distinction between natural and moral ability along with the more traditional Calvinistic perspective on particular redemption to refute White.[49] Yet the fact that, in this controversy between White and Mercer, both sides could appeal to Fuller does reveal how Fuller and his Edwardsian theology could be clearly misunderstood.[50]

"He Always Speaks so Sweetly of Christ"

What is noteworthy about this pathway of Baptist Edwardsianism in America is that by the nineteenth century Andrew Fuller appears to have been the main conduit by which the ideas of Edwards and his New Divinity followers made their way into Baptist life and thought.[51] And by the late 1850s Francis Wayland (1796–1865), the former president of Brown University in Rhode Island, was able to report that adherence to Fuller's brand of Edwardsianism had become "almost universal" among the Baptists in the "northern and eastern States."[52] In the South, though, as has been seen, controversy raised burning questions about the theological viability of the New Divinity, and to a certain degree the orthodoxy of Andrew Fuller, who had been influenced by New Divinity writers. Many of the major Southern Baptist theologians of the latter half of the nineteenth century preferred to find their theological moorings in an older expression of Calvinism, one more tied to the confessional heritage of the seventeenth century than to the revivals of the eighteenth.

Edwards and Fuller continued to be read, but more for their piety—their lives of Brainerd and Pearce, for example. Southern Baptists would have heartily affirmed what the Northern Baptist John Williams (d. 1825), the Welsh pastor of the second-oldest Baptist work in New York City, Oliver Street Baptist Church, said on the day of his death: "I love President Edwards, he always speaks so sweetly of Christ."[53] But many of them would also have endorsed what the influential Georgia Baptist Patrick Hues Mell (1814–1888), twice president of the Southern Baptist Convention, opined about Edwards's confidant and first biographer, Samuel Hopkins: Mell could not view Hopkins as a trustworthy theological guide, for he was sure that Hopkins should not be "acknowledged as a Calvinist at all."[54]

15

"A German Professor Dropped into the American Forests"

BRITISH, FRENCH, AND GERMAN VIEWS OF JONATHAN EDWARDS, 1758–1957

Michael J. McClymond

JONATHAN EDWARDS'S WRITINGS were known on the far side of the Atlantic Ocean from the 1730s onward. English clergymen sponsored the original London publication of the *Faithful Narrative* (1737). John Wesley and the British Methodists were early readers of Edwards's works. Treatises such as *Religious Affections* (1746), *Life of Brainerd* (1749), *Freedom of the Will* (1754), and *Original Sin* (1758)—followed by posthumous works such as the *History of Redemption* (1774) and the *Two Dissertations* (1765)—were all widely read in Britain and in continental Europe. To be sure, the reception accorded to the works was lopsided. The response to *Freedom of the Will*, for instance, was disproportionate compared to Edwards's other writings. Yet the same might be said regarding his American reception. The British and European receptions, though, were neither random nor inexplicable. Interpreters used his texts and ideas to address questions current in trans-Atlantic contexts. This essay seeks to sketch a few of the ways in which British and European authors interpreted Edwards, and, having done so, interpreted themselves as well.

Underlying much of the trans-Atlantic discussions of Edwards—at least prior to the early twentieth century—was a presumption that the British and European cultures were originative and normative while American culture was derivative and imitative. If Britain and Europe were like a Himalayan range of intellectual excellence, then Edwards was Mount Kilimanjaro, rising high above the surrounding plains and conspicuous in his solitary eminence.

On the presumption of British or European cultural superiority, Edwards was an anomaly, the "lonely genius." Immanuel Fichte in 1850 referred to him as "this solitary thinker of North America."[1] In an influential essay first published in 1876, Leslie Stephen wrote, "He was, one might fancy, formed by nature to a German professor, and accidentally dropped into the American forests."[2] British and European authors not only imagined a trans-Atlantic *comparison* but also a *contest* of cultures. Dugald Stewart wrote, "In logical acuteness and subtlety he does not yield to any disputant bred in the universities of Europe."[3] America's David faced off against the European Goliaths. Yet if British and European authors were measuring the stature or greatness of America in their appraisals of Edwards, they were also seeking a core or essence of American thought. Some felt they had discovered in Edwards a "representative man" who embodied a national ethos. Another common trope was to play off Jonathan Edwards and Benjamin Franklin as two "representative men" who together captured American culture in its pious and secular aspects.[4]

The discussion here is limited to works written in three nations: Britain (comprising England, Scotland, and Wales), France, and Germany. In addition, this essay considers American authors who received academic training in Europe, wrote on Edwards in German or French, or primarily engaged a European audience. This includes John Henry McCracken, William Harder Squires, and Mattoon Monroe Curtis. McCracken and Squires wrote dissertations on Edwards in Germany and in German, and Curtis—though writing on Edwards in English—did so under the tutelage of a German philosopher. These American writers shed light on European attitudes toward Edwards.

The ensuing discussion treats just two major themes in the British and European reception of Edwards: his metaphysics and philosophy, and his revivalism and eschatology. Much can and should be said about the impact of Edwards's Calvinism among eighteenth- and nineteenth-century British authors. Yet because of space constraints, and because chapters in this volume by Mark Noll and by Michael Haykin already treat this theme, the present one does not discuss the reception of Edwards's Calvinism except briefly to touch on the British Baptists and their interpretations of Edwards's revival theology and eschatological views.

Since this essay limits itself to the period ending in 1957—the bicentennial of Edwards's death and the commencement of Yale University's *Works of Jonathan Edwards*—it will not engage such contemporary British and European authors as Miklos Vetö and Oliver Crisp, who are both discussed elsewhere.[5] All French- and German-language sources here are cited in English translation, and the translations are my own.

Prisoner of the Past: Leslie Stephen's Interpretation of Edwards

A British man of letters helped to shape American views of Edwards. Among the most influential interpretive essays on Edwards during the nineteenth century was a forty-five-page piece contained in Leslie Stephen's *Hours in a Library* (1876). From the time of its first publication (followed by numerous republications), everyone seriously interested in Edwards felt obliged to read it. Stephen's essay created a template for later American authors, including Alexander V. G. Allen, Vernon Parrington, Ola Winslow, and Perry Miller.

Stephen begins with Edwards and Franklin as two "normal representatives" from which the "genuine Yankee" derives. He notes that Franklin and Edwards took differing attitudes toward the phenomenon of lightning, Edwards seeing it as a manifestation of God's power and Franklin seeking to comprehend it scientifically. Edwards's philosophy thus did "not harmonise with the dominant current of the time." Stephen spoke of Edwards dismissively, calling him "a speculative recluse, with little faculty of literary expression, and given to utter opinions shocking to the popular mind." Stephen's basic approach to Edwards might be described as a salvaging operation, an attempt to find something of value amid the debris. Edwards had merit, said Stephen, as a "connecting link" between the "expiring Calvinism of the old Puritan theocracy" and "what is called transcendentalism."[6]

Stephen portrayed Edwards as a man trapped by his Calvinist heritage and presuppositions: "The Puritan assumptions were so ingrained in his nature that the agony of mind which they caused never led him to question their truth." He was excessively self-conscious and self-analytical yet believed that "this constant cross-examination of all your feelings, this dissection of emotion down to its finest and most intricate convolutions, was of the very essence of religion." Though Edwards's accounts of religious conversions "seem stale and profitless to us," it is "rather touching"—said Stephen—to see the "awe-stricken reverence" with which he accepted them. One notes Stephen's use of "us," in reference to the presumably sympathetic reader.[7] Stephen notes that *Freedom of the Will* is Edwards's "main title to philosophical fame" and yet has "the faults natural to an isolated thinker" or a "philosophical recluse." Chief among these is logical overkill, attempting not only to win the argument but to overturn every aspect of his opponent's arguments. "The book reads," says Stephen, "like a verbatim report of those elaborate dialogues which he was in the habit of holding with himself." Yet it was easy for him to gain the victory in arguments in which he was "at once opponent and respondent." Another mark of Edwards's intellectual isolation, writes Stephen, is that he engages the Arminian and yet "appears to be unconscious of the existence of a genuine sceptic," like Hobbes or Hume, who will not find any appeal to the text of scripture to be convincing. "His mind, acute as it was, yet worked entirely in the groove provided for it."[8]

Stephen turns to Edwards's mystical aspect, insisting that "Calvinism, logically developed, leads to Pantheism." God's sovereignty in salvation may be extended to all of nature. Yet Edwards's error lies in his inconsistency: "He is a kind of Spinoza-Mather . . . he sees God in all nature, and yet believes in the degrading supernaturalism of the Salem witches." Ultimately Edwards remains inexplicable, for it is "as clear as it is singular that so acute a man should have suffered his intellectual activity to be restrained within such narrow fetters." Placed in different circumstances, he might have developed a "system of metaphysics" as influential as those of Hume or Kant. Edwards was "away from the main currents of speculation, ignorant of the conclusions reached by his most cultivated contemporaries, and deriving his intellectual sustenance chiefly from an obsolete theology," and so "his mind never expanded itself freely." In sum, "he is still in bondage to the dogmas of the Pilgrim Fathers." Yet underneath "the crust of ancient superstition," one finds an "ennobling" morality and "elevated" theory of the universe.[9]

Stephen's essay seems to have set a direction for elite opinion on Edwards from the 1870s to the 1940s. Vernon Parrington's 1927 essay "The Anachronism of Jonathan Edwards" echoed Stephen's statements regarding Edwards's outmoded and obsolete theology.[10] Acknowledging Edwards's intellectual potential and his failure to develop it, Stephen laid the groundwork for the later "tragic" interpretation found in Ola Winslow's 1940 biography. She wrote that "his bondage seems almost a tragic pity."[11] Winslow used Leslie Stephen's word—"bondage"—in the same way that Stephen did and to describe the same thing, namely, Edwards's attachment to Calvinist doctrine. Perry Miller sounded the same ideas in 1949, commenting that "the life of Edwards is a tragedy."[12] It would be difficult to prove that Winslow, Parrington, and Miller were directly dependent on Stephen's essay, but there were striking parallels. In any case, it is clear that Stephen anticipated these later authors. His essay seems to be the first to bring together a cluster of related ideas: Edwards's intellectual genius, his "bondage" to Calvinist dogma, the "tragedy" of his life, and his obsolete theology with its flashes of brilliance. No nineteenth-century American interpreter seems to have brought together these ideas in the way Stephen did. British opinion shaped American views.

It is noteworthy that Leslie Stephen was the father of novelist Virginia Woolf and that he bequeathed the house in London in which Bloomsbury artists and authors held their evening *soirées* from the early 1900s into the 1920s.[13]

Stephen's essay on Edwards might be classified as proto-Bloomsbury. Like Lytton Strachey's *Eminent Victorians* (1918), it offered a sophisticated debunking of conventional piety. Edwards's beliefs, for Stephen, were palpably wrong and morally repugnant; they needed no refutation. To say that an idea shocked the sensibilities of a well-bred Englishman was argument enough. Like the later Bloomsbury set, Stephen presupposed that moral sense and aesthetic taste went hand in hand. The culturally evolved would be morally discerning.[14] Thus his critique was largely based on stylistics. Edwards was not so much logically wrong as he was in bad taste—like someone in outmoded clothing. For an Englishman such as Stephen, Edwards's failure was a distant occurrence. Yet, for American interpreters, his failure affected American culture and so took on "tragic" dimensions in Winslow's and Miller's biographies.

Necessitarian Logician: Trans-Atlantic Interpretations of Edwards's Philosophy

The early reception of Edwards's philosophy was shaped by the fact that that "The Mind" was not published prior to 1829 when it appeared within Sereno Dwight's biography of Edwards. This text offered the clearest indication of Edwards's philosophical idealism and yet was not available for about seventy years after Edwards's death. The published selections from the *Miscellanies*— first appearing in 1793—were primarily concerned with apologetics, and there was little there to indicate his broad range of metaphysical arguments, opinions, and speculations. Because of this publication history, the scope of Edwards's philosophical reflection was not known for several generations. What is more, publication of "The Mind" put Edwards philosophically out of step with the dominant trends of American thought in the early 1800s. In America, Scottish commonsense philosophy was well established in most educational institutions by this time. With the exception of some Romantics, followers of Coleridge, and proponents of German philosophy, few readers in the English-speaking world were at first interested in Edwards's idealism. Only toward the end of the 1800s, after philosophical idealism carved out a place for itself in France and England—having then declined in Germany—did one find a surge of interest in Edwards's idealism and its possible sources. Prior to this point, when most authors wrote of his "philosophy" they were referring to the metaphysics of *Freedom of the Will*. That "philosophy" was generally understood as necessitarian.[15]

The stress on *Freedom of the Will* helps to explain a seemingly curious feature in British accounts of Edwards's philosophy. This is the regular association of Edwards with philosophical or religious skeptics such as Thomas Hobbes,

Anthony Collins, and David Hume. Despite Edwards's effort in *Freedom of the Will* to distinguish his theologically based concept of the will's determination from notions of materialistic and physical determinism, the difference Edwards had insisted on was generally lost on his educated British readership. This may have been due in part to differences in the philosophical climate in Britain as compared with America. Among the American elite, Hobbes and Hume never made much headway until well into the twentieth century. A more faith-friendly version of empiricism—offered by Scottish thinkers— carried the day during the nineteenth century. Yet, in the British context, Hume's religious skepticism and his necessitarian views of the will were more of a live option, and they colored much of the philosophical response to Edwards. When *Freedom of the Will* appeared in Scotland, a "curious cross-fight" occurred when "Home [i.e., Henry Home, or Lord Kames] and his friend wished to shelter themselves under the Calvinism of the Church of Scotland."[16] Edwards himself sharply distinguished his views from those of Lord Kames in two 1757 letters he wrote to his Scottish correspondents.[17]

The Unitarian Joseph Priestley held that Calvinism, properly speaking, never denied human choice but simply asserted that human beings chose wrongly. In *The Doctrine of Philosophical Necessity Illustrated* (1777), Priestley traced metaphysical determinism back to Thomas Hobbes rather than to Calvin and the Calvinists. Priestley went on to laud Edwards as the first Calvinist to abandon traditional Calvinistic views and align himself with philosophical necessity as taught by Hobbes and Collins. British defenders and British opponents of Edwards both aligned him with those—like Hobbes and the deists—whom Edwards had disavowed in *Freedom of the Will*.[18]

The Scottish philosopher Dugald Stewart linked Edwards with Collins, commenting, "It is remarkable how completely Collins has anticipated Dr. Jonathan Edwards, the most celebrated, and indisputably the ablest champion of the scheme of Necessity who has since appeared." Stewart spoke of Anthony Collins's necessitarianism (and by implication of Edwards's) as possibly even "more dangerous" than that of Spinoza, because of its "high strain of mystical devotion."[19] Along similar lines, Samuel Taylor Coleridge in *Aids to Reflection* (1829) insisted that man's spiritual life takes place "not *by* the Will of Man alone; but neither *without* the Will." In Coleridge's eyes, "the doctrine of modern Calvinism, as laid down by Jonathan Edwards . . . represents a Will absolutely passive, clay in the hands of the Potter, destroys all Will, takes away its essence and definition." For "the Necessitarian Scheme" errs by "subjecting to its Mechanism the moral World no less than the material or physical," and in effect denies the very notion of "Spirit": "Now as the difference of a captive and enslaved Will, and *no* Will at all, such is the difference between the *Lutheranism* of Calvin and the Calvinism of Jonathan Edwards."[20] A much more positive spin on Edwards's *Freedom of the Will* appeared in William Hazlitt: "No metaphysician can read it without feeling a wish to have been the author of it."[21]

An early French Catholic response to Edwards also highlighted the theme of necessitarianism. M. Gregoire, in *Histoire des sectes religieuses* (1829) offered a catalogue of such religious groups as "Dissenters," "Familists," "Semi-Jews," "Swedenborgians," and "Tremblers." Among them he includes "Necessitarians or Hopkinsians," with the explanation that "one calls 'necessitarians' all those who propose that moral beings are moved by necessity." Edwards's teaching here appears not as a philosophical opinion but as a form of religious deviance. Gregoire regarded philosophical necessity and Calvinistic predestination as virtually identical, and so he classified Edward and Hopkins as necessitarians along with Hobbes, Hume, Kames, and Priestley.[22] Henry Bargy in 1902 mentioned Edwards while discussing "the psychology of fatalism"; "It was the doctrine of necessity," wrote Bargy, "that prolonged Edwards's influence after his death." Aligning Edwards with Ralph Waldo Emerson and Henry James, Bargy saw these American thinkers as teaching that human beings act out of the fullness and intensity of their heart's desires.[23]

Another French work, Frédéric De Rougemont's *Les deux cités* (1874), examined *History of Redemption* as a work in the philosophy of history. Characterizing Edwards as the Augustine or Bishop Bossuet of North America, De Rougemont nonetheless judged that Edwards's idea of the papacy's impending downfall was difficult to justify in light of the events of Edwards's day. From his interpretation of biblical prophecies, Edwards taught that both the papacy and Islam would be overthrown, the Jews would be converted, and a glorious Christian era would follow. De Rougement aptly noted that "the American pastor seems to have had no presentiments of the coming political revolutions" (i.e., the American and French revolutions). De Rougemont's reading was more generous than that of Gregoire, and yet De Rougemont intimated that the facts of history stood against Edwards's anti-Catholicism and his belief in a coming, global triumph of Protestant Christianity. The Catholic Church would endure.[24]

By the late nineteenth century, Edwards's philosophical idealism began to receive attention. James McCosh, in *The Scottish Philosophy* (1875), judged that several Lockean thinkers had shifted toward idealism—George Berkeley, Edwards, Samuel Johnson, etc.—and yet "idealism has never struck deep into the American soil." Scottish philosophy had greater influence in America. Edwards's problem was his intellectual isolation: "His opinions might have been modified, had he been brought more fully into contact and collision with other thinkers." McCosh presumed that Edwards's thought was out of step with that of the earlier Calvinists, making it both philosophically and theologically untenable: "Many think he has overlooked an essential freedom of the mind, acknowledged by Calvin, Owen, and the greatest Calvinistic divines, and revealed by consciousness."[25]

Georges Lyon's *L'Idéalisme en Angleterre au Dix-Huitième Siècle* (1888) was among the most important philosophical studies of Edwards prior to the mid-1900s. Presupposing Edwards's cultural isolation in America, he asked how much Edwards might have accomplished if he had not been born in a "half-savage" region. Under more favorable circumstances he might have taken his place between Leibniz and Kant among the "founders of immortal systems." Instead he offered a "sublime yet barbarous theology that astonishes our reason and offends our heart." A key element in Lyon's argument was his claim that Edwards's idealism was dependent on that of Berkeley, though it was also more problematic than Berkeley's. Lyon discusses Edwards in a way that makes him sound like Spinoza. Rejecting human agency, Edwards left nothing "contingent or arbitrary" and "each soul . . . vanishes into the exhaustible ocean of the Idea." He was no longer able to preserve the distinctness of human beings, and "his immaterialism is inevitably entangled and confounded with pantheism."[26]

Although French-language scholars continued to discuss Edwards in the early twentieth century, there was little new in the French literature for several decades.[27] It was not until Miklos Vetö's *Le pensée de Jonathan Edwards* (1987) that a major French work on his thought appeared.[28]

At the end of the 1800s and into the early and mid-1900s, Edwards's philosophy received heightened attention from German scholars and from American scholars studying in Germany.[29] John Henry McCracken, an American, authored a German-language dissertation on Edwards's idealism that took issue with Lyon's views. A. C. Fraser in 1871 and Georges Lyon in 1888 had argued that Edwards's idealism derived from Berkeley, but McCracken in 1899 affirmed what had become the dominant American view—set forth by Sereno Dwight in 1829, by Moses Coit Tyler in 1878, by George Park Fisher in 1880, and Noah Porter in 1885—that "the idealism of Jonathan Edwards sprang from the same foundation as that of Berkeley," and yet Edwards developed his thinking in parallel with Berkeley and not in dependence on him.[30] The American view ultimately carried the day and became the accepted opinion among editors of the Yale edition of Edwards's *Works*.[31] Nevertheless, one suspects that nineteenth-century American scholars who argued for Edwards's originality were motivated as much by national pride as they were by any textual analysis.

At the outset of the twentieth century, two divergent philosophical inter-pretations of Edwards appeared in Germany, the one comparing him to Schopenhauer, and insisting that Edwards's thought was essentially a philos-ophy of will or volition, and the other comparing him with Kant, and finding points of comparison between their idealisms. In his German language disser-tation, William Harder Squires asserted that "Edwards passed on the most com-plete theory of the will from the standpoint of causality that English-language literature has been able to produce." This was a "pure, pantheistic, speculative teaching on the will" that understood God's essence as consisting in an exercise of volition. The identification of God as will was "the central point in Edwards's speculative metaphysic of the will," which rendered all of nature an expression of the divine will. Schopenhauer conceived of the "universal will" as a "blind force," leading him into a "hopeless pessimism." Though Edwards's thought, like that of Schopenhauer, ended in "gloomy pessimism," it had the advan-tage of affirming that God orders all things according to wisdom.[32] Squires went on to edit a quarterly journal devoted to Edwards—*The Edwardean*—that ran through several issues in 1903–04 before it expired. Though Squires was unsuccessful in recruiting other authors (he wrote all the essays for his own journal!) he sought to demonstrate Edwards's influence on American thought, embed him in a larger history of philosophy, and initiate a new philosophical movement inspired by Edwards that was theistic rather than secular.[33]

Strikingly different from Squires's interpretation was that of Mattoon Monroe Curtis. Seemingly unacquainted with the *Miscellanies*, and attempt-ing to assimilate Edwards to Kant, Curtis wrote that Edwards "does not put forth any demonstration of God's existence, but asserts that the understand-ing is incapable of giving any proof." Curtis claimed as well that "Edwards and Kant make no radical distinction between morality and religion" and that both "have essentially the same doctrines of sin and of grace"—which are startling assertions for those who know the thinkers being compared. Speaking of an "anthropological motive" in Edwards, Curtis wrote "that God is the true self write large and that his attributes are experienced desirable qualities raised to infinity," a statement that makes Edwards sound somewhat like Friedrich Schleiermacher. Yet Curtis was on firmer ground in insisting that value the-ory was fundamental for Edwards, that aesthetic themes dominated, and that God alone existed as a true substance, while nature was permeated with God's presence.[34]

Early-twentieth-century German authors on Edwards's philosophy included Eric Voegelin in 1928 and Gustav Müller in 1950. Voegelin studied in the United States on a scholarship and later emigrated during the Third Reich. Like many European students of America, Voegelin was looking for continuities in American thought, and he found that a "formal affinity exists . . . between the theories of substantive unity of the self and the world in [Charles Sanders] Peirce, [William] James, and [George] Santayana, and Puritan mysticism as espoused by Jonathan Edwards." He saw a "substantive unity of the self and the world" among these American authors. Edwards had commenced a process of "the separation of dogma from mysticism," so that "the perilous superiority [of God] disappears, and the religious life is dissolved in the immediate relationship to divinity, in a sequence of ecstasies that do not require dogma." In support, Voegelin cited Columbia University philosopher Frederick Woodbridge, who asserted that the *Two Dissertations,* written near the end of Edwards's life, represented a break with Calvinism and marked his transition into "mystical pantheism." Voegelin's most sweeping claim was that all of Edwards's "comments and notes serve merely to solidify and explain some of the points touched on in 'On Being.' "[35] Whereas Squires had identified Edwards's God with will, Voegelin identified Edwards's God with being and associated this notion of being with mysticism.

Voegelin's argument anticipated Perry Miller's 1940 essay "From Edwards to Emerson." Miller there proposed that Puritanism had always contained a mystical element and that Transcendentalism effected a separation of mysticism from the Calvinist dogmas hindering its expression.[36] A dozen years before Miller's essay, Voegelin argued that a separation of mysticism from Calvinism was already under way in Edwards's writings.

Gustav E. Müller's *Amerikanische Philosophie* (1950) offered a wide-ranging account of Edwards's thought. Müller described him as "at once the first and last philosophical Puritan in America" and also "the strongest, most original philosophical head [i.e., thinker] in the New World." He identified "necessary being" as Edwards's foundational concept. The core problem in his thought was the reconciliation of his "logical philosophy" with his "mystical, erotic inclination." Müller thus concurred with Voegelin, who saw being as the center of Edwards's philosophy and affirmed a tension between "logic" (or "dogma") and "mysticism." Human dependence on God, for Edwards, concerned an "absolute relationship" and was not about "a subjective feeling" (*subjectives Gefühl*)—wording that suggests a contrast between Edwards and Schleiermacher. For Edwards, human beings were not "made divine" (*Vergottung*), as in some Romantic thinkers. God shared with human beings the fullness of his being and yet remained transcendent in doing so. Müller ended by saying that Edwards's thought showed resemblances to that of Leibniz and Kant.[37]

One of the more unusual appeals to Edwards was in a study of "heredity theory" and "racial hygiene." German authors cited a well-known study of

Edwards's distinguished descendants during the nineteenth century to prove that "it is consistently the rule that the descendents of families of higher standing choose professions that demand an exceptional measure of talent, and that they succeed in these professions."[38]

Great Awakener: Trans-Atlantic Interpretations of Edwards's Revival Writings and Eschatology

In turning to Edwards's revival writings, one is immediately struck by the absence of interest among German-language authors. Beyond a few formulaic references, German sources from the mid-1700s to the mid-1900s seldom mention the theme of revival.[39]

Little known to researchers on Edwards is the appreciative reception and interpretation of his revival writings by the nineteenth-century French Protestant pastor and scholar Jean Frédéric Astié, and the more critical reception among French Protestants at the start of the twentieth century, including Henri Bois and Jacques Kaltenbach. French writings on revival typically arose in response to events outside of France. The Revival of 1857–58 in the United States and the Welsh Revival of 1904–05 generated new discussions. Moreover, the *Reveil* (spiritual "awakening") of the early 1800s—centered in the Netherlands, French-speaking Switzerland, and certain parts of France—aroused curiosity about revivals.[40] An early sign of French interest in Edwards was the 1823 publication of a French translation of the *Humble Attempt*. A French translation of the whole of *History of Redemption*—lacking an introduction—appeared in 1854.[41]

Edwards's revival writings found a French interpreter in Astié (1822–1892), who studied in Geneva, Halle, and Berlin, served as pastor of a French Protestant congregation in New York (1848–1853), taught on the faculty at Lausanne University, and published widely on theology, history, and biblical exegesis.[42] Having learned of the 1857–58 revival that began in New York City—where he had led a French congregation some years earlier—Astié wrote with enthusiasm of the new developments: "Most of the churches in the northern part of the United States, for many weeks, have become the scene of a most remarkable religious movement. The Spirit of God seems to be poured out in great abundance." Commenting that the latest events recalled the Great Awakening that occurred under Jonathan Edwards in 1740, Astié added that Edwards in his day was "the first to perceive the evil" of lax communion, and limited participation in the Lord's Table to those who could supply "an individual profession of their faith." As a result of this strictness, "the consciences of Christians were awakened; a great revival followed." Those congregations rejecting Edwards's reforms sank into worldliness, thus preparing for the rise of American Unitarianism. Astié implied that Edwards's stricter communion policy triggered the New England awakenings, and so his knowledge of the sequence of events in Edwards's parish—at least when writing this essay— was deficient.[43]

Several years later, Astié offered a wide-ranging assessment of Edwards and the Great Awakening in *Histoire de la République des États-Unis* (1865). After describing America's spiritual decline during the early 1700s, the author states, "Very happily for American civilization, and for the welfare of the entire world, there was a movement of reform . . . This was an important development that explains the known difference, that, to our day, profoundly distinguishes the New World from the Old." Although Europe broke with its religious traditions during the eighteenth century, America experienced religious renewal, even if this took place along the "unfortunate path of schism." Jonathan Edwards, "a modest pastor from an obscure town," discovered a message that changed the course of history. Taking aim at Arminianism, Edwards launched "a pure and simple return to the central doctrine of the sixteenth century," namely, justification by faith. Astié noted that Edwards put no confidence in physical manifestations as signs of grace. Unlike other revival participants, Edwards did not fall into hasty judgments regarding others' spiritual state. Whitefield himself afforded an example of "temerarious denunciation" when he "spoke out strongly against the unconverted ministers, denouncing them as a mal-ediction upon the church." A "tragic situation" prevailed when "separatists" broke off from existing churches. Yet Edwards "resolved the delicate problem of finding rapport between the church and the world." He did not insist that the church be composed only of true saints. Human judgment could not sepa-rate the sheep from the goats. Above all, Edwards was a peacemaker amid the conflicts over revivals: "The judicious mediating position that he took had the effect of annulling the positions of the two extreme parties."[44] Astié reflected a European Protestant aversion to separatism, and so he was more critical of Whitefield and the New Lights generally than were most American authors.

At the outset of the twentieth century, modernist theology exerted influ-ence in French Protestant seminaries.[45] Social-scientific analysis also gained ground in theological circles. Henri Bois, a professor in the Protestant Faculty of Theology at Montauban, and Jacques Kaltenbach, the student whose dis-sertation Bois directed, both published extensively on revival in 1905–06 and frequently cited Edwards's writings.[46] Kaltenbach's *Etude psychologique des plus anciens réveils religieux aux États-Unis* (1905) contained no less than sixty-eight references to him. "Edwards was a mystic," wrote Kaltenbach. Like St. Francis of Assisi, he saw "an imprint of divine glory in all of creation."

He was "especially preoccupied with the greatness of God," and he "celebrated the power manifested in nature." Both Kaltenbach and Bois saw differences between Edwards's conversion and those occurring under Edwards's preaching. Kaltenbach explained the "singularity" of Edwards's conversion by saying that his theological ideas, though "long unsettled," became "finally fixed" at the time of the revival. Prior to the revival, Edwards was at war in his own mind between affirming and denying human liberty, and then at last he came to "strict Calvinism" and a belief in the "passivity of conversion."

Twentieth-century modernist Protestants essentially agreed with eighteenth-century Old Light objections to fear-based preaching. To promote revival, Kaltenbach said, Edwards preached "fear," while in later generations Charles Finney preached "duty" and Dwight Moody preached "love." Experience showed the sequel to all revivals was a period of spiritual relaxation or diminution. Kaltenbach noted that American Protestants were gradually turning away from revivalist emotion to embrace educational methods. The revivalists Edwards, Finney, and Moody in their later years went on to become heads of educational institutions (Princeton University, Oberlin College, and Northampton Academy). Revivals were thus phenomena of the past and increasingly marginal.[47] The stress on education as a replacement for revivals aligned Kaltenbach with the religious education movement that was strong among mainline Protestants in this day. [48]

Henri Bois, in *Quelques réflexions sur la psychologie des réveils* (1906), constructed his interpretation of revival on the basis of current psychological theories, including the emerging work on crowd psychology. He cited the work of the American scholar Frederick Davenport, whose *Primitive Traits in Religious Revivals* (1905) offered itself as the first truly "scientific" (i.e., empirical and nontheological) analysis of religious revivals.[49] Bois also cited the American George Coe, the pioneering leader of the "New Psychology" that was altering the relationship between theology and scientific study during the 1890s.[50] For Bois, both past and present revivals might be explained in terms of hypnotism. The declining efficacy of revivals led to deliberate use of hypnotic methods to sustain religious interest. Already in Edwards's revivals there had been, wrote Bois, a "regression to a primitive state" and "animistic mentality." Like Kaltenbach, Bois perceived a dichotomy between education and revivals, so that "progress in theology means decline in revival." His overall assessment of revivals was negative: "An impartial consideration of history shows that the revivals under Jonathan Edwards in America produced very doubtful moral effects. They were followed by a period of religious lethargy, caused in great part by a 'revolt against the excesses of the revivalists and the tumultuous excitements of the Great Awakening.' " Nature inevitably asserted itself after a time of excitement; slow development was preferable. Edwards himself was converted gradually and without any crisis, in Bois's judgment, and he was not passive but actively exerted his own will in the process of conversion.[51]

Those most receptive to Edwards's revival theology outside of America were the British Baptists, for whom the rediscovery of Edwards triggered a theological and missionary awakening during the 1780s and 1790s. These British Baptists interpreted the revival writings in the context of the missionary labors portrayed in the *Life of Brainerd*, the eschatological backdrop and summons to prayer in the *Humble Attempt*, and the notion of moral agency in *Freedom of the Will*. To understand the British Baptist reception of Edwards's revival theology, one must take account of all of these intertwining elements. Reacting against the hyper-Calvinism of their day, they insisted on the duty of all persons to repent and place their faith in Christ. Andrew Fuller's doctrine of "duty faith" became a touchstone of evangelical dissenting orthodoxy in Britain for most of the nineteenth century. In Bebbington's words, Edwards "supplied the intellectual tools" for British evangelicals to reconcile human responsibility before God with divine power and providence over human affairs. Such a reconciliation was evident in William Carey's *Enquiry* (1792), a foundational text for the Protestant missionary movement and a stirring call to the use of "means" for the conversion of nonbelievers.[52]

Yet Edwards's impact went beyond the issue of "duty faith." His expectations for the church's "glorious times" in *History of Redemption*, his summons to prayer in *Humble Attempt*, and the tangible realization of missionary concern in *Life of Brainerd* all fueled the fires of evangelical activism. Though British evangelicals were generally less eager than American evangelicals to embrace millennialist views, Edwards's writings raised interest in biblical prophecy in Britain.[53] The *Humble Attempt* emphasized, in Iain Murray's words, "the links between prayer, prophecy, and the world's evangelization."[54] After John Sutcliff read *Humble Attempt*, he urged fellow Baptists in the Northamptonshire Baptist Association to begin meeting monthly to pray for revival. From these prayer meetings came spiritual renewal. Edwards showed, in Michael Haykin's words, "how to combine a commitment to Calvinism with a passion for revival, fervent evangelism and experiential religion."[55]

Conclusion: The View from Across the Pond

What did British and European scholars see when they looked at Jonathan Edwards?

With the exception of confessional Calvinists, like the British Baptists and Scottish Presbyterians who venerated Edwards for his Christian devotion and intellectual power, most British and European readers came to him with a presumption of cultural superiority. Not surprisingly, they often sought to measure Edwards with European yardsticks. His philosophy of history was like that of St. Augustine or Bishop Jacques Bossuet. His nature mysticism was reminiscent of St. Francis of Assisi. His philosophy was akin to the conceptual systems of Leibniz, Spinoza, Kant, and Schopenhauer. His deterministic theory of the will was analogous to that of Thomas Hobbes and David Hume. The great tragedy of Edwards's life was to have been born on the wrong continent. Had he been situated in Britain or Europe, and given access to superior British or European education, incalculable good might have resulted. Edwards would not have been hindered and burdened with outmoded Puritan beliefs that prevailed in America much longer than they did in Europe. Though Leslie Stephen expressed himself more pointedly than others, British and European authors generally believed that their own culture was more advanced. Beliefs in divine predestination, God's wrath, hell and damnation, original sin, and the enslaving power of sin died out in Britain and in Europe much sooner than they did in America. By 1800, Edwards's beliefs were like a time capsule from a less cultured era. Interpreting him therefore was an exercise in sifting wheat from the chaff. In this scholarly salvaging operation, one looked for material of enduring value—a "usable" Edwards—and left behind what was merely transient.

The debate at the end of the nineteenth century over the sources of his idealism had much to do with British and European assumptions about American cultural dependency. The United States had achieved political independence, but its reliance on trans-Atlantic education and literature made it still a colony in its elite culture. Americans for their part were eager to declare cultural independence and to show that America's greatest intellectual hero was not simply echoing British philosophical opinions as formulated in the immaterialism of Bishop George Berkeley.

Outside of Calvinistic Baptist and Calvinistic Presbyterian circles, Edwards's theological opinions did not find much favor in Britain or Europe. His views were shocking. He was an alarming determinist, who reduced human beings to machinelike status (so Samuel Taylor Coleridge). Alternatively, he was a dreaded pantheist in the vein of Spinoza, for whom all of humanity and all of creation were swallowed up and dissolved in an ocean of divinity (so Georges Lyon). Yet again, he was the terrifying preacher of a frightful message of hell and damnation (so Leslie Stephen). Such views of Edwards were based on limited knowledge of and reading of the primary texts. In part this was because many of his key writings were not available. A deeper problem, however, was that British and European authors did not like what they read of Edwards and so had little motivation to read further. His known views were simply too far from the mainstream to be regarded as intellectual live options. In the American context, a sense of filial devotion to this greatest of American thinkers led even liberal-minded thinkers to acknowledge his greatness and search for something of lasting value in his writings.

Nevertheless, by the end of the nineteenth century, there was a growing sense among elite thinkers on both sides of the Atlantic that the salvaging operation was no longer viable. There was nothing to learn or to retrieve from Edwards. Interest steadily tapered off, and some egregious caricatures began to appear in print.[56] Early-twentieth-century Progressives responded to him with sneers or jeers rather than arguments. A serious reengagement with his ideas did not take place until the later twentieth century. Leslie Stephen's 1876 essay created an interpretive template for scholarly opinions on both sides of the Atlantic. The American author Alexander V. G. Allen may have captured Stephen's core objection when he wrote in 1889: "The great wrong which Edwards did, which haunts us as an evil dream throughout his writings, was to assert God at the expense of humanity."[57]

Sometimes there were flashes of insight in British and European scholarship on Edwards that complemented—or challenged—dominant American perspectives. The British Baptists, for instance, may have had a better grasp on the practical application of his ideas than did the American New Divinity adherents. British interpreters were less preoccupied with the metaphysical intricacies of *Freedom of the Will* and such arcana as the exerciser-taster debates. Reading Edwards's texts more holistically, and finding links among his views on moral agency, religious affection, biblical prophecy, and missionary endeavor, the Brits leaped ahead of the Americans during the 1790s in applying his ideas to gospel preaching and foreign missions. For at least a decade or two, the American Edwardsians appeared introverted and self-involved in comparison with their British counterparts.

German-language scholarship on Edwards underscored features that escaped Anglo-American scrutiny. The Germans, for example, often wrote of his "mysticism" and were intrigued with a possible tension between the logical and experiential aspects of his thought. They asked whether his God should be conceived in terms of being (so Voegelin and Müller) or in terms of will (so Squires). German scholars viewed him as a systematic or speculative thinker—like one of the great German pundits—while Anglo-American readers generally stressed Locke's influence and empiricist epistemology.[58] The most thorough Continental European reading of Edwards to date—Miklos Vetö, *Le pensée de Jonathan Edwards* (1987; 2007, 2nd ed.)—offered a corrective to English-language literature because of its attempt to tackle some big questions (e.g., divine justice, the nature of freedom, the problem of evil, etc.) that generally have gone unexamined in the more specialized and piecemeal readings of Edwards by Anglo-American interpreters.[59]

More than the English and the Germans, the French struggled to make sense of Edwards, and with the exception of such nineteenth-century French Calvinists as Astié there was little empathy with his theological views among French readers and interpreters in the time period we have examined. Yet the French sometimes saw things that the English and Germans missed. They were more aware of his affinities to earlier thinkers (such as Augustine). They found implausible the notion of the impending overthrow and disappearance of the Roman Catholic Church. In a Catholic nation, such a prediction seemed offensive as well. More than the British, the French readers questioned the value of religious revivals, both because of their divisive effects and because they seemed invariably to be followed by periods of spiritual lethargy or decline.

One issue British and European interpreters have seemingly never resolved was Edwards's cultural location and identity in a trans-Atlantic context. Was he, as Leslie Stephen suggested, a "German professor" accidentally dropped into the American forest? Or was Edwards, as Stephen stated in the same essay, a "normal representative" who summed up the American character and genius? It seems impossible to make both claims regarding the same person. The "German professor" perspective viewed him as a one-man outpost of European culture. The "normal representative" perspective sought to find what set Americans apart from the British and the Europeans. Stephen perhaps failed to see the problem entailed in his own interpretation. But it could be this combined sense of kinship and foreignness that made Edwards an engaging, though baffling, figure for British and European interpreters.

16

An Edwardsian Lost and Found

THE LEGACY OF JONATHAN EDWARDS IN ASIA

Anri Morimoto

I FOUND THE book sitting unassumingly on a shelf at the home of a Japanese-American family near Princeton, New Jersey. The house belonged to an elderly woman who was well into her eighties, with a fading memory and declining dexterity. She lived mostly in her memories of prewar Japan, before she and her entire family immigrated to the West Coast. At times, she would go out of the house on foot to buy some tofu at the local store—a store misplaced in her memory from her hometown in rural Okayama to present-day New Jersey. After immigrating to the United States, she experienced unspeakable hardships during World War II in the internment camp. She then moved to the East Coast after the war, where she eventually spent a happy life with successful children. But every time she went out to her imaginary tofu store, she would become lost in the reality of late-twentieth-century urban traffic. One of her daughters, a senior curator at Princeton University's Gest Library, lived with her and decided to hire someone to be her daytime companion while she was at work. Our families knew each other from the church, and so my wife took on the role of caretaker. I myself had just started studying at Princeton Theological Seminary, and that day I had happened to have lunch with them.

The book I found on the shelf, though dusty and tinged yellow-brown over time, still declared its title clearly: *The God of Wrath.*[1] I had barely begun my Edwards studies at the time, but the moment I saw it I knew that it was a volume of Jonathan Edwards's sermons in Japanese translation. Published in 1948, it was the very first translation ever to appear in the Japanese language, and arguably the first in any Asian language, but the book had long been forgotten. I had never seen it in Japan, nor had I seen any mention of it in whatever scant publications there were on Jonathan Edwards, scholarly or otherwise, in Japanese. More than twenty years have passed since my encounter with the book, and I still have not come upon another copy since. In all likelihood, the printing must have been on a very small scale. The paper used is crude in quality, and the author's writing style and orthography follow prewar rules. In 1948, just three years after Japan's unconditional surrender to the Allied Powers, the devastated nation was struggling to survive the postwar resource shortage. At a time when the average monthly salary of a fresh college graduate was about 2,300 yen, 200 yen must have been an extravagant price for a book of sermons by an unknown preacher. The book was published by a small Christian publishing company, which soon merged with another and lost its original name.

For these and other reasons, the book quietly slipped into oblivion in its home country, but it found an unlikely place of preservation in the house of a Japanese immigrant in America. The ailing woman (or perhaps her deceased husband) must have acquired the book, but it was quite some time since she had last read a book in any language. Her children grew up in America and did not read Japanese books, either. I asked her if I could have it, and she readily granted my wish. I felt as if the book were beckoning to me, seeking the attention it had long deserved.

The translator was a young scholar by the name of Mamoru Iga, an English literature major who graduated in 1946 from Kwansei Gakuin University, a Methodist school located in Nishinomiya. After graduation, he was hired by his alma mater to be a tutor in their Department of Commerce. It is not clear how this junior scholar managed to publish a book of 286 pages at such a difficult time. Almost all the men of his age had been drafted and expended in Japan's all-out war effort, so it is miraculous that he was alive and well at the time. Further, because Nishinomiya is not far from Hiroshima, he must have witnessed the horrible effects of the atomic bomb dropped there. Iga seems to have survived everything—the draft, the war, the bombs both atomic and conventional, the postwar shortage of resources—and published the first Japanese translation of Jonathan Edwards merely two years out of school and three years out of the war. At the end of his preface to the sermons, he inscribed the date of the manuscript's submission: "August 15th, 1948." Coincidentally, that date is the third anniversary of Japan's defeat and the end of war.

There are so many questions to be answered about this publication and its author. What motivated him? Why did he publish a book of sermons by a preacher from the distant past of the former enemy country? And why did he publish it during a time when his charred nation was in turmoil, struggling to recover, suffering from a dire shortage of everyday necessities? How did he come to know Edwards to begin with? Was it due to his personal or family background, the education he received at the Methodist school, or the influence of his teachers?

AT FIRST LOOK, the reader is surprised to see the richness and profundity of the content for the first publication on or by Edwards in the Japanese language. Within its 286 pages, it contains the translator's preface (10 pages), a short biography of Edwards (7 pages), seven sermons (234 pages), and "Personal Narrative" (25 pages). The seven sermons he chose were:

- God Glorified in Man's Dependence
- A Divine and Supernatural Light
- Ruth's Resolution
- Many Mansions
- Sinners in the Hands of an Angry God
- God's Awful Judgment in the Breaking and Withering of the Strong Rods of a Community
- A Farewell Sermon

Each sermon is introduced with concise but precise background information that only a scholar well versed in Edwards's works could have written. More than anything, it is simply impressive that these seven were selected out of the many sermons available then in print. Judging from the date of publication, I believe the translator must have had access to several editions of Edwards's collected works. The selection seems to strike a good balance between revival sermons, with the ever-indispensable "Sinners in the Hands of an Angry God" representing many of Edwards's threat-and-damnation sermons, and such occasional sermons as Thursday lecture, funeral, and farewell sermons. But why did he choose these seven in particular?

Inquiries into possible explanations yielded a rather simple answer that may dampen the enthusiasm of history detectives. Experts on the history of Edwardsian scholarship may have already guessed, but it was only through the bibliography of Faust and Johnson's anthology that I detected a possible source for his particular choice of sermons.[2] The anthology's bibliography contains a collection of Edwards's sermons by Harry Norman Gardiner, published in 1904 by Macmillan as a volume in the Pocket Classics series.[3] I did not know the existence of such a collection. I checked with many libraries online and finally determined it was indeed his source book. It contains those exact seven sermons, in the same chronological order, and each sermon is introduced with the kind of background information our translator furnished in his entries. Gardiner's book comes complete with Edwards's short biography, which our translator used to his maximum benefit.[4] Had he given due credit to his source, my search would have been much easier, but he did not even hint at his textual dependence on Gardiner. At any rate, he was not looking for scholarly recognition for himself. Iga seemed to be genuinely eager to bring Edwards's sermons live to the people of postwar Japan.

As for the selection of the seven sermons, Gardiner himself gives a reasonable account. First, they are chosen to represent Edwards the preacher rather than Edwards the theologian, and for that purpose Gardiner insists it must include at least these four: a sermon on man's dependence, another on spiritual light, the Enfield sermon, and the Farewell sermon. They represent "a theology resting ultimately on the principle of a transcendent, righteous, sovereign Will"; "the mystical principle of an immediate, intuitive apprehension, through supernatural illumination, of divine truth"; "pitiless logic and terrible realism of description, arousing, startling, overwhelming the sinner with the sense of impending doom"; and "the rejected minister appealing, without rancor or bitterness, from the judgment of this world to the judgment of an infallible tribunal."[5] To these four, Gardiner added three more sermons: "Ruth's Resolution," for its brevity, to offset the Enfield sermon that loomed so large in the popular imagination regarding Edwards; John Stoddard's funeral sermon, which treats the rare theme of civil government; and "Many Mansions," a sermon whose original manuscript was kept privately by Edwards Amasa Park's family and published for the first time in this collection. Gardiner also maintains in his preface that he took utmost care in reproducing Edwards's original text. He compared all six extant sermons against Edwards's original handwritten manuscripts in the Yale University Library, pointed out some lines and paragraphs missing in previous editions, and even revealed Dwight's textual tampering in some of the passages.[6] One could argue that "The Excellency of Christ," or "Praise, One of the Chief Employments of Heaven," for example, are better choices for the purpose of offsetting the Enfield sermon, but few will disagree that it was the best critical reproduction of Edwards's sermons one could ever hope for, prior to the arrival of the Yale Edition. Indeed, Iga as a translator picked an excellent source for his job, though unwittingly and unannounced.

THUS THE MYSTERY has been unraveled—for the most part. There remains a portion of Iga's writing that is genuinely original: the preface. In the first ten pages of the book, Iga makes his own evaluation of Jonathan Edwards, set in the context of late Colonial America, and explains why he thought Edwards's sermons could give much-needed inspiration to Japan's postwar spirituality.[7]

He begins with Josiah Royce's exalted evaluation of Edwards. In a lecture delivered at Harvard University in 1911, Royce counted Edwards and Emerson as America's two premier philosophers before William James.[8] Iga regards this as an indication of the high profile that the empirical philosophy of Edwards has achieved among twentieth-century American intellectuals but gives even higher praise to his theology. Iga says Edwards's theological genius was most vividly exhibited in the contradictions he struggled unsuccessfully to resolve. First, he was a defender of traditional doctrines, in opposition to modern Deistic thoughts. At the same time, he was progressive in explicating the mystical universe that later inspired Emerson's transcendentalism. Second, his revolutionary and experiential congregationalism did not square with his strict ecclesiastical vision to build a Puritan community of saints. That vision eventually demolished existing church orders for more open and independent administration. And third, his absolutist faith in orthodox Calvinism sits ill at ease with the empiricist principles he learned from Locke and other modern philosophers. These contradictions suggest Edwards faithfully lived out an age of immense upheaval, from the traditional Puritan commonwealth to the modern democratic Republic. Furthermore, Iga explains that Edwards wanted to lead the society into a new era of rationality and science, but inside him there was a vigorous Puritan sentiment that reason could not contain. This ambivalent sentiment was due mainly to his social position as the last pillar of the collapsing Puritan regime.

Iga states that the essence of Puritanism was itself divided by conflicting attempts, one aiming at individual assertiveness and the other imposing social order. He therefore describes Puritanism in a number of ways: religiously, it was a reform movement against the absolutist episcopacy; socially, it was an ethical movement that enforced austere civil codes on citizenry; economically, it was a liberating movement of the middle-class gentry formerly shackled by feudal system; and politically, it was a democratic movement rejecting absolutism in favor of parliamentary governance by liberal individuals. Although Edwards's personal disposition was cultivated and sustained by the emerging bourgeois class mentality of the age, his social stance was more in solidarity with the ruling Tories and their colonial counterparts who represented the interest of the old regime. Since Edwards found it difficult to reverse the liberal trend of his day with "reason," he relied on "experience," the ultimate realm of living faith unapproachable by mere metaphysical speculation. Thus, Iga interprets the true grandeur of Edwards's thought to be in the inevitable and insurmountable contradictions he encountered and faithfully grappled with, using all of his intellectual power.

And that, I believe, is how our translator saw postwar Japan and its predicament: he saw the feudal system of politics literally collapse and the overbearing hierarchical structure of society liquefied by the tumultuous earthquake called World War II. He did not have the keys to resolve all the contradictions of the imperial regime made painfully bare by Japan's total defeat, but he was personally witnessing a national landslide into a much publicized "democratic" and "egalitarian" society that no Japanese had ever experienced. Japan's new Constitution, under the patent influence of America's occupying forces, was proposed and ratified and then took effect in 1947, a year before publication of Iga's work. Postwar Japan, as he perceived it, was experiencing an unprecedented societal change. Contrary to everyone's expectations, Japanese citizens quickly abandoned their animosity and resentment and embraced the defeat.[9] They eagerly welcomed the occupation army, which was mostly composed of American forces, as a liberating force. The defeat must have been the one and only chance for Japan to go through such a radical change. Understandably, a number of intellectuals rejoiced in the demise of imperial Japan and embraced their new life in a supposedly free and democratic regime.

Iga must have been among the intellectuals who rejoiced at the nation's liberation from its ancient regime, but at the same time uncertain of the direction in which his nation was moving. Overwhelmed by the frivolous celebration of "freedom" and "democracy," he must have been disturbed by the rosy prospects that American liberalism fed to the undoubting masses of postwar Japan. This explains why he further compared Edwards to Karl Barth and Friedrich Gogarten. Barth's emphasis on the "between-the-times" imminence of eschaton and Gogarten's social application of "dialectical theology" both represent a transcendental view of reality that was sorely lacking in Iga's Japan. By presenting Edwards's sober and chilling sermons, Iga wanted to express his refusal to believe in the prevalent optimistic Enlightenment mentality. Each in his own time and place, Edwards and these German theologians offered testimonies to the profound faith that squarely faced human despair and social predicament.[10]

Iga acknowledges that Edwards, a product of unresolved contradictions, showed signs of subjective experientialism bordering on the modern divinization of human sentimentality. In his opinion, this was what made his revivalist sermons effective, as the Enfield sermon vividly illustrates. Yet at the same time, he pursued an unquenchable search for truthfulness born from his Puritan heritage, which drove him into conflict with the Northampton river-gods. He did not retreat from his rebellion and staked his ministry in a fight against the mainstream. According to Iga, these efforts are a noble example of the Great Spirit that endured conflict and persevered to lasting victory beyond his earthly defeat.

Because he was a literature major, Iga seems to have some familiarity with works of American writers such as Hawthorne, Emerson, Dreiser, and O'Neill. Though some of these writers can hardly be called "Puritan" by lineage, Iga still sees manifestations of the Puritan drive for truthfulness in them. The very fabric of American literature is characterized by its bourgeois utilitarian spirit and sentimental emotionalism, which Edwards occasionally punctures with his quest for truthfulness. In America, there has always been a set of opposing spirits, Puritanism and Pragmatism, each keeping the other in check. When the spirit of Pragmatism dominates the nation, the Puritan spirit compels it to sincere self-reflection. This dichotomy is the very thing Iga wanted to introduce to postwar Japan:

> I only wish to confirm that the greatest value of American literature, truthfulness, is derived from Puritanism, and that Edwards is the most profound example of this heritage. We contemporary Japanese do not have spiritual grounds of such depth, and that is the reason we cannot see things without the veil of sentimentalism. I hereby offer my translation of his sermons in the hope that, whether Christian, humanist or Marxist, we would all be able to think through truthfully and live out the truth in Japan today.[11]

By introducing Edwards's works to the Japanese public, Iga wished that the vigorous sense of truthfulness present in the sermons would imbue a fresh spirit into the deceptive romanticism stagnant in the minds of the postwar Japanese people.

Thus, Mamoru Iga became Japan's first Edwardsian. But what happened to him after this publication? Did he continue the same studies? Why didn't he wish to reprint his book? There is a postlude to my findings. For all his admirable efforts in translating Jonathan Edwards for the first time into Japanese, he may have felt hesitant about being called an "Edwardsian in Asia," because his life changed abruptly after publication of the book. Iga crossed the Pacific Ocean and enrolled in Brigham Young University, and then in the University of Utah, where he received his Ph.D. in 1955. He found a teaching position and became a professor of sociology at California State University, Northridge. Its College of Social and Behavioral Sciences lists him as an emeritus professor, and in response to my recent inquiry the administrative assistant of the College kindly informed me that he passed away in 1998.[12] Apparently, he switched his field of study from Jonathan Edwards to social psychology and became a specialist researching and writing on issues of suicide in Japan.[13] No further writing on Edwards appeared in either English or Japanese, and one can only guess what he felt about his earlier publication in Japan. He may once have been an Edwardsian in Asia, but after his immigration to the United States he was no longer an Edwardsian; nor was he in Asia.

Nevertheless, one must remember that Edwards himself was deeply engaged in psychological observation of Northampton society during the revivals. He was also a keen observer of the societal maladies epitomized by the suicide of Joseph Hawley. In his own manner and function, one might be able to say, Iga was indeed a legitimate heir to Edwards's legacy.

I COULD END my chapter at this point. However, since I was asked to introduce "Edwardsians in Asia," I should add a few words of explanation about the present state of this scholarship outside of Japan. From the outset, researching the current state of affairs was a near-impossible task for a person who knows no Asian language other than his own, but with the help of valuable resources and people in different regions of Asia, I am able to present a basic picture.

By far, the largest group of Asian Edwardsians reside in Korea. This may not be surprising, given the size of the Christian population in Korea, especially its evangelical Protestant quarters. The breadth of Edwards's works in Korean is impressive. At the center of the Korean Edwards industry is the Revival and Reformation Press in Seoul, established in 1999 for the purpose of promoting M'Cheyne's method of Bible reading. In response to my recent inquiries, the incumbent chair of the company, Rev. Keumsan Baek, kindly explained the history and vision of the press.[14] The large collection of the Edwardsian corpus is part of its overall publishing mission to provide spiritual nourishment for Korean evangelical Christians and promote the work of revival in Korea. According to the Press, the best-selling book has sold more than twenty thousand copies. Other books on Edwards run around three hundred copies every year.

At present, there are four translations from the Yale edition: *Religious Affections* (YE 2), translated by Sungwook Jung (2005); *A History of the Work of Redemption* (YE 7), translated by Gyutak Kim (2007); *The Great Awakening* (YE 4), translated by Nakheung Yang (2005); and *The Sermons of Jonathan Edwards: A Reader*, translated by Keumsan Baek (2005). In addition to these Yale volumes, the Revival and Reformation Press has published Edwards's writings in the form of single volumes: *A Faithful Narrative*, translated by Keumsan Baek (2006); *The Distinguishing Marks of a Work of the Spirit of God*, translated by Beunggi No (2004); *Some Thoughts Concerning the Revival*, translated by Nakheung Yang (2005); *Concerts of Prayer*, translated by Sungwook Jung (2004); *The Nature of True Virtue*, translated by Beunggi No (2005); *Watchman for Souls*, translated by Yongjung Lee (2006); and *Can We Live Like Jonathan Edwards? Biography, Resolutions, and Diary*, translated and compiled by Keumsan Baek (2003). Some notable sermons are also made available by the same publisher. They are "Sinners in the Hands of an Angry God," "A Divine and Supernatural Light," "God Glorified in the Work of Redemption," "The Importance and Advantage of a Thorough Knowledge of Divine Truth," "Heaven Is a World of Love," "A Farewell Sermon," and "Much in Deeds of Charity," all translated by Keumsan Baek and printed as separate booklets.

Other publishers have translated Edwards from independent English texts: *Charity and Its Fruits*, translated by Mungang Seo (Seoul: Jeongeum, 1984); *Freedom of the Will*, translated by Jaehwi Chae (Seoul: Yale Munhwasa, 1987); and *The Life and Diary of David Brainerd*, translated by Gihyang Yun (Seoul: Christian Digest, 1995).

With one exception, these Korean translations have escaped M. X. Lesser's bibliographical attention.[15] In one of his last articles, "An Honor Too Great: Jonathan Edwards in Print Abroad," Lesser notes a Korean translation, *Faithful Narrative*, as published "in Seoul in 1997."[16] However, it is not listed in his second enlarged edition. The book must be one of the few translations printed prior to establishment of the Revival and Reformation Press.

Translations of secondary sources on Edwards are also abundant. Among them are Conrad Cherry, *The Theology of Jonathan Edwards*, translated by Doheung Ju (Seoul: Ireseowon, 2001); Edna Gerstner, *Jonathan and Sarah: An Uncommon Union*, translated by Gyuil Hwang (Seoul: Christian Literature Mission, 1999); Iain H. Murray, *Jonathan Edwards: A New Biography*, translated by Sangmun Yun and Gwanggyu (Seoul: Ireseowon, 2006); Stephen J. Nichols, *Jonathan Edwards: A Guided Tour of His Life and Thought*, translated by Cheonseok Chae (Seoul: Christian Literature Mission, 2005); Ralph Turnbull and Don Kistler, eds., *Devotions from the Pen of Jonathan Edwards*, translated by Gyegwang Jo (Seoul: Word of Life Press, 2003); and David J. Vaughan, *Jonathan Edwards*, translated by Eunheung Kim (Seoul: Gidokshinmun, 2004).

More recent publications on Edwards are made available through the Revival and Reformation Press: D. G. Hart, Sean Michael Lucas, and Stephen J. Nichols, eds., *The Legacy of Jonathan Edwards: American Religion and the Evangelical Tradition*, translated by Hoik Jang (2009); John Piper and Justin Taylor, eds., *A God-Entranced Vision of All Things: The Legacy of Jonathan Edwards*, translated by Yongjung Lee (2007); John Piper, *God's Passion for His Glory: Living the Vision of Jonathan Edwards* (with the complete text of *The End for Which God Created the World*), translated by Keumsan Baek (2003); Sang

Hyun Lee, ed., *The Princeton Companion to Jonathan Edwards*, translated by Yongjung Lee (2008); and George Marsden's *Jonathan Edwards: A Life,* translated by Dongsoo Han (2006). The five-volume work by Owen Strachen and Doug Sweeney, *The Essential Edwards Collection,* is being translated by Yongnam Kim and Chanyoung Kim.

Secondary sources on Edwards written first in Korean include Buheung Jeong, *A Life of Jonathan Edwards* (Seoul: Christian Literature Mission, 1996). Nak-Heong Yang, a professor of historical theology at Kosin Theological Seminary, is the author of *The Life and Theology of Jonathan Edwards* (Seoul: Revival and Reformation Press, 2003). Sang Woong Lee, who teaches Edwards at Daeshin University and runs an online Edwards club (http://jonathanedwards.cyworld.com), has published his dissertation under the title of *The Pneumatology of Jonathan Edwards* (Seoul: Revival and Reformation Press, 2009). Hyun-Jin Cho, a professor of church history and theology at the Westminster Graduate School of Theology, will soon publish his dissertation on Edwards's doctrine of justification from the University Press of America. Kevin Woongsan Kang, who teaches Edwards at Chongshin Theological Seminary, and Jin Rak Lee, who wrote a dissertation at Chongshin Seminary on Edwards' *Religious Affections*, should also be mentioned among these younger scholars.[17]

In the Chinese language, an evangelical publishing company based in Hong Kong, Chinese Christian Literature Council, has published *Selected Writings of Jonathan Edwards, Sr.,* translated by Ping-Teh Hsieh (1960; second edition, 1996) in a series called Christian Classics Library. This must be the book M. X. Lesser mentioned in his 2003 article as "a 425-page selection published in Hong Kong in 1960."[18] In 2003, Yu Daxin Carver published a biographical introduction, *A Thinker in the Affection of the Holy Spirit: Jonathan Edwards,* from the same publisher. Reformation Translation Fellowship Publishing in Taipei published two books by Edwards: *The Experience That Counts* (the Chinese title of *Religious Affections*), translated by Theological Translation Fellowship (1994; second edition, 2007); and *The Distinguishing Marks of a Work of the Spirit of God,* translated by Charles Chao (2003).[19] Part of the second book is made available online, with permission from the original publisher, by Church China (https://www.churchchina.org/n0070906). This web magazine ministry is operated by a Massachusetts-based organization called Chinese Christian Internet Mission. A work of more scholarly nature, Helen K. Hosier's *Jonathan Edwards: The Great Awakener,* is translated by Cao Wen Li and published in mainland China (Beijing: HuaXia, 2006).[20]

A number of scholars from Asia have studied Edwards in the United States, but their primary activities and publications are based outside of Asia.

Seng-Kong Tan may be a precious exception here. He has written a number of articles on Edwards's theology as an independent scholar now based in Singapore. Originally trained in Singapore as an architect, he became interested in Edwards while studying Pentecostal spirituality at Regent College, Canada. He then discovered that Edwards was "much more than a revivalist theologian," and began writing articles on his theology in English.[21]

Japanese scholarship on Edwards is in its budding stage. Since Iga's legendary translation, only two booklets have been released in Japanese, each containing one sermon: "Sinners in the Hands of an Angry God" (1991) and "The Excellency of Christ" (1993). The translator is Toru Iijima, a former English professor at a junior college in Tokyo. So far my own book, a Japanese version expanded from the English, is the only monograph ever published in Japanese.[22] Occasionally, articles of an introductory nature have appeared in various forms, among which "Jonathan Edwards and the Great Awakening" by Kayoko Kodama, in an anthology on *Puritanism and America* (1969), deserves special attention for its balanced presentation of Edwards's life and thought in context. On a lighter side, the recent illustrated edition of *Jonathan Edwards for Armchair Theologians* by James P. Byrd is translated and published in 2011. I served as translator, hoping to make these works accessible to readers intimidated by the bulky Yale edition. The Armchair Theologians series has seen Japanese translations of Luther, Calvin, and Barth so far. Since no Japanese intellectual would foresee Edwards following these monumental theologians, this translation will hopefully enhance the general perception of his status in Japanese scholarship.

In 2008, the 250th anniversary of Edwards's death, a Christian publishing company finally committed itself to releasing a multivolume Japanese edition of Edwards. I consulted Kenneth Minkema, who kindly gave me suggestions as to the selection of texts to be included as well as other practical information regarding copyright issues. Here is the content of the seven volumes: vol. 1, *Freedom of the Will* (YE1); vol. 2, *Nature and Beauty* ("Images of Divine Things" and "Types of the Messiah" from YE11, "Beauty of the World" and "The Mind" from YE6); vol. 3, *Original Sin* (YE3); vol. 4, *The Great Awakening and Ecclesiology* ("Faithful Narrative" and "Some Thoughts Concerning the Revival" from YE4, and "Narrative of Communion Controversy" from YE12); vol. 5, *History of the Work of Redemption* (YE9); vol. 6, *Theological Writings* ("The End for Which God Created the World" and "The Nature of True Virtue" from YE8, "Discourse on the Trinity," "Treatise on Grace," and "Controversies Notebook on Justification" from YE21); and vol. 7, *Sermons* (fourteen sermons from *The Sermons of Jonathan Edwards: A Reader*, "Personal Writings," and letters from *A Jonathan Edwards Reader*).

I have organized a team of able translators for this daunting task: Naoki Onishi, an American literature professor at International Christian University, who has published several articles on Edwards and other early American literary figures; Shitsuyo Masui, a professor in Sophia University's English Department, who has been writing articles on evangelism and revivals in early America; Mikayo Sakuma, also an American literature professor, teaching at Wayo Women's University; and Masakata Okubo, an English philosophy professor at Sugino Fashion College.

A word of explanation as to why the project does not include *Religious Affection* or *Charity and Its Fruits*: these have already been provided in Japanese, albeit exclusively on the internet. An independent translator has a large online collection of evangelical Christian writers in Japanese translation.[23] His site boasts collections of John Owen, Richard Sibbes, Thomas Watson, John Newton, Charles Hodge, and Charles Spurgeon in modern readable Japanese. On the page devoted to Edwards, there are translations of *Religious Affection*, *Charity and Its Fruits*, and *Resolutions*, all based on the texts from the Banner of Truth edition. Our publisher contacted the site owner and asked if he would join in the new publication project, but he respectfully declined. He is convinced that it is his personal ministry to provide these translations online, free of charge for anyone interested, and he wishes to remain independent of the major publishing business. The incident testifies to the continuing presence of the Edwardsian legacy in a small but vibrant evangelical segment among Japanese Christians. In one way or another, Edwards has been and will be provided for the Japanese public.

As for the publisher of our project, I felt deeply obliged to call the publishing company that produced Mamoru Iga's mysterious translation more than sixty years ago. The original publisher, Nishimura Shoten, had merged with Nagasaki Shoten and renamed itself Shinkyo Shuppan-sha, or the Protestant Publishing Company. Thus the early efforts of Professor Mamoru Iga will soon be honored with publication of Edwards' multivolume works. Destiny fulfilled, though long overdue.

Before the Young, Restless, and Reformed

EDWARDS'S APPEAL TO POST–WORLD WAR II EVANGELICALS

D. G. Hart

HAD JOSEPH A. Conforti written his thoughtful book *Jonathan Edwards, Religious Tradition, and American Culture* (1995) in 2010, he would have had to add at least a chapter and possibly reorganize his material. When Conforti wrote his study of the reception of Edwards's thought and writings since the revolutionary era, the most visible effort to recover and maintain the legacy was Yale University Press's critical edition of the Massachusetts pastor's works. Indeed, the original director of the Yale project, Perry Miller, makes only a cameo appearance in Conforti's epilogue as an example of midtwentieth-century existentialist, American studies, and neo-orthodox invocations of Edwards, whose speculative and philosophically engaged Calvinist theology gave American academics an ample leash to appropriate the Massachusetts pastor for a culture that had plenty of reasons to fear a world without a sovereign who was divine. Of course, the tercentenary of Edwards's birth in 2003 would change the editorial landscape.

But aside from the outpouring of books and dissertations inspired by the anniversary of Jonathan's birth to Timothy and Esther on October 5, 1703, was the rise of a cohort of evangelicals dubbed by one of its members as "young, restless, and reformed." Adolescents and young adults were flocking to inspirational conferences where, after singing rock 'n' roll inspired praise songs, they listened to middle-aged pastors and teachers speak about the transcendence and glory of God in ways inspired by Edwards and the Puritans more generally. The young people's interest in Calvin led the editors at *Time* magazine in 2009 to claim that Calvinism was evangelical Protestantism's "latest success story," and to place this set of Protestant convictions at number three on the magazine's list of "top ten ideas changing the world right now." The editors explained, "In the 1700s, Puritan preacher Jonathan Edwards invested Calvinism with a rapturous near mysticism," but the movement soon faltered after Methodism cultivated a faith "more impressed with human will." But Calvinism in the first decade of the new millennium roared back to occupy the spot where, according to one of the editors at *Christianity Today*, "the energy and the passion are in the Evangelical world."[1]

Had Conforti included this expression of Calvinism in his study, he would have had to look away from stone monuments, critical editions, and educational institutions to one of the chief expressions of youth culture: the T-shirt. And what he would have found printed on these items of clothing (formerly covered by dress shirts, ties, and jackets) was a phrase that testified to the urban hipster affectations of those restless, young Calvinists: "Jonathan Edwards Is My Homeboy."[2] The adolescents and young adults wearing those T-shirts were the same ones attending conferences and services to hear R. Albert Mohler, the president of Southern Baptist Theological Seminary (the oldest seminary in the largest Protestant denomination in the United States); John Piper, the senior pastor of Bethlehem Baptist Church in Minneapolis and accessible to millions through his website and publications at Desiring God ministries; and Mark Driscoll, a Seattle-based pastor with a large following thanks to his own hip style and a network of churches called Acts 29—some of the popular American figures who found in Calvinism a deity big and strong enough to tackle all human problems.

In point of fact, recent appropriation of Edwards's legacy was not confined to T-shirts or to the decade or so after publication of Conforti's book. At the same time that Miller, Joseph Haroutunian, and H. Richard Niebuhr were using Edwards at midcentury to score points among the mainstream Protestant churches and universities they patronized, evangelical Protestants were appropriating Edwards for purposes much closer to those of the Northampton pastor himself, namely, to help believers appreciate better the glory and majesty of God and understand their dependence on that divinity especially for genuine faith and holiness. This born-again Protestant recovery of Edwards's legacy functioned as the subtext to the monographs and critical editions that began to surface in the 1950s within academic circles. Conforti may have missed this contemporary evangelical Edwardsian revival because its authors did not publish with presses from which university librarians usually ordered their books. But from the Presbyterian church historian Jonathan

Gerstner, Gordon-Conwell Seminary professor Richard Lovelace, the Scottish Presbyterian minister Iain Murray, and the Baptist pastor John Piper to the historians Mark A. Noll and George M. Marsden, evangelical Protestants have created still another chapter in the ongoing American reclamation of a theologian, who despite obscure references, dated philosophical nomenclature, and bracing doctrine, has functioned for the brainier evangelicals as Jay Gatsby's beckoning green light—that longed-for but impossible-to-attain philosophical mind illuminated by the Holy Spirit. What follows is an overview and assessment of the recent recovery of Edwards for evangelical Protestants by pastors and academics. As it turns out, this religious and academic revival of Edwards has great appeal to the academically inclined but is a tough sell to born-again Protestants who know they can experience God's power without the philosophical rigmarole.

Edwards Revived

Before John H. Gerstner wrote *Steps to Salvation: The Evangelistic Message of Jonathan Edwards* (1959), the production of books on Edwards averaged in the low single digits throughout the 1950s. (Only in 1963 would the number of works about the Massachusetts pastor—whether books or theses and dissertations—climb into double figures and never go back.) For instance, the year prior to the appearance Gerstner's book—the first to rise above ten titles since 1904, when the bicentennial of Edwards's birth was still generating commemorative publications—saw publication of five books and seven dissertations. Among those books was a prosopography by Adam Leroy James of early American philosophers, which included Edwards, and another for evangelical readers from Ralph G. Turnbull.[3] In fact, one indication of the seeming lack of interest in Edwards during the post–World War II era was the paucity of materials produced for the 250th anniversary of his birth in 1953. No books were published. Meanwhile graduate students in that year defended seven theses or dissertations, among them Charles Peter MacGregor's Th.D. dissertation at Boston University on the relevance of Edwards for contemporary churches and Lloyd Sheridan Walker's analysis of Edwards's understanding of conversion, written for an undergraduate degree in divinity at Butler University.[4]

This is not to imply that Gerstner was single-handedly responsible for reviving an interest in Edwards for evangelicals. But until 1968, when Edwards studies began to lift from the runway to the cruising altitude of 2003 levels of publication and interest, the study of the Puritan pastor for classroom purposes or attempts to resurrect his theology and piety for contemporary church life were marginal at best. For instance, 1968 witnessed publication of several works by university presses, and even more dissertations.⁵ But for the trend that would emerge among evangelical authors, publishers and editors, Gerstner's book was effectively groundbreaking.

Born in Tampa, Florida, the son of German immigrants, Gerstner grew up in a nominally Lutheran home. He became active in Presbyterian churches, work that would characterize his entire life, only through a romantic interest. By the time he was in high school, the family had moved to Philadelphia and he was interested in a classmate who attended a congregation in the United Presbyterian Church of North America. He parted company with the girl but remained interested in Reformed Protestantism, first attending the UPCNA's college in western Pennsylvania, Westminster, and then preparing for the ministry at Westminster Seminary (same name but different wing of American Presbyterianism). He eventually earned a doctorate at Harvard University, where he wrote a dissertation on the influences of Immanuel Kant and Charles Darwin on James McCosh.⁶

Fresh from his doctorate, Gerstner pastored in two UPCNA congregations in Pennsylvania before taking a job offer to teach church history at Pittsburgh-Xenia Seminary. Prior to his academic appointment he had not studied Edwards, but while preparing for courses Gerstner devoted more attention to the Massachusetts pastor, perhaps second only to Calvin in his studies. When Gerstner started to write on Edwards, the UPCNA was undergoing merger negotiations with the Presbyterian Church U.S.A., the mainline body that was to the doctrinal left of the United Presbyterians. Gerstner opposed this merger because he feared it would liberalize his own communion. Still, aside from regarding Edwards as a source of Reformed orthodoxy, his decision to write on Edwards did not reveal necessarily an effort to use the colonial defender of Calvinism to oppose twentieth-century liberal Protestantism (or Barthianism).

Gerstner's aim in *Steps to Salvation* (1960) was to show that Edwards, who was one of the great evangelists of North America, was both a consistent Calvinist and a covenant theologian. This description, he conceded, was surprising since "many men, learned and unlearned," supposed that predestination and evangelism were inherently incompatible.⁷ In point of fact, he argued, many evangelists throughout the history of Christianity in the United States had been predestinarians, and Edwards was arguably the best example. Without an index, footnotes, or bibliography, readers could not tell if Gerstner had a contemporary problem in mind when he wrote *Steps to Salvation*. His preface was equally elusive; he mentioned only recent biographies by Turnbull, Ola Winslow, and Perry Miller, whom he faulted for neglecting Edwards's sermon manuscripts.⁸ But since Gerstner was writing at a time when Billy

Graham was achieving fame as the era's premier evangelist, readers might well have speculated that the author was using Edwards's Calvinism as a foil to a decision-based understanding of conversion that in the eyes of some Reformed Protestants took Graham too close for comfort to Arminianism.

This interpretation would not easily fit a second difficulty that Gerstner addressed, namely, the supposed tension between covenant theology and the "high Calvinism of John Calvin." According to this view, Edwards rejected a covenant theology that specified the rights and duties of God and believers in the scheme of salvation, calling the Puritan tradition back to understanding salvation within "the framework of divine decrees, without any violation of the decrees." To this perspective, Gerstner simply replied that Edwards was a covenant theologian who saw no "compromise whatever with Arminianism."[9] The rest of the book proceeded to explore Edwards's sermons to prove his bona fides as a Calvinistic evangelist. Gerstner concluded the book with the observation that Edwards preached whatever he found in the Bible: divine sovereignty and human responsibility, hell and heaven, grace and law, individual duty and social obligation, terror and comfort. As such "he was a consistent preacher of Calvinism." To be sure, Edwards "called no man master—not John Calvin or any other man," but in the main he clearly saw the Bible "as Calvin did."[10]

Steps To Salvation was the beginning of Gerstner's lifelong study of Edwards, which would culminate in the multivolume work *The Rational Biblical Theology of Jonathan Edwards* (1991–1993). Because that labor of love was privately published, it did not circulate as widely as Gerstner's digest of his magnum opus, published in 1987 as *Jonathan Edwards: A Mini-Theology*. The thrust of this short book, which divided Edwards's thought into the historic categories of church dogmatics, from the doctrine of Scripture to the last things (or eschatology), was again to emphasize the colonial pastor's genius in combining faith and reason. To this end, Gerstner commented on the flowering of Edwardsian studies, from Perry Miller to Robert C. Whittemore, which all questioned whether an orthodox Calvinist could combine insights from contemporary philosophy with faithful doctrine. "The assumption that an orthodox theologian devoted to the theology of the past," Gerstner wrote, "could not also gain insights from contemporary philosophy is based on a misconception of traditional Christian orthodoxy." As such, Edwards functioned for Gerstner in the 1980s as he had three decades earlier, as a proponent of both head-informed and heartfelt religion:

Many today misunderstand Edwards and Christianity precisely at this point. The historic Christian position has been, in spite of the prevailing contemporary notion to the contrary, a reason-plus-faith synthesis.

Many today think that faith-minus-reason is the Christian position because it is so common in our time. That, however, is a caricature of Christian belief. . . . If one looks at the whole history of Christian thought, it is the reason-plus-faith synthesis of Edwards which emerges dominant.[11]

At roughly the same time Gerstner was recovering Edwards as one of the greatest theologians in the history of Christianity, another Presbyterian pastor-turned-seminary-professor, Richard Lovelace of Gordon-Conwell Theological Seminary, was appropriating Edwards for renewal within contemporary evangelicalism. A graduate of Yale University, like Gerstner Lovelace attended seminary at Westminster before pursuing doctoral work at Princeton Theological Seminary. In 1969 he joined the faculty at Gordon-Conwell and continued his work on pietism in North America, which he began in his dissertation, a study of Cotton Mather eventually published in a revised form in 1979 as *The American Pietism of Cotton Mather*.[12] That same year, Lovelace came out with *Dynamics of Spiritual Life: An Evangelical Theology of Renewal*, which as the subtitle suggested was an attempt to accomplish for evangelicals what Roman Catholics already had in the form of spiritual theology, or a historical theology of Christian experience. Without surprise, Lovelace turned to Edwards as one of the sources for constructing such a theology of renewal. As he wrote in his preface, "Edwards' theology of revival is . . . another prototype for this book and a source of wisdom on which I have constantly drawn."[13]

In anticipation of the later phase of the contemporary evangelical recovery of Edwards, Lovelace started his book by appealing to a younger readership with a first chapter entitled "Jonathan Edwards and the Jesus Movement." Despite that hook, Lovelace opened with a fairly depressing account of American society:

The situation in this country seems to call for a jeremiad, not a celebration. The worst scandal in our government's history stilling lingers in our memories. Race prejudice, latent under the surface of political campaigns, seems intensified by our very efforts to correct it. The crime rate is outstripping police restraint and turning private surveillance into a growth sector. Pornography and violence fill the media, and a host of other social problems run in counterpoint with an uncertain economy.[14]

Despite such an inauspicious time for a book on revival, Lovelace plowed ahead. Contemporaneous with the country's woes were stirrings of Christian renewal movements, spearheaded by Vatican II, which may have also indirectly prompted the evangelical renewal movement of born-again teenagers and young adults known as Jesus People.

For this manual of spiritual theology, Lovelace did not follow Edwards slavishly. On the cover of the book, the New England pastor had to compete for space with John Wesley, Dwight L. Moody, and Billy Graham. But the Gordon-Conwell professor did interact carefully with Edwards on questions regarding when revivals "go wrong," and on the nature of spiritual gifts in renewal movements. The greatest threat to revivals, according to Lovelace's reading of Edwards, was spiritual pride. Here Lovelace credited Charles Chauncy with several valuable insights about the Great Awakening that Edwards apparently appropriated to discern genuine from false spirituality. Paraphrasing Edwards's *Thoughts on Revival*, Lovelace wrote: "Under the guise of prophetic righteousness, pride can move awakened believers to censorious attacks on other Christians, a lack of meekness in rebuking those who really need it and a hair-trigger readiness to separate from those less holy or less orthodox." Lovelace detected this form of pride in "the institutionalized strangeness of Fundamentalism" and the "invented strangeness of the Jesus movement."[15] He also discerned that Chauncy had been correct to call for "spiritual reality more than emotional fireworks" during the events of the 1740s in Massachusetts. But Edwards "incorporated" Chauncy's critique and passed it on in a revival-friendly form that "would have prevented the abuse of cheap grace in American revivalist culture" had later revivalists not followed Edwards's understanding of the intellect, will, and emotion as essentially one, "controlling every aspect of the soul."[16]

When Lovelace explored charismatic gifts, such as prophecy and new revelations, he was less willing to follow Edwards uncritically. For instance, he observed that Edwards was rightfully dismissive of extraordinary operations of the Holy Spirit since the apostle Paul himself identified charity as the supreme mark of true spirituality. Lovelace saw dangers in exalting the gifts of the Spirit: "People who begin by being open to extrabiblical revelation will give Satan an opportunity to wean them gradually away from Scripture and establish himself as ultimate authority."[17] But so long as subjective experience operated alongside the control and critique of reason, Lovelace did not see any reason to dismiss spiritual gifts as mere enthusiasm. "If the direction of our lives is reduced to a function of reason alone," Lovelace wrote, "there is something wanting, something which does not harmonize well with Paul's description of Christians as those 'who are led by the Spirit of God' (Rom. 8:14)."[18] In the end, Lovelace could not go all the way with Edwards's assertion that Spirit-filled displays were pertinent only for the apostolic age. This argument solved some practical problems but proceeded from an "exceedingly theoretical base," derived "not from the plain sense of Scripture but from the Reformers' necessity to fight a two-front war against papists and enthusiasts."[19]

If Lovelace looked to Edwards for the foundation of spiritual theology, Iain H. Murray, whose labors resulted in *Jonathan Edwards: A New Biography* (1987), looked to the Northampton pastor, much as Gerstner had, as the font of theological orthodoxy. Born in 1931 in Lancashire, England, to parents of Scottish descent, Murray trained at King William's College on the Isle of Man and the University of Durham for the ministry. When Martin Lloyd-Jones, one of the leading figures in midtwentieth-century British evangelicalism, recruited Murray to assist him at Westminster Chapel in London, Murray was only twenty-five years old. During this time, with encouragement and support from Lloyd-Jones, Murray started (1957) Banner of Truth publications, which for evangelicals in the United Kingdom and the United States was the best inexpensive source for Edwards's writings; in 1974 the Banner brought out an 1834 London edition of Edwards's works, which, though not the best of texts or the easiest on the eyes, allowed evangelicals to have most of his writings in roughly six inches of shelf-space. Murray remained active as a pastor, taking calls to London in the 1960s and Sydney, Australia, in the 1980s. But his chief outlet was the Banner of Truth, which through publications and conferences kept alive for evangelicals of a Reformed perspective the zeal and intensity of experimental Calvinism.

Murray authored studies of other evangelical figures, including Lloyd-Jones, John Wesley, A. W. Pink, and John Murray, but his regard for Edwards was unmistakable. In his 1987 biography, he explained that his purpose was to speak to "the contemporary state of the Christian church." Murray believed that Christians, at least in the English-speaking world, needed to read Edwards because he was first and foremost a pastor, "speaking to the rank and file membership of the churches," and because of the "gifts God gave him in the exposition of Scripture." These accomplishments meant that Edwards remained "one of the foremost teachers of the church."[20]

Edwards's significance for Murray indicated that the biographer was not bashful about the religious character either of his subject or his book. In his introduction, Murray interacted with the major biographers of Edwards, including contemporaries of the Northampton pastor, and was struck by the diversity of interpretations. Several academics (e.g., Peter Gay and Herbert W. Schneider) recognized his brilliance as a philosopher but believed his Calvinist theology obscured that intellectual grandeur. Murray also noticed how differently students of Edwards had judged his character, with Gilbert Tennent stressing his candor and Perry Miller noticing a deceptive streak. To explain these antagonistic assessments, Murray went to Edwards himself on the nature of Christianity, the importance of religious experience, and the unbelief inherent in unregenerate reason. To appreciate his faith and teaching, interpreters in effect needed to be converted. "According to the New Testament, and therefore to Edwards also," Murray wrote, "the difference between the regenerate Christian and the remainder of men constitutes the most radical of all divisions." In other words, "what is revealed to babes is hidden from the proud." As such, Murray's assessment of Edwards would proceed from the starting point that his subject's faith was in fact true and biblical. Without that, interpreters would inevitably be divided because "the saving knowledge of God inevitably brings division."[21]

Despite that presupposition, Murray treated Edwards's life straightforwardly, though sometimes digressing to defend a contested point of doctrine or to show accordance between Edwards and biblical teaching. The biography was designed primarily to orient readers of his works to his life. It was effectively a book-length companion to the Banner of Truth's edition of Edwards's works. And for that reason, Murray concluded with considerations of his "continuing ministry": "The ministry of Jonathan Edwards is, very clearly, not yet concluded. He is being read today as he has not been read for over a century and in more countries than ever. Such a recovery of truth has commonly been a forerunner of revival."[22] Since Murray would eventually write a book on the difference between real revival and faux revivalism, he believed his biography might produce what Edwards himself worked to accomplish: proclamation of biblical religion for the sake of an awakened and faithful church.[23]

Although Murray's biography treated Edwards's various works roughly the same—with perhaps more space devoted to *Religious Affections* than the other treatises—John Piper's contribution to the late-twentieth-century Edwards revival was to reprint the posthumous work *The End for Which God Created the World* (1765), in Piper's estimation the book that captured best "the heart and center" of Edwards's thought and faith.[24] Piper grew up in the home of an evangelist and church planter in Tennessee before enrolling at Wheaton College, where he graduated in the same class as the evangelical historians Mark A. Noll and Nathan O. Hatch. Only while training for the ministry at Fuller Theological Seminary in Pasadena, California, did Piper begin his passionate preoccupation with Edwards. A theology professor there encouraged students to identify and study one theologian as an avocational outlet and supplement to exegesis, preaching, and pastoral counseling. Piper started with a paper for Geoffrey Bromiley on Edwards's essay on the Trinity and moved on to *The Freedom of the Will* and *The Nature of True Virtue*. While studying for a doctorate in New Testament at the University of Munich, Piper maintained his interest and plowed through *Dissertation Concerning the End for Which God Created the World*. That treatise captivated Piper and would provoke, once he took a call to pastor Bethlehem Baptist Church in Minneapolis, a lifelong interaction with Edwards, with Piper as the secondary teacher learning from the primary instruction of the Northampton pastor. [25]

Aside from Piper's own fascination with Edwards, his purpose was to encourage evangelicals to encounter the eighteenth-century New England minister and resist the theological hollowness and pragmatism that Piper believed was afflicting contemporary evangelicalism. The reprint of *End for Which God Created the World* came out in 1998, a few years after the splash created by David F. Wells's indictment of evangelicalism, *No Place for Truth*, and the ripples sustained in Os Guinness's *Fit Bodies, Fat Minds*. Piper regarded Edwards as the antidote to what ailed born-again Protestantism.[26]

In many respects, Piper continued to find in Edwards what had been appealing to his predecessors in this evangelical Edwardsian revival: a theologian who lent depth to both the born-again Protestant desire for evangelism and the individual evangelical's religious experience. But Piper's fascination with Edwards went beyond these shared evangelical ideals to zero in on some of the most abstract aspects of Christian doctrine, and a prevailing theme in Edwards, the glory of God. His ability to craft a theology that combined the believer's experience and God's glory was particularly appealing. "The *rejoicing* of all peoples in God, and the *magnifying* of God's glory are one end, not two," he wrote. "Why this is so, how it can be, and what difference it makes is what this book, and my life and Jonathan Edwards' theology, are about." Whether or not Piper's prose could create in readers what he had himself experienced while contemplating God's glory in Edwards is open to question, though Piper's own earnestness as a conference speaker would clearly persuade listeners to become buyers, if not readers, of Edwards' *End for Which God Created the World*. At the same time, someone could well imagine a contemporary evangelical reader struggling to make concrete Piper's quotation from Timothy Dwight's description of this book by Edwards: "From the purest principles of reason, as well as from the fountain of revealed truth, he demonstrates that the *chief* and *ultimate* end of the Supreme Being, in the works of creation and providence, was the manifestation of his own glory in the highest happiness of his creatures."[27]

A further curiosity of this theme in Edwards and Piper's attraction to it was how few times either one mentioned Christ. A discussion of the life and ministry of the second person of the Trinity could actually put some concreteness into the abstract notion of the supreme being's radiance and still retain Piper's concern for doctrinal recovery. But the glory of God in the experience of his creatures was sufficient for Piper and best captured Edwards's theology and devotion. The Baptist pastor quoted the following as the core of Edwards's thought:

> It appears that all that is ever spoken of in the Scripture as an ultimate end of God's works is included in that one phrase, *the glory of God*. . . . In the creature's knowing, esteeming, loving, rejoicing in, and praising God, the glory of God is both *exhibited* and *acknowledged*; his fullness is *received* and *returned*. Here is both an *emanation* and *remanation*. The refulgence shines upon and into the creature, and is reflected back to the luminary. The beams of glory come from God, are something of God, and are refunded back again to their original. So that the whole is *of* God, and *in* God, and *to* God; and he is the beginning, and the middle, and the end.[28]

Through passages such as this, Piper confessed, Edwards had taught him, "as one modern evangelical—that our concern with truth is an inevitable expression of our concern with God." He added that to love God "passionately" is to love truth with the same passion, and to be "God-centered in life" meant "being truth-driven in ministry." The reason was that "what is not true is not of God" and "what is false is anti-God."[29]

Edwards Reexamined

At the same time these seminary faculty and pastors were finding in Edwards relief for late-twentieth-century evangelicalism's woes, evangelical historians were turning to Edwards not so much for inspiration but as part of a larger effort to understand Protestant evangelicalism in North America. The number of multiauthor collections on Edwards from discernibly evangelical academics easily surpassed anything that the midtwentieth century, neo-orthodox recovery of Edwards produced. It began with a volume stemming from a conference sponsored by the Institute for the Study of American Evangelicals at Wheaton College, *Jonathan Edwards and the American Experience* (1983), and included *Edwards in Our Time: Jonathan Edwards and the Shaping of American Religion* (1999), *The Legacy of Jonathan Edwards: American Religion and the Evangelical Tradition* (2003), *Jonathan Edwards at Home and Abroad* (2003), and *A God Entranced Vision of All Things* (2004).[30] Even more impressive for the study and recovery of Edwards by evangelicals was the dent that the eighteenth-century pastor made on the research and writing of evangelicalism's two most prolific religious historians, Mark A. Noll and George M. Marsden.

Noll contributed an essay to the ISAE's volume on Edwards that was part of his larger project on nineteenth-century Protestant theology in the United States. Like the evangelical academic interest in Edwards more generally, Noll tried to limit his assessments of Edwards and his successors in the development of American Reformed theology to scholarly criteria of intellectual consistency, connections to broader currents of thought, and the size and scope of influence. For instance, in his book on the College of New Jersey, where Edwards finished his career, Noll observed the significant shift in teaching and metaphysics that accompanied the arrival of John Witherspoon and the school's subsequent identification with the philosophical traditions of the Scottish Enlightenment. Witherspoon clearly affirmed Edwards's theology, but he regarded the former president's philosophical idealism as tainted and his theology as speculative, and perhaps he suspected "that Edwards' fiercely revelational ethics was not quite respectable in an age of reason and science."[31] The subtext of this transition from Edwards to Witherspoon was a change "from idealism, metaphysics, and conversion to realism, ethics, and morality, a change that profoundly affected the college and its place in the wider world."[32] Part of the consequences of this change, Noll wrote in his conclusion, was a fundamental tension between the ideals of science and Calvinist theology. Witherspoon and others

> enlisted the procedures of the Enlightenment as apologetic means to sustain the Christian faith and thereby opened the door to the spread of naturalistic thought in America. With great optimism they affirmed their ability to discern the ends and means of social well-being and to engineer events for the perpetuation of public virtue. Yet principles accepted eagerly as if to herald the millennium soon showed them the decay of their own institutions and the prospect of apocalypse.[33]

In a word, as noble as Witherspoon's enlightened Protestantism was, it was also a failure, with the implication that it did not measure up to Edwards's own combination of Reformed orthodoxy and philosophical idealism.

The scale of the shift that uprooted American Protestant theology from Edwardsian influences was in effect the message of Noll's big book on nineteenth-century Protestant divinity, *America's God: From Jonathan Edwards to Abraham Lincoln*. Not only did Edwards function as the starting point in Noll's chronological mapping of American theology, but the Northampton pastor also supplied the benchmark for Noll's verdict of doctrinal declension. In his conclusion, he pointed out a number of contrasts between Edwards and his successors, Charles Finney and Nathaniel Taylor. One indication was the subject of virtue. In Edwards's day it was an inclination ("love to God"), but for Taylor and Finney it was an activity (self-governance or obedience to divine law). The departure from Edwards was successful on one level; American Protestant theologians thereafter "translated the historic Christian message into the dominant cultural languages of politics and intellectual life."[34] But for Noll this post-Edwardsian theology was too successful:

> Attentive readers of these pages will realize that if I had to recommend only one American theologian for the purposes of understanding God, the self, and the world as they really are, I would respond as the Separatist Congregationalist minister, Israel Holly did in 1770 when he found himself engaged in theological battle: "Sir, if I was to engage with you in this controversy, I would say *Read Edwards!* And if you wrote again, I would tell you to *Read Edwards!* And if you wrote again, I would still tell you to *Read Edwards!*"

Having reiterated Holly, Noll resumed his dispassionate pose by conceding that, as "rigorously doxological" as Edwards was, his successors "did more to Christianize and civilize unchurched Americans in a free-form liberal society than Edwards could ever have done."[35]

In his big biography of Edwards, Marsden did not let down his guard of objectivity, as Noll seemed to at the end of *America's God*. In the last chapter of *Jonathan Edwards: A Life* (2003), Marsden surveyed how various American religious figures and academics had attempted to appropriate Edwards for contemporary readers, from the first biographers down to Perry Miller and Ola Winslow. Marsden knew that his own audience and editors were not predisposed to appreciate Edwards's Calvinism. He conceded that everyone could find something in his theology, biblical exegesis, or social attitudes that appeared to be "antiquated beyond recovery." At the same time, Marsden implicitly implored his readers to leave behind "naïve assumptions" that the most recent ideas and arguments were "best." If they were to "contemplate Edwards' view of reality with its awesome implications" they would be doing "well." Marsden went farther, to suggest that the part of Edwards most valuable for contemplation was his understanding that reality was basically a "communication of affections, ultimately of God's love and creatures' responses." In other words, material things were "transitory and ephemeral" and found their meaning only "in relation to the loves at the center of reality." In this sense, Edwards offered an important correction to modern men and women who were generally preoccupied with the physical side of reality. According to Marsden, Edwards challenges "us to see the universe as most essentially God's unceasing action."[36]

This was a much more modest plea than John Piper's instruction to evangelicals, but when Marsden spoke or wrote about Edwards beyond the confines of a university press audience he was willing to suggest Edwards's relevance for contemporary Christians. For instance, in the collection of essays entitled *Jonathan Edwards at 300*, Marsden drew the assignment of appropriating Edwards for the twenty-first century. He refashioned some of his remarks from the end of his biography to challenge contemporary Christians to see the material world as a manifestation of deeper spiritual realities, including the ever-present danger of believing in God primarily as existing "to protect our happiness and to prevent calamities." Marsden also addressed evangelical believers when he warned how an "emphasis on conversion and testimony gets turned into celebration of one's own experience."[37] The proper antidote to a "truly God-centered" experience was whether it conformed, according to Edwards's own instruction, to the fruit of the Holy Spirit and obedience to God's revealed will. Marsden added: "Ironically, today's American evangelicals seem to be more followers of Benjamin Franklin than of Edwards. They admire practicality, friendliness, moralism, easy formulas, and quantifiable results. While these Franklinesque traits are not all bad, they sometimes contribute to evangelical superficiality. . . . Awareness and respect for the Edwardsean part of their heritage would be a healthy balance."[38]

Marsden's appropriation of Edwards did not by any means speak for all evangelical academics who were busy lecturing and writing on the eighteenth-century pastor in connection at least with his tercentenary. But the use to which both Marsden and Noll put Edwards for their understanding of Christian history in the United States added a layer of depth to the appreciation that had been building since the 1960s among seminary professors, pastors, and lay believers. When the generation of evangelical historians—Marsden, Noll, Nathan O. Hatch, Harry S. Stout, and Grant Wacker among others—began around 1980 to produce substantial work and collaborate on American religious history, Edwards was a significant figure who shared the stage with other important evangelical leaders, notably Charles Finney, Dwight L. Moody, Billy Sunday, Charles Fuller, and Billy Graham. But by the beginning of the twenty-first century, Edwards had, through the efforts of historians such as Marsden and Noll, become the standard by which to judge subsequent evangelical developments.

Young, Restless, and Edwardsian

Whether the efforts of Gerstner, Lovelace, Murray, Piper, Noll, and Marsden were simply those of forerunners to the recent revival of Calvinism is in the eye of the beholder, but the interest in Edwards cultivated during the last half of the twentieth century has been decisive for a contemporary revival of Reformed theology. Collin Hansen, a reporter for *Christianity Today*, documented the breadth of the resurgence of Calvinism in his book *Young, Restless, and Reformed: A Journalist's Journey with the New Calvinists* (2008). Of the figures explored here, Murray, Noll, and Marsden make cameo appearances in Hansen's reporting. Piper, in contrast, receives almost as much attention as Edwards, the "homeboy" of the young students flocking to hear Piper's Calvinistic sidekicks, who range from R. Albert Mohler, Jr., the president of Southern Baptist Theological Seminary in Louisville; to Mark Driscoll, the Seattle-based leader of the emergent church movement, Acts 29. According to Hansen, J. I. Packer, who was urging a recovery of Puritanism at the same time Gerstner was beginning to write on Edwards, said of Piper's ministry, *Desiring God*, that "Jonathan Edwards, whose ghost walks through most of Piper's pages, would be delighted with his disciple."[39]

As much as Hansen sprinkled Piper's presence and remarks throughout the book, the young journalist devoted an entire chapter to Edwards, the "Big Man on Campus." The student body reference stemmed in part from Hansen's journey to New Haven to see Yale's Beinecke Rare Book and Manuscript Library, the Divinity School, Edwards College, the Jonathan Edwards Center, and the pastor's papers—Hansen even held "Sinners in the Hands of an Angry God" in his own hands. To be sure, Piper provided the frame of reference for Hansen's trip to Edwards's alma mater. The reporter quoted Piper on the significance of Edwards before interviewing the various academics and pastors responsible for Calvinist teaching and practice in New Haven: "What Edwards saw in God and in the universe because of God, through the lens of Scripture, was breathtaking."[40] Somewhat more restrained was the regard that Caleb Maskell, the associate director of the Edwards Center, expressed for arguably Yale's most notable graduate: "To have Edwards on your shelf—better yet to read him—is to say, 'I want to be deeply connected to the church that has come before . . . with the orthodoxy that the church has espoused.' "[41] Hansen also interviewed Calvinistic pastors in the vicinity of Yale, including Josh Moody, a Baptist pastor, originally from the United Kingdom, who wrote a dissertation on Edwards en route to a Ph.D. from Cambridge University. Moody explained that part of the reason for the resurgence of interest in Edwards owed to a larger set of reservations about the Enlightenment. According to Moody, "It's taken us two hundred years to realize, as Edwards did, that we should not be bowled over by the Enlightenment." "Edwards helps us with that," Moody added, "particularly with issues of the emotions. He does really good surgery on the heart and mind."[42]

As useful as Edwards was for intellectually inclined seekers and believers, both Moody and Hansen expressed worries about the gap between his soaring thoughts and run-of-the-mill evangelical piety. Hansen admitted to reading *Religious Affections*—all four hundred pages in the Banner of Truth edition—closely, but he had not "dared" to pick up *Freedom of the Will*. Moody extended those misgivings: "Even if reading Edwards makes someone think, *This is too much for me*, I'm quite glad it does, because it makes them feel there's something they should be shooting for that's a little more profound than cheesy Christianity."[43] Distress over the intellectual prowess needed to read and reflect on Edwards was appropriately enough the dark cloud on the horizon of Hansen's sunny young Calvinist phenomenon. The appeal of Edwards to academics, pastors, and Yale students involved in campus ministries made perfect sense. But would such academically inclined evangelicals find churches, pastors, or co-religionists with whom to bask in the glow of Edwards's glorious God?

Indeed, ever since the Great Awakening that Edwards defended and in which he participated, born-again Protestantism has thrived on forms of reflection and devotion geared to mass appeal rather than metaphysical grandeur. H. L. Mencken captured well evangelicalism's ability to appeal to the common and unlearned in a piece he wrote about the twentieth-century revivalist Billy Sunday, which also spoke volumes about similar evangelists before and since:

> Even setting aside [Sunday's] painstaking avoidance of anything suggesting clerical garb and his indulgence in obviously unclerical gyration on his sacred stump, he comes down so palpably to the level of his audience, both in the matter and the manner of his discourse, that he quickly disarms the old suspicion of the holy clerk and gets the discussion going on the familiar and easy terms of a debate in a barroom. The raciness of his slang is not the whole story by any means; his attitude of mind lies behind it, and is more important. . . . It is marked, above all, by a contemptuous disregard of the theoretical and mystifying; an angry casting aside of what may be called the ecclesiastical mask, an eagerness to reduce all the abstrusities of Christian theology to a few and simple and (to the ingenuous) self-evident propositions, a violent determination to make of religion a practical, an imminent, an everyday concern.[44]

To be sure, Edwards was the one significant exception to this observation— the one evangelist more suitable to the classroom than the barroom. But this also makes him the exception that proves the rule. The revival of Calvinism since the 1950s among evangelical Protestants has shown remarkable growth. But just as the fires of awakening cooled in Edwards's own church and town, the Edwardsian revival among born-again Protestants may likely follow a similar course. In this case, the end of revival, if it comes, will have less to do with the work of the third person of the Trinity and more with a philosophical idiom that only compounds the "abstrusities of theology" against which evangelicals instinctively rebel.

Postscript

Douglas A. Sweeney and Oliver D. Crisp

DESPITE THIRTY YEARS of scholarship on Jonathan Edwards's vast legacy, represented ably in the volume now before you, many continue to assume that his work proved largely feckless till American evangelicals conscripted it for service in the culture wars of the late twentieth century. Even magisterial histories of American Christianity, such as the recent one by Gary Wills, a scholar and media spokesman for religious literati, claim with confidence that in spite of Edwards's vaunted reputation "he had no great impact on American religious practice or thought"—let alone the practice and thought of people in other parts of the world.[1] But as this book has demonstrated beyond the shadow of a doubt, such assumptions cannot last. That impact has been great, both in America and beyond. It has been rural and cosmopolitan, religious, social, and cultural, American, British, broadly Western, and non-Western too. In short, Edwards has become one of the few Protestant leaders who have changed the world forever—through his ministry, his writings, and the labors of his followers.

The contributors to this volume disagree among themselves about how best to interpret the nature, value, and history of Edwards's legacy. But all agree on this: it has been larger, far more global, and more enduring than we knew—or than we even know today. Edwardsian Calvinism did not decline but flourished in the decades of the early nineteenth century, spreading quickly to Britain and Europe through a network that we might well call the Christian republic of letters,[2] and to other parts of the world by means of the modern missions movement (which Edwards himself helped to inspire).[3] Indeed, Edwards may well be America's most popular serious theologian even now.

And we will need more work on his legacy if we are to come to terms with this, the difference it makes in the world, and the attraction of his Calvinism to millions of modern believers.[4]

This volume is not intended as a conversation stopper. Rather, we hope it will incite further academic interest in the courses of Edwardsian theology. Many of those courses have been charted briefly here. Others have not been mentioned, either because they want an explorer or because they remain too novel for reliable assessment. All of them need more travelers, cartographers, and scribes. In conclusion, then, we offer a few suggestions to scholars interested in helping us interpret and improve on the legacy.

Of the courses mapped out summarily in this volume, we suggest that those in Asia and Europe need the most attention. Anri Morimoto has admitted in his chapter that there is no one, including himself, who has the language skills requisite to survey Edwards's legacy in Asia comprehensively. An international team of academics is required, with diverse language skills and methods, to study his legacy in the world's most varied region. Edwards has attracted the most interest in Japan, Korea, and China. The Koreans, in fact, are reading him more fervently and productively than anyone beyond the borders of Britain and the United States. But Edwards is also read in Arabic, and in parts of southern Asia. (He is read in Australia too, which is, of course, another continent on which his star is rising.)[5] We need a group of younger scholars to follow the leads that are provided in the Morimoto chapter and explore the legacy in the whole of modern Asia, the continent Edwards deemed most central to the history of redemption.[6]

As Michael McClymond makes clear, there is also much to do on Edwards's legacy in Europe. McClymond's is perhaps the most original essay bound within the covers of this book, yet it only scratches the surface of the continent of Europe. A recent Edwards conference in Budapest attracted due attention to his legacies in central, southern, and even eastern Europe, yielding publications in English and Hungarian. As we compose these very words, scholars in Poland are preparing to host an Edwards conference there. And Edwards Centers are emerging in Poland, Benelux (Leuven), and Germany, all satellites of the Edwards Center at Yale. It is time to pay attention to appropriations of Edwards not only in Scotland, England, and Holland but in Hungary, Slovakia, France, the Czech Republic, Poland, Italy, and other parts of Europe—where he is studied today not only for religious edification but for import in theology, English language and literature, and American history and culture. It is time to chart his legacy on the continent he knew best.[7]

Regarding the courses of Edwards' legacy that are not addressed here, there are several deserving increased attention. None has attracted enough notice yet for summative analysis (at least not of the sort provided in these chapters), but all of them contain a wide array of raw materials, some of which are rich enough for use by theologians, and a few of which are mentioned in other secondary sources.

We need much more work on Edwardsian women. Beginning with New England's Great Awakening and continuing at least through the antebellum period, there were far more women than men who converted in the revivals led by Edwards and his followers, feminizing the movement in ways that complement and sometimes contradict the "feminization" limned more famously by scholars in the train of Ann Douglas.[8] Edwards recommended the piety of parishioner Abigail Hutchinson, the precocious Phebe Bartlet, and his own wife, Sarah, in his writings on revival.[9] Sarah Edwards, her daughter Mary, Susanna Anthony, Sarah Osborn, and the elderly Phebe Bartlet shaped the ministries of Edwardsians such as Edwards, Samuel Hopkins, Timothy Dwight, Elias Cornelius, and Andover's Justin Edwards.[10] Many Edwardsian women helped to lead revival conference meetings, Sunday schools, missions groups, and benevolent societies.[11] Osborn and Anthony led the women's prayer group that undergirded Newport's First Church. Osborn led a revival there (1766–67) and pioneered in ministry to local black Americans. With Anthony, she became a key player in her church's call of Hopkins to its pastorate (1770) and served as his advisor and confidante when he arrived.[12] Nathanael Emmons's wife, Martha, performed her husband's pastoral calls.[13] The Edwardsian Mary Lyon established Mount Holyoke Seminary in 1837, leading eleven revivals and preparing scores of missionaries and Christian social workers before she died young in 1849.[14] This striking list could well be rounded out. It should be rounded out. We hope that others will help us navigate this course.

Another course for further work is Native American Christianity. The new Indian history is moving beyond the tired cliché of European-Native encounters in which white people are always and only exploitative agents of religiously fueled imperialism and Indians are weak and passive victims. Of course, white Christians did exploit America's aboriginal people. But recent studies also suggest that Native Americans appropriated Edwards for themselves. We ought to know why this took place and what they did with Edwards's thought. Rachel Wheeler has worked carefully on these questions for many years, producing a pathbreaking book, *To Live upon Hope: Mohicans and Missionaries in the Eighteenth-Century Northeast* (2008). Joel Martin and Mark Nicholas offer other intriguing leads, though few with theological substance, in *Native Americans, Christianity, and the Reshaping of the American Religious Landscape* (2010). Oxford University Press has published the writings of the Mohegan Edwardsian pastor Samson Occom. But we still know very little about this subject.[15]

Black Edwardsian theology deserves attention too. A few academics and clergy have studied the black New Divinity parson and public intellectual Lemuel Haynes, and the Edwardsian roots of modern black theology.[16] Others have examined Edwardsian roles in the antislavery and colonization movements, and the faith of black colonists in Liberia and beyond.[17] But there has also been a recent surge of interest in Edwards's thought among Reformed black Christians in the United States and the Caribbean.[18] And a Jonathan Edwards Centre has arisen in South Africa, promising further work on his legacy there.[19] We have more work, that is, to perform on black Edwardsian theology, especially beyond New England.

Finally, Edwards is gaining readers in many Latin American countries. Although Central and South America remain largely Catholic, evangelicalism is growing there and some of its adherents have appropriated Edwards. A couple of his writings are now available in Spanish, even more in Portuguese. Most of these publications are popular and aimed at shaping piety. But a fledgling Edwards Center based in São Paulo, Brazil, hopes to promote research and academic writing as well. Edwards scholar Gerald McDermott recently spoke in Cuba to a large group of clergy. A few Latin American scholars also plan to work on Edwards. But very few academics north of the border know about this. It is time for an assessment of the prospects of Edwardsian thought among Latino scholars and practitioners.[20]

Our aim here is not to impose a comprehensive agenda for the work of future scholars. Rather, our aim, in conclusion, is to emphasize the vast scope of Edwards's varied legacies and the courses of Edwardsian theology. North American scholars often cite the large number of books and articles written on him, as if to suggest that we now know more than we need to know about him. But as this volume has displayed, there is far more to his reach than anyone knew or even imagined only a decade ago, when we commemorated the Edwards tercentennial. He has been studied and put to use among a wide—indeed, surprising and ironic—array of people, in nearly every part of the world. If we are to understand his legacy and historical significance, we have more work to do. And if we are to make good on his legacy in theology today, we must improve our view of the paths on which it has reached us over time. Much of the work that lies before us will require a new, more global, intellectual orientation. So we call for teachable scholars with impressive language skills, intercultural experience, and a creative, energetic, and intrepid curiosity. Come and join us on a fascinating voyage of discovery as we navigate the history and the future of Edwards's thought.

Notes

INTRODUCTION

1. Edwards Amasa Park, "New England Theology," *Bibliotheca Sacra* 9 (1852), 169–217. This essay was part of the "paper war" between Park and Charles Hodge (and others), about which theological school actually represented the legitimate developments of Edwards's ideas. Although Hodge and the "Old Light" Presbyterians expended considerable energy in trying to wrest Edwards from the New England theologians, Park seems to have had the better part of the controversy. His essay offers a sophisticated and nuanced treatment of topics in Edwardsian theology, which Hodge was unable to match. It is, as Douglas Sweeney and Allen Guelzo have recently put it, "the *Urtext* for those assessing Edwards's role in New England's theological ancestry." From Sweeney and Guelzo, eds. *The New England Theology: From Jonathan Edwards to Edwards Amasa Park* (Grand Rapids: Baker Academic, 2006), 257.
2. Park, "New England Theology."
3. Gerald McDermott and Michael McClymond explain the history and development of different designations for the New England Theology and offer an overview of the debate about when the movement actually began in *The Theology of Jonathan Edwards* (New York: Oxford University Press, 2011), chap. 38.
4. YE1: 362–363.
5. Ibid., 179.
6. See Edwards Jr. "Three Sermons on the Necessity of Atonement and the Consistency Between that and Free Grace in Forgiveness," in Edwards Amasa Park, *The Atonement: Discourses and Treatises by Edwards, Smalley, Maxcy, Emmons, Griffin, Burge and Weeks* (Boston: Congregational Board of Publication, 1859), 1–42.

7. Samuel Hopkins, "System of Doctrines," in *The Works of Samuel Hopkins, D.D., in 3 Vols.* (Boston: Doctrinal Tract and Book Society, 1852 [1793]), Vols. 1–2.

8. Harriet Beecher Stowe, *The Minister's Wooing* (New York: Derby and Jackson, 1859), chap. XXIII, 332.

9. Ibid., 334.

10. For the historiography of New England Theology, see Mark A. Noll, "Jonathan Edwards and Nineteenth Century Theology," in Nathan O. Hatch and Harry S. Stout, eds. *Jonathan Edwards and the American Experience* (New York: Oxford University Press, 1988), 260–287; and Douglas A. Sweeney, "Edwards and His Mantle: The Historiography of the New England Theology," in *New England Quarterly* 74.1 (1998), 97–119. Representative of the recent (and more appreciative) revisionist accounts of the New England Theology are William Breitenbach, "Piety and Moralism: Edwards and the New Divinity," in *Jonathan Edwards and the American Experience*, 177–204; Joseph A. Conforti, *Jonathan Edwards, Religious Tradition, and American Culture* (Chapel Hill: University of North Carolina Press, 1995); and Conforti, *Samuel Hopkins and the New Divinity Movement: Calvinism, the Congregational Ministry, and Reform in New England Between the Great Awakenings* (Grand Rapids: Eerdmans, 1981); Allen Guelzo, *Edwards on the Will: A Century of American Theological Debate* (Eugene, OR: Wipf and Stock, 2007 [1989]); Bruce Kuklick, *Churchmen and Philosophers: From Jonathan Edwards to John Dewey* (New Haven: Yale University Press, 1985); Douglas A. Sweeney, *Nathaniel Taylor, New England Theology, and the Legacy of Jonathan Edwards* (New York: Oxford University Press, 2003); Sweeney and Guelzo, "Introduction," in *The New England Theology*, 13–24; and Mark Valeri, *Law and Providence in Joseph Bellamy's New England: The Origins of the New Divinity in Revolutionary America* (New York: Oxford University Press, 1994).

11. George A. Gordon, writing in 1908, says quite plainly that "[t]his age is characterized by a strong aversion to severe thinking. Immediacy has become a habit, perhaps a disease. Its motto is, He that runs may read; and the reader who intends to run as he reads must not choose for his race-course the New England divinity." Gordon, "The Collapse of the New England Theology," in *Harvard Theological Review* 1.2 (1908): 133.

12. The two standard treatments of the New England Theology were written within a decade of one another at the turn of the twentieth century. See George Nye Boardman, *A History of New England Theology* (New York: A. D. F. Radolph, 1899); and Frank Hugh Foster, *A History of the New England Theology* (Chicago: University of Chicago Press, 1907).

13. The *locus classicus* is Joseph Haroutunian, *Piety Versus Moralism: The Passing of New England Theology from Edwards to Taylor* (Eugene, OR: Wipf and Stock, 2006 [1932]). But in some respects Boardman and Foster might be thought to offer precursors to this interpretation. Similar sentiments are to be found in Benjamin Warfield, "Edwards and the New England Theology," reprinted in

The Works of Benjamin B. Warfield (New York: Oxford University Press, 1932 [1912]), 515–538.

14. Anri Morimoto, *Jonathan Edwards and the Catholic View of Salvation* (University Park: Pennsylvania State University Press, 1995).

15. Park, "New England Theology," 211.

CHAPTER 1

1. Samuel Hopkins, *The Life and Character of the Late Reverend Mr. Jonathan Edwards... Together with a Number of his Sermons* (Boston, 1765), A2.

2. Hopkins, *Life and Character of Edwards*, 40–42, 53.

3. For a list of New Divinity pastors, see Joseph A. Conforti, *Samuel Hopkins and the New Divinity Movement: Calvinism, the Congregational Ministry, and Reform in New England Between the Great Awakenings* (Grand Rapids, MI: Eerdmans, 1981), 227–232. For evidence of the public voice and intellectual influence of the New Divinity, see Conforti, *Samuel Hopkins*, 95–158; Mark Valeri, *Law and Providence in Joseph Bellamy's New England: The Origins of the New Divinity in Revolutionary America* (New York: Oxford University Press, 1994); and Bruce Kuklick, *Churchmen and Philosophers: From Jonathan Edwards to John Dewey* (New Haven: Yale University Press, 1985), 43–65.

4. David W. Kling, *A Field of Divine Wonders: The New Divinity and Village Revivals in Northwestern Connecticut, 1792–1822* (University Park: University of Pennsylvania Press, 1993); Mark Valeri, "The New Divinity and the American Revolution," *William and Mary Quarterly*, 3rd ser., 46 (1989): 741–769; William K. Breitenbach, "Unregenerate Doings: Selflessness and Selfishness in New Divinity Theology," *American Quarterly* 34 (1982): 479–502; and Conforti, *Samuel Hopkins*, 109–158.

5. For quite different answers to these questions, see Frank Hugh Foster, *A Genetic History of the New England Theology* (Chicago: University of Chicago Press, 1907); Joseph Haroutunian, *Piety Versus Moralism: The Passing of the New England Theology* (New York: Holt, 1932); and Allen C. Guelzo, *Edwards on the Will: A Century of American Theological Debate* (Middletown, CT: Wesleyan University Press, 1989).

6. A helpful survey is provided in the "Introduction" to and commentary on primary sources in Douglas A. Sweeney and Allen C. Guelzo, *The New England Theology: From Jonathan Edwards to Edwards Amasa Park* (Grand Rapids, MI: Baker Academic, 2006), esp. 13–24.

7. For the narrative of the revivals, their aftermath, and Edwards's role in them, on which the following paragraphs are based, see George M. Marsden, *Jonathan Edwards: A Life* (New Haven: Yale University Press, 2003), 201–252.

8. Edwards, "Personal Narrative," in YE16:797. For Edwards's reading, see the "Editor's Introduction" to YE26: 1–113, esp. 26. For the Boston clergy, see John Corrigan,

The Prism of Piety: Catholic Congregational Clergy at the Beginning of the Enlightenment (New York: Oxford University Press, 1991).

9. Joseph Bellamy, "Student Notebook," 1736, Joseph Bellamy Papers, Miscellaneous Personal Papers, Ms. Group 30, Box 179, Yale Divinity School, New Haven, Connecticut. John Edwards's *Theologia Reformata* was first published in London in 1713 and enlarged for a 1726 edition: see Peter J. Thuesen, YE26: 27, 142, 227.

10. Douglas L. Winiarski, "Jonathan Edwards, Enthusiast? Radical Revivalism and the Great Awakening in the Connecticut Valley," *Church History* 74 (2005): 683–739.

11. Valeri, *Law and Providence*, 13–33.

12. See the "Editor's Introduction" to YE4: 1–89.

13. The covenant is contained in Edwards to Thomas Prince, 1742, in YE4: 551.

14. Conforti, *Samuel Hopkins*, 30–31; Valeri, *Law and Providence*, 57, n. 39.

15. Jonathan Edwards, *A Treatise Concerning Religious Affections* (Boston, 1746), in YE2, esp. 383–461.

16. Bellamy, quoted in Valeri, *Law and Providence*, 48. For the point about Edwards's religious agenda, see William K. Breitenbach, "Piety and Moralism: Edwards and the New Divinity" in *Jonathan Edwards and the American Experience*, ed. Nathan O. Hatch and Harry S. Stout (New York: Oxford University Press, 1988), 177–204.

17. Most historians of the Great Awakening are quick to make distinctions between what they call "moderate" and "radical" New Lights, but they stress differences in revival techniques or understandings of ordained ministry rather than, as I have done here, the Edwardsian confidence in formal theological thought. See Thomas Kidd, *The Great Awakening*, and Mark A. Noll, *A History of Evangelicalism: People, Movements and Ideas in the English Speaking World, Vol. 1: The Rise of Evangelicalism: The Age of Edwards, Whitefield and the Wesleys* (Downers Grove, IL: InterVarsity Press, 2003).

18. For civility, reasonableness, and politeness, see David S. Shields, *Civil Tongues and Polite Letters in British America* (Chapel Hill: University of North Carolina Press, 1997); and Michael J. Rozbicki, *The Complete Colonial Gentleman: Cultural Legitimacy in Plantation America* (Charlottesville: University of Virginia Press, 1998).

19. Thuesen, "Editor's Introduction" and subsequent entries in YE26: 33–34, 76, 157–158, 248, 326–327, 343.

20. There is an extensive literature documenting Edwards's use of these Enlightenment figures to promote the evangelical message, including Norman Fiering, *Jonathan Edwards's Moral Thought and Its British Context* (Chapel Hill: University of North Carolina Press, 1981); Leon Chai, *Jonathan Edwards and the Limits of Enlightenment Philosophy* (New York: Oxford University Press, 1998); and Avihu Zakai, *Jonathan Edwards's Philosophy of History: The Reenchantment of the World in the Age of Enlightenment* (Princeton: Princeton University

Press, 2003). Edwards's large and comprehensive reading list, which includes all of the authors listed here, is described in Thuesen, "Editor's Introduction" in YE26.

21. Jonathan Edwards, "Preface" to Bellamy, *True Religion Delineated* (Boston, 1750), i, vii–viii.

22. The "paper war" is evident in the publication records from this period; see also M. X. Lesser, *Reading Jonathan Edwards: An Annotated Bibliography in Three Parts, 1729–2005* (Grand Rapids, MI: Eerdmans, 2008), 50–55.

23. The quote from the rural admirer is cited in Valeri, *Law and Providence*, 56; see also 45–51; Conforti, *Samuel Hopkins*, 37, Robert L. Ferm, *Jonathan Edwards the Younger, 1745–1801: A Colonial Pastor* (Grand Rapids, MI: Eerdmans, 1976), 66–67. Hopkins tellingly entitled his magnum opus *The System of Doctrines*, 2 vols. (Boston, 1793).

24. John Clarke, *An Essay upon Study* (London, 1731; 2nd ed. London, 1737), 59; James Burgh, *Youth's Friendly Monitor* (London, 1754), last page (unnumbered). For Edwards's mention of these works, see Thuesen, "Editor's Introduction," in YE26: 27–28, and 243, 283–284.

25. Hopkins, *Jonathan Edwards*, 40; Valeri, *Law and Providence*, 48.

26. Thuesen, "Editor's Introduction," in YE26: 47–49, 68–70; Valeri, *Law and Providence*, 48–49.

27. This is the central point of Edwards's *Nature of True Virtue*.

28. Hopkins, *Jonathan Edwards*, 52.

29. Samuel Hopkins, *A Bold Push* (Boston, 1758), 6, 11.

30. Joseph Bellamy, *True Religion Delineated* (Boston 1750), in *The Works of The Rev. Joseph Bellamy, D. D.* (New York, 1811), 3 vols., 1: 48, 50–51; and Joseph Bellamy, *Essay on the Nature and Glory of the Gospel* (Boston, 1762), in Works, 2: 337.

31. Jonathan Edwards the Younger, "Remarks on the Improvements Made in Theology by His Father; President Edwards," in *The Works of Jonathan Edwards, D. D., Late President of Union College* (Boston, 1854), 2 vols.: 1: 484, 488.

32. Nathanael Emmons: "Autobiography," in *The Works of Nathanael Emmons, D.D.... With a Memoir of His Life*, ed. Jacob Ide (Boston, 1842), 6 vols., I: xix–xxiii, xxix.

33. For one example of urban disdain, see Edmund S. Morgan, *The Gentle Puritan: A Life of Ezra Stiles, 1727–1795* (New Haven: Yale University Press, 1962), 444–450.

CHAPTER 2

1. For treatments of Edwards's *education*, as opposed to him as an *educator*, see Mary Gambrell, *Ministerial Training in Eighteenth-Century New England* (New York: Columbia University Press, 1937); Richard Warch, *School of Prophets: Yale*

College, 1701–1733 (New Haven: Yale University Press, 1973); Wallace E. Anderson, "Editor's Introduction" to YE6; and William M. Sparks, *The Young Jonathan Edwards: A Reconstruction* (Eugene, OR: Wipf & Stock, 2005).

2. On the age cohorts in Edwards's developmental model, see Kenneth P. Minkema, "Old Age and Religion in the Writings and Life of Jonathan Edwards," *Church History* 70 (December 2001), 674–704.

3. Quotes in this section from Edwards's letter to Pepperrell can be found in YE16: 406–414.

4. The long and convoluted saga of the boarding schools at Stockbridge, beginning with John Sargeant, is told in George M. Marsden, *Jonathan Edwards: A Life* (New Haven: Yale University Press, 2003), chap. 23.

5. See, for example, Kenneth A. Lockridge, *Literacy in Colonial New England* (New York: Norton, 1974), 43–71; David Hackett Fischer, *Albion's Seed: Four British Folkways in America* (New York: Oxford University Press, 1989), 130–134.

6. Locke, *Some Thoughts Concerning Education* (London, 1690), was in the Dummer Collection (*Eighteenth-Century Catalogues of the Yale College Library*, ed. James Mooney, New Haven, Yale University Press, 2001, A41) and was cited by Edwards in "Miscellanies" no. 1210, from George Turnbull, *Principles of Moral and Christian Philosophy* (2 vols., London, 1740); on Edwards's acquaintance with the scholastic disputation, see his M. A. *Quaestio*, YE14: 47–66.

7. Edwards, *Freedom of the Will*, YE1: 148.

8. On the Edwards's preparatory school in their East Windsor, Connecticut, home, see John Stoughton, *Windsor Farmes, 1694–1750: A Glimpse of an Old Parish* (Hartford, 1883), 76–80; Ola Winslow, *Jonathan Edwards, 1703–1758: A Biography* (New York: Macmillan, 1941), 40–41; Kenneth P. Minkema, "Sisterhood, Courtship, and Marriage in the Edwards Family in the Early Eighteenth Century," *New England Historic and Genealogical Register* CXLVI (Jan. 1992), 35–56.

9. Edwards, "Personal Narrative," in YE16: 794.

10. Samuel Hopkins, *Life and Character of the Late Rev. Mr. Jonathan Edwards* (Boston, 1765), 46–47.

11. See Roland A. Delattre, *Beauty and Sensibility in the Thought of Jonathan Edwards: An Essay in Aesthetics and Theological Ethics* (New Haven: Yale University Press, 1968); Louis J. Mitchell, "Jonathan Edwards on the Experience of Beauty." *Studies in Reformed Theology and History*, no. 9 (2003): 1–115; and Amy Plantinga Pauw, *The Supreme Harmony of All: The Trinitarian Theology of Jonathan Edwards* (Grand Rapids: Eerdmans, 2003).

12. MS, Gen. Mss. 151, f. 1263, Beinecke Rare Book and Manuscript Library, Yale University; transcript in WJEO 39.

13. On the generational nature of the revivals, see Patricia J. Tracy, *Jonathan Edwards, Pastor: Religion and Society in Eighteenth-Century Northampton* (New York, Hill & Wang, 1980), chaps. 4 and 5.

14. Edwards, MS Sermon on Is. 53:3 (no. 93), n.d. [late 1728–early 1729], Gen. Mss. 151, f. 321, Beinecke Library.

15. *A Valedictorian Oration by John Sargeant, Delivered at Yale College in the Year 1729* (New York, 1882), 22–24.

16. Samuel Hopkins confirms this when he states that Edwards thought "with his pen in his hand." Hopkins, *Life and Character*, 44.

17. Edwards to Trustees of the College of New Jersey, October 19, 1757, YE16: 726, 729. For an early engagement of JE with Hebrew during his college years, see his parsing, in Latin, of Ps. 1, Edwards Mss., f. ND5.11, Franklin Trask Library, Andover Newton Theological School; and on his interest in Hebrew late in life, see the MS "Hebrew Idioms," Gen. Mss. 151, f. 1211, Beinecke Library.

18. *Ibid.*, 84.

19. Edwards, MS sermon no. 443 (originally preached at Northampton, Aug. 1737; repreached Feb. 1758), Gen. Mss. 151, f. 863, Beinecke Library.

20. Edwards, MS sermon no. 742 (originally preached at Northampton May 1744, repreached July 8, 1744, at Southampton; January 1754 to the Stockbridge Indians; and Feb. 1758), Gen. Mss. 151, f. 878, Beinecke Library.

21. Hopkins, *Life and Character*, pp. 24–25.

22. MS, Gen. Mss. 151, f. 1263, Beinecke Library; transcript in WJE 39.

23. Providence, 1822; transcript in WJE 39. The origin of this pamphlet is something of a mystery, but we can speculate that Sereno Dwight, Edwards' great-grandson, had a hand in it, since at this time he was preparing the ten-volume edition of Edwards's *Works* published in New York, 1829.

24. *Bibliotheca Sacra*, XXXIX (April 1882), 367–381.

25. Ordination sermons by Edwards include those for Jonathan Judd, at Southampton, Massachusetts, published as *The Great Concern of a Watchman for Souls* (Boston, 1743); Robert Abercrombie, at Pelham, Massachusetts, published as *The True Excellency of a Minister of the Gospel* (Boston, 1744); Samuel Buell, at Easthampton, Long Island, New York, published as *The Church's Marriage to Her Sons, and to Her God* (Boston, 1746); Job Strong, at Portsmouth, New Hampshire, published as *Christ the Great Example of Gospel Ministers* (Boston, 1750); Edward Billing, at Greenfield, Massachusetts, 1754, and Cornelius Jones, at Sandisfield, Massachusetts, 1756, published as *Christ's Sacrifice an Inducement to His Ministers*. All of these are collected in YE25; other ordination sermons available are in Richard A. Bailey and Gregory A. Wills, eds., *The Salvation of Souls: Nine Previously Unpublished Sermons on the Call of Ministry and the Gospel by Jonathan Edwards* (Wheaton, IL: Crossway, 2002): David White, at Lambstown (Hardwick), Massachusetts, 1736, published as *The Minister Before the Judgment Seat of Christ*; Edward Billing, at Cold Spring, Massachusetts, 1740, published as *Ministers Not to Preach Their Own Wisdom But the Word of God*; Chester Williams, at Hadley, Massachusetts, 1741, published as *Pastor and People Must Look to God*.

26. See "Preface to the Period," in WJE 25:14–19.

27. YE25: 443–456.

28. YE25: 466.

29. YE25: 92–93.

30. MS, "Joseph Bellamy H. B. 1736," Yale Divinity School, Special Collections, pp. 3–4. I have made use of a transcript kindly provided by Mark Valeri.

31. Ibid., p. 13.

32. These include Robert Jenkin's *The Reasonable and Certainty of the Christian Religion* (2 vols., London, 1698); Samuel Willard's *A compleat body of divinity in two hundred and fifty expository lectures on the Assembly's Shorter Catechism* (Boston, 1726); Sir Walter Raleigh, *The historie of the world* (London, 1614); Humphrey Ditton, *A Discourse Concerning the Resurrection of Jesus Christ* (London, 1712, though Edwards used the third edition, 1722); and John Anderson's *A defence of the church-government, faith, worship & spirit of the Presbyterians* (Glasgow, 1714).

33. Edwards, Preface to *Discourses on Various Important Subjects*, YE19: 797.

34. For general background on the role of the "parsonage seminary" in the New Divinity movement, see Melvin B. Endy, Jr., "Theology and Learning in Early America," in *Schools of Thought in the Christian Tradition*, ed. Patrick Henry (Philadelphia, Fortress Press, 1984), 125–151.

35. "Memoir," in *The Works of Joseph Bellamy, D.D.* (2 vols., New Haven, 1811), 1: 34.

36. Mark Valeri, *Law and Providence in Joseph Bellamy's New England* (New York: Oxford University Press, 1994), 56–57; Glenn P. Anderson, "Joseph Bellamy (1719–1790): The Man and His Work," Ph. D. diss., Boston University, 1971, pp. 651–657.

37. On the New Divinity dominance of New England pulpits, see David Kling, *A Field of Divine Wonders: The New Divinity and Village Revivals in Northwestern Connecticut, 1792–1822* (University Park: Pennsylvania State University Press, 1993).

38. Gambrell, *Ministerial Training in Eighteenth-Century New England*, 111.

39. Stephen West, *Sketches of the Life of the Late Rev. Samuel Hopkins, D.D.* (Hartford, 1805), 41–43.

40. Edinburgh imprints include *History of the Work of Redemption* (1774), *Practical Sermons Never Before Published* (1788), *Twenty Sermons on Various Subjects* (1789), *Miscellaneous Observations on Important Theological Subjects* (1793), and *Remarks on Important Theological Controversies* (1796). On the popularity of Edwards's printed works in nineteenth-century America, see Joseph Conforti, *Jonathan Edwards, Religious Tradition, and American Culture* (Chapel Hill, University of North Carolina, 1995), chap. 2.

41. Joseph Conforti, *Samuel Hopkins and the New Divinity Movement* (Grand Rapids: Eerdmans, 1981), chaps. 8 and 9; Kenneth P. Minkema and Harry S. Stout, "The Edwardsean Tradition and the Antislavery Debate, 1740–1865," *Journal of*

American History 92 (June 2005), 1–28; John Saillant, *Black Puritan, Black Republican: The Life and Thought of Lemuel Haynes, 1753–1833* (New York: Oxford University Press, 2003).

42. *Familiar letters, written by Mrs. Sarah Osborn, and Miss Susanna Anthony* (Newport, RI, 1807); Hopkins, *The life and character of Miss Susanna Anthony* (Worcester, 1796).

43. See, for example, Amanda Porterfield, *Feminine Spirituality in America: From Sarah Edwards to Martha Graham* (Philadelphia: Temple University Press, 1980); Genevieve McCoy, "The Women of the ABCFM Oregon Mission and the Conflicted Language of Calvinism.," *Church History* 64 (March 1995): 62–82; and Sharon Y. Kim, "Beyond the Men in Black: Jonathan Edwards and Nineteenth-Century Women's Fiction," in David W. Kling and Douglas A. Sweeney, eds., *Jonathan Edwards at Home and Abroad: Historical Memories, Cultural Movements, Global Horizons* (Columbia: University of South Carolina Press, 2003), 137–153.

44. Sarah Pierpont Edwards had given sermons and some of the "long papers" to Hopkins for eventual publication and a biography. See Samuel Hopkins to Joseph Bellamy, January 19, 1758, Hartford Seminary Foundation. As the leading intellectual of the family, Jonathan Jr. was given the bulk of his father's library, and in 1767 he was officially recognized by his siblings as the caretaker. Timothy Edwards et al., "Presentment," March 27, 1767, Gen. Mss. 151, f. 1666, Beinecke Library.

45. William Patten, *Reminiscences of the Late Rev. Samuel Hopkins, D.D., of Newport, R.I.* (Providence, 1843), 47. Edwards Jr. nonetheless retained some differences in his thought from his father, such as on atonement and on "Mentor's scheme of the introduction of evil." See "Remarks on the Improvements Made in Theology by His Father, Pres. Edwards," in *Works of Jonathan Edwards, D.D.* (2 vols., Boston, 1842), 1: 481–492; and Jonathan Edwards Jr. to Joseph Bellamy, January 25, 1770, Gen. Mss. 151, f. 1414, Beinecke Library.

46. Jedidiah Morse, *A sermon, preached at Charlestown, November 29, 1798, on the anniversary thanksgiving in Massachusetts. With an appendix, designed to illustrate some parts of the discourse; exhibiting proofs of the early existence, progress, and deleterious effects of French intrigue and influence in the United States* (Boston, 1798).

47. Robert L. Ferm, *Jonathan Edwards the Younger, 1745–1801* (Grand Rapids: Eerdmans, 1976), 88.

48. The earliest version we have of Edwards the Younger's list is a copy from 1794 in the hand of one of his students, Maltby Gelston, titled "A Systematic Collection of Questions and Answers in Divinity." Yale University Manuscript and Archives Division, Misc. MSS Collection, MS 353, Series III. E-G, box 5, f. 499.

49. Dorus P. Rudisill, *The Doctrine of the Atonement in Jonathan Edwards and His Successors* (New York: Poseidon Books, 1971).

50. Samuel Nott, "The Life of the Rev. Samuel Nott, D.D.," typescript, p. 87, Congregational House, Hartford, Connecticut.

51. That Edwards Jr. drew up these items for his students is suggested by the existence of a separate list of directions for his *own* preaching, including not speaking too fast, or in "too high a key," or—echoing the last point in the "Observations"—warning himself against "preaching metaphysically." "Corrigenda," Franklin Trask Library.

52. Samuel Dutton, *A History of the North Church in New Haven* (New Haven, 1842), 72n; William Sprague, *Annals of the American Pulpit* (New York, 1857), 1: 657.

53. Jonathan Edwards, Jr., "On the Abridgement of Blair," Edwards Mss., f. ND3.1, Franklin Trask Library.

54. That is, confused or thrown into disorder.

55. Jonathan Edwards, Jr., "Order of Commencement, May 6, 1801," Edwards Mss., f. ND 3.4, Franklin Trask Library.

56. Jonathan Edwards, Jr., "Address to the Graduates," n.d., Edwards Mss., f. ND 3.4, Franklin Trask Library, pp. 14–15.

57. Conforti, *Jonathan Edwards, Religious Tradition, and American Culture*, chap. 4; Amanda Porterfield, *Mary Lyon and the Mt. Holyoke Missionaries* (New York: Oxford University Press, 1997); David W. Kling, "The New Divinity and Williams College, 1793–1836," *Religion and American Culture* 6 (1996), 195–223; Charles Phillips, "The Last Edwardsean: Edwards Amasa Park and the Rhetoric of Improved Calvinism," Ph.D. diss., University of Stirling, 2005.

CHAPTER 3

1. Gerald R. McDermott, *One Holy and Happy Society: The Public Theology of Jonathan Edwards* (University Park: Pennsylvania State University Press, 1992), 65; JE, "A Faithful Narrative" and "Some Thoughts Concerning the Revival," in YE4: 168, 353, 510, 520, 540.

2. JE, "The Mind" no. 17, in YE6: 345; JE, "Account Book," in YE26: 339–340, 350; William S. Morris, "The Genius of Jonathan Edwards," in *Reinterpretations in American Church History*, ed. Jerold Brauer (Chicago: University of Chicago Press, 1968), 29–36; and Morris, *The Young Jonathan Edwards: A Reconstruction* (Brooklyn: Carlson, 1991), 79–80.

3. JE, "Personal Narrative," in YE16: 791–792, 799; Thomas S. Kidd, *The Great Awakening: The Roots of Evangelical Christianity in Colonial America* (New Haven, CT: Yale University Press, 2007), 13–15.

4. JE, "A Faithful Narrative" and "Some Thoughts Concerning the Revival," in YE4: 168, 503.

5. Jonathan Dickinson, *The True Scripture Doctrine Concerning Some Important Points of Christian Faith* (Boston: D. Fowle, 1741); Bryan F. LeBeau, *Jonathan Dickinson and the Formative Years of American Presbyterianism* (Lexington: University Press of Kentucky, 1997), 153–154. On Edwards's place in the larger context of deterministic thought in the eighteenth century, see Norman Fiering,

Jonathan Edwards's Moral Thought in Its British Context (Chapel Hill: University of North Carolina Press, 1981), 261–321.

6. Mettrie, *Man A Machine*, ed. G. C. Bussey (LaSalle, IL: Open Court, 1921; originally published 1748), 94–95, 133; Benjamin Franklin, "A Dissertation of Liberty and Necessity," (1725), in *The Papers of Benjamin Franklin, Vol. One*, ed. Leonard Labaree (New Haven, CT: Yale University Press, 1959), 62; and Franklin, *The Autobiography and Other Writings*, ed. Jesse Lemisch (New York: Signet, 1961), 56.

7. Edwards, "Miscellanies" nos. 363 and 436, in YE13: 435, 484–485; Fiering, *Jonathan Edwards's Moral Thought*, 283.

8. Edwards, "Miscellanies" no. 657, in YE18: 197; Edwards to John Erskine (August 31, 1748), to Joseph Bellamy (January 15, 1750), and to Thomas Foxcroft (May 24, 1753), in YE16: 248–249.

9. Edwards, YE1: 137, 138, 141–143; Philip F. Gura, *Jonathan Edwards: America's Evangelical* (New York: Hill & Wang, 2005), 187–192.

10. YE1: 164.

11. *Ibid.*, 172, 176, 207; Clyde A. Holbrook, *The Ethics of Jonathan Edwards: Morality and Aesthetics* (Ann Arbor: University of Michigan Press, 1973), 40–43.

12. YE1: 150.

13. *Ibid.*, 156, 157, 159, 162.; John E. Smith, *Jonathan Edwards: Puritan, Preacher, Philosopher* (Notre Dame: University of Notre Dame Press, 1992), 68–69.

14. Edwards, YE3: 107.

15. *Ibid.*, 120, 128, 134, 164, 184, 207, 210, 262, 264.

16. *Ibid.*, 383, 399, 404; Conrad Cherry, *The Theology of Jonathan Edwards: A Reappraisal* (1966; Gloucester, MA: Peter Smith, 1974), 92–94.

17. Joseph Conforti, "Edwards A. Park and the Creation of the New England Theology, 1840–1870," in *Jonathan Edwards's Writings: Text, Context, Interpretation*, ed. Stephen J. Stein (Bloomington: Indiana University Press, 1996), 196–203; Mark A. Noll, "Edwards' Theology After Edwards," in *The Princeton Companion to Jonathan Edwards*, ed. Sang Hyun Lee (Princeton: Princeton University Press, 2005), 296–298.

18. Margaret Oliphant, *Thomas Chalmers: Preacher, Philosopher and Statesman* (New York: Houghton Mifflin, 1893), 6; Sir James Mackintosh, "Jonathan Edwards," in *The Miscellaneous Works of the Rt. Hon. Sir James Mackintosh* (Philadelphia: Carey & Hart, 1846), 130; R. J. Mackintosh, *Memoirs of the Life of the Right Honourable Sir James Mackintosh* (London: Edward Moxon, 1835), 1: 13; Hall, "Preface" to "Help to Zion's Travellers," in *The Works of the Rev. Robert Hall, A.M.* (New York: G. & C. Carvill, 1830), 2: 335; Knapp, *Lectures on American Literature: With Remarks on Some Passages of American History* (New York: Elam Bliss, 1829), 82; Rowland G. Hazard, *Freedom of Mind in Willing, or Every Being That Wills a Creative First Cause* (New York: D. Appleton, 1864), 173.

19. James T. Kloppenberg, "The Virtues of Liberalism: Christianity, Republicanism and Ethics in Early American Political Discourse," *Journal of American History* 74 (1987), 28.

CHAPTER 4

1. John Brown, *John Brown, Liberator of Kansas and Martyr of Virginia: Life and Letters*, ed. Franklin B. Sanborn (Cedar Rapids, IA: Torch, 1910), 10–11; Evan Carton, *Patriotic Treason: John Brown and the Soul of America* (New York: Simon and Schuster, 2006), 22–23; Louis A. DeCaro, *"Fire from the Midst of You": A Religious Life of John Brown* (New York: New York University Press, 2002), 23; D. S. Reynolds, *John Brown, Abolitionist: The Man Who Killed Slavery, Sparked the Civil War, and Seeded Civil Rights* (Vintage, 2006), 19, 21, 25–27, 41, 43, 47–48, 151–152.

2. Samuel West, *Essays on Liberty and Necessity* (New Bedford, MA: John Spooner, 1795), 19. This section summarizes some of the arguments that I covered in James P. Byrd, *Jonathan Edwards for Armchair Theologians* (Louisville, KY: Westminster John Knox Press, 2008), especially chapters 2, 4, and 6.

3. YE1: 362–363, 156–162; Allen C. Guelzo, *Edwards on the Will: A Century of Theological Debate*, 1st ed. (Middletown, CT: Wesleyan University Press, 1989), 46–50.

4. YE2: 191–208. See also Jonathan Edwards, "A Divine and Supernatural Light," in *The Sermons of Jonathan Edwards*, ed. Wilson Kimnach, Kenneth Minkema, and Douglas Sweeney (New Haven, CT: Yale University Press, 1999), 126–127; George M. Marsden, *Jonathan Edwards: A Life* (New Haven, CT: Yale University Press, 2003), 96.

5. YE2: 256.

6. YE2: 383–411, especially 393–394, 407, 411.

7. James Hutson, *The Founders on Religion: A Book of Quotations* (Princeton, NJ: Princeton University Press, 2003), 147; George Marsden, *Jonathan Edwards*, 464–468.

8. YE16: 552.

9. YE16: 539.

10. YE16: 540.

11. YE16: 550.

12. YE16: 550, 552, 554–555; Avihu Zakai, "The Age of Enlightenment," in *The Cambridge Companion to Jonathan Edwards*, ed. Stephen J. Stein (Cambridge: Cambridge University Press, 2007), 91–95.

13. YE16: 589–590, 597; Norman Fiering, *Jonathan Edwards' Moral Thought and Its British Context* (Chapel Hill: University of North Carolina Press, 1981), 105–149; Stephen H. Daniel, "Edwards as a Philosopher," in *The Cambridge Companion to Jonathan Edwards*, ed. Stephen J. Stein (Cambridge: Cambridge University Press, 2007), 174–177; John E. Smith, "Christian Virtue and Common Morality," in *The Princeton Companion to Jonathan Edwards* (Princeton, NJ: Princeton University Press, 2005), 147–166.

14. William Breitenbach, "The Consistent Calvinism of the New Divinity Movement," *William and Mary Quarterly* 41(2), 3rd series (1984): 242.

15. Breitenbach, "Consistent," 244; Joseph A. Conforti, *Samuel Hopkins and the New Divinity Movement: Calvinism, the Congregational Ministry, and Reform in New England Between the Great Awakenings* (Grand Rapids, MI: Christian University Press, 1981), chapters 1 and 2.

16. E. Brooks Holifield, *Theology in America: Christian Thought from the Age of the Puritans to the Civil War* (New Haven, CT: Yale University Press, 2003), 138.

17. Breitenbach, "Consistent," 143; Holifield, *Theology*, 127, 136.

18. Joseph Bellamy reflected the polemical opponents of the New Divinity in the title of his *True Religion delineated; or, Experimental Religion, As distinguished from Formality on the one Hand, and Enthusiasm on the other, set in a Scriptural and Rational Light. In Two Discourses. In which some of the principal Errors both of the Arminians and the Antinomians are confuted, the Foundation and Superstructure of their different Schemes demolished, and the Truth as it is in Jesus, explained and Proved* (Boston: S. Kneeland, 1750). Edwards contributed the preface to Bellamy's treatise. Holifield, *Theology*, 137.

19. William Hart, *Remarks on President Edwards' Dissertations concerning the Nature of true Virtue* (New Haven, CT: T. and S. Green, 1771).

20. William Hart, *Brief Remarks on a Number of False Propositions, and Dangerous Errors, Which Are Spreading in the Country* (New London, CT: Timothy Green, 1769), 49; Joseph Haroutunian, *Piety Versus Moralism: The Passing of the New England Theology* (New York: Holt, 1932), 67–68.

21. William Hart, *A Letter to the Rev. Samuel Hopkins, Occasioned by His Animadversions on Mr. Hart's Late Dialogue.* (New London, CT: T. Green, 1770), 11.

22. Hart, *Letter*, 15; Hart, *Remarks on President Edwards' Dissertations*, 8–9, 19, 21, 30–31, 34.

23. Hart, *Remarks on President Edwards' Dissertations*, 40–41.

24. Samuel Hopkins, *Works: With a Memoir of His Life and Character*, vol. 3 (Boston: Doctrinal Tract and Book Society, 1854), 6–7; Conforti, *Hopkins*, 117–118.

25. Among the New Divinity discussions of this important distinction, two by John Smalley were distinctive: *The Consistency of the Sinner's Inability to Comply with the Gospel; with His Inexcusable Guilt in Not Complying with It* (Hartford, CT: Green & Watson, 1769); and *The Inability of the Sinner to Comply with the Gospel, His Inexcusable Guilt in Not Complying with It, and the Consistency of These with Each Other, Illustrated, in Two Discourses* (Boston: John Kneeland, 1772).

26. This was a controversial point, with New Divinity ministers such as Hopkins receiving criticism for their belief that "human depravity is a moral, and not a natural, disorder." Ebenezer Bradford, *Strictures on the Remarks of Dr. Samuel Langdon on the Leading Sentiments in the Rev. Dr. Hopkins' System of Doctrines* (Boston: I. Thomas and E. T. Andrews, 1794), 18. William Breitenbach, "Unregenerate Doings: Selflessness and Selfishness in New Divinity Theology," *American Quarterly* 34(5) (1982): 484; Samuel Hopkins, *A New Edition of Two Discourses, Delivered by Samuel Hopkins* (Bennington, VT: Anthony Haswell, 1793), 57.

27. Hopkins, *Works*, 3: 85. See also Nathanael Emmons, *The Works of Nathanael Emmons, D.D.*, 3 vols. (Boston: Congregational Board of Publication, 1860), 3: 106.

28. Hopkins, *Works*, 3: 81, 84.

29. Hopkins, *Works*, 3: 82; Hopkins, *An Enquiry Concerning the Promises of the Gospel* (Boston: 1765), 76–77; Holifield, *Theology*, 141; Douglas A. Sweeney and Allen C. Guelzo, eds., *The New England Theology: From Jonathan Edwards to Edwards Amasa Park* (Grand Rapids, MI: Baker Academic, 2006), 118–119.

30. Hopkins, *Two Discourses*, 60.

31. As Hopkins wrote, "In conversion man is active, and it wholly consists in his act: but in regeneration the spirit of God is the only active cause." Hopkins, *Two Discourses*, 58–59. Nathanael Emmons went even further in stressing the moral ability of humanity in both regeneration and conversion. He asserted that "sinners are not *passive*, but *active* in regeneration." Moreover, "sinners may be as active in regeneration as in conversion," even though sinners acted not of themselves but "under a divine influence," in renegotiation as well as in sanctification. Emmons, *Works*, 3: 109–110.

32. Hopkins, *An Enquiry*, 76–81, 124–125; Hopkins, *Two Discourses*, 30, 32–33; Holifield, *Theology*, 139–141.

33. Hopkins, *Works*, 3: 18, 26, 28–29, 30, 33, 70.

34. Hopkins, *Works*, 3: 31, 34, 41, 48, 63.

35. Hopkins, *Works*, 3: 148, 156–157.

36. Hopkins, *Works*, 3: 65–66. Hopkins's colleague Joseph Bellamy expressed a similar view, arguing that many so-called Christians of the day sought religion "only to get just Grace enough to carry them to Heaven; as a lazy Hireling that is for doing only just Work enough...that he may get his Wages...which is all he wants." Bellamy, *True Religion*, 90.

37. New Divinity activists for missions included Samuel Hopkins (who pursued mission in Africa), Jonathan Edwards the Younger (who helped launch the Connecticut Missionary Society), and Nathanael Emmons (who assisted in founding the Massachusetts Missionary Society). Several New Divinity ministers also helped to launch the American Board of Commissioners for Foreign Missions; Sweeney and Guelzo, *New England Theology*, 150. The Edwardsian zeal for missions influenced American evangelicals throughout the nineteenth century. See especially the work of Joseph A. Conforti in several books and articles, including "Samuel Hopkins and the New Divinity: Theology, Ethics, and Social Reform in Eighteenth-Century New England," *William and Mary Quarterly* 34(4), 3rd series (October 1977): 572–589; "Mary Lyon, the Founding of Mount Holyoke College, and the Cultural Revival of Jonathan Edwards," *Religion and American Culture* 3(1) (1993): 69–89; "Jonathan Edward's Most Popular Work: 'The Life of David Brainerd' and Nineteenth-Century Evangelical Culture," *Church History: Studies in Christianity and Culture* 54(2) (2009): 188–201; and *Jonathan Edwards, Religious Tradition, & American Culture* (Chapel Hill: University of North Carolina Press, 1995).

38. Kenneth P. Minkema, "Jonathan Edwards on Slavery and the Slave Trade," *William and Mary Quarterly* 54(4), 3rd series (October 1, 1997): 823–834; Kenneth P. Minkema and Harry S. Stout, "The Edwardsean Tradition and the Antislavery Debate, 1740–1865," *Journal of American History* 92(1) (2005): 47–74; Ava Chamberlain, "Edwards and Social Issues," in *The Cambridge Companion to Jonathan Edwards*, ed. Stephen J. Stein (Cambridge: Cambridge University Press, 2007), 340–342.

39. Hopkins's letter to Moses Brown, April 29, 1784, quoted in Conforti, *Hopkins*, 134.

40. Hopkins, *Works*, 2: 562–565. Hopkins argued against pro-slavery interpretations of several biblical texts, including the famous "curse of Noah." For a history of interpretation of this text in relation to slavery, see Stephen R. Haynes, *Noah's Curse: The Biblical Justification of American Slavery* (New York: Oxford University Press, 2007).

41. Minkema and Stout, 52; Conforti, *Hopkins*, 125–127.

42. Hopkins, *Works*, 2: 559–562; Conforti, *Hopkins*, 127–128; David Brion Davis, *The Problem of Slavery in the Age of Revolution, 1770–1823* (New York: Oxford University Press, 1999), 280–281. Hopkins's *Dialogue Concerning the Slavery of the Africans* was printed in Samuel Hopkins, *The Works of Samuel Hopkins: With a Memoir of His Life and Character*, ed. Edwards Amasa Park, vol. 2 (Boston: Doctrinal Tract and Book Society, 1854), 547–588.

43. Quotation is from Hopkins, *Works*, 3: 23. For his full discussion of the three types of self-love, see pp. 22–27. As historian William Breitenbach argued, New Divinity theology "allowed a person to purse his self-interest by redefining it as a form of disinterested benevolence." Breitenbach, "Unregenerate Doings," 501–502. See also James D. German, "The Social Utility of Wicked Self-Love: Calvinism, Capitalism, and Public Policy in Revolutionary New England," *Journal of American History* 82(3) (December 1995): 965–998; Mark Valeri, "Jonathan Edwards, The Edwardsians, and the Sacred Cause of Free Trade," in *Jonathan Edwards at Home and Abroad: Historical Memories, Cultural Movements, Global Horizons*, ed. David W. Kling and Douglas A Sweeney (Columbia: University of South Carolina Press, 2003), 85–100.

44. Edwards, Jr., *Injustice*, 10–13, 33.

45. Hopkins, *Works*, 2: 550–552, 584–585.

46. Hopkins, *Works*, 2: 570–571. See also Davis, *Slavery*, 275–276.

47. Hopkins, *Works*, 2: 556–557.

48. Hopkins, *Works*, 2: 572–574.

49. Sweeney and Guelzo, *New England Theology*, 151.

CHAPTER 5

1. Dorus Paul Rudisill makes much the same point when he says: "The Atonement was not a theological issue in New England during Edwards's ministerial career.

Opportunity for the articulation of his polemic predilection was afforded by other issues." *The Doctrine of Atonement in Jonathan Edwards and His Successors* (New York: Poseidon Books, 1971), 20–21.

2. The most important historic discussion of this matter is Edwards Amasa Park's Introduction to *The Atonement: Discourses and Treatises by Edwards, Smalley, Maxcy, Emmons, Griffin, Burge and Weeks* (Boston: Congregational Board of Publication, 1859), which also contains treatment of the topic by a number of key New England theologians, including Jonathan Edwards, Jr., and John Smalley. What emerges from this work is the fact that there was some difference of views about how to understand the atonement within the New England theology. Rudisill's *The Doctrine of The Atonement* is the most accessible published treatment in the modern secondary literature.

3. The *locus classicus* of this "decline and fall" reading of the development of New England theology away from the piety and genius of Edwards, to a moribund moralism, is Joseph Haroutunian, *Piety Versus Moralism: The Passing of New England Theology from Edwards to Taylor* (Eugene, OR: Wipf and Stock, 2006, originally published 1932). This monograph set the tone for much subsequent twentieth-century commentary on the movement, but it has been superseded by more nuanced treatments of New England Theology. A helpful account of the vicissitudes attending the historiography of the New England Theology can be found in Douglas A. Sweeney, "Edwards and His Mantle: The Historiography of the New England Theology," in *New England Quarterly* 74.1 (1998), 97–119. My own reading of the New Divinity is closer to that of such scholars as William Breitenbach, who argues (*contra* Haroutunian) that "the leading tendencies of Edwards's system can be discovered by tracing the trajectory of his ideas in the theology of his New Divinity successors." Moreover, "this Edwardsean theology, for all its originality, should be seen as maintaining the fundamental commitment of New England Puritanism to the reconciliation of grace and law." Breitenbach, "Piety and Moralism: Edwards and the New Divinity," in Nathan O. Hatch and Harry S. Stout, eds. *Jonathan Edwards and the American Experience* (New York: Oxford University Press, 1988), 178. Also of use in this regard is Joseph A. Conforti, *Jonathan Edwards, Religious Tradition, and American Culture* (Chapel Hill: University of North Carolina Press, 1995), 123–126; and Mark Valeri, *Law and Providence in Joseph Bellamy's New England: The Origins of the New Divinity in Revolutionary America* (New York: Oxford University Press, 1994), especially 14–15 on his debt to Edwards and 123–125 on the atonement.

4. Something of this changing social context is described by Mark Noll in *America's God: From Jonathan Edwards to Abraham Lincoln* (New York Oxford University Press, 2005), especially chap. 7.

5. *The New England Theology, from Jonathan Edwards to Edwards Amasa Park*, eds. Douglas A. Sweeney and Allen C. Guelzo (Grand Rapids, MI: Baker Academic, 2006), 133–134. See also Guelzo's *Edwards on the Will: A Century of American*

Theological Debate (Eugene, OR: Wipf and Stock, 2007 [1989]). He seizes on the New Divinity view as an instance of doctrinal development that was decidedly non-Calvinist, especially in the matter of the scope of the atonement, commenting that "the most startling departure from received Calvinist doctrine which the New Divinity undertook concerned the central doctrine of Christian theology, the atonement" (129). Note, however, that Sweeney is sympathetic to the view expressed in this chapter elsewhere in his work. See, e.g., his *Nathaniel Taylor, New England Theology, and the Legacy of Jonathan Edwards* (New York: Oxford University Press, 2002), chap. 5.

6. Hypothetical universalism is the dogmatic genus of which English hypothetical universalism and the Amyraldism of the School of Saumur (following the Scot John Cameron and his French disciple, Moise Amyraut) are different species—a point that has not always been entirely clear in the literature. An excellent discussion of this can be found in Jonathan D. Moore, *English Hypothetical Universalism: John Preston and the Softening of Reformed Theology* (Grand Rapids, MI: Eerdmans, 2007).

7. See Garry Williams's "A Critical Exposition of Hugo Grotius' Doctrine of the Atonement in *De Satisfactione Christi*" (D. Phil. thesis, Oxford University, 1999). I discuss this in "Penal Non-Substitution," *Journal of Theological Studies* NS, 59.1 (2008): 140–168.

8. As G. Michael Thomas has recently pointed out, it cannot be claimed "on the basis of the Reformation and classical period [of the development of Reformed confessionalism subsequently] that there was ever such a thing as a coherent and agreed 'Reformed position' on the extent of the atonement"; *The Extent of the Atonement: A Dilemma for Reformed Theology from Calvin to the Consensus (1536–1675)* (Milton Keynes: Paternoster, 1997), 249–250. There were a number of different, related views on a spectrum that were permissible in early Reformed theology, including doctrines that allowed a universal scope to the atonement, favored by the Amyraldians, Anglican hypothetical universalists and such continental divines as Matthias Martinius, who was a member of the Bremen delegation to the Synod of Dordt, where he distinguished himself by vociferously defending this doctrine. (See Thomas, *Extent of the Atonement*, chap. 7, especially 137–138.)

9. This was a strategy Hodge adopted in other controversies too, e.g., when dealing with the sacramental Calvinism of John Williamson Nevin—but that is another story. Sweeney discusses the "paper war" between Charles Hodge and Edwards Amasa Park in the midnineteenth century about who was the rightful theological heir of Jonathan Edwards, in " 'Falling Away from the General Faith of the Reformation?': The Contest over Calvinism in Nineteenth-Century America," in Thomas J. Davis, ed. *John Calvin's American Legacy* (New York: Oxford University Press, 2010), 111–146. Hodge makes oblique reference to this dispute in *Systematic Theology Vol. II.* (Grand Rapids, MI: Eerdmans, 1940 [1871]),

578–579. Benjamin Warfield adopts essentially the same position in "Edwards and the New England Theology," reprinted in *The Works of Benjamin B. Warfield* (New York: Oxford University Press, 1932 [1912]), 515–538. There he speaks of the New England theologians' "substitution of the Governmental (Grotian) for the Satisfaction doctrine of the Atonement"; ibid., 535. This is inaccurate. The New England governmental theory of atonement was not identical to the Grotian version, as I have argued in "Penal Non-Substitution."

10. Robert W. Jenson, *America's Theologian: A Recommendation of Jonathan Edwards* (New York: Oxford University Press, 1988), 124.

11. See, e.g., Miscellany entries t, oo, 21, 25, 32, 306, 319, 321b, 357, 366, 388, 398, 424, 449, 451, 506, 516, 589, 594, 622, 698, 728, 764a, 772, 779, 781, 798, 898, 915, 1035, 1076, 1083, 1145, 1211–1214, 1217, 1295, 1352.

12. Edwards, *Miscellany* 774 in YE18: 437.

13. Jonathan Edwards, *"Controversies" Notebook*, WJEO 27, located at http://edwards. yale.edu/ (last accessed April 13, 2011). I am grateful to Mark Hamilton for this reference. Compare sermon 14 in *A History of the Work of Redemption*, where Edwards says that Christ's purchase of redemption includes two things: his satisfaction and merit. His work "pays our debt and so it satisfies by its intrinsic value and agreement between the Father and the Son; it procures a title for us to happiness and so it merits. The satisfaction of Christ is to free us from misery, and the merit of Christ is to purchase happiness for us." In YE9: 304.

14. Park, Introduction, *Atonement,* xi–xii.

15. Edwards seems to think all sin is sin against God, irrespective of who the sin is aimed at, because all sin is a failure of benevolence to being in general, and being in general is identified with God (in his dissertation on *True Virtue*). This seems implausible. Exploring it would take us too far afield from our present concern. So, to avoid this inconvenience I offer this weaker premise: that humans normally commit at least one such sin. This leaves open the question of limit cases such as humans who die in childbirth, or in the womb, or who are morally incapable, such as the severely mentally handicapped. The claim that all sin is directed against God is discussed by Jonathan L. Kvanvig in "Jonathan Edwards on Hell" and William J. Wainwright in "Jonathan Edwards on the Doctrine of Hell," both in Paul Helm and Oliver D. Crisp, eds., *Jonathan Edwards: Philosophical Theologian* (Aldershot: Ashgate, 2003), 1–12 and 13–26, respectively.

16. This is the preponderant view one finds in Edwards's remarks on this subject. However, John Gerstner thinks Miscellany 306 may be an exception because Edwards says there that if God did not punish sin, no one could accuse him of wrongdoing. "How could an Anselmian like Edwards say that?" asks Gerstner. But the aim of the Miscellany is to establish on what basis it is true to say God must punish sin; Edwards reasons that it cannot be merely on the basis of bare justice. Rather, it must be that he is obliged "in holiness and wisdom" to punish

sin because it would not be a "prudent, decent or beautiful" thing for God to fail so to act. But God is essentially prudent, decent, and beautiful, as well as holy and wise. So he must punish sin. The claim that God could fail to punish sin without being accused of wrongdoing is puzzling to be sure. But in context, it is clear that whatever he may mean by that, Edwards is not abandoning the Anselmian notion that God must punish sin. His worry seems to be that justice alone, without this richer moral understanding of the divine nature, is not a sufficient reason for thinking that God must punish sin. But taken together with this rich account of the divine nature, it is necessary and sufficient to the task. See Miscellany 306 in YE13: 391; and Gerstner, *The Rational Biblical Theology of Jonathan Edwards Vol. II* (Powhatan, VA: Berea, 1992), 435–436.

17. Jonathan Edwards, YE1: 362–363.

18. Harriet Beecher Stowe, *Oldtown Folks* (Boston: Fields, Osgood and Co., 1869), 374; chap. XXIX, entitled "My Grandmother's Blue Book" (which is her copy of *True Religion Delineated* wrapped in a blue dust cover) is concerned with the influence of the New Divinity through Edwards and Bellamy. Her story is based on recollections of the period in which the New Divinity flourished.

19. See Crisp, "Penal Non-substitution." This article is a prequel to this essay.

20. Jonathan Edwards, Preface to Joseph Bellamy, *True Religion Delineated* (Boston: S. Kneeland, 1750), vi–vii.

21. See letter 117, to the Rev. John Erskine in YE16: 347–356. Edwards remarks, "I have had opportunity to read the manuscript and, in my humble opinion, it has a tendency to give as much light in this matter as anything that ever I saw" (YE16: 348). He goes on to say that he is "persuaded his book might serve to give the church of God considerable light as to the nature of true religion, and many important doctrines of Christianity" (YE16: 349). See also letter 106 to Joseph Bellamy, in the same volume.

22. *True Religion Delineated* (Morris-Town: Henry P. Russell, 1804 [1750]), 352. All subsequent references are to this edition.

23. Bellamy, *An Essay on The Nature and Glory of The Gospel of Jesus Christ*, §IV, in *The Works of Joseph Bellamy, DD., Vol. 2* (Boston: Doctrinal Tract and Book Society, 1853), 313. Later he says, "Thus the whole mediatorial scheme is designed, and in its own nature adapted, to do honor to the divine law" (315). Similar sentiments are expressed in *True Religion Delineated*, where he says, "The death of Christ was not designed, at all, to take away the evil nature of sin, or its ill deserts.... But the death of Christ was rather, on the contrary, to acknowledge and manifest the evil nature and ill desert of sin, to the end that pardoning mercy might not make it seem to be less evil than it really is: So that God may freely pardon all our sins, and entitle us to eternal life for Christ's sake" (339; cf. 333, 343).

24. "The truth is, that when Christ laid down his life a ransom for all, he only accomplished what he undertook at the beginning. Christ actually interposed as Mediator immediately upon the fall of man, and undertook to secure the divine

honor, by obeying and suffering in the room of a guilty world; and therefore, through him, God did offer mercy to Cain as well as to Abel, and show common favor to the world in general, as well as grant special grace to the elect." *True Religion Delineated*, 355.

25. Bellamy, *True Religion Delineated*, 354.

26. If the purchase of sinful humanity by the atonement were unconditional, then Bellamy would have a problem with double payment. As it is, by making the effectiveness of the atonement conditional on its appropriation by faith, he elides this objection. Christ's work makes human salvation possible; it is made effectual only through the gift of faith, which all humans can ask for (natural ability), though only the elect will avail themselves of it (moral inability). Part of the problem in understanding exactly what Bellamy commits himself to is that his language in *True Religion Delineated* is popular, somewhat repetitious, and less rigorous than that of, say, Edwards's *Freedom of the Will*.

27. *True Religion Delineated*, 361. Emphasis added.

28. "Arminianism" included a wider group than theological Arminianism. For Edwards it was a term that encapsulated a range of theologically liberalizing tendencies in the New England churches, of which theological libertarianism was one particular instance. For discussion of this, see Paul Ramsey's Introduction to *Freedom of the Will*, 3.

29. Two examples of this can be found in Charles Mingus's Blue Note album *Moanin'* (1958), which contains two "takes" on the piece, and in the Mingus Big Band version of *Moanin'* in the album *The Essential Mingus Big Band* (2001).

30. *Miscellany* t says this: "Now Arminians, when [they] say that Christ died for all, cannot mean, with any sense, that he died for all any otherwise than to give all an opportunity to be saved; and that, Calvinists themselves never denied. He did die for all in this sense; 'tis past all contradiction." YE13: 175.

31. In this respect, Bellamy's view is similar to Amyraldism, the adherents of which typically adopt a "multiple intentions" account of the atonement: God first intends to save all, but his decree is ineffectual because of human sin; so, in a consequent decree he intends to save the elect only, via the faith they are given. For discussion of this in the case of John Davenant, see Moore, *English Hypothetical Universalism*, 205–208.

32. Guelzo, *Edwards on the Will*, 135. He goes on, "It would not have been difficult at all for Edwards or anyone else to have embraced such an idea of the atonement—indefinite in theoretical scope, limited in actual application—and still insist that he was within the ambit of Westminster Calvinism" (ibid.). That is precisely my point: Edwards would not have thought Bellamy's doctrine beyond the bounds of what was doctrinally permissible for a Reformed theologian.

33. Compare Guelzo, who maintains that "a little reflection will show that the New Divinity doctrine of the atonement represented hardly more than an elaboration of what Edwards himself had laid the foundations for." *Edwards on the Will*, 134.

34. I am grateful to Mark Hamilton, Paul Helm, and Douglas Sweeney for comments on a previous draft of this essay.

CHAPTER 6

1. YE1: 131.
2. Edwards to the Reverend Joseph Bellamy, January 15, 1747, in YE16: 211.
3. Aza Goudriaan, *Reformed Orthodoxy and Philosophy*, 1625–1750, Brill's Series in Church History ed. Wim Janse, vol. XXVI (Leiden: Brill, 2006), 14ff. Goudriaan's book is an excellent comparative study of three Reformed theologians, Gisbertus Voetius, Van Mastricht, and Antonius Driessen, especially their attitude to scholastic philosophy and the rise of Cartesianism in Holland. It is a useful sourcebook for details of the theological outlook of Van Mastricht.
4. Jonathan Edwards to the Trustees of the College of New Jersey, October 1757, YE26: 727.
5. John Gill, *A Body of Divinity*, 2 vols., 1769.
6. For a discussion of this influence, see Paul Helm, "A Forensic Dilemma: John Locke and Jonathan Edwards on Personal Identity," in Paul Helm and Oliver D Crisp, eds., *Jonathan Edwards, Philosophical Theologian* (Aldershot: Ashgate, 2003), 45–59.
7. *Pneumatologia, or, A Discourse on the Holy Spirit* (1674), *The Works of John Owen*, ed. W. H. Goold (Edinburgh: Banner of Truth, 1966 [1853]), III: 329–330.
8. Isaac Watts was one of those instrumental in circulating in England, in 1737, Edwards's *A Faithful Narrative of the Surprising Work of God*. For details, see George M. Marsden, *Jonathan Edwards: A Life* (New Haven: Yale University Press, 2003), 170–173.
9. For further discussion on these issues, see Paul Helm, *John Calvin's Ideas* (Oxford: Oxford University Press, 2004), chap. 6; and *Calvin at the Centre* (Oxford: Oxford University Press, 2010) chap. 8.
10. *Ethic.Ni*. 3.1. *The Bondage and Liberation of the Will*, ed. A. N. S. Lane, trans. G. I. Davies (Grand Rapids, MI: Baker, 1996), 250.
11. *Inst*. I.16.4. See also I.16.8, where he denies chance or causal contingency.
12. *Freedom of the Will*, part I, sect. 5, 163.
13. Chubb and Whitby were at the rationalist end of Arminianism, not its evangelical end. This also is significant. Edwards's target was not Wesleyan Arminianism, but the basic metaphysics of libertarianism on which Arminianism drew.
14. *Freedom of the Will*, part II, sect. 8, 213.
15. Of course Edwards's thinking does not stop at this point. The actual operation of such a metaphysical principle is due to the creative and sustaining activity of God. Yet not even God can ordain a causeless event.
16. *Inst*. II.4.2.

17. For discussion of this, see Paul Helm, *John Calvin's Ideas*, 171. For a somewhat different view, see Stephen A. Wilson, *Virtue Reformed: Rereading Jonathan Edwards's Ethics* (Leiden: Brill, 2005). For Van Mastricht's position regarding primary and secondary causation, see Aza Goudriaan, *Reformed Orthodoxy and Philosophy, 1625–1750*, 156–157.

18. For their use, see the evidence gathered together in *Reformed Thought on Freedom: The Concept of Free Choice in Early Modern Reformed Theology*, eds. Willem J. van Asselt, J Martin Bac, and Roelf T. te Velde (Grand Rapids, MI: Baker, 2010). However, Edwards would not have shared the innovative view of the editors that the liberty of indifference was a hallmark of Reformed Orthodoxy! On this, see Paul Helm, "*Reformed Thought on Freedom:* Some Further Thoughts," in *Journal of Reformed Theology* 4.3 (2010): 185–207.

19. For Calvin's use, see, for example, *Institutes of the Christian Religion* I. 16. 9; *Concerning the Eternal Predestination of God* (1552), trans. J. K. S Reid (London, James Clarke 1961), 170.

20. *Freedom of the Will*, part I, sect. 3, 153.

21. On Edwards's occasionalism, see, for example, Oliver Crisp, "How 'Occasional' Was Edwards's Occasionalism?" in Helm and Crisp, eds. *Jonathan Edwards, Philosophical Theologian*, 61–77.

22. Thanks to the editors, Oliver Crisp and Doug Sweeney, for helpful suggestions.

CHAPTER 7

1. Mark A. Noll, *America's God: From Jonathan Edwards to Abraham Lincoln* (New York: Oxford University Press, 2002), 270.

2. Hopkins, "Sin, through Divine Interposition, an Advantage to the Universe," in *The Works of Samuel Hopkins, D.D.*, 3 vols. (Boston: Doctrinal Tract and Book Society, 1852), II, 503–504, 506, 508, 527–528. Cf. Jonathan Edwards, YE1: 407–409, 411; Joseph Bellamy, "The Wisdom of God in the Permission of Sin," in *The Works of Joseph Bellamy*, 2 vols. (Boston: Doctrinal Tract and Book Society, 1853), II, 35.

3. Bellamy, "The Wisdom of God," 9; Hopkins, "Sin, through Divine Interposition," 529–530. Conforti misreads Hopkins's position here. See Joseph Conforti, *Samuel Hopkins and the New Divinity Movement* (Grand Rapids, MI: Christian University Press, 1981), 61, 66. For Hopkins and previous Reformed theologians, there was no difference between permitting sin and *willing* or *determining* to permit sin. Both implied a willful act of God. See, for example, Johannes Wollebius, *Compendium Theologiae Christianae*, in John W. Beardslee III, ed., *Reformed Dogmatics* (New York: Oxford University Press, 1965), 47–49, 59–61; Francis Turretin, *Institutes of Elentic Theology*, ed. James T. Dennison, Jr., trans. George Musgrave Giger, 3 vols. (Phillipsburg, NJ: Presbyterian and Reformed Publishing, 1992), I, 515–522; YE13, no. u.

4. Hopkins, "System of Doctrines," in *Works*, I, 41, 55.

5. Heinrich Heppe, *Reformed Dogmatics*, ed. Ernst Bizer, trans. G. T. Thomson (London; Allen and Unwin, 1950), 92; Turretin, *Institutes*, I, 245, 246, 250.

6. Hopkins, "System of Doctrines," in *Works*, I, 41–42, 49, 51; "The Nature of True Holiness," in *Works*, III, 40–41.

7. Hopkins, "System of Doctrines," in *Works*, I, 51. Cf. Jonathan Edwards, "The End for which God Created the World," in YE8: 436, 440, 461 (hereafter referred to as "The End of Creation").

8. Hopkins, "System of Doctrines," in *Works*, I, 52, 56.

9. Hopkins, "An Inquiry concerning the Future State of Those Who Die in Their Sins; or, Endless Punishment consistent with Divine Justice, Wisdom, and Goodness," in *Works*, II, 436–437, 451–454, 457, 459–462.

10. Ibid., 459, 465, 471–473. See Joseph Bellamy, "The Millennium," in *Works*, I, 455–457.

11. Jonathan Mayhew, *Striving to enter in at the strait Gate explain'd and inculcated* (Boston: Richard Draper, 1761), 6–22, 28, 68–69, 81.

12. Samuel Hopkins, "An Inquiry concerning the Promises of the Gospel," in *Works*, III, 199–200, 204–206, 209–210, 216–217, 221, 235. Implicit in Hopkins's argument was Edwards's distinction between natural and moral inability. The unregenerate were not constrained by any *natural* inability to repent but by a *moral* one that was due to their depraved wills. William Breitenbach, "Unregenerate Doings: Selflessness and Selfishness in New Divinity Theology," *American Quarterly* 34 (Winter, 1982), 479–502.

13. Hopkins, "The Promises of the Gospel," 263–264. Hopkins deviated from the standards of the Westminster Confession, which declared that although all unregenerate acts were evil, the "neglect" of such works was "more sinful and displeasing unto God." John H. Leith, ed., *Creeds of the Churches*, 3rd ed. (Atlanta: John Knox Press, 1982), 211.

14. Jedidiah Mills, *An Inquiry concerning the State of the Unregenerate under the Gospel* (New Haven, CT: B. Mecom, 1767), 5; William Hart, *A Sermon of a New Kind, Never preached, nor ever will be; Containing a Collection of Doctrines, Belonging to the Hopkintonian Scheme of Orthodoxy* (New Haven, CT: T. and S. Green, 1769), iii–iv; *Brief Remarks on a Number of False Propositions and Dangerous errors which are spreading in the Country* (New London, CT: Timothy Green, 1769), 4, 37, 40, 48–49.

15. Hopkins, "The Promises of the Gospel," 264; Bellamy, "True Religion Delineated," in *Works*, I, 116; YE3, 181–182.

16. Jonathan Edwards, "The Folly of Looking Back in Fleeing Out of Sodom," in YE19: 332–334.

17. Turretin, *Institutes*, II, 515; Clarke, "The Inexcusableness of rejecting the Gospel," in *The Works of Samuel Clarke, D.D.*, 4 vols. (London, 1738; reprint, New York: Garland, 1978), I, 490–494; Conforti, *Samuel Hopkins*, 61.

18. See Bellamy, "True Religion Delineated," 13ff; Jonathan Edwards, Jr., "The Law Not Made Void Through Faith," in *The Works of Jonathan Edwards*, 2 vols. (Andover, MA: Allen, Morrill and Wardwell, 1842; reprint, New York: Garland, 1987), II, 361–377; Nathanael Emmons, "Love the Essence of Obedience," in *The Works of Nathanael Emmons, D.D.*, 6 vols., ed. Jacob Ide (Boston: Congregational Board of Publication, 1860–1871), III, 173–187.

19. Samuel Hopkins, "The Knowledge of God's Law Necessary in Order to the Knowledge of Sin," in *Works*, III, 521, 530–531.

20. The New Divinity notion of a temporal interval between regeneration and justification was drawn from Edwards and was absent from Puritan-era Reformed thought. See Edwards, *Miscellanies*, nos. 27b, 78, 393. See also Anri Morimoto, *Jonathan Edwards and the Catholic Vision of Salvation* (University Park: Penn State Press, 1995), 30–35.

21. Hopkins, "The Knowledge of God's Law," 536 footnote. As Breitenbach has observed, by insisting that some holy act precedes pardon, "the Hopkinsians began to move beyond Puritan standards, for they were asserting not merely that people performed a condition or qualification for justification (i.e., an act of faith) but that performance was an act of personal, inherent holiness." See Breitenbach, "Unregenerate Doings," 491.

22. Hopkins, "The Knowledge of God's Law," 532 footnote, 540; 547 footnote; "The True State and Character of the Unregenerate," 424–425. Cf. Breitenbach, "Unregenerate Doings," 490–492.

23. Jonathan Edwards, "The Nature of True Virtue," in YE8: 540–541, 544–545.

24. William Hart, *Remarks on President Edwards's Dissertation concerning the Nature of True Virtue* (New Haven, CT: T. and S. Green, 1771), 5, 7–10, 16–18, 24, 31, 37, 45–46, 49–52.

25. Hopkins, "An Inquiry into the Nature of True Holiness," in *Works*, III, 10. Cf. Edwards, "True Virtue," in YE8: 541.

26. Hopkins, "True Holiness," 12–14.

27. Ibid., 11, 16–17.

28. Ibid., 42–43; Edwards, "The End of Creation," in YE8: 433–435, 442, 528, 531.

29. Hopkins, "True Holiness," 22–24, 29–30.

30. Ibid., 112, 26.

31. Edwards, *The "Miscellanies,"* no. 530 in YE18.

32. Edwards, "True Virtue," 545.

33. Hopkins, "True Holiness," 46.

34. Samuel Hopkins, "A Dialogue Between a Calvinist and a Semi-Calvinist," in *Works*, III, 143–144. Emphasis added.

35. Ibid., 147, 157; cf. "True Holiness," 62.

36. Hopkins, "System of Doctrines," in *Works*, I, 211, 212, 218. Cf. Edwards, YE3: 399, 408, 387.

37. Hopkins, "System of Doctrines," in *Works*, I, 224.

38. Ibid., footnote.

39. Noll, *America's God*, 273, 135.

40. Hopkins, "System of Doctrines," in *Works*, I, 323–324, 328, 364–365, 461.

41. William Bentley, *The Diary of William Bentley*, 4 vols. (Salem, MA, 1905–1914), III, 364; IV, 302; Conforti, *Samuel Hopkins*, 181–183.

42. Conforti, *Samuel Hopkins*, 173–186; Joseph A. Conforti, *Jonathan Edwards, Religious Tradition, & American Culture* (Chapel Hill: University of North Carolina Press, 1995), 108–144.

CHAPTER 8

1. *Works of Nathanael Emmons, D.D.*, ed. Jacob Ide, 6 vols. (Boston: Congregational Board of Publication, 1861), 1: 383; 3: 10; 6: 305; 3: 108, 215. Hereafter this six-volume set is referred to as the *Works*.

2. Gerald McDermott, "The Public Theology of Nathanael Emmons: Continuing the Edwardsean Tradition of Dissent," unpublished paper delivered at Southeastern Commission for the Study of Religion in Atlanta, March 14, 1992.

3. Henry F. May, *The Divided Heart: Essays on Protestantism and the Enlightenment in America* (New York: Oxford University Press), 86.

4. Bruce Kuklick, "Jonathan Edwards and American Philosophy," in Nathan O. Hatch and Harry S. Stout, eds., *Jonathan Edwards and the American Experience* (New York: Oxford University Press, 1988), 257.

5. This is the Ide edition of the *Works* cited in note 1. It was reissued by Garland (New York) in 1987 as part of a thirty-two-volume set edited by Bruce Kuklick: *American Religious Thought of the 18th and 19th Centuries*. This chapter uses the Garland reprint of the Ide edition.

6. Edwards A. Park, *Memoir of Nathanael Emmons, D.D.*, in *Works* 1: 330–331.

7. Henry F. May, introduction to Harriet Beecher Stowe, *Oldtown Folks* (Cambridge: Harvard University Press, 1966), 33, 404, 417.

8. Stowe, *Oldtown Folks*, 402. Stowe was writing of "Dr. Stern," who was a thinly veiled characterization of Emmons. See May, introduction, 11, 14–20.

9. Of course what Emmons took to be intellectual consistency and reason itself were shaped by his own cultural context, in which the Enlightenment's various incarnations—especially those embodied by John Locke and Thomas Reid—had washed over colonial and early Republic minds. For more on how the Enlightenment helped shape this intellectual culture by direct influence and reaction against it, see Avihu Zakai, "Jonathan Edwards, the Enlightenment, and the Form of Protestant Tradition in America," in Elizabeth Mancke and Carole Shammas, eds. *The Creation of the British Atlantic World* (Baltimore: Johns Hopkins University Press, 2005), 182–208.

10. *Works* 2: 429.

11. *Works* 2: 683; 1: 454. Original emphasis.

12. *Works* 2: 441.

13. *Works* 2: 420, 412. Though Edwards also taught moral necessity in all sin, unlike Emmons he held for a mediating principle in sinful affections and wrote of God's permitting rather than directly ordaining evil. See McClymond and McDermott, *The Theology of Jonathan Edwards* (New York: Oxford University Press, 2011), 321–356.

14. *Works* 1: 453.

15. *Works* 1: 453; 2: 553, 590. According to Edwards, God saw that Adam's descendants fully "consented" to and "concurred" with Adam's sin, and on that basis he imputed Adam's sin to them: "Therefore the sin of the apostasy is not theirs, merely because God *imputes* it to them; but it is *truly* and *properly* theirs, and on that ground, God imputes it to them." God deals with Adam's posterity "as having *all sinned in him.*" He treats our relation to Adam as so many branches coming from a common root: "All are looked upon as sinning in and with their common root." So wicked men go to hell "not according to the behavior of their particular ancestors; but every one is dealt with according to the sin of his own wicked heart, or sinful nature and practice." Therefore the imputation of Adam's sin is not unjust because we consented to it and in some way participated in it. YE3: 408, 383, 387, 409; original emphases.

16. *Works* 2: 590, 596, 597, 600.

17. *Works* 1: sermons 193. The first volume in this reprint of the six-volume edition begins with a 468-page memoir by Edwards Amasa Park and then restarts page numbering with a 331-page collection of sermons.

18. *Works* 3: 103–104.

19. *Works* 3: 110.

20. *Works* 3: 106–107; 4: 304.

21. These were the words of Henry Boynton Smith in his "Theological System of Emmons," in *Faith and Philosophy* (New York: Garland, 1987; originally published 1877), 253. As far as I know, Emmons never said that human beings are the efficient cause of their own actions. If Emmons did indeed refrain from saying the latter, it is probably because he realized that this would contradict his oft-repeated claim that God is the efficient cause of human willing. For if God is truly the efficient cause of our willing, then it would seem his willing is necessary and sufficient for our willing. Consequently, our own willing would not be necessary but an accidental effect of his willing. Our being efficient causes of our willing and God's efficiency in that willing would be contradictory. Yet Emmons's persistently strong rhetoric about our ability suggests human efficiency and therefore that very contradiction. Thanks to Michael McClymond for helping me see this problem.

22. *Works* 3: 117.

23. *Works* 3: 92.

24. *Works* 1: 415; 1: sermon 200. On this Emmons seems to have been inconsistent, for he said Paul had both holy and unholy affections and spoke of having a "sense" and "taste" of divine goodness. *Works* 4: 321, 402, 399.

25. *Works* 2: 335.
26. *Works* 2: 340.
27. *Works* 2: 402. Emmons treated reprobation as finally a matter of the divine will in eternity—creating some from the get-go to be damned. Edwards carefully distinguished the order of the divine decrees, saying that creation came from the divine goodness. First was the decree to create free creatures to share the divine love, and only after God saw that some would abuse that freedom came the decree of damnation. For Emmons, see sermon 27 in vol. 2 of the *Works*; for Edwards, see McClymond and McDermott, *The Theology of Jonathan Edwards*, 321–356. Emmons saw no contradiction between the divine decrees and free will because, by his lights, human beings acted from divine necessity and also from natural freedom; God determined their choices but not by compulsion, so that they still chose voluntarily. *Works* 2: 417–447.
28. *Works* 2: 814; 3: 5, 28, 54, 26. For Edwards on these issues, see McClymond and McDermott, *Theology of Jonathan Edwards*, 244–261, 321–338, 357–409.
29. *Works* 1: sermon 160; 1: 388; 2: 671, 811, 817–818, 814; 3: 22; 2: 813.
30. McClymond and McDermott, *Theology of Jonathan Edwards*, 389–409.
31. *Religious Affections*, ed. John E. Smith (New Haven, CT: Yale University Press, 1959), 274.
32. *Works* 4: 401.
33. *Works* 2: 600; 3: 124; 2: 124; 4: 74. On Edwards and mystery, see McClymond and McDermott, *Theology of Jonathan Edwards*, 130–148.
34. *Works* 1: 364–365.
35. *Works* 1: 365.
36. *Works* 3: 101.
37. *Works* 1: 39; 2: 189.
38. *Works* 1: sermon 300.
39. *Works* 2: 124, original emphasis; ibid.
40. *Works* 1: 229.
41. *Works* 2: 137.
42. *Works* 2: 142.
43. *Works* 2. 812–813.
44. E. Brooks Holifield, *Theology in America: Christian Thought from the Age of the Puritans to the Civil War* (New Haven, CT: Yale University Press, 2003), 159, 175–177, 172–175.
45. *Works* 2: 5.
46. *Works* 2: 473.
47. *Works* 3: 85.
48. *Works* 3: 314.
49. William Breitenbach, "The Consistent Calvinism of the New Divinity Movement," *William and Mary Quarterly* 41 (1984), 257.
50. *Works* 1: 157.
51. *Works* 2: 35, 38.

52. *Works* 1: 70; 2: 36, 37.

53. *Works* 1: 82.

54. *Works* 2: 42, 39; 1: 288.

55. *Works* 2: 38.

56. *Works* 1: sermon 317.

57. *Works* 1: sermon 323.

58. Nathan O. Hatch, *The Democratization of American* Christianity (New Haven, CT: Yale University Press, 1989); see especially chap. 6: "The Right to Think for Oneself."

59. Charles Chauncy, *The Mystery hid from Ages and Generations, made manifest by the Gospel-Revelation* (Boston, 1784).

60. Alexander Campbell, *The Christian Baptist*, April 3, 1826, 3; quoted in Hatch, 179.

61. Hatch, 162–166.

62. *Works* 1: 156–167.

63. See William Gerald McLoughlin, *The Meaning of Henry Ward Beecher: An Essay on the Shifting Values of Mid-Victorian America, 1840–1870* (New York: Knopf, 1970); J. A. Elsmere, *Henry Ward Beecher: The Indiana Years, 1837–1847* (Indianapolis: Indiana Historical Society, 1973); and Debby Applegate, *The Most Famous Man in America: The Biography of Henry Ward Beecher* (New York: Doubleday, 2006).

64. Harriet Beecher Stowe, *Oldtown Folks* (Boston: Fields, Osgood, 1869), 389.

65. Ibid.

66. Stowe, *Oldtown Folks*, 386–387. Stowe's rejection of Emmons, Edwards, and Hopkinsonian Calvinism seems to have solidified after the 1857 drowning of her son Henry in the Connecticut River, and her subsequent doubts about whether he had experienced an evangelical conversion. See Joan D. Hedrick, *Harriet Beecher Stowe: A Life* (New York: Oxford University Press, 1994), 272–287, esp. 279–284. Thanks to Joe Conforti for alerting me to Hedrick and this event.

67. May, *Divided Heart*, 111.

68. May, *Divided Heart*, 93. I say "most" because one sees in their writing and preaching the lasting impact of Edwardsian "disinterested benevolence"—both divine and human—on their thinking.

69. Nathaniel Taylor, *Lectures on the Moral Government of God*, 2 vols. (New York, 1859), 1: 195; 2: 344.

70. Mark Noll, "Jonathan Edwards and Nineteenth-Century Theology," in Hatch and Stout, eds., *Jonathan Edwards and the American Experience*, 261, 275–277; Frank Hugh Foster, *A Genetic History of the New England Theology* (Chicago: University of Chicago Press, 1907), 543; Bruce Kuklick, *Churchmen and Philosophers: From Jonathan Edwards to John Dewey* (New Haven, CT: Yale University Press, 1985), 224. Park protested the Progressive Orthodoxy of "Andover liberalism." See Charles W. Phillips, "The Last Edwardsean: Edwards Amasa Park and the Rhetoric of Improved Calvinism," (University of Stirling Ph.D. diss., 2005), chap. 6.

71. Holifield, *Theology in America,* 507; Joseph A. Conforti, *Jonathan Edwards, Religious Tradition, and American Culture* (Chapel Hill: University of North Carolina Press, 1995), 161; Kuklick, *Churchmen and Philosophers,* 252, 255–257.

72. Sweeney, "Taylorites, Tylerites, and the Dissolution of the New England Theology," in D. G. Hart, Sean Michael Lucas, and Stephen J. Nichols eds., *The Legacy of Jonathan Edwards: American Religion and the Evangelical Tradition* (Grand Rapids, MI: Baker Academic, 2003), 198–199; David W. Bebbington, *The Dominance of Evangelicalism: The Age of Spurgeon and Moody* (Downers Grove, IL: InterVarsity Press, 2005), 148–183; Allen C. Guelzo, *Edwards on the Will: A Century of American Theological Debate* (Middletown, CT.: Wesleyan University Press, 1989), 277; Kuklick, *Churchmen and Philosophers,* 222–223; Holifield, *Theology in America,* 501–502. The quote about Darwin's materialism is from Kuklick, *Churchmen and Philosophers,* 223.

73. Holmes dismissed Edwards's theology as a "system that would consign innocent babes to the fires of everlasting torment"; Weber, 121, 147, 148, 153. Stowe referred to Edwards's sermons as "refined poetry of torture" in *The Minister's Wooing* (Boston and New York, 1859, 1896), 245.

74. Bebbington, *The Dominance of Evangelicalism,* 191.

75. Alexander V. G. Allen, *Jonathan Edwards* (Boston, 1889), 380, 386, 388.

76. See the other chapters in this volume, plus 625–648 in McClymond and McDermott, *The Theology of Jonathan Edwards.*

77. Smith, "Theological System of Emmons," 244.

CHAPTER 9

1. *A History of the Work of Redemption,* in YE9: 121.

2. YE9: 514, 460.

3. A cursory review of "revivals" in *WJE Online* (http://edwards.yale.edu/archive) reveals Edwards's use of these adjectives.

4. Jonathan Edwards, "The Reality of Conversion" (1740), in *The Sermons of Jonathan Edwards: A Reader,* ed. Wilson H. Kimnach, Kenneth P. Minkema, and Douglas A. Sweeney (New Haven, CT, and London: Yale University Press, 1999), 92.

5. For recent sampling of articles on Edwards and revival, see Walter L. Eversley, "The Pastor as Revivalist," in *Edwards in Our Time: Jonathan Edwards and the Shaping of American Religion,* ed. Sang Hyun Lee and Allen C. Guelzo (Grand Rapids, MI: Eerdmans, 1999), 113–130; Helen P. Westra, "Divinity's Design: Edwards and the Work of Revival," in *Edwards in Our Time,* 131–157; Amy Plantinga Pauw, "Edwards as American Theologian: Grand Narratives and Pastoral Narratives," in Harry S. Stout, Kenneth P. Minkema, Caleb J. D. Maskell, eds., *Jonathan Edwards at 300: Essays on the Tercentenary of His Birth* (Lanham, MD: University Press of America, 2005), 14–124; Harry S. Stout, "Edwards as Revivalist," in Stephen J. Stein, ed., *The Cambridge Companion to Jonathan*

Edwards (Cambridge: Cambridge University Press, 2007), 125–143; Douglas A. Sweeney, "Evangelical Tradition in America," in *Cambridge Companion to Jonathan Edwards*, 217–238; Harry S. Stout, "Edwards and Revival," in Gerald R. McDermott, ed., *Understanding Jonathan Edwards: An Introduction to America's Theologian* (New York: Oxford University Press, 2009), 37–52; Willem van Vlastuin, "Alternative Viewpoint: Edwards and Revival," in *Understanding Jonathan Edwards*, 53–61.

6. Avihu Zakai, *Jonathan Edwards's Philosophy of History: The Reenchantment of the World in the Age of Enlightenment* (Princeton, NJ: Princeton University Press, 2003), 330; see also Joseph A. Conforti, *Jonathan Edwards, Religious Tradition, and American Culture* (Chapel Hill: University of North Carolina Press, 1995), 47–48.

7. Stout, "Edwards and Revival," in *Understanding Jonathan Edwards*, 38.

8. Recent studies include David W. Kling, *A Field of Divine Wonders: The New Divinity and Village Revivals in Northwestern Connecticut, 1791–1822* (University Park: Pennsylvania State University Press, 1993); James R. Rohrer, *Keepers of the Covenant: Frontier Missions and the Decline of Congregationalism, 1774–1818* (New York: Oxford University Press, 1995); Conforti, *Jonathan Edwards, Religious Tradition, and American Culture*, chap. 2; Jonathan D. Sassi, *A Republic of Righteousness: The Public Christianity of the Post-Revolutionary New England Clergy* (New York: Oxford University Press, 2001), esp. 133–135; Douglas A. Sweeney, *Nathaniel Taylor, New Haven Theology, and the Legacy of Jonathan Edwards* (New York: Oxford University Press, 2003), esp. 39–42; Sweeney, "Evangelical Tradition in America," 219–225.

9. YE9: 433–436; YE5: 363–364.

10. For a more expansive treatment of the relationship between Edwards's millennialism and missions, see Sidney H. Rooy, *The Theology of Missions in the Puritan Tradition* (Grand Rapids, MI: Eerdmans), 294–309; James A. De Jong, *As the Waters Cover the Sea: Millennial Expectations in the Rise of Anglo-American Missions, 1640–1810* (Kampen, Neth.: J. H. Kok, 1970), 120–137; Charles L. Chaney, *The Birth of Missions in America* (South Pasadena, CA.: William Carey Library, 1976), 65–70.

11. The Connecticut Missionary Society (1797–1798) and Massachusetts Missionary Society (1798)—merged later into the American Home Missionary Society (1826)—were primarily New Divinity creations.

12. "Miscellanies," no. 810, in YE18: 518, quoted in Pauw, "Edwards as American Theologian," 15; see also YE4: 374.

13. *An Humble Attempt*, in YE5: 329.

14. There is no Ph.D. dissertation dealing with Griffin, though Mark Rogers of Trinity Evangelical Divinity School is currently writing one. The most extensive treatment of Griffin is found in Kling, *Field of Divine Wonders*, passim; and Kling, "The New Divinity and Williams College, 1793–1836," *Religion and American*

Culture 6(2) (summer 1996): 210–213. Nettleton has been the subject of two dissertations: George Hugh Birney, Jr., "The Life and Letters of Asahel Nettleton, 1783–1844" (Ph. D. diss., Hartford Theological Seminary, 1943); Sherry Pierpont May, "Asahel Nettleton: Nineteenth-Century American Revivalist" (Ph.D. diss., Drew University, 1969). Several recent dissertations from Southwestern Baptist Seminary (SBS) deal with Nettleton and Charles G. Finney: Ricky Charles Nelson, "The Relationship Between Soteriology and Evangelistic Methodologies in the Ministries of Asahel Nettleton and Charles G. Finney" (Ph.D. diss, SBS, 1997); Sung Ho Kand, "The Evangelistic Preaching of Asahel Nettleton and Charles G. Finney in the Second Great Awakening and Applications for Contemporary Evangelism" (Ph.D. diss., SBS, 2004); Sung Chul Hwang, "The Bible and Christian Experience in the Revival Movements of Charles G. Finney and Asahel Nettleton" (Ph.D. diss., SBS, 2006). A solid though somewhat uncritical biography is John F. Thornbury, *God Sent Revival: The Story of Asahel Nettleton and the Second Great Awakening* (Grand Rapids, MI: Evangelical Press, 1977). Other recent semischolarly articles on Nettleton include James Ehrhard, "Asahel Nettleton: The Forgotten Evangelist," *Reformation and Revival* 6(1) (winter 1997): 67–93; and John F. Thornbury, "Asahel Nettleton's Conflict with Finneyism," *Reformation and Revival* 8(2) (spring 1999): 103–119.

15. Gardiner Spring, "Death and Heaven: A Sermon preached in Newark at the interment of the Rev. Edward D. Griffin, D.D." (New York, 1838), 31, 32–33.

16. *The Autobiography of Lyman Beecher*, ed. Barbara M. Cross, 2 vols. (Cambridge, MA: Belknap Press of Harvard University Press, 1961), 2: 363. For a similar estimate by Francis Wayland, the Baptist president of Brown, see Thornbury, *God Sent Revival*, 55.

17. See Jonathan D. Sassi, *A Republic of Righteousness*. Griffin held official positions in or delivered sermons to the African School (Synod of New York and New Jersey), American Bible Society, ABCFM, American Education Society, American Society for Meliorating the Condition of the Jews, American Sunday School Union, Marine Missionary Society, Portsmouth Female Asylum, Presbyterian Education Society, and the United Foreign Missionary Society.

18. Owen Peterson, *A Divine Discontent: The Life of Nathan S. S. Beman* (Macon: Mercer University Press, 1986), 106.

19. Ironically, Nettleton became wealthier than Griffin, thanks to profits from his *Village Hymns* (1824), but he gave away the proceeds to various New Divinity–inspired organizations such as the American Board of Commissioners for Foreign Missions (ABCFM) and the Theological Institute of Connecticut (TIC). See Bennet Tyler, *Nettleton and His Labours: The Memoirs of Dr. Asahel Nettleton*, remodeled in some parts by Andrew A. Bonar (1854; reprint, Carlisle: Banner of Truth Trust, 1975), 422–423, hereafter Tyler, *Memoirs of Nettleton*.

20. Griffin communicated with Nettleton regarding an 1827 Finney revival in Troy, New York (Tyler, *Memoirs of Nettleton*, 343). When Griffin was informed about

the founding of TIC—a foil to Taylor's New Haven Theology at Yale and an institution to which Nettleton gave time and money—he responded: "I rejoice exceedingly in the firm stand which the brethren of Connecticut have taken against the New Haven school...I vote for the new school with all my heart" (quoted in Birney, "The Life and Letters of Asahel Nettleton," 363). Nettleton also asked Griffin to send Williams students to TIC (Asahel Nettleton to Edward Dorr Griffin, July 29, 1836, Gratz Collection, Historical Society of Pennsylvania). In his correspondence, Nettleton thanked Griffin for his anti-Taylor theological work, *The Doctrine of Divine Efficiency* (1833), and recommended it to others (Asahel Nettleton to Edward Dorr Griffin, September 30, 1833, Gratz Collection; Asahel Nettleton to William Swan Plumer, January 29, 1836, William Swan Plumer Papers, PCUSA, Dept. of History, Montreal, NC, hereafter, Plumer Papers).

21. *Sermons of the late Rev. Edward D. Griffin, D.D., to which is prefixed a memoir of his life*, 2 vols. (Albany, 1838), 1: 242–243.

22. Edward D. Griffin to Mark Tucker, August 29, 1837, Gratz Collection.

23. Kling, *Field of Divine Wonders*, 126–137.

24. The literature on Edwards's contribution to missions is extensive. For a recent article, see Stuart Piggin, "The Expanding Knowledge of God: Jonathan Edwards's Influence on Missionary Thinking and Promotion," in David W. Kling and Douglas A. Sweeney, eds. *Jonathan Edwards at Home and Abroad: Historical Memories, Cultural Movements, Global Horizons* (Columbia: University of South Carolina Press, 2003), 266–296.

25. See David W. Kling, "The New Divinity and the Origins of the American Board of Commissioners for Foreign Missions," *Church History* 72(4) (December 2003): 791–819.

26. On Edwards and the millennium, see John F. Wilson, "History, Redemption, and the Millennium," in Nathan O. Hatch and Harry S. Stout, eds., *Jonathan Edwards and the American Experience* (New York: Oxford University Press, 1988), 132; Gerald R. McDermott, *One Holy and Happy Society: The Public Theology of Jonathan Edwards* (University Park: Pennsylvania State University Press, 1992), 37–92.

27. Ernest R. Sandeen, *The Roots of Fundamentalism: British and American Millenarianism, 1800–1930* (1970; reprint, Grand Rapids, MI: Baker, 1978), 42.

28. Edward D. Griffin, "A Sermon, preached October 20, 1813, at Sandwich, Massachusetts, at the Dedication of the Meeting House" (Boston, 1813), 28. On millennial fervor among the New Divinity, see Kling, *Field of Divine Wonders*, 57–62; on millennialism in general, see James West Davidson, *The Logic of Millennial Thought: Eighteenth-Century New England* (New Haven, CT: Yale University Press, 1977); Ruth H. Bloch, *Visionary Republic: Millennial Themes in American Thought, 1756–1800* (New York: Cambridge University Press, 1985).

29. Griffin, "Sermon preached at Sandwich," 31. See also his "A Sermon preached September 14, 1826, before the American Board of Missions at Middletown,

Connecticut," 24; and "Letter to the Rev. Dr. William Sprague," in *Lectures on Revivals of Religion*, 359–360.

30. See "Foreign Missions: A Sermon, preached May 9, 1819, ... in the Garden-Street Church, New York"; and "A Sermon preached September 14, 1826, before the American Board of Missions at Middletown, Connecticut."

31. John Ryland to Edward D. Griffin, May 12, 1807, Gratz Collection, Historical Society of Pennsylvania. Edwards's sermon was "The Duty of Ministers of the Gospel to Preach the Truth..." (Hartford, 1795).

32. Clifton J. Phillips, *Protestant America and the Pagan World: The First Half Century of the American Board of Commissioners for Foreign Missions, 1810–1860* (Cambridge, MA: East Asia Research Center, Harvard University, 1969), 26; Chaney, *Birth of Missions in America*, 220.

33. Quoted in Conforti, *Jonathan Edwards, Religious Tradition, and American Culture*, 48.

34. I cite from the reprint edition published by the Andover Society of Inquiry Respecting Missions: Edward D. Griffin, "The Kingdom of Christ. A Missionary Sermon preached before the General Assembly of the Presbyterian Church in Philadelphia, May 23, 1805" (Andover, 1821).

35. For examples of Edwards's use of "propensity" (or "disposition," the word he uses more often), "fullness," and "fountain" metaphor, see YE8: 433–435, 438–442.

36. On "end of creation," see *Concerning the End for Which God Created the World*, in YE8, esp. 428–444; on "holy and happy," one of Edwards's favorite phrases, see *Humble Attempt*, in YE5: 338, 339, 365, 446.

37. According to Edwards, "all the decrees of God do some way or other belong to that eternal covenant of redemption that was between the Father and Son before the foundation of the world" (YE9: 513; see also 516 and "Editor's Introduction," 40–41).

38. In *Work of Redemption*, Edwards used two metaphors to describe the "many parts": rivers and streams that fed into the great providential ocean (YE9: 517); and a building with its many constituent facets (ground preparation, materials, foundation, and superstructure), which, when completed with the top stone, demonstrates God's providential design of redemption (121–122).

39. YE9: 130–132, 344–356.

40. On "paradise restored," see *Humble Attempt*, in YE5: 337.

41. According to Edwards, God's work of redemption "will be accomplished by means, by the preaching of the gospel, and the use of the ordinary means of grace" (YE9: 459).

42. Tyler, *Memoir of Nettleton*, 17. According to Thornbury, *God Sent Revival*, twenty-five thousand is a more "conservative estimate" (233), but given the number of converts supplied in Tyler's *Memoirs of Nettleton* and R. Smith's *Recollections of Nettleton, and the Great Revival of 1820* (Albany, 1848), even Thornbury's calculation seems high. A range of ten to fifteen thousand seems more reasonable.

43. YE4: 161.

44. The two paragraphs below are taken from Tyler, *Memoir of Nettleton*, 17–30, 293 (Tyler quote).

45. Edward Dorr Griffin, "A Letter to the Rev. Dr. William Sprague," in William Buell Sprague, *Lectures on Revivals of Religion*, 2nd ed. (New York, 1833), 360.

46. Smith, *Recollections of Nettleton*, 135. Note: emphasis where seen in all subsequent quotes from Nettleton is his.

47. Tyler, *Memoir of Nettleton*, 145.

48. Edward Dorr Griffin, "Sermon, preached September 2, 1827, before the Candidates for the Bachelor's Degree in Williams College" (Williamstown, 1827), 15.

49. Tyler, *Memoir of Nettleton*, 296, 294–295; see also *Remains of the Late Asahel Nettleton, D.D.*, comp. Bennet Tyler (Hartford, 1865), 309.

50. *Remains of Nettleton*, 132, 21, 135.

51. Tyler, *Memoir of Nettleton*, 245.

52. *Remains of Nettleton*, 60; see also 352–358.

53. Ibid., 122; see also 66–70, 116–127.

54. Ibid., 375, 295. For a summary of this view, see Kling, *Field of Divine Wonders*, 103–108. For selective primary sources, see Douglas A. Sweeney and Allen C. Guelzo, *The New England Theology: From Jonathan Edwards to Edwards Amasa Park* (Grand Rapids, MI: Baker, 2006), 133–148.

55. Nettleton to Plumer, March 3, 1836, Plumer Papers.

56. Quoted in Tyler, *Memoirs of Nettleton*, 360, 362.

57. Nettleton to Plumer, September 5, 1838, Plumer Papers.

58. Edward D. Griffin, "The Causal Power in Regeneration Proper upon the mind" (North-Adams, Mass., 1834), 9; Griffin, *The Doctrine of Divine Efficiency, defended against certain Modern Speculations* (New York, 1833), 43, 45.

59. Edward Dorr Griffin, "A Letter to the Rev. Ansel D. Eddy...on the Narrative of the Late Revivals of Religion" (Williamstown, 1832), 9, 6, 7.

60. Edward Dorr Griffin, "A Letter to a Friend on the Connexion between the New Doctrines and the New Measures" (Albany, 1833).

61. Asahel Nettleton, "Temperance and Revivals" (New York, 1829), 2.

CHAPTER 10

1. Perry Miller, *The New England Mind: The Seventeenth Century* (Cambridge, MA: Harvard University Press, 1954), 1–5; Nathan O. Hatch, *The Democratization of American Christianity* (New Haven, CT: Yale University Press, 1989); and Joseph Haroutunian, *Piety Versus Moralism: The Passing of the New England Theology* (New York: Holt, 1932). On the historiography of the New England Theology, see Douglas A. Sweeney, "Edwards and His Mantle: The Historiography of the New England Theology," *New England Quarterly* 71 (March 1998): 97–119.

2. On the interpretations of Haroutunian and his followers, see Sweeney, "Edwards and His Mantle," 108–12. The literature depicting the Taylorites as "Old Calvinists" (or moderate-to-liberal Congregationalists most interested in maintaining what they deemed the religious status quo, in shoring up the clerical establishment, and thus in opposing the theological innovations and religious zeal of the "New Divinity") includes Sidney Mead, *Nathaniel William Taylor, 1786–1858: A Connecticut Liberal* (Chicago: University of Chicago Press, 1942), 12–23, 95–127; Mark A. Noll, "Moses Mather (Old Calvinist) and the Evolution of Edwardseanism," *Church History* 49 (September 1980): passim; Allen C. Guelzo, *Edwards on the Will: A Century of American Theological Debate* (Middletown, CT: Wesleyan University Press, 1989), 218–271; David W. Kling, *A Field of Divine Wonders: The New Divinity and Village Revivals in Northwestern Connecticut, 1792–1822* (University Park: Pennsylvania State University Press, 1993), 91–93, 232–243; and William R. Sutton, "Benevolent Calvinism and the Moral Government of God: The Influence of Nathaniel W. Taylor on Revivalism in the Second Great Awakening," *Religion and American Culture* 2 (Winter 1992): 28–29, 40.

3. See especially Joseph Conforti, *Jonathan Edwards, Religious Tradition, and American Culture* (Chapel Hill: University of North Carolina Press, 1995); and Kling, *A Field of Divine Wonders*.

4. Douglas A. Sweeney, *Nathaniel Taylor, New Haven Theology, and the Legacy of Jonathan Edwards*; and Sweeney and Allen C. Guelzo, eds., *The New England Theology: From Jonathan Edwards to Edwards Amasa Park* (Grand Rapids, MI: Baker Academic, 2006), 187–218.

5. *The Diary of William Bentley, D.D., Pastor of the East Church, Salem, Massachusetts*, 4 vols. (1905; reprint, Gloucester, MA: Peter Smith, 1962), 4: 302 (for further supercilious testimony from Bentley concerning the prevalence of Edwardsianism, see 1: 160, 196–197, and 3: 113, 364–365, 412); David D. Field, ed., *A History of the County of Berkshire, Massachusetts; In Two parts: The First Being a General View of the County; The Second, an Account of the Several Towns* (Pittsfield, MA: Samuel W. Bush, 1829), 229; [Archibald Alexander], "An Inquiry into That Inability under Which the Sinner Labours, and Whether It Furnishes Any Excuse for His Neglect of Duty," *Biblical Repertory and Theological Review*, n.s., 3 (July 1831): 362; Samuel Miller, *Life of Jonathan Edwards* (Boston: Hilliard, Gray, 1837), 215; Bennet Tyler, *Memoir of the Life and Character of Rev. Asahel Nettleton, D.D.*, 2nd ed. (Hartford, CT: Robbins and Smith, 1845; 1st ed., 1844), 274; Samuel M. Worcester, *The Life and Labors of Rev. Samuel Worcester, D.D.*, 2 vols. (Boston: Crocker and Brewster, 1852), 1: 211; and Mortimer Blake, *A Centurial History of the Mendon Association of Congregational Ministers, with the Centennial Address, Delivered at Franklin, Mass., November 19, 1851, and Biographical Sketches of the Members and Licentiates* (Boston: S. Harding, 1853), 31.

6. Rebecca Taylor Hatch, *Personal Reminiscences and Memorials* (New York: n.p., 1905), 11, 28, 34; Noah Porter, introduction to *Lectures on the Moral Government*

of God, by Nathaniel W. Taylor, 2 vols. (New York: Clark, Austin & Smith, 1859), 1: vi; Porter, "Dr. Taylor and His Theology," in *The Semi-Centennial Anniversary of the Divinity School of Yale College, May 15th and 16th, 1872* (New Haven, CT: Tuttle, Morehouse and Taylor, 1872), 92–97; Porter, "Philosophy in Great Britain and America: A Supplementary Sketch," appendix I in *History of Philosophy from Thales to the Present Time,* vol. 2 of *History of Modern Philosophy,* by Friedrich Ueberweg, trans. George S. Morris (New York: Scribner, Armstrong, 1874), 452; Leonard Bacon, "A Sermon at the Funeral of Nathaniel W. Taylor, D.D., in the Center Church, March 12, 1858," in *Memorial of Nathaniel W. Taylor, D.D.: Three Sermons* (New Haven, CT: Thomas H. Pease, 1858), 8; George P. Fisher, "A Sermon Preached in the Chapel of Yale College, March 14, 1858, the First Sunday after the Death of Rev. Nathaniel W. Taylor, D.D...," in ibid., 32, 35; George P. Fisher, "Historical Address," in *Semi-Centennial Anniversary of the Divinity School of Yale College,* 20, 27–28; and George Park Fisher, *History of Christian Doctrine* (1896; reprint, Edinburgh: Clark, 1949), 414–417.

7. For ample documentation, consult Sweeney, *Nathaniel Taylor, New Haven Theology, and the Legacy of Jonathan Edwards.*

8. Nathaniel W. Taylor, *Concio ad Clerum: A Sermon Delivered in the Chapel of Yale College, September 10, 1828* (New Haven, CT: Hezekiah Howe, 1828).

9. Lyman Beecher, *The Autobiography of Lyman Beecher,* ed. Barbara M. Cross, 2 vols. (Cambridge, MA: Harvard University Press, 1961), 2: 117, 1: 410. For more on this opposition to Finney, see Beecher to Nettleton, January 30, 1827, folder 63, box 2, Beecher-Scoville Family Papers, Sterling Memorial Library, Yale University (SML); Beecher, *To the Congregational Ministers and Churches of Connecticut...* (Boston: n.p., 1827); and the published *Letters of the Rev. Dr. Beecher and Rev. Mr. Nettleton on the "New Measures" in Conducting Revivals of Religion...* (New York: G. and C. Carvill, 1828). On the new Lebanon Conference, see Beecher, *Autobiography,* 2: 89–108; Garth M. Rosell and Richard A. G. Dupuis, eds., *The Memoirs of Charles G. Finney: The Complete Restored Text* (Grand Rapids, MI: Zondervan, 1989), 216–225; Mead, *Nathaniel William Taylor,* 200–210; Charles E. Hambrick-Stowe, *Charles G. Finney and the Spirit of American Evangelicalism* (Grand Rapids, MI: Eerdmans, 1996), 46–73; George Hugh Birney, Jr., "The Life and Letters of Asahel Nettleton 1783–1844" (Ph.D. diss., Hartford Theological Seminary, 1943), 114–154; and the published minutes of the conference in the Unitarian *Christian Examiner and Theological Review* 4 (July and August 1827): 357–370. Significantly, even the Princetonians proved friendly to the Taylorites before the end of the 1820s, as evidenced in Samuel Miller's urgent plea to Beecher to settle in a recently vacated Philadelphia pulpit. See Miller to Beecher, April 2, 1828, Stowe-Day Foundation, Hartford.

10. The best evidence of Nettleton's now-frenzied opposition to Finney is found in his own correspondence. See the letters collected in Birney, Jr., "The Life and Letters of Asahel Nettleton," 269–278, 279–295, 307–320, 408–415; and

Hambrick-Stowe, *Charles G. Finney*, 67, who states that, in going after Finney, "Nettleton aimed to kill."

11. Sherry Pierpont May, "Asahel Nettleton: Nineteenth Century American Revivalist" (Ph.D. diss., Drew University, 1969), 323.

12. Examples may be found in Birney, Jr., "Life and Letters of Asahel Nettleton," 330–346, 353–355, 366–369; and Tyler, *Memoir of the Life and Character of Rev. Asahel Nettleton*, 291–294, 297–301.

13. See Leonard Woods, "Letters to Rev. Nathaniel W Taylor," in *The Works of Leonard Woods, D.D.*, 5 vols. (Andover: John D. Flagg, 1850), 4:343–459. On the meeting in Porter's study, see Bennet Tyler, *Letters on the Origin and Progress of the New Haven Theology* (New York: Robert Carter and Ezra Collier, 1837), 24ff; and Birney, Jr., "Life and Letters of Asahel Nettleton," 155–194. See also Asahel Nettleton to Charles Hodge, December 7, 1837, folder 2, box 18, ser. 14, Charles Hodge Papers, Princeton University Library (PUL). Nettleton notes that Beecher "was the great apologist [and] advocate of Dr. Taylor" at this meeting, "as will be recollected by all present." On Porter's opposition to Taylor, see his letter to Beecher, May 22, 1829, printed in *The Presbyterian* (Philadelphia) 6 (December 24, 1836): 202; Lyman Matthews, *Memoir of the Life and Character of Ebenezer Porter, D.D.* (Boston: Perkins & Marvin, 1837), 219–225; and Tyler, *Letters on the Origin and Progress of the New Haven Theology*, 33–34.

14. Beecher to Porter, June 1829, and Beecher to Taylor, September 6, 1830, both in Beecher, *Autobiography*, 2: 128, 171–172.

15. See Beecher, *Autobiography*, 2: 287–288; and Nettleton to Charles Hodge, December 7, 1837, folder 2, box 18, ser. 14, Charles Hodge Papers, PUL.

16. The exchange (including Taylor's eleven-point creed) was published in Hartford's *Connecticut Observer* (February 20, 1832): 1–8; New Haven's *Religious Intelligencer* (*RI*) 16 (February 25, 1832): 614–616; Boston's *Spirit of the Pilgrims* (*SP*) 5 (March 1832): 173–179; and New Haven's *Quarterly Christian Spectator* (*QCS*) 4 (March 1832): 171–176. This exchange led to a major paper war over Taylor's annotations, waged between Taylor and Tyler in *SP* 5–6 (1832–33), after which an anonymous Taylorite, exhausted, wrote in New Haven's *RI* 18 (November 16, 1833): 392, "There are no doubt wolves in sheep's clothing, but we have seen with pain, a growing disposition among Christians of the present day, to dress every sheep that they can catch out of their own fold, in wolves' clothing, and set the dogs upon them."

17. He did this in an exchange of three pairs of letters in *SP* 5–6 (1832–33). Of Beecher's Edwardsian-Calvinist creed, Woods wrote, "I cordially agree.... The cordial belief of these doctrines is, I think, a solid basis of ministerial fellowship and cooperation, though there may be a variety of opinions on other subjects, and on some subjects which are by no means unimportant" (*SP* 5, September 1832: 505).

18. See Noah Porter et al., "Report on Articles of Faith," August 1, 1834, folder 38, box 7, Divinity School Papers, SML; as well as Nathaniel W. Taylor, "Dr. Taylor's

Statement" and "Dr. Taylor's Explanation," August 21, 1834, in the same folder at Yale (Taylor's formal response to Dow's complaints submitted to the Yale Corporation). Cf. Taylor's original "Declaration of Assent to Saybrook," December 31, 1822, folder 38, box 7, Divinity School Papers, SML, which includes a creed submitted by Taylor verifying that he did subscribe originally to the Saybrook Platform only "for substance of doctrine." Illuminating early assessments of this controversy at Yale may be found all over the contemporary periodical literature, but see Daniel Dow (who left the Yale Corporation and eventually became a board member at the Tylerites' Theological Institute of Connecticut), *New Haven Theology, Alias Taylorism, Alias Neology; In Its Own Language* (Thompson, CT: George Roberts, 1834), 52–56 and passim; Tyler, *Letters on the Origin and Progress of the New Haven Theology,* 78–85; and Zebulon Crocker, *The Catastrophe of the Presbyterian Church, in 1837, Including a Full View of the Recent Theological Controversies in New England* (New Haven, CT: B. and W. Noyes, 1838), 244–250.

19. "Who Are the True Conservatives?" *QCS* 10 (November 1838): 616; Chauncey A. Goodrich to Charles Hodge, March 9, 1831, folder 9, box 16, Charles Hodge Papers, PUL; Bacon, "A Sermon at the Funeral of Nathaniel W. Taylor," 8; and Nathaniel W. Taylor, "Letter to the Editor from the Rev. Dr. Taylor," *QCS* 5 (September 1833): 448. Nettleton, who had suffered from poor health throughout his life, did not actually die until May 16, 1844. On the Taylorites' Edwardsian ecumenism, see also Chauncey A. Goodrich to Bennet Tyler, October 1, 1832, MS Vault File, Beinecke Rare Book and Manuscript Library, Yale University (Beinecke), in which Goodrich laments that "no opportunities have been afforded us of comparing our views in *conversation*, where misapprehensions can be removed and objections obviated in a moment"; Nathaniel W. Taylor to Asahel Nettleton, June 4, 1834, folder 2851, box 180, Nettleton Papers, Case Memorial Library, Hartford Seminary (CML); "On Christian Union," *QCS* 9 (March 1837: 65–93, and June 1837: 289–313); and "On Dissensions among Christian Brethren," *QCS* 9 (December 1837): 554–569.

20. There are various indicators of Taylorite success. Throughout the Taylorite controversy, for example, enrollment increased at Yale Divinity School and always outnumbered that at the Tylerites' Theological Institute of Connecticut. By 1840 there were seventy-two students at Yale, making it the second-largest divinity school in New England (behind the older and more established Andover Seminary). As Yale's George Park Fisher would note, "The more that young men in other colleges and schools of theology were warned against Dr. Taylor, the more they flocked to his lecture-room." Taylor also remained a very popular churchman throughout the controversy, serving as both moderator and preacher at the annual meeting of the General Association of Connecticut in 1830 (in Wethersfield) and as moderator of the annual meetings of 1838 (in Norwalk) and 1841 (in New Haven). Tyler, by comparison, served as preacher only in 1837

and never served as moderator. Nettleton never served in either capacity. Well after Taylor's death, an anonymous reviewer for the *New Englander* (*NE*) would characterize Taylor's resilience by noting that "the attempt to proscribe men for sympathizing with Dr. Taylor's theology is [now] almost as obsolete in New England as the custom of hanging witches." See Fisher, "Historical Address," 21; John T. Wayland, *The Theological Department in Yale College 1822–1858* (1933; reprint, New York: Garland, 1987), 123 and passim; Glenn T. Miller, *Piety and Intellect: The Aims and Purposes of Ante-Bellum Theological Education* (Atlanta: Scholars Press, 1990), 201–202; *Contributions to the Ecclesiastical History of Connecticut,* 145–146; and "The Princeton Review for January," *NE* 28 (April 1869): 408.

21. The strengthening of ties between the Tylerites and Old School Presbyterians is most evident in the fraternal correspondence that developed among such clergymen as Leonard Woods and Asahel Nettleton of New England and Ashbel Green, Charles Hodge, and Samuel Miller to the south. A good number of their letters remain in collections such as the Simon Gratz Autograph Collection of the Historical Society of Pennsylvania and the Ashbel Green and Charles Hodge Papers at PUL. In one such letter, Miller wrote to Nettleton, speaking for himself and Princeton's patriarch, Archibald Alexander: "Our views [and] feelings with respect to the 'Pastoral Union of Con.' are not only amicable, but cordial [and] fraternal. We view it as a most desirable [and] important association, embarked in a great [and] good cause, [and] likely to accomplish a very important object. True, indeed, in looking over their published Confession of Faith, we do not find every word exactly as we could have wished; but we find quite enough in it that we approve, to be a basis of affectionate confidence, [and] unfeigned good will" (Miller to Nettleton, March 14, 1834, folder 6, box 3, ser. 2, Samuel Miller Papers, PUL). As demonstrated by May ("Asahel Nettleton," 390–397), the Tylerites sought a formal alliance with moderate Old School Presbyterians that would not only fortify their efforts in New England but might also help to avert a Presbyterian schism. And after the Presbyterians did divide in 1837–38, Connecticut's Congregationalists disagreed strenuously on how to relate to the Old and New School bodies. See Leonard Bacon, *Seven Letters to the Rev. George A. Calhoun, concerning the Pastoral Union of Connecticut . . .* (New Haven, CT: B. L. Hamlen, 1840), 9–42.

22. *An Address, to the Congregational Churches in Connecticut, on the Present State of Their Religious Concerns* (Hartford: Peter B. Gleason, 1833), 54, 58.

23. On these institutional developments, see especially Crocker, *The Catastrophe of the Presbyterian Church,* 234–268; George A. Calhoun, *Letters to the Rev. Leonard Bacon, in Reply to His Attack on the Pastoral Union and Theological Institute of Connecticut* (Hartford: Elihu Geer, 1840), 72–79; Charles Hyde, "Theological Institute of Connecticut," in *Contributions to the Ecclesiastical History of Connecticut,* 185–189; Curtis Manning Geer, *The Hartford Theological Seminary, 1834–1934* (Hartford, CT: Case, Lockwood & Brainard, 1934), 26–67; and May, "Asahel Nettleton," 368ff.

24. This skirmish began with a letter to the editor of the *New Haven Record* (August 31, 1839), in which Calhoun opposed the *Record's* recent coverage of the annual meeting of Connecticut's General Association. It culminated in a lengthy exchange concerning a wide range of ecclesiastical developments that had to be published in pamphlet form after the *Record* was criticized for encouraging controversy. See Bacon, *Seven Letters to the Rev. George A. Calhoun;* Calhoun, *Letters to the Rev. Leonard Bacon;* and Bacon, *An Appeal to the Congregational Ministers of Connecticut against a Division...*(New Haven, CT: B. L. Hamlen, 1840). On Bacon's role in the Taylorite controversy, see also Hugh Davis, *Leonard Bacon: New England Reformer and Antislavery Moderate* (Baton Rouge: Louisiana State University Press, 1998), 102–106.

25. In 1854–55, Bennet Tyler and Joseph Harvey debated the classic Edwardsian question concerning the ability of the unregenerate to turn to God in faith. Tyler argued in typical Edwardsian terms for the sinner's "natural" (though not moral) ability to repent and believe the gospel, while Harvey concluded in more traditional Calvinist language that "the *entire* impotence and hopelessness of man in himself is a vital truth in the economy of redemption" (emphasis mine). See Tyler, *Discourse on Human Ability and Inability* (Hartford, CT: Case, Tiffany, 1854); Harvey, *A Letter to the Rev. Dr. Tyler in Reply to His Discourse on Human Ability and Inability* (Springfield, MA: S. Bowles, 1855); Tyler, *A Letter to the Rev. Joseph Harvey, D.D....* (Hartford, CT: Case, Tiffany, 1855); and [Harvey], *A Review of Recent Publications on Human Ability and Inability* (Hartford: n.p., 1855), quotation from 29.

26. On these developments, see Leonard Bacon to Noah Porter, January 15, 1856, and Porter to unidentified, March 1, 1856, both in folder 29, box 5, Divinity School Papers, SML; "Meeting of Alumni of Yale Theological Seminary," *Independent* (August 7, 1856): 256; Hyde, "Theological Institute of Connecticut," 188; Fisher, "Historical Address," 21–22; Gerald Everett Knoff, "The Yale Divinity School, 1858–1899" (Ph.D. diss., Yale University, 1936), 8, 14–26, 45–57; Wayland, *The Theological Department in Yale College,* 120–124, 160–170, 409, 414–416; Geer, *Hartford Theological Seminary,* 99–100; Roland H. Bainton, *Yale and the Ministry: A History of Education for the Christian Ministry at Yale from the Founding in 1701* (San Francisco: Harper, 1957), 161; Theodore Davenport Bacon, *Leonard Bacon: A Statesman in the Church,* ed. Benjamin W. Bacon (New Haven: Yale University Press, 1931), 515–516; and Davis, *Leonard Bacon,* 227–228. As Donald M. Scott has shown in *From Office to Profession: The New England Ministry, 1750–1850* (Philadelphia: University of Pennsylvania Press, 1978), the period after the height of the Taylorite controversy was one of socioeconomic decline for New England clergy generally. Many poor and rural students entering the ministry could not afford to attend schools like Yale and consequently often did most of their preparation at smaller, regional colleges.

CHAPTER 11

1. C. C. Carpenter, *Congregationalist*, January 5, 1899 (reprint in Andover-Harvard Theological Library, Harvard University), n.p. See also Samuel Clarke, *A Demonstration of the Being and Attributes of God* (1705).

2. Edward Dwight Eaton to Owen Gates, November 16, 1928 (MS in Trask Library, Andover-Newton Theological School).

3. George P. Fisher, *Congregationalist*, June 14, 1900, 871.

4. Richard Salter Storrs, *Congregationalist*, June 7, 1900, 831.

5. Elizabeth Stuart Phelps, *Chapters from a Life* (Boston: Houghton Mifflin, 1897), 196.

6. See Mark A. Noll, *America's God: From Jonathan Edwards to Abraham Lincoln* (New York: Oxford University Press, 2002) on Park, 264, 265, 522 (note 4), 531 (note 99). Noll has shown elsewhere that he is more than able to write perceptively about Park.

7. See Joseph Haroutunian, *Piety Versus Moralism: The Passing of the New England Theology* (New York: Holt, 1932), xxiii.

8. Frank Hugh Foster, *A Genetic History of the New England Theology* (Chicago: University of Chicago Press, 1907), 473.

9. Douglas A. Sweeney, *Nathaniel Taylor, New Haven Theology, and the Legacy of Jonathan Edwards* (New York: Oxford University Press, 2003), 147.

10. Edwards Park, "The Fitness of the Church to a Constitution of Renewed Men," in *Addresses of Rev. Drs. Park, Post and Bacon at the Anniversary of the American Congregational Union, May 1854* (New York: Clark, Austin and Smith, 1854), 41 (emphasis in original).

11. Edwards Park, "New England Theology; with Comments on a Third Article in the *Biblical Repertory and Princeton Review*, Relating to a Convention Sermon," *Bibliotheca Sacra* 9 (1852), 184.

12. Edwards Park, "Autobiographical Fragments," in Frank Hugh Foster, *The Life of Edwards Amasa Park* (New York: Fleming H. Revell, 1936), 31.

13. Richard Salter Storrs, *Edwards A. Park: Memorial Address* (Boston: Samuel Usher, 1900), 21.

14. Park, "New England Theology," 184.

15. Samuel Hopkins, *The System of Doctrines, contained in Divine Revelation, explained and defended, Showing their Consistence and Connection with each other, by Samuel Hopkins, D.D., Pastor of the First Congregational Church in Newport, in Two Volumes* (Boston: I. Thomas and E. Andrews, 1793), vol. I, 337.

16. Edward Chipman Guild, "Lecture Notes on Systematic Theology" (1855–56), 4 vols. (MS in Andover-Harvard Theological Library [Archives reference: "bMS 466/1–2 Edwards Amasa Park, 1808–1900"], Harvard University), vol. III, 223.

17. Smith Norton, "Park's Lectures on Systematic Theology" (1856–57), 4 vols. (MS in Oberlin College Library, Oberlin College), vol. I, 59.

18. Edwards Park to George Bancroft, June 27, 1859 (MS in Massachusetts Historical Society, Boston; emphasis in original).

19. Edwards Park, "Review of Reid's *Essays on the Intellectual and Moral Powers*," *Bibliotheca Sacra* 7 (1850), 602.

20. Edwards Park, "Unity Amid Diversities of Belief," *Bibliotheca Sacra* 8 (1851), 599.

21. Robert Coit Learned, "Notes on Sacred Rhetoric" (1840–41), 1 vol. (MS in Trask Library, Andover-Newton Theological School, 210; emphasis in original).

22. Park, "Fitness of the Church," 41.

23. See Edwards Park, "Connection Between Theological Study and Pulpit Eloquence," *American Biblical Repository* 10 (1837), 169–191; Park, "The Mode of Exhibiting Theological Truth," *American Biblical Repository* 10 (1837), 436–478; Park, "The Duties of a Theologian," *American Biblical Repository* 2 (Second series, 1839), 347–380.

24. Park, "Mode of Exhibiting Theological Truth," 436, 442.

25. Edwards Park, "The Theology of the Intellect and That of the Feelings," *Bibliotheca Sacra* 7 (1850), 543, 534.

26. Park, "Theology of the Intellect," 534, 542–543.

27. Ebenezer Porter, *Lectures on Eloquence and Style*, ed. Lyman Matthews (Andover: Gould and Newman, 1836, 20; emphasis in original).

28. George Campbell, *Lectures on Systematic Theology and Pulpit Eloquence*, ed. Henry J. Ripley (Boston: Lincoln and Edmands, 1832), 132.

29. Hugh Blair, *Lectures on Rhetoric and Belles Lettres*, ed. Harold F. Harding, 2 vols. (Carbondale: Southern Illinois University Press, 1965), vol. II, 226–227.

30. Park, "Theology of the Intellect," 567, note F.

31. See D. G. Hart, "The Critical Period for Protestant Thought in America," in D. G. Hart, ed., *Reckoning with the Past: Historical Essays on American Evangelism from the Institute for the Study of American Evangelicals* (Grand Rapids, MI: Baker Books, 1995), 194.

32. See Horace Bushnell, "A Discourse on Dogma and Spirit; or the True Reviving of Religion," in *God in Christ: Three Discourses Delivered at New Haven, Cambridge, and Andover, with a Preliminary Dissertation on Language* (New York: Scribner, Armstrong, 1877).

33. Bushnell, "Preliminary Dissertation on the Nature of Language," in *God in Christ*, 94.

34. Park, "Theology of the Intellect," 567, note F.

35. James L. Hill, "Park's Lectures" (1872–1875), 3 vols. (MS in Trask Library, Andover-Newton Theological School), vol. I, 68.

36. See B. B. Edwards and E. A. Park, eds., *Selections from German Literature* (New York: Gould, Newman and Saxton, 1839).

37. See Charles Hodge, "The Theology of the Intellect and that of the Feelings," *Biblical Repertory and Princeton Review* 22 (1850), 642–674.

38. Jonathan Edwards to Thomas Gillespie, April 2, 1750, in John E. Smith, ed., *Religious Affections, The Works of Jonathan Edwards*, vol. 2 (New Haven, CT: Yale University Press, 1959), 511.

39. See Park, "New England Theology," 170–220.

40. Park, "New England Theology," 174, 212, 181, 177, 178, 181, 185.

41. Edwards Park, "Remarks on the *Biblical Repertory and Princeton Review*," *Bibliotheca Sacra* 8 (1851), 137.

42. Enoch Pond, "Dr. Hodge and the New England Theology," *Bibliotheca Sacra* 30 (1873), 379.

43. See Edwards Park, *Memoir of Nathanael Emmons; with Sketches of His Friends and Pupils* (Boston: Congregational Board of Publication, 1861).

44. George P. Fisher, "Professor Park's Memoir of Dr. Emmons," *New Englander* 19 (1861), 721.

45. Henry Boynton Smith, "The Theological System of Emmons," *American Theological Review* 4 (1862), 8.

46. Jonathan Edwards in Paul Ramsey, ed., *Freedom of the Will, The Works of Jonathan Edwards*, vol. 1 (New Haven, CT: Yale University Press, 1957), 144.

47. See William C. Davis, "Thomas Reid on Moral Epistemology and the Moral Sense" (unpublished Ph.D. diss., University of Notre Dame, 1992), 100–152.

48. Guild, "Notes," vol. III, 109, 127, 68.

49. Frank Hugh Foster, "New England Theology," in Samuel M. Jackson, ed., *The New Schaff-Herzog Encyclopedia of Religious Knowledge*, 12 vols. (New York: Funk and Wagnalls, 1910), vol. 8, 138.

50. Foster, *Genetic History*, 525.

51. Guild, "Notes," vol. III, 126.

52. Nathanael Emmons to Edwards Park, August 7, 1838 (MS in Yale University Library).

53. See Charles C. Carpenter, ed., *General Catalogue of the Theological Seminary, Andover, Massachusetts* (Boston: Thomas Todd, 1909).

54. See Daniel Day Williams, *The Andover Liberals: A Study in American Theology* (New York: King's Crown Press, 1941).

55. Steven R. Pointer, *Joseph Cook, Boston Lecturer and Evangelical Apologist: A Bridge Between Popular Culture and Academia in Late Nineteenth-Century America* (Lewiston, NY.: Edwin Mellen Press, 1991), 26.

56. Washington Gladden in Frank Hugh Foster, *The Modern Movement in American Theology: Sketches in the History of American Thought from the Civil War to the World War* (New York: Fleming H. Revell, 1939), 22.

57. See Joseph Conforti, "The Creation and Collapse of the New England Theology: Edwards A. Park and Andover Seminary, 1840–1881," in *Jonathan Edwards, Religious Tradition and American Culture* (Chapel Hill: University of North Carolina Press, 1995), 108–144. Conforti's work is the best published material on Edwards Park.

58. B. B. Warfield, "Edwards and the New England Theology," in *Studies in Theology, The Works of Benjamin B. Warfield* (New York: Oxford University Press, 1932; reprint, Grand Rapids, MI: Baker, 2000), vol. IX, 536.

59. Park, "Fitness of the Church," 41.

60. Smith, "Theological System of Emmons," 34.

61. Harriet Beecher Stowe to Henry Ward Beecher, August 30, 1859 (MS in Beecher Family Papers, Yale University Library).

CHAPTER 12

1. See especially Thomas S. Kidd, *The Great Awakening: The Roots of Evangelical Christianity in Colonial America* (New Haven: Yale University Press, 2007) and Charles Hambrick-Stowe, "The Spirit of the Old Writers: The Great Awakening and the Persistence of Puritan Piety," in Francis J. Bremer ed., *Puritanism: Transatlantic Perspectives on a Seventeenth-Century Anglo-American Faith* (Boston: Massachusetts Historical Society, 1993), 277–291.

2. Douglas A. Sweeney and Allen C. Guelzo, eds., *The New England Theology: From Jonathan Edwards to Edwards Amasa Park* (Grand Rapids: Baker Academic, 2006), 17. See also Joseph A. Conforti, *Samuel Hopkins and the New Divinity Movement* (Grand Rapids: Christian University Press, 1981), 1–7.

3. Mark A. Noll, *America's God: From Jonathan Edwards to Abraham Lincoln* (New York: Oxford University Press, 2002), 270. E. Brooks Holifield, *Theology in America: Christian Thought from the Age of the Puritans to the Civil War* (New Haven: Yale University Press, 2003), 342.

4. Allen C. Guelzo, *Edwards On the Will: A Century of American Theological Debate* (Middletown, CT.: Wesleyan University Press, 1989), 146. Conforti, *Samuel Hopkins and the New Divinity Movement*, 33–34, 181, 185–186. David W. Kling, *A Field of Divine Wonders: The New Divinity and Village Revivals in Northwestern Connecticut, 1792–1822* (University Park: The Pennsylvania State University Press, 1993), 29.

5. Sweeney and Guelzo, eds., *The New England Theology*, 187–190; Guelzo, *Edwards On the Will*, 221–229; William B. Sprague, *Annals of the American Pulpit*, vol. 2 (New York: Robert Carter and Bros., 1857), 152–165; Franklin Bowditch Dexter, *Biographical Sketches of the Graduates of Yale College*, vol. 3 (New York: Henry Holt and Co., 1903), 321–333.

6. Conforti, *Samuel Hopkins and the New Divinity Movement*, 15, 227–232.

7. Kling, *Field of Divine Wonders*, 245–250.

8. Samuel Hopkins, *The System of Doctrines, Contained in Divine Revelation, Explained and Defended* (Boston: Isaiah Thomas and Ebenezer T. Andrews, 1793), iii–vi.

9. J. Rixey Ruffin, *A Paradise of Reason: William Bentley and Enlightenment Christianity in the Early Republic* (Oxford: Oxford University Press, 2007);

Dr. Bentley's Salem: Diary of a Town (Salem, Mass.: Essex Institute, 1977); Sprague, *Annals of the American Pulpit*, vol. 8 (New York: Robert Carter & Bros., 1865), 35–37; *The Christian Examiner*, vol. 42, May, 1847 (http://books.google. com), 466–467.

10. *The Diary of William Bentley*, quoted in Conforti, *Samuel Hopkins and the New Divinity Movement*, 182.

11. Sprague, *Annals of the American Pulpit*, vol. 2, 247–256; Franklin Bowditch Dexter, *Biographical Sketches of the Graduates of Yale College*, vol. 4 (New York: Henry Holt and Co., 1907), 295–304.

12. Sprague, *Annals of the American Pulpit*, vol. 2, 137–139. Richard A. Harrison, *Princetonians, 1769–1775: A Biographical Dictionary* (Princeton: Princeton University Press, 1980), 206–209; Kling, *Field of Divine Wonders*, 29–33.

13. William B. Sprague, *Annals of the American Pulpit*, vol. 1 (New York: Robert Carter and Bros., 1859), 693–706; vol. 2, 34–41, 559–565. See also Dexter, *Biographical Sketches of the Graduates of Yale College*, vol. 3, 216–230.

14. Kling, *Divine Field of Wonders*, 16–42.

15. Sprague, *Annals of the American Pulpit*, vol. 1, 697; vol. 2, 87, 221–228. See also Dexter, *Biographical Sketches of the Graduates of Yale College*, vol. 3, 305–310; vol. 4, 248–257.

16. Mary Kupiec Cayton, "The Expanding World of Jacob Norton: Reading, Revivalism, and the Construction of a 'Second Great Awakening' in New England, 1787–1804," *Journal of the Early Republic*, 26 (Summer 2006), 221–248.

17. Sprague, *Annals of the American Pulpit*, vol. 2, 300–306, 216–221, 268–272, 20–23, 275–276; Brown Thurston, *Thurston Genealogies, 1635–1892* (Portland, Maine: Brown Thurston, 1892), 79 (http://books.google.com).

18. Sprague, *Annals of the American Pulpit*, vol. 1, 573–574, 548–556; Franklin Bowditch Dexter, *Biographical Sketches of the Graduates of Yale College*, vol. 2 (New York: Henry Holt and Co., 1896), 424–428, 388–394.

19. Kling, *Field of Divine Wonders*, 248.

20. Conforti, *Samuel Hopkins and the New Divinity Movement*, 231. http://jefferson-countyms.org/bios.htm#bullen. Sprague, *Annals of the American Pulpit*, vol. 2, 140–147, 288–291; Dexter, *Biographical Sketches of the Graduates of Yale College*, vol. 3, 438–440; vol. 4, 351–355.

21. John Saillant, *Black Puritan, Black Republican: The Life and Thought of Lemuel Haynes, 1753–1833* (New York: Oxford University Press, 2003). See also Richard Newman, ed., *Black Preacher to White America: The Collected Writings of Lemuel Haynes, 1774–1833* (New York: Carlson, 1990); Charles Hambrick-Stowe, "'All Things Were New and Astonishing;' Edwardsian Piety, the New Divinity, and Race," in David W. Kling and Douglas A. Sweeney, eds., *Jonathan Edwards at Home and Abroad: Historical Memories, Cultural Movements, Global Horizons* (Columbia: University of South Carolina Press, 2003), 120–136; Sprague, *Annals of the American Pulpit*, vol. 2, 176–187.

22. For the Providence churches, see Arthur Edward Wilson, *Weybosset Bridge in Providence Plantations, 1700–1790* (Boston: Pilgrim Press, 1947).

23. Conforti, *Samuel Hopkins and the New Divinity Movement*, 125–158.

24. Charles Hambrick-Stowe, "The Spiritual Pilgrimage of Sarah Osborn (1714–1796)," *Church History*, 61 (December, 1992), 408–421; Catherine A. Breckus, ed., *The Religious History of American Women* (Chapel Hill: University of North Carolina Press, 2007), 108–141; Sweeney and Guelzo, eds., *The New England Theology*, 98–105.

CHAPTER 13

1. Edwards to John Erskine, July 5, 1750, in YE16: 355.

2. For recent engagement with Edwards from widely varying points on the spectrum of contemporary Presbyterian theology, see John H. Gerstner, *The Rational Biblical Theology of Jonathan Edwards* (Orlando, FL: Ligonier, 1991); D. G. Hart, "Jonathan Edwards and the Origins of Experimental Calvinism," in Hart et al., eds., *The Legacy of Jonathan Edwards: American Religion and the Evangelical Tradition* (Grand Rapids, MI: Baker, 1903), 161–180; Sang Hyun Lee, *The Philosophical Theology of Jonathan Edwards* (Princeton, NJ: Princeton University Press, 1988); Samuel T. Logan, "Puritans, Presbyterians, and Jonathan Edwards," in S. Donald Fortson, ed., *Colonial Presbyterians: Old Faith in a New Land* (Eugene, OR: Pickwick, 2007), 1–25; Ian R. K. Paisley M.P., *Jonathan Edwards: Theologian of Revival* (Belfast: Martyrs Memorial Free Presbyterian Church, 1987); and Amy Plantinga Pauw, *"The Supreme Harmony of All": The Trinitarian Theology of Jonathan Edwards* (Grand Rapids, MI: Eerdmans, 2002).

3. For background on these matters as they related to Presbyterian theological development, see Mark A. Noll, "Revival, Enlightenment, Civic Humanism, and the Evolution of Calvinism in Scotland and America, 1735–1843," in Noll and George A. Rawlyk, eds., *Amazing Grace: Evangelicalism in Australia, Britain, Canada, and the United States* (Grand Rapids, MI: Baker; and Montreal and Kingston, Ont.: McGill-Queen's University Press, 1994), 73–107; and Noll, *America's God: From Jonathan Edwards to Abraham Lincoln* (New York: Oxford University Press, 2002), 253–329.

4. Indispensable for all efforts to trace Edwards's influence over time is M. X. Lesser, *Reading Jonathan Edwards: An Annotated Bibliography in Three Parts, 1729–2005* (Grand Rapids, MI: Eerdmans, 2008). For the development of Presbyterian theology in America, a superb account is found in E. Brooks Holifield, *Theology in America: Christian Thought from the Age of the Puritans to the Civil War* (New Haven, CT: Yale University Press, 2003).

5. Lefferts A. Loetscher, *Facing the Enlightenment and Pietism: Archibald Alexander and the Founding of Princeton Seminary* (Westport, CT: Greenwood, 1983), 44–46.

6. Samuel Miller, *A Brief Retrospect of the Eighteenth Century*, 2 vols. (New York: T. & J. Swords, 1803), 2: 30.

7. Ibid., 231.

8. S. C. Aiken to Lyman Beecher, April 20, 1827, in *The Autobiography of Lyman Beecher*, ed. Barbara M. Cross, 2 vols. (Cambridge, MA: Harvard University Press, 1961), 2: 67–68.

9. Charles G. Finney, *Lectures on Systematic Theology*, ed. J. H. Fairchild (New York: George H. Doran, n.d., originally published 1878), 323.

10. Charles G. Finney, *Lectures on Revivals of Religion*, 2nd ed. (New York: Leavitt, Lord, 1835), 241–242.

11. *Letters of the Rev. Dr. Beecher and Rev. Mr. Nettleton, on the "New Measures" in Conducting Revivals of Religion* (New York: G. & C. Carvill, 1828), 29.

12. Miller to W. B. Sprague, March 8, 1832, in Sprague, *Lectures on Revivals of Religion* (London: Banner of Truth, 1959, originally published 1832), 29, 41 of separately numbered Appendix.

13. Albert Dod, "Finney's Lectures," *Princeton Review* 7 (October 1835), 657–658.

14. Ibid., 656–657.

15. Samuel Miller, *The Life of Jonathan Edwards* (New York: Harper, 1837), 191. Further page references to this work are noted in parentheses.

16. On mediate and immediate imputation, see below in the paragraphs on H. B. Smith.

17. Albert Dod and J. W. Alexander, "Transcendentalism," *Princeton Review* 11 (Jan. 1839): 95, 97. Further page references to this work are noted in parentheses.

18. Hodge, "The Theology of the Intellect and That of the Feelings—Article III" (1851), in *Essays and Reviews* (New York: Robert Carter & Brothers), (1857), 631.

19. Hodge, *Systematic Theology*, 3 vols. (Grand Rapids, MI: Eerdmans, 1979, originally published 1871–72), 3: 116–117, 148; *The Constitutional History of the Presbyterian Church in the United States of America* (Philadelphia: Presbyterian Board of Publication, 1840), 48n. Further page references to the *Constitutional History* are noted in parentheses.

20. George M. Marsden, *The Evangelical Mind and the New School Presbyterian Experience* (New Haven, CT: Yale University Press, 1970), 218.

21. Lyman Atwater, "The Power of Contrary Choice," *Princeton Review* 12 (October 1840): 549.

22. For fuller treatment of this exchange, as well as for an account of the Scottish reactions explained below, see Mark A. Noll, "Jonathan Edwards and Nineteenth-Century Theology," in Nathan O. Hatch and Harry S. Stout, eds., *Jonathan Edwards and American Experience* (New York: Oxford University Press, 1988), 260–287; and Noll, "Edwards's Theology After Edwards," in Sang Hyun Lee, ed., *The Princeton Companion to Jonathan Edwards* (Princeton, NJ: Princeton University Press, 2005), 292–308.

23. Charles Hodge, "Prof. Park and the Princeton Review," *Princeton Review* 23 (Oct. 1851): 631.

24. Edwards, *Dissertation II: The Nature of True Virtue*, in YE8: 596. For Paul Ramsey's description of what he called Edwards's account of "The Splendor of Common Morality," see the Editor's Introduction, ibid., 33–53; and for Ramsey's careful unpacking of knotty issues on the relationship of Edwards to the moral philosophy of his day, ibid., "Appendix II: Jonathan Edwards on Moral Sense, and the Sentimentalists," 689–705. An outstanding contemporary assessment that explains why both the Princeton and New England theologians of the nineteenth century misconstrued the theological and philosophical discriminations that Edwards tried to preserve is Henry Boynton Smith, "The Theological System of Emmons" (1862), in *Faith and Philosophy: Discourses and Essays* (Edinburgh: T. & T. Clark, 1878), 215–264.

25. Loetscher, *Facing the Enlightenment*, 182–184.

26. See Mark A. Noll, *Princeton and the Republic, 1768–1822* (Princeton, NJ: Princeton University Press), 36–40.

27. Anon., "President Edwards's Dissertation on the Nature of True Virtue," *Bibliotheca Sacra* 10 (Oct. 1853): 727–728.

28. Ibid., 728–729 n8.

29. Lyman Atwater, "Outlines of Moral Science by Alexander," *Princeton Review* 25 (January 1853): 13.

30. Ibid., 19, 25.

31. E. A. Park, "New England Theology," *Bibliotheca Sacra* 9 (Jan. 1852): 191, 192, 210.

32. Noah Porter, "The Princeton Review on Dr. Taylor and the Edwardean Theology," *New Englander* 18 (August 1860): 744.

33. Ibid., 772.

34. Ibid., 769.

35. These judgments are found in Samuel Baird, "Edwards and the Theology of New England," *Southern Presbyterian Review* 10 (1858): 581–582, 586–590; *The First Adam and the Second: Elohim Revealed in the Creation and Redemption of Man* (Philadelphia: Lindsay, 1860), 161; and *A History of the New School* (Philadelphia: Claxton, Remsen, and Hafflefinger, 1868), 182.

36. James Henley Thornwell, "Nature of Our Relation to Adam in his First Sin," in *The Collected Writings of James Henley Thornwell*, 4 vols. (Richmond, VA: Presbyterian Committee of Publication, 1871), 1: 517.

37. Thornwell, "Theological Lectures," in ibid., 250, 333, 350, 381.

38. See Sean Michael Lucas, "'He Cuts Up Edwardsism by the Roots': Robert Lewis Dabney and the Edwardsian Legacy in the Nineteenth-Century South," in *The Legacy of Jonathan Edwards*, 200–214.

39. Henry B. Smith, "Nature and Worth of the Science of Church History" (1851), in *Faith and Philosophy*, 59–61; Smith, "The Reformed Churches of Europe and America in Relation to General Church History" (1855), in ibid., 90.

40. Expert guidance on these issues is provided in George P. Hutchinson, *The Problem of Original Sin in American Presbyterian Theology* (n.p.: Presbyterian and Reformed, 1972).

41. A later Princeton theologian, who was further removed from the earlier polemics, joined Smith in seeing this dual focus in Edwards; B. B. Warfield, "Edwards and the New England Theology" (1912), *The Works of Benjamin B. Warfield, vol. 9: Studies in Theology* (New York: Oxford University Press, 1932), 530–531.

42. Smith, "The Idea of Christian Theology as a System" (1855), in *Faith and Philosophy*, 151.

43. Ibid., 149.

44. Smith, "The Relations of Faith and Philosophy," in *Faith and Philosophy*, 16.

45. This formula follows Marsden, *Evangelical Mind*, 163.

46. The Erskine-Edwards connection is thoroughly explored in Jonathan Yeager, *Enlightened Evangelicalism: The Life and Thought of John Erskine* (New York: Oxford University Press, 2011).

47. William Hanna, *Memoirs of the Life and Writings of Thomas Chalmers*, 4 vols. (Edinburgh: Thomas Constable, 1851), 1: 16.

48. Chalmers to William B. Sprague, *Annals of the American Pulpit: Trinitarian Congregational*, 2 vols. (New York: Robert Carter & Brothers, 1857), 1: 334.

49. Chalmers, *The Christian and Civic Economy of Large Towns*, 3 vols. (Glasgow: Chalmers and Collins, 1821), 1: 334.

50. James Orr, "The Influence of Edwards," in John Winthrop Platner, ed., *Exercises Commemorating the Two-Hundredth Anniversary of the Birth of Jonathan Edwards* (Andover, MA: Andover Press, 1904), 108, 111.

51. Hanna, *Memoirs of Chalmers*, 17.

52. Orr, "The Influence of Edwards," 123, 124.

53. John McLeod Campbell, *The Nature of the Atonement and Its Relation to Remission of Sins and Eternal Life* (London: James Clarke, 1959, originally published 1856), 51–75.

54. Ibid., 137.

55. Two turn-of-the-century American Presbyterian reviews of Edwards and New England theological history that replicated the main Princeton arguments, but with less passion and more discernment, were Warfield, "Edwards and the New England Theology"; and Henry Collin Minton, "President Jonathan Edwards," *Presbyterian Quarterly* 13 (1899): 68–94.

CHAPTER 14

1. Letter to Samuel Hopkins, February 21, 1803 (personal possession of Craig Fries, Amsterdam, NY).

2. William Newman, *Rylandiana: Reminiscences Relating to the Rev. John Ryland, A.M.* (London: George Wightman, 1835), 3.

3. For Beddome's association with Whitefield, see Geoffrey F. Nuttall, "George Whitefield's 'Curate': Gloucestershire Dissent and the Revival," *Journal of Ecclesiastical History*, 27 (1976), 382–384. Occom preached at Bourton in April 1767, during an extensive trip that the Native American evangelist made to Britain; Roger Hayden, *Continuity and Change: Evangelical Calvinism Among Eighteenth-Century Baptist Ministers Trained at Bristol Academy, 1690–1791* (Milton under Wychwood, Chipping Norton, Oxfordshire: Nigel Lynn for Rev. Roger Hayden and the Baptist Historical Society, 2006), 88.

4. Beddome's personal copy of this book may be seen in the Angus Library, Regent's Park College, University of Oxford. On the title page Beddome has written the date "Apr. 1742," which would indicate either when he purchased the book or the date by which he had read it.

5. [John Fawcett, Jr.], *An Account of The Life, Ministry, and Writings of the Late Rev. John Fawcett, D.D.* (London: Baldwin, Cradock, and Joy, and Halifax: P. K. Holden, 1818), 155–156, n.*. According to this note, Wood was said to have been "much attached to the writings of the late President Edwards."

6. Michael A. G. Haykin, *One Heart and One Soul: John Sutcliff of Olney, His Friends, and His Times* (Darlington, Co. Durham: Evangelical Press, 1994), 55; Hayden, *Continuity and Change*, xii–xiii. For the younger Hall, Edwards was an "amazing genius"; "Preface" to Robert Hall, Sr., "Help to Zion's Travellers," in *The Works of Rev. Robert Hall, A.M.* (New York: Harper & Brothers, 1854), II, 450.

7. For Edwards's acquaintance with Gill, see for example Jonathan Edwards, YE26: 55–56, 72, 74, 246, 260, 330, 443. See also Stephen R. Holmes, *God of Grace and God of Glory: An Account of the Theology of Jonathan Edwards* (Grand Rapids, MI: Eerdmans, 2000), ix.

8. For studies of the influence of Edwards on Fuller, see especially Thomas J. Nettles, "The Influence of Jonathan Edwards on Andrew Fuller," *Eusebeia: The Bulletin of The Andrew Fuller Center for Baptist Studies*, 9 (Spring 2008), 97–116; Chris Chun, "'Sense of the Heart': Jonathan Edwards' Legacy in the Writings of Andrew Fuller," *Eusebeia: The Bulletin of The Andrew Fuller Center for Baptist Studies*, 9 (Spring 2008), 117–134; idem, "The Greatest Instruction Received from Human Writings: The Legacy of Jonathan Edwards in the Theology of Andrew Fuller" (unpublished Ph.D. thesis, University of St. Andrews, 2008).

9. "Preface to the Complete American Edition," in his ed., *The Complete Works of the Rev. Andrew Fuller*, ed. Andrew Gunton Fuller and revised Joseph Belcher (1845 ed.; reprinted Harrisonburg, VA: Sprinkle, 1988), I, viii. This preface was written by Belcher in November 1844.

10. Hawkins had been recommended to Fuller by the Baptist pastor Joseph Kinghorn (1766–1832). See William Hawkins, letter to Joseph Kinghorn, January 15, 1815 (MS 4281, T143, Norfolk Record Office, Norwich); Charles B. Jewson, "William Hawkins, 1790–1853," *Baptist Quarterly*, 26 (1975–76), 276.

11. William Hawkins, letter to Joseph Kinghorn, April 4, 1815 (Norfolk Record Office).

12. Joseph A. Conforti, "Samuel Hopkins and the New Divinity: Theology, Ethics, and Social Reform in Eighteenth-Century New England," *William and Mary Quarterly*, 34 (1977), 581–583.

13. William Hawkins, letter to Joseph Kinghorn, April 17, 1815 (Norfolk Record Office).

14. Olney Church Book III, Sutcliff Baptist Church, Olney, Buckinghamshire.

15. For details about the influence of Edwards on Sutcliff, see Haykin, *One Heart and One Soul*, 13, 55, 139–140, 153–155, 158–169, 209–210, 259, 273–274, 300–302. Also see Tom J. Nettles, "Edwards and His Impact on Baptists," *Founders Journal*, 53 (Summer 2003), 7; D. Bruce Hindmarsh, "The Reception of Jonathan Edwards by Early Evangelicals in England," in David W. Kling and Douglas A. Sweeney, eds., *Jonathan Edwards at Home and Abroad: Historical Memories, Cultural Movements, Global Horizons* (Columbia: University of South Carolina Press, 2003), 207–210; and Michael J. McClymond, "'A German Professor Dropped into the American Forests': British, French, and German Views of Jonathan Edwards, 1758–1957," Chapter 15 in this volume.

16. Letter to John Ryland, April 28, 1815; cited by John Ryland, *The Indwelling and Righteousness of Christ no Security against Corporeal Death, but the Source of Spiritual and Eternal Life* (London: W. Button & Son, 1815), 34.

17. Ryland, *Indwelling and Righteousness of Christ*, 47.

18. For Edwards's impact on Ryland, see also Hindmarsh, "Reception of Jonathan Edwards" in Kling and Sweeney, eds., *Jonathan Edwards at Home and Abroad*, 201–203, 207–210.

19. For the second edition of *The Gospel Worthy of All Acceptation*, see *Complete Works of the Rev. Andrew Fuller*, II, 328–416. For studies of this work, see E. F. Clipsham, "Andrew Fuller and Fullerism: A Study in Evangelical Calvinism," *Baptist Quarterly*, 20 (1963–1964), 214–225; Peter J. Morden, *Offering Christ to the World: Andrew Fuller (1754–1815) and the Revival of Eighteenth-Century Particular Baptist Life* (Carlisle, Cumbria, UK, Waynesboro, GA: Paternoster Press, 2003), 23–76. Extremely helpful in tracing the differences between the two editions is Robert W. Oliver, *History of the English Calvinistic Baptists 1771–1892: From John Gill to C. H. Spurgeon* (Edinburgh/Carlisle: Banner of Truth, 2006), 156–172. On Edwards's influence on Fuller, see E. Brooks Holifield, *Theology in America: Christian Thought from the Age of the Puritans to the Civil War* (New Haven, CT, and London: Yale University Press, 2003), 280–281; Mark Noll, "Jonathan Edwards's *Freedom of the Will* Abroad," in Harry S. Stout, Kenneth P. Minkema, and Caleb J. D. Maskell, eds., *Jonathan Edwards at 300: Essays on the Tercentenary of His Birth* (Lanham, MD: University Press of America, 2005), 102–104.

20. Andrew Fuller, *Strictures on Sandemanianism* (*Complete Works of the Rev. Andrew Fuller*), II, 602. See also his *Gospel Worthy of All Acceptation* (*Complete Works of the Rev. Andrew Fuller*), II, 399–400.

21. Fuller, *Strictures on Sandemanianism*, II, 602.

22. John E. Smith, "Puritanism and Enlightenment: Edwards and Franklin," in William M. Shea and Peter A. Huff, eds., *Knowledge and Belief in America: Enlightenment Traditions and Modern Religious Thought* (Washington, DC: Woodrow Wilson Center Press, and Cambridge: Cambridge University Press, 1995), 201.

23. Letter to Samuel Hopkins, February 21, 1803. For Hopkins's detailed response to Ryland, see his letter to John Ryland, September 1803; *The Works of Samuel Hopkins, D.D.* (Boston: Doctrinal Tract Society, 1865), II, 752–758.

24. "The Serampore Form of Agreement," para. 10, *Baptist Quarterly*, 12 (1947), 125–138. For Brainerd's influence on Carey and Fuller, see also A. de M. Chesterman, "The Journals of David Brainerd and of William Carey," *Baptist Quarterly*, 19 (1961–62), 147–156; John A. Grigg, *The Lives of David Brainerd: The Making of an American Evangelical Icon* (Oxford: Oxford University Press, 2009), 165–168.

25. Andrew Walls, "The Evangelical Revival, The Missionary Movement, and Africa," in Mark A. Noll, David W. Bebbington, and George A. Rawlyk, eds., *Evangelicalism: Comparative Studies of Popular Protestantism in North America, the British Isles, and Beyond, 1700–1900* (New York and Oxford: Oxford University Press, 1994), 310.

26. Letter to Sarah Pearce, October 19, 1799, cited in S. Pearce Carey, *Samuel Pearce, M.A., The Baptist Brainerd* (London: Carey Press, n.d.), 214.

27. Letter to Sarah Pearce, October 19, 1799.

28. See, for instance, "The Future Perfection of the Church" (*Complete Works of the Rev. Andrew Fuller*, I, 250); "Justification" (*Complete Works of the Rev. Andrew Fuller*, I, 280); "The Believer's Review of His State" (*Complete Works of the Rev. Andrew Fuller*, I, 303).

29. See Oliver D. Crisp, "Penal non-Substitution," *Journal of Theological Studies*, 59 (2008), 140–168, for details regarding these two strands of the governmental view of the atonement. For the thinking of the New Divinity movement about the atonement, see also E. Brooks Holifield, *The Gentleman Theologians: American Theology in Southern Culture 1795–1860* (Durham, NC: Duke University Press, 1978), 193–194; William Breitenbach, "The Consistent Calvinism of the New Divinity Movement," *William and Mary Quarterly*, 41 (1984), 247–255; Allen C. Guelzo, "Jonathan Edwards and the New Divinity: Change and Continuity in New England Calvinism, 1758–1858," in Charles G. Dennison and Richard C. Gamble, eds., *Pressing Toward the Mark: Essays Commemorating Fifty Years of the Orthodox Presbyterian Church* (Philadelphia: Committee for the Historian of the Orthodox Presbyterian Church, 1986), 160–162; idem, *Edwards on the Will: A Century of American Theological Debate* (Middletown, CT: Wesleyan University Press, 1989), 129–135.

30. *Edwards on the Will*, 134–135.

31. Benjamin B. Warfield, "Edwards and the New England Theology," *Studies in Theology* (1932 ed.; reprinted Grand Rapids, MI: Baker Book House, 1981), IX, 532–536; George M. Ella, "John Sutcliff (1752–1814) and His Friends," *New Focus*, 1(1) (June/July 1996), 8; idem, *Law and Gospel in the Theology of Andrew Fuller* (Eggleston, Co. Durham: Go, 1996), 167–168.

32. Letter to John Ryland, April 21, 1794, in John Ryland, Jr., *The Work of Faith, the Labour of Love, and the Patience of Hope Illustrated; in the Life and Death of the Reverend Andrew Fuller* (London: Button & Son, 1816), 365–366; letter to John Sutcliff, January 22, 1795 (Letters of Andrew Fuller, typescript transcript, Angus Library, Regent's Park College, Oxford).

33. "The Calvinistic and Socinian Systems Examined and Compared" (*Complete Works of the Rev. Andrew Fuller*, II, 154–155). See also "Calvinistic and Socinian Systems" (*Complete Works of the Rev. Andrew Fuller*, II, 157): "God, . . . in the punishment of sin, is not to be considered as acting in a merely private capacity, but as the universal moral Governor."

34. *Theology in America*, 281.

35. Nettles, "Edwards and His Impact on Baptists," 7–9; Holifield, *Theology in America*, 282–283; Sweeney, "Evangelical Tradition in America," in Stein, ed., *Cambridge Companion to Jonathan Edwards*, 227. On his response to the Arminianism of John Wesley (1703–1791), see, for example, Backus's *The Doctrine of Particular Election and Final Perseverance, explained and vindicated* (Boston, 1789). And see his *The Sovereign Decrees of God Set in a Scriptural Light* (Boston: Philip Freeman, 1773), 14–15, where, using Edwards's distinction between natural and moral inability, he refutes the argument put forward by the "carnal reasoners of our world" that "either men are able to obey and serve God, or else if they cannot do it, they are not to blame for neglecting of it, until God is pleased to convert them." Similarly, see his *Truth is Great, and Will Prevail* (Boston, 1781), 6–7, where he cites Edwards's treatise on the freedom of the will.

36. "A Discourse, Designed to Explain the Doctrine of Atonement. In Two Parts" (Providence, 1796), 25, 33. For the reference to Edwards, see *Doctrine of Atonement*, 33, n.*. See also Holifield, *Theology in America*, 283.

37. Gregory A. Wills, *The First Baptist Church of Columbia, South Carolina 1809 to 2002* (Brentwood, TN: Baptist History and Heritage Society, and Nashville, TN: Fields, 2003), 48. For the description of Johnson, see Thomas J. Nettles, *By His Grace and for His Glory: A Historical, Theological and Practical Study of the Doctrines of Grace in Baptist Life* (Grand Rapids, MI: Baker, 1986), 161.

38. "Love Characteristic of the Deity" (Charleston, SC, 1823), 17. For a discussion of the other main themes of this sermon, see Nettles, "Edwards and His Impact on Baptists," 12–14.

39. Letter to James S. Mims, March 25, 1848 (William B. Johnson Papers, James B. Duke Library, Furman University); cited in Gregory A. Wills, "The *SBJT*

Forum: Overlooked Shapers of Evangelicalism," *Southern Baptist Journal of Theology*, 3(1) (Spring 1999), 87.

40. Wills, *First Baptist Church of Columbia*, 46–50.

41. *First Baptist Church of Columbia*, 50.

42. *Abstract of Systematic Theology* (1887 ed.; reprinted Cape Coral, FL: Founders Press, 2006), 312.

43. Holifield, *Theology in America*, 285.

44. *A Scriptural View of the Atonement* (Milledgeville, GA: Statesman and Patriot, 1830). On White's views, see Jarrett Burch, *Adiel Sherwood: Baptist Antebellum Pioneer in Georgia* (Macon, GA: Mercer University Press, 2003), 90–92; Peter Beck, "A Southern Exposure: The Theology of Jonathan Edwards in the Writings of Jesse Mercer," *Journal of Baptist Studies*, 1 (2007), 23–24.

45. "Ten Letters, Addressed to the Rev. Cyrus White, in reference to his Scriptural View of the Atonement" (Washington, GA, 1830), i–ii. William T. Brantly (1787–1845) reprinted the letters—though not the two-page introduction, what Mercer called "The Apology"—in the *Columbian Star and Christian Index* (henceforth *CSCI*). The first installment is simply entitled "Letters on the Atonement," *CSCI* (August 28, 1830), 137–139. The next five installments are called "Mercer's Letters to White on the Atonement": October 23, 1830, 259–262; October 30, 1830, 276–279; November 6, 1830, 293–296; November 13, 1830, 307–309; November 20, 1830, 326–328. I am indebted to these discussions of Mercer's tract: Anthony L. Chute, *A Piety Above the Common Standard: Jesse Mercer and the Defense of Evangelical Calvinism* (Macon, GA: Mercer University Press, 2004), 83–92; Robert A. Snyder, "William T. Brantly (1787–1845): A Southern Unionist and the Breakup of the Triennial Convention" (unpublished Ph.D. thesis, Southern Baptist Theological Seminary, 2005), 127–149; Beck, "Southern Exposure," 20–37, *passim*.

46. "Review of the *Complete Works of the Rev. Andrew Fuller, with a Memoir of his Life*," *American Baptist Magazine*, 13 (1833), 388.

47. "Ten Letters," 11 (Letter IV).

48. "Ten Letters," 37 (Letter IX). Mercer has rightly read Fuller. See Michael A. G. Haykin, "Particular Redemption in the Writings of Andrew Fuller (1754–1815)," in David Bebbington, ed., *The Gospel in the World: International Baptist Studies* (Carlisle, Cumbria, and Waynesboro, GA: Paternoster Press, 2002), 107–128.

49. Burch, *Adiel Sherwood*, 91.

50. Snyder, "William T. Brantly (1787–1845)," 133–135.

51. Wills, "Overlooked Shapers of Evangelicalism," 88. Cf. Holifield, *Theology in America*, 280–286.

52. *Notes on the Principles and Practices of Baptist Churches* (New York: Sheldon, Blakeman, 1857), 18.

53. Cited in Wayland, *Principles and Practices of Baptist Churches*, 21.

54. Cited in Holifield, *Theology in America*, 284.

CHAPTER 15

1. Immanuel Hermann von Fichte, *System der Ethik*, 2 vols. (Leipzig: Dyk, 1850–1853), 1: 544–545; cited in Mattoon Monroe Curtis, "Kantean Elements in Jonathan Edwards," in *Philosophische Abhandlungen: Max Heinze zum 70. Geburtstage* (Berlin: Ernst Siegfried Mittler and Sohn, 1906), 35.

2. Leslie Stephen, *Hours in a Library*, 3 vols. (London: Smith, Elder, 1892 [1876]), 1: 343.

3. Dugald Stewart, cited in Curtis, "Kantean Elements," 34.

4. Philarète Charles, *Études sur la literature et les moeurs des Anglo-Américains au XIXe Siècle* (Paris: Amyot, 1851), speaks of Benjamin Franklin as a "type of the national genius" and "a consummate politician, subtle dialectician, amorous and useful" (10). By contrast Edwards is "a logician whose celebrity does not seem to have been propagated to Europe" (12). Richard Paul Wülker, in *Geschichte der englischen Literatur*, vol. 2 (Leipzig: Verlag des Biographischen Instituts, 1907), speaks of Franklin as the "first American author who became world renowned" (422), while Edwards's "significance as logician and metaphysician is uncontested" (421). See also Barbara B. Oberg and Harry S. Stout, ed., *Benjamin Franklin, Jonathan Edwards, and the Representation of American Culture* (New York: Oxford University Press, 1993).

5. On Miklos Vetö and Oliver Crisp, see Michael J. McClymond and Gerald R. McDermott, *The Theology of Jonathan Edwards* (New York: Oxford University Press, 2012), 658–662.

6. Stephen, *Hours in a Library*, 300, 305, 301–302.

7. Stephen, *Hours in a Library*, 305, 307, 314, 309.

8. Stephen, *Hours in a Library*, 315, 317, 316, 320, 322, 326–328.

9. Stephen, *Hours in a Library*, 329, 343–344.

10. Vernon L. Parrington, "The Anachronism of Jonathan Edwards," in his *Main Currents of American Thought*, vol. 1 (New York: Harcourt, Brace, 1927), 148–163.

11. Ola Winslow, *Jonathan Edwards, 1703–1758: A Life* (New York: Octagon Books, 1973 [1940]), 327.

12. Perry Miller, *Jonathan Edwards* (New York: William Sloane, 1949), 16, cf. 148.

13. On Bloomsbury, see Christine Froula, *Virginia Woolf and the Bloomsbury Avant-Garde: War, Civilization, Modernity* (New York: Columbia University Press, 2005); and Robert Skidelsky, *John Maynard Keynes, 1883–1946: Economist, Philosopher, Statesman* (New York: Penguin, 2003), 142–148.

14. G. E. Moore's *Principia Ethica* (1903) was a manifesto for the Cambridge avant-garde and Bloomsbury group, insisting that ethical judgments are self-evident and not justified through argumentation (Skidelsky, *Keynes*, 1).

15. On freedom in early Continental Calvinism, see Willem J. van Asselt, J. Martin Bac, and Roelf T. te Velde, eds., *Reformed Thought on Freedom: The Concept of Free Choice in Early Modern Reformed Theology* (Grand Rapids, MI: Baker Academic,

2010). Richard A. Muller distinguishes Edwards from other Calvinists on free choice in "Jonathan Edwards and the Absence of Free Choice: A Parting of Ways in the Reformed Tradition," *Jonathan Edwards Studies*, forthcoming.

16. James McCosh, *The Scottish Philosophy* (New York: Robert Carter, 1875), 183.

17. Jonathan Edwards, *Freedom of the Will: The Works of Jonathan Edwards, Volume 1* (New Haven: Yale University Press, 1957), 445–470.

18. Muller, "Jonathan Edwards and the Absence of Free Choice," 3–5.

19. Dugald Stewart, "Dissertation, Exhibiting a General View of the Progress of Metaphysical, Ethical, and Political Philosophy," in *The Works of Dugald Steward*, 7 vols. (Cambridge, UK: Hilliard and Brown, 1829), 6: 281–283.

20. Samuel Taylor Coleridge, *Aids to Reflection* (1829), 105–107.

21. William Hazlitt, *Literary Remains of the Late William Hazlitt* (London: Saunders and Otley, 1836), 1: 207. Hazlitt preferred Edwards to Priestley: "Dr. Priestley's whole aim seems to be to evade the difficulties of his subject, Edwards's to answer them" (208).

22. M. Gregoire, *Histoire des sectes religieuses*, vol. 5, new ed. (Paris: Baudouin, 1829), 235–244.

23. Henry Bargy, *La Religion dans la société aux États-Unis* (Paris: Librairie Armand Collin, 1902), 94, 98. The chapter on Emerson bears the paradoxical title "Freedom Without Free Will" (99–105).

24. Frédéric De Rougemont, *Les deux cités; philosophie de l'histoire*, vol. 2 (Paris: Sandoz et Fischbacher, 1874), 589–592. Similarly, Rudolf Rocholl, in *Die Philosophie der Geschichte* (Göttingen: Vandenhoek and Ruprecht, 1878), commented on *History of Redemption* and added that "Edwards is the Augustine of the new continent" (261).

25. James McCosh, *The Scottish Philosophy* (New York: Robert Carter, 1875), 183–184.

26. Georges Lyon, *L'Idéalisme en Angleterre au Dix-Huitième Siècle* (Paris: Felix Alcan, 1888), 406–407, 436–439.

27. Worth mentioning is Edward Gregory Lawrence van Becelaere's *La philosophie en Amérique* (New York: Eclectic, 1904), 33–48. William Girard, in "Du transcendentalisme considéré essentiellement dans sa définition," in *University of California Publications in Modern Philology* 4 (1916) 353–498, judged that "the essential merit of Jonathan Edwards was to establish the conceptual foundation for a Calvinistic philosophy" (364). Neither author broke new ground.

28. Miklos Vetö, *Le pensée de Jonathan Edwards* (Paris: Cerf, 1987; 2007, 2nd ed.); see also Vetö's "Edwards and Philosophy," in Gerald R. McDermott, ed., *Understanding Jonathan Edwards* (New York: Oxford University Press, 2009), 151–170.

29. An early German essay is by Dr. [Calvin] Stowe at Andover Seminary, "Edwards (Jonathan)," in Johann Jakob Herzog, ed., *Real-enzyklopädie für protestantische Theologie und Kirche*, vol. 3 (Stuttgart and Hamburg, Rudolf Besser, 1855), 652–658.

30. John Henry MacCracken, *Jonathan Edwards Idealismus; Inaugural-Dissertation,* Friedrichs-Universitat Halle-Wittenburg (Halle: C. A. Kammerer, 1899), 16–25, quoting 17, with references.

31. Wallace E. Anderson asserts Edwards's independence of Berkeley's idealism in his "Editor's Introduction," in *Scientific and Philosophical Writings; The Works of Jonathan Edwards, Volume 6* (New Haven: Yale University Press, 1980), 1–143.

32. William Harder Squires, *Jonathan Edwards und Seine Willenslehre, Inaugural-Dissertation* (Leipzig: University of Leipzig, 1901), 8, 15, 42–43.

33. See Richard Hall, "Introduction," in William Harder Squires, *The Edwardean: A Quarterly Devoted to the History of Thought in America* (Lewiston, NY: Edwin Mellen Press, 1991), vii–xv; and the discussion of Squires in McClymond and McDermott, *Theology of Jonathan Edwards,* 657–658.

34. Mattoon Monroe Curtis, "Kantean Elements in Jonathan Edwards," in *Philosophische Abhandlungen: Max Heinze zum 70. Geburtstage* (Berlin: Ernst Siegfried Mittler and Sohn, 1906), 34–62, citing 47, 62, 40, 34–35, 46, 36.

35. Eric Voegelin, "A Formal Relationship with Puritan Mysticism," *The Collected Works of Eric Voegelin; Volume 1: On the Form of the American Mind* (Baton Rouge: Louisiana State University Press, 1987 [1928]), 126–143, citing 127, 131–133, 136, 139. Much like Voegelin, Wolfgang Keller and Bernhard Fehr, in *Die englische Literatur von der Renaissance biz zur Aufklärung* (Akademische Verlagsgesellschaft Athenaion, 1927), found mysticism in Edwards as something distinct from his Calvinism: "Edwards's effort to place Calvinism on a modern, rational foundation came to its completion in a deep inclination toward mysticism" (20).

36. Perry Miller, "Jonathan Edwards to Emerson," *New England Quarterly* 13 (1940) 589–617. Miller wrote that "Unitarianism had stripped off the dogmas, and Emerson was free to celebrate purely and simply the presence of God in the soul and in nature, the pure metaphysical essence of the New England tradition" (609).

37. Gustav E. Müller, *Amerikanische Philosophie* (Stuttgart: Fr. Frommanns Verlag, 1950), 17–38, citing 17, 25, 19, 26–27, 38.

38. Erwin Baur, Eugen Fischer, and Fritz Lenz, *Grundriss der menschlichen Erblichkeitslehre und Rassenhygiene,* vol. 1 (München: J. F. Lehmanns Verlag, 1921), 55. There is similar reference in I. Facaoaru, *Soziale Auslese: Ihre biologischen und psychologischen Grundlagen* (Huber, 1933). The study on which the German authors based their comments was A. E. Winship, *Jukes-Edwards: A Study in Education and Heredity* (Harrisburg, PA: R. L. Myers, 1900).

39. More recently there is Benedikt Peters, *Der Geist der Erweckung: Die grosse Erweckung und die charismatische Bewegung* (Bielefeld, Ger.: Betanien Verlag, 2001). Yet this short book is mostly a reworking of English-language literature on revival.

40. An extensive bibliography on religious revivals appears in Michael J. McClymond, ed., *Encyclopedia of Religious Revivals in America,* 2 vols. (Westport, CT: Greenwood

Press, 2007), 387–602, with separate listings for North America, Britain, and Europe. The *Reveil* in France and French-speaking Switzerland is treated in Alice Wemyss, *Histoire du Reveil, 1790–1849* (Paris: Les Bergers et Les Mages, 1977).

41. Published as Edwards, *L'union dans la prière pour la propagation de l'Evangile* (Paris, 1823); and Edwards, *Histoire de l'oeuvre de la redemption* (Toulouse: Société des Livres Religieux, 1854).

42. Information on Astié is based on the Spanish language webpage (accessed January 10, 2011) http://www.iglesiapueblonuevo.es/historia.php?pagina=bio_astie.

43. J.-F. Astié, "Grand réveil aux Etats-Unis," in *Le Chrétien Évangélique* 1 (1858) 129–133, citing 129, 132.

44. J. Astié, *Histoire de la République des États-Unis*, vol. 2 (Paris: Grasart, 1865), 338–376, citing 342–344, 352–354, 363–364, 367, and 370.

45. A representative French Protestant theologian of this era was Louis Auguste Sabatier (1839–1901), whose books reflected a modernist agenda.

46. Jacques Kaltenbach, *Etude psychologique des plus anciens réveils religieux aux Etats-Unis; Thèse... Bachelier en Théologie* (Geneva: W. Kündig, 1905); Henri Bois, *Quelques réflexions sur la psychologie des réveils* (Paris: Librairie Fischbaher, 1906).

47. Kaltenbach, *Etude psychologique*, 71, 74, 80, 100–109, 144–145. Emmanuel Pétaval-Olliff commented that "our fathers have inherited from the Middle Ages a philosophy and theology that assigns an exorbitant place to the motive of fear." In this account, Edwards's "Sinners in the Hands of an Angry God" was a prime expression of fear-based religion (*Le problème de l'immortalité*; Paris: Librairie Fischbacher, 1892; 281, 308).

48. On revivals versus Christian nurture and religious education, see Michael A. Farley, "Christian Nurture Debate," in McClymond, ed., *Encyclopedia of Religious Revivals in America*, 1: 106–109.

49. Davenport's book is excerpted and its significance is discussed in McClymond, ed., *Encyclopedia of Religious Revivals in America*, 2: 237–241.

50. See Ian Nicholson, "Academic Professionalization and Protestant Reconstruction, 1890–1902: George Albert Coe's Psychology of Religion," *Journal of the History of the Behavioral Sciences* 30 (1994) 348–368.

51. Bois, *Quelques réflexions* 7 n, 84–85 n. 2, 143–144, 170 n. 1, 342 n. 1.

52. David W. Bebbington, *Evangelicalism in Modern Britain: A History from the 1730s to the 1980s* (London: Unwin Hyman, 1989), 64–65.

53. Bebbington, *Evangelicalism*, 62, notes that Edwards's *Some Thoughts on the Revival* (1743) anticipated the possible dawning of the millennium in America. Bebbington writes: "Perhaps more congenial to British readers was his subsequent argument, in *An Humble Attempt* (1747), that unfulfilled prophecy is an incentive to prayer." When *Humble Attempt* was republished in 1784 it did much to foster millennial expectations in Britain, according to Bebbington.

54. Iain H. Murray, *The Puritan Hope: A Study in Revival and the Interpretation of Prophecy* (London: Banner of Truth Trust, 1970), 152. Murray also notes

(see 150–155, 175–178) that Edwards's writings may have helped to stir British hopes for Christian conversion of the Jewish people.

55. Michael A. G. Haykin, *One Heart and One Soul: John Sutcliff of Olney, His Friends and His Times* (Darlington, Durham, UK: Evangelical Press, 1994), 13, 55.

56. On the nineteenth- and twentieth-century receptions, see McClymond and McDermott, *Theology of Jonathan Edwards*, 601–648. Among the most extreme caricatures were Joseph Crooker, "Jonathan Edwards: A Psychological Study," *New England Magazine* 2 (1890), 159–172; and Henry Bamford Parkes, *Jonathan Edwards: The Fiery Puritan* (New York: Minton, Balch, 1930).

57. Alexander V. G. Allen, *Jonathan Edwards* (Boston: Houghton, Mifflin, 1889), 388.

58. It seems no accident that Müller's *Amerikanische Philosophie* treats Edwards in a chapter called "Das System: Jonathan Edwards" (17–38).

59. See the discussion of Vetö in McClymond and McDermott, *Theology of Jonathan Edwards*, 658–659.

CHAPTER 16

1. Mamoru Iga, ed. and trans., *Ikari no Kami: Edowazu Sekkyoshu* (The God of Wrath: Sermons of Edwards) (Tokyo: Nishimura Shoten, 1948), in Japanese.

2. Clarence H. Faust and Thomas H. Johnson, ed., *Jonathan Edwards: Representative Selections, with Introduction, Bibliography, and Notes* (New York: American Books, 1935), cxx. Ava Chamberlain kindly informed me that the entry appears only in the first edition, not in later editions, of Faust and Johnson's anthology.

3. The book is duly recognized in M. X. Lesser's *Jonathan Edwards: A Reference Guide* (Boston: G. K. Hall, 1981), 121 (1904: no. 7); and idem, *Reading Jonathan Edwards: An Annotated Bibliography in Three Parts, 1729–2005* (Grand Rapids, MI: Eerdmans, 2008), 140 (1904: no. 7). Lesser does not recognize Iga's work in either book.

4. Harry Norman Gardiner, ed., *Selected Sermons of Jonathan Edwards* (London: Macmillan, 1904), "Introduction," vii–xv. Iga's textual dependence is evidenced in his verbatim translation of Gardiner's comparison of Sarah Pierpont to Dante's Beatrice: "Dante's description of Beatrice, which in pure lyric quality it certainly equals, though it lacks the latter's sensuous coloring and imaginative idealization."

5. Ibid., xxv.

6. Gardiner, "Introduction," xxvii.

7. Mamoru Iga, "Preface," 7–16.

8. Josiah Royce, *William James and the Philosophy of Life, Phi Beta Kappa Oration Delivered at Harvard University, June, 1911* (New York: Macmillan, 1911), 5. Royce's intention was to add James to this hall of fame as the third, but this is "in order of time," as he explicitly qualifies, not necessarily in degree as Iga seems to suggest.

9. See John W. Dower, *Embracing Defeat: Japan in the Wake of World War II* (New York: Norton, 1999).

10. At one point, the author mentions the name "McGiffert" with reference to the later American reception of Ritschlian experientialism. No specific passage, however, could be identified as stemming from McGiffert's biography of Edwards.

11. Iga, "Preface," 13 (my translation).

12. E-mail correspondence with Tina Kotin-Savitch, administrative staff at College of Social and Behavioral Sciences, California State University, Northridge, August 23, 2010.

13. His major publication is *The Thorn in the Chrysanthemum: Suicide and Economic Success in Modern Japan* (Berkeley: University of California Press, 1986).

14. Email correspondence with Keumsan Baek, August 25–29, 2010, and January 27, 2011.

15. See Lesser, *Annotated Bibliography*, 590 (2004: no. 32).

16. M. X. Lesser, "An Honor Too Great: Jonathan Edwards in Print Abroad," in David W. Kling and Douglas A. Sweeney, eds., *Jonathan Edwards at Home and Abroad: Historical Memories, Cultural Movements, Global Horizons* (Columbia: University of South Carolina Press, 2003), 304, 318–319.

17. I am indebted to Douglas Sweeney for the information provided here regarding Korean Edwards scholarship. Johannes Unsok Ro of International Christian University kindly helped me confirm the publication data.

18. Lesser, "An Honor Too Great," 304.

19. Lesser mentions the first book as "an abridged *Religious Affections* published in Taipei in 1994" (Lesser, "An Honor Too Great," 319). However, neither *Selected Writings of Jonathan Edwards* nor *The Experience That Counts* is recognized in his 2008 annotated bibliography.

20. I am thankful to Yang-en Cheng of Taiwan Theological College and Seminary, Enoch Yile Wang of Church China, Sze Wai of Chinese Christian Literature Council, and Yeo Wee Yong of the Reformation Translation Fellowship for providing information concerning Edwardsian studies in Chinese.

21. His article is included in Don Schweitzer, ed., *Jonathan Edwards as Contemporary: Essays in Honor of Sang Hyun Lee* (New York: Peter Lang Publishing, 2010), along with mine.

22. Anri Morimoto, *Jonasan Edowazu Kenkyu: Amerika Puritanisumu no Sonzairon to Kyusairon (Jonathan Edwards Studies: The Ontology and Soteriology of American Puritanism)* (Tokyo: Sobunsha, 1995), in Japanese. This is an enlarged edition of *Jonathan Edwards and the Catholic Vision of Salvation* (University Park, Pa.: Pennsylvania State University Press, 1995) by the same author. Lesser lists both versions in his bibliography. Lesser, *Annotated Bibliography*, 494 (1995: #35 and #36).

23. "Budo no Mi Translation Ministry" (http://homepage2.nifty.com/grapes/), accessed August 23, 2010.

CHAPTER 17

1. "10 Ideas Changing the World Right Now," http://www.time.com/time/specials/packages/completelist/0,29569,1884779,00.html; retrieved February 4, 2012.

2. I do not know if vendors sold such T-shirts at conferences, but an example of one is on the cover of Collin Hansen's *Young, Restless, and Reformed: A Journalist's Journey with the New Calvinists* (Wheaton, IL: Crossway Books, 2008).

3. Adam Leroy James, *Early American Philosophers* (New York: Ungar, 1958); and Turnbull, *Jonathan Edwards, the Preacher* (Grand Rapids, MI: Baker Books, 1958).

4. Charles Peter MacGregor, "The Life and Service of Jonathan Edwards and His Message to the Church of Our Day" (Th.D. diss., Boston University, 1953); and Walker, "Jonathan Edwards' Psychology of Conversion" (B.D. thesis, Butler University, 1953).

5. Among the works produced in 1968 were Edward H. Davidson, *Jonathan Edwards: The Narrative of a Puritan Mind* (1966; Cambridge, MA: Harvard University Press, 1968); Roland Andre Delattre, *Beauty and Sensibility in the Thought of Jonathan Edwards* (New Haven, CT: Yale University Press, 1968); David Levin, *The Puritan and the Enlightenment: Franklin and Edwards* (Chicago: Rand McNally, 1968); William Henry Parker, "The Social Theory of Jonathan Edwards as Developed in His Works on Revivalism" (Ph.D. diss., Syracuse University, 1968); and Joseph Crawford Williamson, "The Excellency of Christ: A Study in the Christology of Jonathan Edwards" (Ph.D. diss., Harvard University, 1968).

6. John H. Gerstner, "Scotch Realism, Kant and Darwin in the Philosophy of James McCosh," (Ph.D. diss., Harvard University, 1945).

7. Gerstner, *Steps to Salvation* (Philadelphia: Westminster Press, 1960), 13.

8. Ibid., 9–10.

9. Ibid., 14.

10. Ibid., 190.

11. Gerstner, *Jonathan Edwards: A Mini-Theology* (Wheaton, IL: Tyndale House, 1987), 14, 18–19.

12. Richard F. Lovelace, *The American Pietism of Cotton Mather: Origins of American Evangelicalism* (Grand Rapids, MI: Christian University Press, 1979).

13. Lovelace, *Dynamics of Spiritual Life: An Evangelical Theology of Renewal* (Downers Grove, IL: InterVarsity Press, 1979), 12.

14. Ibid., 25.

15. Ibid., 246, 248. Lovelace, it should be noted, also interacts closely with Edwards on social activism and eschatology, but for the sake of brevity I examine only the inherent destructiveness of spiritual pride and charismatic gifts.

16. Ibid., 250.

17. Ibid., 264.

18. Ibid., 265.

19. Ibid., 269.

20. Murray, *Jonathan Edwards: A New Biography* (Carlisle, PA: Banner of Truth Trust, 1987), xxx.

21. Ibid., xxv–xxvi.

22. Ibid., 472.

23. Iain H. Murray, *Revival and Revivalism: The Making and Marring of American Evangelicalism, 1750–1858* (Carlisle, PA: Banner of Truth, 1994).

24. John Piper, *God's Passion for His Glory: Living the Vision of Jonathan Edwards with the Complete Text of* The End for Which God Created the World (Wheaton, IL: Crossway Books, 1998), 92.

25. Ibid., 87–92, xi.

26. Wells, *No Place for Truth: Or Whatever Happened to Evangelical Theology* (Grand Rapids, MI: Eerdmans, 1993); and Guinness, *Fit Bodies, Fat Minds: Why Evangelicals Don't Think and What to Do About It* (Grand Rapids, MI: Baker Books, 1994).

27. Piper, *God's Passion*, 31 (italics Piper's).

28. Ibid., 92.

29. Ibid., 97.

30. Nathan O. Hatch and Harry S. Stout, eds., *Jonathan Edwards and the American Experience* (New York: Oxford University Press, 1983); Sang Hyun Lee and Allen C. Guelzo, eds., *Edwards in Our Time: Jonathan Edwards and the Shaping of American Religion* (Grand Rapids, MI: Eerdmans, 1999); D. G. Hart, Sean Michael Lucas, and Stephen J. Nichols, eds., *The Legacy of Jonathan Edwards: American Religion and the Evangelical Tradition* (Grand Rapids, MI: Baker, 2003); David W. Kling and Douglas A. Sweeney, eds., *Jonathan Edwards at Home and Abroad: Historical Memories, Cultural Movements, Global Horizons* (Columbia: University of South Carolina Press, 2003); and John Piper and Justin Taylor, eds., *A God Entranced Vision of All Things: The Legacy of Jonathan Edwards* (Wheaton, IL: Crossway Books, 2004).

31. Mark A. Noll, *Princeton and the Republic, 1768–1822: The Search for a Christian Enlightenment in the Era of Samuel Stanhope Smith* (Princeton: Princeton University Press, 1989), 44.

32. Ibid., 47.

33. Ibid., 298.

34. Noll, *America's God: From Jonathan Edwards to Abraham Lincoln* (New York: Oxford University Press, 2002), 440, 443.

35. Ibid., 444.

36. George M. Marsden, *Jonathan Edwards: A Life* (New Haven, CT: Yale University Press, 2003), 503, 504.

37. George M. Marsden, "Jonathan Edwards in the Twenty-First Century," in Harry S. Stout, Kenneth P. Minkema, and Caleb J. D. Maskell, eds., *Jonathan Edwards at 300: Essays on the Tercentenary of His Birth* (Lanham, MD: University Press of America, 2005), 158, 162.

38. Ibid., 161.
39. Packer quoted in Hansen, *Young, Restless, and Reformed,* 35.
40. Piper quoted in ibid., 49.
41. Maskell quoted in ibid., 57.
42. Moody quoted in ibid., 61.
43. Ibid.
44. H. L. Mencken, "Doctor Seraphicus et Ecstaticus," Baltimore *Evening Sun,* March 14, 1916.

POSTSCRIPT

1. Gary Wills, *Head and Heart: A History of Christianity in America* (New York: Penguin Books, 2007), 114.
2. For more on this literary network, see the excellent recent book on one of its most prolific facilitators, Jonathan M. Yeager, *Enlightened Evangelicalism: The Life and Thought of John Erskine* (New York: Oxford University Press, 2011).
3. For more on Edwards and his legacy in the global missions movement, see William E. Strong, *The Story of the American Board: An Account of the First Hundred Years of the American Board of Commissioners for Foreign Missions* (Boston: Pilgrim Press, 1910); Oliver W. Elsbree, *The Rise of the Missionary Spirit in America, 1790–1815* (Williamsport, PA: Williamsport Printing, 1928); Wolfgang E. Lowe, "The First American Foreign Missionaries: The Students, 1810–1829: An Inquiry into Their Theological Motives" (Ph.D. diss., Brown University, 1962); J. A. de Jong, *As the Waters Cover the Sea: Millennial Expectations in the Rise of Anglo-American Missions* (Kampen, Neth.: J. H. Kok, 1970); Charles L. Chaney, "God's Glorious Work: The Theological Foundations of the Early Missionary Societies in America, 1787–1817" (Ph.D. diss., University of Chicago, 1973); John A. Andrew III, *Rebuilding the Christian Commonwealth: New England Congregationalists and Foreign Missions, 1800–1830* (Lexington: University Press of Kentucky, 1976); Joseph Conforti, "David Brainerd and the Nineteenth-Century Missionary Movement," *Journal of the Early Republic* 5 (Fall 1985): 309–329; Ronald E. Davies, *Jonathan Edwards and His Influence on the Development of the Missionary Movement from Britain* (Cambridge, UK: Currents in World Christianity Project, 1996); Andrew F. Walls, "Missions and Historical Memory: Jonathan Edwards and David Brainerd," and Stuart Piggin, "The Expanding Knowledge of God: Jonathan Edwards's Influence on Missionary Thinking and Promotion," both in *Jonathan Edwards at Home and Abroad: Historical Memories, Cultural Movements, Global Horizons,* ed. David W. Kling and Douglas A. Sweeney (Columbia: University of South Carolina Press, 2003), 248–296; David W. Kling, "The New Divinity and the Origins of the American Board of Commissioners for Foreign Missions," *Church History* 72 (December 2003): 791–819; Ussama Samir Makdisi, *Artillery of Heaven: American Missionaries and the Failed Conversion of the Middle East* (Ithaca, NY: Cornell

University Press, 2008); Douglas A. Sweeney, *Jonathan Edwards and the Ministry of the Word: A Model of Faith and Thought* (Downers Grove, IL: IVP Academic, 2009), 165–186; and the work on Mount Holyoke cited below.

4. There is a small but growing literature on Edwards's global reach on which this volume has been built. See especially Kling and Sweeney, eds., *Jonathan Edwards at Home and Abroad*; Mark A. Noll, "Jonathan Edwards's *Freedom of the Will* Abroad," in *Jonathan Edwards at 300: Essays on the Tercentenary of His Birth*, ed. Harry S. Stout, Kenneth P. Minkema, and Caleb J. D. Maskell (Lanham, MD: University Press of America, 2005), 98–110; and D. W. Bebbington, "The Reputation of Edwards Abroad," in *The Cambridge Companion to Jonathan Edwards*, ed. Stephen J. Stein (New York: Cambridge University Press, 2007), 239–261. Also helpful in this regard are the "Index of Translations" and the index of "Printers and Publishers" in M. X. Lesser, *The Printed Writings of Jonathan Edwards, 1703–1758: A Bibliography*, rev. ed. (Princeton, NJ: Princeton Theological Seminary, 2003), 241–248.

5. For evidence of Edwards's popularity in Australia, start with the work of Stuart Piggin, Rhys Bezzant, and the fledgling Jonathan Edwards Centre in Melbourne. See especially Stuart Piggin, "Domestic Spirituality: Jonathan Edwards on Love, Marriage and Family Life," in *The Bible and the Business of Life: Essays in Honour of Robert J. Banks's Sixty-fifth Birthday*, ed. Simon Carey Holt and Gordon Preece, ATF Series (Adelaide: ATF Press, 2004), 149–163; Rhys Stewart Bezzant, "Orderly But Not Ordinary: Jonathan Edwards's Evangelical Ecclesiology" (Th.D. thesis, Australian College of Theology, 2010), which will be published in revised form by Oxford University Press; and the website of the Jonathan Edwards Centre in Australia, jec@ridley.edu.au.

6. For further bibliographical leads, see Lesser, *The Printed Writings of Jonathan Edwards*, items 45, 106, 126, 183, 186, 354, 487; but note that Lesser's catalogue of Edwards's writings in translation is already obsolete, as new translations are appearing every year.

7. The Edwards conference in Budapest yielded Tibor Fabiny, ed., *Introducing America's Theologian: Jonathan Edwards and the European Prospect* (Budapest: Karoli Gaspar University Press, 2008; this reference translates the original Hungarian); and Gerald R. McDermott, ed., *Understanding Jonathan Edwards: An Introduction to America's Theologian* (New York: Oxford University Press, 2009). The Edwards conference in Poland is "Christianity in Today's World: The Legacy of Jonathan Edwards," hosted by the Jonathan Edwards Center-Poland and the Evangelical School of Theology (EWST) in Wroclaw, May 31–June 1, 2011. Conference organizers intend to publish a book based on the conference. Cf. Kelly Van Andel, Adriaan C. Neele, and Kenneth P. Minkema, eds., *Jonathan Edwards and Scotland* (Edinburgh: Dunedin Academic Press, 2011), which emerged from a conference at the University of Glasgow. For more on the Edwards Centers in Europe, go to http://edwards.yale.edu/Global+centers.

8. For Douglas's view of feminization, see Ann Douglas, *The Feminization of American Culture* (New York: Knopf, 1977). The most important critiques of Douglas that treat American religion are David S. Reynolds, "The Feminization Controversy: Sexual Stereotypes and the Paradoxes of Piety in Nineteenth-Century America," *New England Quarterly* 53 (March 1980): 96–106; Terry D. Billhartz, "Sex and the Second Great Awakening: The Feminization of American Religion Reconsidered," in *Belief and Behavior: Essays in the New Religious History*, ed. Philip R. VanderMeer and Robert P. Swierenga (New Brunswick, NJ: Rutgers University Press, 1991), 117–135; Ann D. Braude, "Women's History *Is* American Religious History," in *Retelling U.S. Religious History*, ed. Thomas A. Tweed (Berkeley: University of California Press, 1997), 87–107; and Catherine A. Brekus, *Strangers and Pilgrims: Female Preaching in America, 1740–1845*, Gender and American Culture series (Chapel Hill: University of North Carolina Press, 1998), 207–216. On the issue of "feminization" in New England in this period, see also Richard D. Shiels, "The Feminization of American Congregationalism, 1730–1835," *American Quarterly* 33 (Spring 1981): 46–62; Stephen R. Grossbart, "Seeking the Divine Favor: Conversion and Church Admission in Eastern Connecticut, 1711–1832," *William and Mary Quarterly* 46 (October 1989): 732–735; Harry Stout and Catherine Brekus, "Declension, Gender, and the 'New Religious History,'" in *Belief and Behavior*, eds. VanderMeer and Swierenga, 28; David W. Kling, *A Field of Divine Wonders: The New Divinity and Village Revivals in Northwestern Connecticut, 1792–1822* (University Park: Pennsylvania State University Press, 1993), 10, 179, 206, 230–231; and Genevieve McCoy, "'Reason for a Hope': Evangelical Women Making Sense of Late Edwardsian Calvinism," in *Jonathan Edwards's Writings: Text, Context, Interpretation*, ed. Stephen J. Stein (Bloomington: Indiana University Press, 1996), 175–192. Cf. Sharon Y. Kim, "Beyond the Men in Black: Jonathan Edwards and Nineteenth-Century Woman's Fiction," in *Jonathan Edwards at Home and Abroad*, ed. Kling and Sweeney, 137–153, a source that shows the need for further scholarship on Edwards and female writers in America, from Hannah Foster, Susan Warner, and Harriet Beecher Stowe to Marilynne Robinson today. For further leads in this regard, see the Edwardsian-Stowe sources listed in Douglas A. Sweeney and Allen C. Guelzo, eds., *The New England Theology: From Jonathan Edwards to Edwards Amasa Park* (Grand Rapids, MI: Baker Academic, 2006), 288, 317; Thomas J. Davis, "The Death of Adam, the Resurrection of Calvin: Marilynne Robinson's Alternative to an American Ideograph," in *Sober, Strict, and Scriptural: Collective Memories of John Calvin, 1800–2000*, eds. Johan de Niet, Herman Paul, and Bart Wallet (Leiden: Brill, 2009), 357–384; and Thomas Davis, "John Calvin at 'Home' in American Culture," in *John Calvin's American Legacy*, ed. Thomas J. Davis (New York: Oxford University Press, 2010), 267–271.

9. See especially his *Faithful Narrative* and *Some Thoughts Concerning the Revival*, in Yale 4: 191–205, 331–341.

10. See Edwards Amasa Park, *Memoir of the Life and Character of Samuel Hopkins, D.D.*, in *The Works of Samuel Hopkins, D.D.*, 3 vols. (Boston: Doctrinal Tract Society, 1852), 1: 22, who notes the influence that Sarah Edwards's willingness to be damned for the greater glory of God had on Hopkins's commitment to the doctrine of resignation; Charles Cuningham, *Timothy Dwight, 1752–1817, A Biography* (New York: Macmillan, 1942), 10–18, who discusses the major role of Mary Dwight, Timothy's mother, in preparing her son for college and inculcating her father's thought; B. B. Edwards, *Memoir of the Rev. Elias Cornelius* (Boston: Perkins and Marvin, 1833), 22, who says that Cornelius used Hopkins's *Life and Character of Miss Susanna Anthony* (1796) to navigate the straits of his conversion during college (at Yale in 1813); William A. Hallock, *"Light and Love": A Sketch of the Life and Labors of the Rev. Justin Edwards, D.D.* (New York: American Tract Society, 1855), 11–12, who reports that Justin Edwards, the social reformer and president of Andover from 1836 to 1842, was converted under the influence of the elderly Phebe Bartlet. On the rise of women's influence as nurturers of piety, or moral mothers, in this period, see Ruth H. Bloch, "American Feminine Ideals in Transition: The Rise of the Moral Mother, 1785–1815," *Feminist Studies* 4 (June 1978): 101–126.

11. On the role of women in Edwardsian revivalism, see especially Kling, *A Field of Divine Wonders*, 215–227. On women in the rise of the Sunday School movement, see Anne M. Boylan, *Sunday School: The Formation of an American Institution 1790–1880* (New Haven, CT: Yale University Press, 1988), 114–126. On Edwardsian women in missions, see Genevieve McCoy, "The Women of the ABCFM Oregon Mission and the Conflicted Language of Calvinism," *Church History* 64 (March 1995): 62–82; and Dana L. Robert, *American Women in Mission: A Social History of Their Thought and Practice*, The Modern Mission Era, 1792–1992, an Appraisal (Macon, GA: Mercer University Press, 1996), 1–124.

12. See the personal correspondence among Hopkins, Osborn, and Anthony in the Samuel Hopkins Papers of the Franklin Trask Library (Andover-Newton Theological School); the Simon Gratz and American Colonial Clergy Collections of the Historical Society of Pennsylvania; and the Boston Public Library; the correspondence in the Sarah Osborn collection of the American Antiquarian Society; and the Osborn diaries at the Newport Historical Society, the Beinecke Rare Book and Manuscript Library (Yale University), and the Connecticut Historical Society. For more on Osborn, see Sheryl Anne Kujawa, "'A Precious Season at the Throne of Grace': Sarah Haggar Wheaten Osborn, 1714–1796" (Ph.D. diss., Boston College, 1993); Mary Beth Norton, ed., "'My Resting Reaping Times': Sarah Osborn's Defense of Her 'Unfeminine' Activities, 1767," *Signs: Journal of Women in Culture and Society* 2 (Winter 1976): 515–529; Joseph A. Conforti, *Samuel Hopkins and the New Divinity Movement: Calvinism, the Congregational Ministry, and Reform in New England Between the Great Awakenings* (Grand Rapids, MI: Christian University Press), 102–108; Charles E. Hambrick-Stowe,

"The Spiritual Pilgrimage of Sarah Osborn (1714–1796)," *Church History* 61 (December 1992): 408–421; Charles E. Hambrick-Stowe, "All Things Were New and Astonishing: Edwardsian Piety, the New Divinity, and Race," in *Jonathan Edwards at Home and Abroad,* ed. Kling and Sweeney, 121–136; and Catherine Brekus, *Sarah Osborn's World: Popular Christianity in Early America* (New York: Knopf, forthcoming).

13. Edwards Amasa Park, *Memoir of Nathanael Emmons; with Sketches of His Friends and Pupils* (Boston: Congregational Board of Publication, 1861), 96–97.

14. Joseph A. Conforti, "Mary Lyon, the Founding of Mount Holyoke College, and the Cultural Revival of Jonathan Edwards," *Religion and American Culture* 3 (Winter 1993): 69–89; and Amanda Porterfield, *Mary Lyon and the Mount Holyoke Missionaries* (New York: Oxford University Press, 1997).

15. Rachel Wheeler, *To Live upon Hope: Mohicans and Missionaries in the Eighteenth-Century Northeast* (Ithaca, NY: Cornell University Press, 2008); Joel W. Martin and Mark A. Nicholas, eds., *Native Americans, Christianity, and the Reshaping of the American Religious Landscape* (Chapel Hill: University of North Carolina Press, 2010); and Samson Occom, *The Collected Writings of Samson Occom, Mohegan: Leadership and Literature in Eighteenth-Century Native America,* ed. Joanna Brooks (New York: Oxford University Press, 2006). On Edwardsians and Indians, consult the bibliographies in Gerald R. McDermott, "Missions and Native Americans," in *The Princeton Companion to Jonathan Edwards,* ed. Sang Hyun Lee (Princeton: Princeton University Press, 2005), 258–273; Occom, *Collected Writings of Samson Occom*; and John A. Grigg, *The Lives of David Brainerd: The Making of an American Evangelical Icon,* Religion in America Series (New York: Oxford University Press, 2009). See the articles written against U.S. treatment of the Indians in the heavily Edwardsian *The Spirit of the Pilgrims (SP)*: "Review of an Article in the North American Review," *SP* 3 (March 1830): 141–161; "Speeches on the Indian Bill," *SP* 3 (September 1830): 492–500, and (October 1830): 517–32; "Review of the Case of the Cherokees against Georgia," *SP* 4 (September 1831): 492–513; "Review of Pamphlets on the Death of Jeremiah Evarts, Esq.," *SP* 4 (November 1831): 599–613; and "Review of Thatcher's Lives of the Indians," *SP* 6 (January 1833): 41–47. And see Althea Bass, *Cherokee Messenger* (Norman: University of Oklahoma Press, 1936); William G. McLoughlin, *Cherokees and Missionaries, 1789–1839* (New Haven, CT: Yale University Press, 1984), 239–265; John A. Andrew III, *From Revivals to Removal: Jeremiah Evarts, the Cherokee Nation, and the Search for the Soul of America* (Athens: University of Georgia Press, 1991); William G. McLoughlin, "Two Bostonian Missions to the Frontier Indians, 1810–1860," in *Massachusetts and the New Nation,* ed. Conrad Edick Wright, Studies in American History and Culture (Boston: Massachusetts Historical Society, 1992), 175–180; Gerald R. McDermott, *Jonathan Edwards Confronts the Gods: Christian Theology, Enlightenment Religion, and Non-Christian Faiths* (New York: Oxford University Press, 2000),

194–206; Rachel Wheeler, "Lessons from Stockbridge: Jonathan Edwards and the Stockbridge Indians," in *Jonathan Edwards at 300: Essays on the Tercentenary of His Birth*, ed. Harry S. Stout, Kenneth P. Minkema, and Caleb J. D. Maskell (Lanham, MD: University Press of America, 2005), 131–140; Rachel M. Wheeler, "Edwards as Missionary," in *Cambridge Companion to Jonathan Edwards*, ed. Stein, 196–214; Denise T. Askin, " 'Strange Providence': Indigenist Calvinism in the Writings of Mohegan Minister Samson Occom (1723–1792)," in *John Calvin's American Legacy*, ed. Davis, 191–217; David J. Silverman, *Red Brethren: The Brothertown and Stockbridge Indians and the Problem of Race in Early America* (Ithaca, NY: Cornell University Press, 2010); Richard A. Bailey, *Race and Redemption in Puritan New England*, Religion in America Series (New York: Oxford University Press, 2011); Kelly Van Andel, "The Geography of Sinfulness: Mapping Subjectivity on the Mission Frontier," in *Jonathan Edwards in Scotland*, eds. Van Andel, Neele, and Minkema; and Linford Fisher, *The Indian Great Awakening: Religion and the Shaping of Native Cultures in Early America* (New York: Oxford University Press, forthcoming).

16. See especially John Saillant, "Lemuel Haynes and the Revolutionary Origins of Black Theology, 1776–1801," *Religion and American Culture* 2 (Winter 1992): 79–102; John Saillant, "A Doctrinal Controversy Between the Hopkintonian (Lemuel Haynes) and the Universalist (Hosea Ballou)," *Vermont Historical Review* 61 (Fall 1993): 177–216; John Saillant, "Slavery and Divine Providence in New England Congregationalism: The New Divinity and a Black Protest, 1775–1805," *New England Quarterly* 68 (December 1995): 584–608; John Saillant, " 'Wipe Away All Tears from Their Eyes': John Marrant's Theology in the Black Atlantic, 1785–1808," *Journal of Millennial Studies* 1 (Winter 1999): n.p. (online); John Saillant, *Black Puritan, Black Republican: The Life and Thought of Lemuel Haynes, 1753–1833*, Religion in America Series (New York: Oxford University Press, 2003); Hambrick-Stowe, "All Things Were New and Astonishing," in *Jonathan Edwards at Home and Abroad*, eds. Kling and Sweeney; John Saillant, "African American Engagements with Edwards in the Era of the Slave Trade," in *Jonathan Edwards at 300*, eds. Stout, Minkema, and Maskell, 141–151; Thabiti M. Anyabwile, *The Decline of African American Theology: From Biblical Faith to Cultural Captivity* (Downers Grove, IL: IVP Academic, 2007); Anyabwile, *The Faithful Preacher: Recapturing the Vision of Three Pioneering African-American Pastors* (Wheaton, IL: Crossway Books, 2007); and Anyabwile, *May We Meet in the Heavenly World: The Piety of Lemuel Haynes* (Grand Rapids, MI: Reformation Heritage Books, 2009).

17. See especially David S. Lovejoy, "Samuel Hopkins: Religion, Slavery, and the Revolution," *New England Quarterly* 40 (June 1967): 227–243; Bertram Wyatt-Brown, *Lewis Tappan and the Evangelical War Against Slavery* (Cleveland: Press of Case Western Reserve University, 1969); Lawrence Thomas Lesick, *The Lane Rebels: Evangelicalism and Antislavery in Antebellum America*, Studies in

Evangelicalism (Metuchen, NJ: Scarecrow Press, 1980); Conforti, *Samuel Hopkins and the New Divinity Movement*; James D. Essig, *The Bonds of Wickedness: American Evangelicals Against Slavery, 1770–1808* (Philadelphia: Temple University Press, 1982); Ruth Bogin, " 'Liberty Further Extended': A 1776 Antislavery Manuscript by Lemuel Haynes," *William and Mary Quarterly* 40 (January 1983): 85–105; John R. McKivigan, *The War Against Proslavery Religion: Abolitionism and the Northern Churches, 1830–1865* (Ithaca, NY: Cornell University Press, 1984); Victor B. Howard, *Conscience and Slavery: The Evangelistic Calvinist Domestic Missions, 1837–1861* (Kent, Ohio: Kent State University Press, 1990); John Saillant, *Black, White, and "The Charitable Blessed": Race and Philanthropy in the American Early Republic* (Bloomington: Indiana University Center on Philanthropy, 1993); Saillant, "Slavery and Divine Providence in New England Congregationalism"; Hugh Davis, "Leonard Bacon, the Congregational Church, and Slavery, 1845–1861," in *Religion and the Antebellum Debate over Slavery*, ed. John R. McKivigan (Athens: University of Georgia Press, 1998); Hugh Davis, *Leonard Bacon: New England Reformer and Antislavery Moderate* (Baton Rouge: Louisiana State University Press, 1998); Lamin O. Sanneh, *Abolitionists Abroad: American Blacks and the Making of Modern West Africa* (Cambridge, MA: Harvard University Press, 1999); Janet Duitsman Cornelius, *Slave Missions and the Black Church in the Antebellum South* (Columbia: University of South Carolina Press, 1999); Jonathan D. Sassi, " 'This Whole Country Have Their Hands Full of Blood This Day': Transcription and Introduction of an Antislavery Sermon Manuscript Attributed to the Reverend Samuel Hopkins," *Proceedings of the American Antiquarian Society* 112 (2004): 24–92; Kenneth P. Minkema and Harry S. Stout, "The Edwardsean Tradition and the Antislavery Debate, 1740–1865," *Journal of American History* 92 (June 2005): 47–74; and Eric Burin, *Slavery and the Peculiar Solution: A History of the American Colonization Society*, Southern Dissent (Gainesville: University Press of Florida, 2005).

18. A movement of Edwards-inspired black Reformed evangelicals has emerged in recent years. Its best-known leaders are the Revs. Anthony Carter (East Point, GA) and Thabiti Anyabwile (Grand Cayman). Its best-known institution is Reformed Blacks of America (http://www.reformedblacksofamerica.org/links.php). Other members of this network are Reddit Andrews, Anthony Bradley, Sherard Burns, Ken Jones, Michael Leach, Lance Lewis, Louis Love, Eric Redmond, and Roger Skipple. See the works of Anyabwile cited in note 16; Anthony Carter, *On Being Black and Reformed: A New Perspective on the African-American Christian Experience* (Phillipsburg, NJ: P & R, 2003); Sherard Burns, "Trusting the Theology of a Slaveowner," in *A God Entranced Vision of All Things: The Legacy of Jonathan Edwards*, ed. John Piper and Justin Taylor (Wheaton, IL: Crossway Books, 2004), 145–171; Anthony J. Carter, ed., *Experiencing the Truth: Bringing the Reformation to the African-American Church* (Wheaton, IL: Crossway Books, 2008); Anthony J. Carter, ed., *Glory Road: The Journeys of 10 African-Americans*

into Reformed Christianity (Wheaton, IL: Crossway Books, 2009); and Anthony B. Bradley, *Liberating Black Theology: The Bible and the Black Experience in America* (Wheaton, IL: Crossway Books, 2010).

19. For more on the new "Jonathan Edwards Centre Africa," based at the University of the Free State, Bloemfontein, visit its multilingual website: http://edwards.yale.edu/node/115.

20. For Edwards in Spanish, see Jonathan Edwards, *Pecadores en Manos de Un Dios Airado (1741)*, ed. José Antonio Gurpegui, trans. Julio César Santoyo, Taller de Escudos Norteamericanos (Léon, Spain: University of Léon, 2000); Jonathan Edwards, *Los Afectos Religiosos: La Válida Experiencia Espiritual* (Ciudad de México: Faro de Gracia, 2000); and Jonathan Edwards, *Características de Un Auténtico Avivamiento, Presentando a Jonathan Edwards al Contexto Latino*, ed. Ernie Klassen (Lima, Peru: Grafitec y Cia, 2002). For Edwards in Portuguese, see Jonathan Edwards, *A genuína experiência espiritual* (São Paulo: Publicações Evangélicas Selecionadas, 1993); Jonathan Edwards, *A soberania de Deus na salvação* (São Paulo: Publicações Evangélicas Selecionadas, 2004); Jonathan Edwards, *Pecadores nas mãos de um Deus irado e outros sermões* (Rio de Janeiro: CPAD, 2004); Jonathan Edwards, *O dom maior* (São José dos Campos: FIEL, 2005); Jonathan Edwards, *A vida de David Brainerd* (São José dos Campos: FIEL, 2005); Jonathan Edwards, *Uma fé mais forte que as emoções: discernindo a essência da verdadeira espiritualidade* (Distrito Federal: Editora Palavra, 2008); Jonathan Edwards, *Pecadores nas mãos de um Deus irado* (São Paulo: Publicações Evangélicas Selecionadas, 2008); Jonathan Edwards, *A verdadeira obra do Espírito: sinais e autenticidade* (São Paulo: Edições Vida Nova, 2010); Jonathan Edwards, *A busca do avivamento* (São Paulo: Cultura Cristã, 2010); Jonathan Edwards, *A busca da santidade* (São Paulo: Cultura Cristã, 2010); Jonathan Edwards, *A busca do crescimento* (São Paulo: Cultura Cristã, 2010); and see the Edwards material online at www.jonathanedwards.com.br. Edwards scholarship written/translated for Latin American readers includes Luiz Roberto França de Mattos, *Jonathan Edwards e o avivamento brasileiro* (São Paulo: Cultura Cristã, 2006); John Piper, *A paixão de Deus por sua glória: vivendo a visão de Jonathan Edwards* (São Paulo: Cultura Cristã, 2008); José Moreno Berrocal, Jonathan Edwards: La Pasión por la Glória de Dios (Barcelona: Publicaciones Andamio, 2008); Steven J. Lawson, *As firmes resoluções de Jonathan Edwards* (São José dos Campos: FIEL, 2010); Gerald R. McDermott, *Viendo A Dios*, trans. David Gomero and Yaima Gutierrez (Camagüey, Cuba: Christian Pentecostal Church of Cuba, 2011); and D. M. Lloyd-Jones, *Jonathan Edwards e a crucial importância do avivamento* (São Paulo: Publicações Evangélicas Selecionadas, s.d.). On the Brazilian Edwards Center, see its website: http://www.mackenzie.br/unidades_universitrias.html.

Index